Johnston County North Carolina

MARRIAGES

1764–1867

Charlotte D. Meldrum

HERITAGE BOOKS
2012

HERITAGE BOOKS
AN IMPRINT OF HERITAGE BOOKS, INC.

Books, CDs, and more—Worldwide

For our listing of thousands of titles see our website at
www.HeritageBooks.com

Published 2012 by
HERITAGE BOOKS, INC.
Publishing Division
100 Railroad Ave. #104
Westminster, Maryland 21157

Copyright © 1994 Charlotte D. Meldrum

All rights reserved. No part of this book may be reproduced or transmitted in any form or by any means, electronic or mechanical, including photocopying, recording or by any information storage and retrieval system without written permission from the author, except for the inclusion of brief quotations in a review.

International Standard Book Numbers
Paperbound: 978-1-58549-281-7
Clothbound: 978-0-7884-9301-0

CONTENTS

Introduction v
Johnston County Marriage Bonds 1
Johnston County Marriage Records 118
Index 135

INTRODUCTION

In this volume there are 4,355 marriage bonds and marriage records for Johnston County, North Carolina, covering the years 1768-1868. These were abstracted from a microfilm prepared by the North Carolina Department of Archives and History, Raleigh, North Carolina (1903).

The records have been arranged in the same order as appearing in the original records. Care has been taken to record the exact spelling as shown, noting that many of the same names are spelled differently throughout the records.

In 1669 a law was enacted requiring each marriage to be registered, but before 1868 not all marriages were recorded. Oft times marriages were performed after the publication of banns, which precluded the need for a license. When a marriage was by license, the groom would execute a bond in the bride's county of residence. The existence or absence of a marriage bond or record does not mean that a marriage did or did not take place.

The purpose of the bond was to prevent couples who were not qualified to be married. The bondsman (bdsm), who was often the groom or a relative of the groom and/or bride, was guaranteeing that there was no obstruction to the marriage.

The second part of this book is a collection of records of the actual marriages performed by the Justices of the Peace (JP) and/or ministers beginning around 1854. Although the law required that marriages be recorded, it appears to that this did not happen regularly until the latter period.

Charlotte D. Meldrum
Columbia, Maryland 1994

ACKNOWLEDGEMENTS

I wish to thank my publisher, who guided me in all aspects of publishing and editing, and my husband and daughter who encouraged me to finish the book.

JOHNSTON COUNTY, NORTH CAROLINA, MARRIAGES
1764 - 1867

JESSE JOHNSON to ELIZABETH LEWIS 14 Dec 1778. Bdsm Jesse Johnson and Zadock Stallings.
REUBIN ROGERS to TEMPIA JAMES 4 Dec 1767. Bdsm Reubin Rogers and James Wooten.
JOHN SMITH to EDITH AVERA 23 Jun 1778. Bdsm John Smith.
ASA BRYAN to ANNE LEE 18 Jun 1778. Bdsm Asa Bryan and James Lee.
JOHN COTTON to CHARITY WRIGHT 25 Jul 1769. Bdsm John Cotton and Dionysius Wright.
MECHAJAH ONEAL to CLARA RICHARDSON 2 Jan 1768. Bdsm Thomas Tomlinson and Isome Oneal.
ELISHA THOMAS to LUCY MASSEY 16 Feb 1764. Bdsm Elisha Thomas, Drury Vinson and Benjamin Scott.
MARKE SIMS to ELISABETH WATSON 3 Nov 1767. Bdsm Marke Sims and James Wooten.
BALAAM JOHNSON to MARY INMAM 10 Jul 1778. Bdsm Balaam Johncon and Thomas Spight.
JOHN BUSH to SUSANNAH BRYAN 15 Mar 1779. Bdsm John Bush and Bryan Whitfield.
THOMAS ROBERTS to WINNOWFIELD BUSBY 29 May 1764. Bdsm Thomas Busby and Jeremiah Hendrick.
MALACHI WIMBERLY to CHARITY HORN 10 Oct 1778. Bdsm Malachi Wimberly and Richard Horn.
SAMUEL WILLIAMS to FERABA McCULLERS 22 Dec 1779. Bdsm Samuel Williams and Saul Smith.
ELIJAH WARREN to POLLY INGRAM 16 Oct 1779. Bdsm Richard Warren and Elijah Warren.
WILLIS WIGGINS to MOURNIG STEVENS 17 Dec 1779. Bdsm Willis Wiggins and Jacob Stevens.
ARTHUR BRYAN to MARY McCULLERS 10 Dec 1773. Bdsm Arthur Bryan and Needham Bryan.
THOMAS CHIANS to GRACE BRADY 1 Mar 1771. Bdsm Thomas Chians and William Rand, Jr.
JOHN McCULLERS to ANN SANDERS 19 Sep 1778. Bdsm John McCullers and Zadock Stallings.
LEWIS MOON to ELIZABETH SANDERS 11 May 1779. Bdsm Lewis Moon and John Moon.
JESSE VICK to MOLLEY ROBERTSON 12 Feb 1778. Bdsm Thomas Robertson and John Gerrald.
SAMUEL COLLINS to MARTHA NOWEL 15 Sep 1778. Bdsm Samuel Collins and James Holliman.
JOSIAH SASSER to ELIZABETH BRYAN 10 Dec 1770. Bdsm Josiah Sasser and William Bryan, Jr.
HARRY PHILIPS to SARAH LAWHORN 1 Dec 1778. Bdsm Harry Philips and William Dodd.
PHILLIP PEARCE to PATIENCE OLIVER 3 Jul 1778. Bdsm John Pearce and Averet Pearce.
WILLIAM MOBLEY to LUCY ALLEN 1 Mar 1770. Bdsm William Mobley, Edward Mobley and Young Allen.
ISHAM ONEAL to ANN ARRUNDEL 23 Apr 1779. Bdsm Elisha Thomas.

JOHNSTON COUNTY MARRIAGES

WILLIAM TALTON to JUDITH STALLINGS ? 1779. Bdsm William Talton and Zadoc Stallings.

JACOB YELVINTON to CHARITY CANWELL 1 Dec 1778. Bdsm Jacob Yelvinton and Charles Wilkinson.

SHADRACK VINNING to PHEREBE RATCLIFF 13 Apr 1778. Bdsm Shadrack Vinning and Porter Ratcliff.

WILLIAM SULLIVANT to TABITHA LEE 19 Feb 1772. Bdsm William Sullivant and John Smith and John Pope.

MOSES JOHNSON to ANN BAGLEY 14 Nov 1778. Bdsm Moses Johnson and John Garrald.

AVINGTON MICKLEROY to SARAH DAWSON 17 Mar 1770. Bdsm Avington Mickleroy, William Dawson, William Mickleroy.

FELPS SMITH to BARSHEBY COBB 12 May 1778. Bdsm Felps Smith and Benjamin Wilkerson.

WILLIAM WALTON to ELIZABETH SMITH 28 Nov 1767. Bdsm William Walton and David Smith.

ISAAC FERRELL to EDITH PEPKIN 25 Jul 1778. Bdsm Isaac Ferrell and James Butler.

ARTHUR BAILE JOHNSON to CLOE THOMAS 25 Jan 1779. Bdsm Arthur Baile Johnson and David B. Bailey.

LEWIS BRADY to ELISABETH GILES 13 Feb 1770. Bdsm Lewis Brady and John Brady.

ROBERT DODD to LYDIA WOOD 29 May 1778. Bdsm Robert Dodd and John Wood.

DAVID BELL to ? 28 Sep 1778. Bdsm David Bell and Zalok Stallings.

JOSEPH BOON to LYDEY PORVEL 12 Mar 1779. Bdsm Joseph Boon and Joseph Sims.

ELIAS GEORGE to SARAH RAINS 1 Jan 1779. Bdsm Elias George and Charles Wilkerson.

JAMES HALLIMAN to ELIZABETH BRYAN 16 Apr 1772. Bdsm James Halliman and Charles Jones.

ROBERT GULLEY to ELIZABETH STALLION 23 May 1778. Bdsm Robert Gulley and Felps Smith.

ARTHUR JERNIGAN to WINIFRED CRAFFORD 6 Dec 1779. Bdsm Arthur Jernigan and John Raiford.

LEWIS BRYAN to SARAH HINTON 26 Oct 1769. Bdsm Lewis Bryan and Samuel Smith, Jr.

JESSE JONES to WINIFRED SPIGHT 1 May 1775. Bdsm Jesse Jones and Etheldred Jones.

GIDION ALLEN to MARY EASON 14 Dec 1771. Bdsm Gidion Allen and John Smith.

OTHORIAL EASON to ANN NORRISS 9 Dec 1767. Bdsm Othorial Eason and John Norriss.

JACOB AVERA to ANNE FAILE 14 Feb 1764. Bdsm Jacob Avera, William Bryan and John Smith, Jr.

SAMUEL AVERA to ZILPHIA INGRAM 11 Feb 1779. Bdsm Samuel Avera and John Smith.

JAMES LANGDON to PATTEY STEVENS 13 Sep 1778. Bdsm James Langdon and Richard Whitington.

WILLIAM WATSON to ELIZABETH TANNER 20 Oct 1763. Bdsm James Watson, Henry Rains and David Holleman.

RICHARD HOLLEMAN to ASPTIE BRYAN 8 Jan 1768. Bdsm Richard Holleman

MARRIAGE BONDS

and David Holleman.
JONATHAN AVERA to MARY DRAPER 20 May 1768. Bdsm Jonathan Avera and Alexander Avera.
DANIEL HIGDON to MARY CALVET 30 Jan 1762. Bdsm Daniel Higdon, Joshua Houghton and John Higdon.
LEWIS BRYANT to CELIA HOLLEMAN 18 Nov 1767. Bdsm Lewis Bryant.
JOSHUA HOUGHTON to ? 19 Apr 1764. Bdsm Joshua Houghton, Thomas Houghton and Carl Heith.
THOMAS JONES to EASTER NORRISS 13 Aug 1795. Bdsm Thomas Jones and James Norriss.
ALLAN WATKINS to RHODA GODWIN 4 Aug 1795. Bdsm John Pearce and James Kirby.
JOHN DELOACH to ISABEL HODGSON 25 Feb 1762. Bdsm John Deloach and Samuel Pearson.
DRURY DEES to SALLIE STEVENS 20 Jun 1795. Bdsm John Pool and John Smith, Jr.
REUBEN NORRISS to ELIZABETH BRITT 14 Jan 1797. Bdsm Reuben Norriss and Thomas Tolson.
ELIAS ATKINSON to SARAH ? 6 Oct 1795. Bdsm Benjamin Hill.
DEMPSEY DODD to PHEREBY DODD 14 Jan 1796. Bdsm Dempsey Dodd and William Durham.
THOMAS FOLSOM to CHARITY NORRISS 18 Aug 1795. Bdsm Thomas Folsom and James Norriss.
STEPHEN OLIVER to POLLY BRASWELL 7 Oct 1795. Bdsm John Oliver.
WILLIAM ROADS to MARY SEARL 2 Oct 1797. Bdsm Abraham Web.
JOHN LANGSTON to MARY RANDAL 25 Feb 1794. Bdsm Joseph Langston.
WILEY WATKINS to ALSEY JOHNSON 19 Jun 1794. Bdsm Aaron Johnson and Hardy Bryan.
JOHN HAYLES to ELIZABETH SPICER 12 Aug 1795. Bdsm John Hayles and Nathan Gulley.
BENJAMIN BRIDGERS TO BERSHEBA GILES 19 Jun 1794. Bdsm Benjamin Bridgers and Hardy Bryan.
HENRY HARRELL to ELIZABETH BAKER 8 Jan 1796. Bdsm John Roads.
GILLEY WHITE to SARAH JOHNSON 27 Sep 192. Bdsm James Langdon and Isaac Johnson.
HENRY FAULK to SARAH STOAVON 11 May 1795. Bdsm Henry Faulk and John Faulk.
WILLIAM BAKER to WAMMER BAKER 22 Jul 1795. Bdsm John Blackman, Jr.
JACOB JOHNSON to NANCY COATS 20 Jul 1795. Bdsm Isaac Johnson and Noel Johnson.
ELIJAH SOLOMON to LETTY DURHAM 22 Aug 1797. Bdsm Edmond Tomlinson.
WILEY JOHNSON to WINIFRED CARRELL 13 Aug 1792. Bdsm Amos Johnson.
DENNIS CARRELL to ELIZABETH SOLOMON 23 May 1795. Bdsm Dennis Carrell and John Carrell.
JESSE BAILEY to SARAH THORN 12 Jan 1779. Bdsm Jesse Bailey and James Glasglow.
WILLIAM BRANNON to MARY GREEN 27 Nov 1793. Bdsm William Brannan and John Watson.
WILLIAM DURHAM to SURARY JOHNSON 27 Nov 1797. Bdsm William Durham and Joseph Deloach.
JAMES PINDER to PATTY EDWARDS 23 Dec 1795. Bdsm Jesse Spencer.
CHARLES STEVENS to MARY HOLLEMON 8 Oct 1795. Bdsm Frederick

JOHNSTON COUNTY MARRIAGES

Hollemon.
MOSES JOHNSTON to EDITH MARSHALL 24 Dec 1795 Bdsm Moses Johnston and William Peebles.
JACOB DELK to PEGGY SMITH 26 Jun 1794. Bdsm Jacob Delk, Abner Jordan and Drury Massey.
EDWARD STEVENS, JR to TABITHA RIVERS 19 Dec 1792. Bdsm Edward Stevens Jr. and Richard Rivers.
JOHN HOLT to MARY JORDAN 18 Feb 1795. Bdsm John Holt and Thomas Price.
AMOS JOHNSON to DESA BEDERYFIELD 27 Feb 1797. Bdsm John Jarrell.
JOHN BEDINGFIELD, JR. to MARY ANN PRICE 2 Jan 1792. Bdsm John Bedingfield, Jr. and John Price Jr.
HENRY STEVENS to SALLY WHITE 13 May 1794. Bdsm Henry Stevens and William Coats.
JAMES DURHAM to DRUZILLA TOMLINSON 20 Dec 1797. Bdsm Henry Avera.
HOWELL ADAMS to ELIZABETH SOWELL 26 Jul 1799. Bdsm Howell Adams and Clayton Sowell.
JAMES CARRELL to RHODA STEVENS 30 Jan 1792. Bdsm John Carrell.
WILLIAM AVERA, JR to SARAH PRICHET 9 Sep 1794. Bdsm William Avera, Jr. and Robert Whittington.
NATHAN LEE to WINIFRED SELLERS 20 Jul 1796. Bdsm Ichabod Blackman.
THOMAS ONEAL to BARSHEBY RICHARDSON 7 Oct 1795. Bdsm William Hackney.
STEPHEN POWELL to CHARLOTTE HARRELL 19 Nov 1796. Bdsm Hugh Cravy.
AMOS PEEDIN to ANN RETOR HOWELL 27 Nov 1793. Bdsm Joseph Edwards.
THOMAS ALLEN to BEDITH SMITH 9 Apr 1797. Bdsm Thomas Allen and Bryant Adams.
JOHN ELLIS to MARY FERRELL 9 Feb 1793. Bdsm John Tinner.
WILLIAM SPERRY to NAMMY POOL 12 Apr 1794. Bdsm Reuben Wilkinson.
WILLIAM CANADY to TABITHY BRATCHER 27 Jun 1793. Bdsm William Canady and Robert Whittington.
MATTHEW CHILIS to NAMMY TAILOR 18 Nov 1795. Bdsm Matthew Chilis and Samuel Avera.
JOEL ALTMAN to NAMMY BLACKMAN 21 Mar 1797. Bdsm John Lee.
RUI PRICE, JR to MARINEY MOORE 24 Feb 1795. Bdsm Dixon Price.
LEAVY PEARCE to NAMMY DAVIS 4 Jun 1795. Bdsm James Davis.
MATCHET HERRING to BETSY BRASWELL 26 Aug 1793. Bdsm Benjamin Strickland and Jarrot Thompson.
SOLOMON THOMAS to REDLEY BRYAN 25 Feb 1792. Bdsm Solomon Thomas and Isaac Hinton.
MICAJAH ADKERSON to MARY ADKERSON 7 Jun 1796. Bdsm Benjamin Bryan.
BENJAMIN JONES to MARY CLIMMY 1 Apr 1793. Bdsm Benjamin Jones and Jesse Morgan.
JESSE MORGAN to ESTHER ALLEN 2 Jan 1795. Bdsm Jesse Morgan and James Woodall.
JONATHAN HOLDER to PATTY FINET 14 Aug 1795. Bdsm Jonathan Holder and Henry Smith.
JOHN EASON to OLIVE AVERA 28 Oct 1795. Bdsm John Eason and Hardy Bryan.
NAHOR NORRISS to SALLY AVERGET 22 Feb 1797. Bdsm John Sanders.
JOHN W. TIGH to SALLY COBB 15 Sep 1793. Bdsm John W. Tigh and Samuel Oneal.

MARRIAGE BONDS

JAMES BRADDY to MARTHA ROBERTS 30 Aug 1791. Bdsm Linzery Roberts and Barnaby Bulls.
MILES SEVEANEY to JANE DODD 7 Mar 1795. Bdsm Miles Seveaney and John Dodd.
WILLIAM McGLAWHON to MARGARET DEMONT 26 Oct 1793. Bdsm William McGlawhon and Ryan Ward.
JOSEPH EDWARDS to PATTY COLLERS 27 May 1794. Bdsm Joseph Ingram.
BAAL WATSON to MARY DOWNING 25 Feb 1794. Bdsm Archeleus Barnes and Jesse Barnes.
FRANCIS YOUNG to SALLY TOMLINSON 30 Jan 1796. Bdsm Francis Young and Abner Sands.
GEORGE KEEN to CATERN GOODRICH 28 Jan 1793. Bdsm Drenny Bryan.
WILLIAM GILES to LYDIA WOOD 27 Aug 1793. Bdsm John Wood.
JESSE EVANS to MARGARET POWELL 6 Mar 1794. Bdsm Jesse Evans and Nathaniel Giles.
GEORGE MASSINGIL to ELIZABETH BLACKMAN 6 ? 1797 Bdsm Etheldred Massingil.
MECHAJAH LILES to NANCY WOODARD 9 Aug 1793. Bdsm Mecahaj Liles and John Roper.
WILLIAM WILDER to MARY WHITINGTON 2 Nov 1795. Bdsm James Langdon.
JOHN HAYES to APSILLA PEARCE 6 Feb 1795. Bdsm Nichols Tompson.
JOSEPH DELOACH to LEACY JOHNSON 10 Apr 1795. Bdsm Joseph Deloach and William Spier.
EPHRAIM GODWIN to PENELEPY THAUGHN 25 Sep 1795. Bdsm Thomas Cockran.
MICHAEL REYNOLDS to POLLY CHAMBERS 16 May 1783 Bdsm Michael Reynolds and Joseph Edwards.
FREEMAN KITTINGSWORTH to POLLY RAIFORD 20 Apr 1798. Bdsm Freeman Kittingsworth and Philip Raiford.
JACOB GILES to LELAH AVERA 11 Feb 1788. Bdsm Jacob Giles and David Bell.
JOHN LEAREY to LUCY TEMPLE 19 Dec 1795. Bdsm John Learey and Salathiel Holton.
JEREMIAH STRICKLAND to ELIZABETH GURLEY 1 Apr 1783. Bdsm Jeremiah Strickland and Benjamin Strickland.
JOHN OLIVER to SARAH EDWARDS 22 Jan 1783. Bdsm John Oliver and Elisha Thomas.
WILLIAM ONEAL, JR to ELIZABETH STEVENS 29 Jan 1788. Bdsm William Oneal Jr. and Frederick Hollimon.
WILLIAM ONEAL to PHEREBY CLANEY 1 Dec 1784. Bdsm Thomas Gray.
THOMAS HILL to ELIZABETH GARNER 5 Jan 1782. Bdsm John Garner and Richard Bailey.
DRURY PEOPLES to ANN COALTS 26 Mar 1786. Bdsm Drury Peoples and John Eliot.
JOHN CORE PENDER to THENEY STEVENS 2 Feb 1784. Bdsm John Core Pender and William Fillion.
FRANCIS EVANS TO JENNY BREWER 20 Mar 1784. Bdsm Francis Evans and Ambrose Rams.
EDWARD PENNY TO EDITH BAGGET 1 SEP 1784. Bdsm Edward Penny and William Ryals.
ZACHARIAH PRICE to MOLLY MOORE 1 Dec 1784. Bdsm Zachariah Price and Thomas Gray.

JOHNSTON COUNTY MARRIAGES

THOMAS PRICE to ANN RYALS 23 Jan 1784. Bdsm Thomas Price and Charles Ryals.
ALEXANDER PENNY to PHEREBY JOHNSON 28 Aug 1787. Bdsm James Penny and Caleb Johnson.
JAMES PURVIS to RODIA ROBERTS 14 Aug 1786. Bdsm James Purvis and Benjamin Sellars.
WILLIAM COPELAND to ANN MEEKS 17 Mar 1785. Bdsm William Copeland and Samuel Smith.
LUCIUS PRICE to MARY ONEAL 17 May 1780. Bdsm Lucius Price and Isham Oneal.
BENJAMIN TAYLOR to ALSEY PRITCHET 27 Feb 1787. Bdsm Benjamin Taylor and David Bell.
JAMES LEE to ELIZABETH RAINS 6 Jul 1782. Bdsm James Lee and Stephen Lee.
GIDION YELVINGTON to BEEDY HATCHER 14 May 1785. Bdsm Gidion Yelvington and John Hatcher.
ADAM TAPLEY to ANNE BRANNON 16 Feb 1786. Bdsm Adam Tapley and William Hobbs.
WILLIAM ROBERTS to MARGARET TUCKER 20 Aug 1782. Bdsm William Roberts and Charles Parish.
WILLIAM CAPPS to TILPHRIA BULLS 26 Jan 1788. Bdsm Daniel Dees.
EDWARD PRICE to MARY JONES ? Bdsm Edward Price and Jesse Wall.
JACOB STALLINGS to EDITH AVERA 13 Apr 1784. Bdsm Jacob Stallings and Isaac Stallings.
JOHN HINTON to LUCY BEDINGFIELD 14 Dec 178? Bdsm Hardy Hinton and John Bedingfield.
HARBARD GILMAN to WINIFRED GARNER 16 Aug 1787. Bdsm Harbard Gilman and Benjamin Crumpler.
CHARLES COPELAND, JR. to BARBABY JONES 1 Mar 1784. Bdsm Charles Copeland, Jr. and Charles Copeland, Sr.
SETH HOLLEMAN to URIAH GODWIN 20 Aug 1786. Bdsm Seth Holleman and Frederick Holleman.
WILLIAM JACKSON to PRISCILLA PRICE 26 Aug 1784. Bdsm William Jackson and John Brady.
THOMAS CHAMBERS to MARY STANLEY 22 Sep 1786. Bdsm Thomas Chambers and Deal Collins.
WILLIAM GARNER to MARY HATCHER 29 Nov 1785. Bdsm William Garner and Reuben Wilkerson.
JOHN KEARSI to ELIZABETH WHITINGTON 25 Jul 1783. Bdsm John Kearsi and Aaron Vinson.
WILLIAM BULLS to REBECKAH CAPSE 25 Oct 1785. Bdsm Jethro Bulls.
THOMAS GREEN to AMITY YELVINTON 2 Sep 1782. Bdsm Thomas Green and Amos Atkerson.
JOHN MATTHEWS to POLLY WILLIAMS 19 Dec 1787. Bdsm John Matthews and Thomas Matthews.
RICHARD JOHNSON to MARTHA JOHNSON 10 Oct 1785. Bdsm Richard Johnson and Abner Sauls.
MECAJAH HICKS to SUSANNAH OVERBY 29 Jun 1786. Bdsm Mecajah Hicks and Joseph Edwards.
ROBERT HOOKS to SARAH RAIFORD 10 Mar 1784. Bdsm Robert Hooks and Needham Whitley.
NATHANIEL HOOD to SUSANNAH GURLEY 13 Nov 1782. Bdsm Nathaniel Hood

MARRIAGE BONDS

and Kedar Powell.
SAMUEL BALDWIN to ELIZABETH REVIS 15 Jan 1783. Bdsm Samuel Baldwin.
BENJAMIN HILL to MARY WOOTEN 28 Nov 1787. Bdsm John Green.
ELISHA BROWN to ANN BULLOCK 9 Oct 1783. Bdsm Elisha Brown and Nicholas Thompson.
WILLIAM BRIDGERS to ELIZABETH SMITH 21 Dec 1785. Bdsm William Bridgers.
NATHANIEL GULLEY TO TEMPORAM THOMAS 30 Nov 1780. Bdsm Nathaniel Gulley, Robin Gulley and George Warren.
SOLOMON GALES to MIRIAM FERRELL 7 Mar 1787. Bdsm Solomon Gales and John Turner.
JAMES BACKHAM to SARAH ROGERS 3 Jan 1780. Bdsm James Backham and Green Rogers.
EZEKIEL BELLINGTON to ELIZABETH PENNY 8 Nov 1784. Bdsm Ezekiel Bellington and Edward Penny.
JAMES BRANNON to ROSE MARTIN 27 Jan 1783. Bdsm James Brannon and William Green.
WILLIAM DURHAM to ANN NICHOLS 5 May 1780. Bdsm William Durham and Britain Smith.
GREEN ROGERS to TABITHA MARCH 16 Jan 1786. Bdsm Green Rogers and James Barrison.
WILLIAM RAINWATER to MEDLEY RIVES 16 Nov 1787. Bdsm Samuel Baldwin.
HENRY BLURTON to EDITH AVERET 5 Jan 1785. Bdsm Henry Blurton and Zadoc Stallings.
LUCIUS PRICE to MARY AVEALS 17 May 1780. Bdsm Lucius Price and Isham Aveals.
MILES LANGLERY to ANN CLARK 21 Sep 1782. Bdsm Miles Langlery and James Lockhart.
BRYANT LEE to ELIZABETH FAULK 3 Feb 1784. Bdsm Bryant Lee and Elisha Woodard.
JAMES LEE, JR. to ANN INGRAM 20 Sep 1785. Bdsm James Lee, Jr and William Ballenger.
WILLIAM LEE to MILLEY NARON 3 Feb 1784. Bdsm William Lee and Richard Price.
BENJAMIN TAYLOR to ALSEY PRITCHET 27 Feb 1787. Bdsm Benjamin Taylor and David Bull.
ROBERT JOHNSON to ANN GARRALD 26 Mar 1785. Bdsm Robert Johnson and William Johnson.
JOHN EDWARDS to SARAH ONEAL 27 Nov 1787. Bdsm John Edwards and Benjamin Oneal.
THOMAS JOINER to MARY HINNIARD 8 Mar 1786. Bdsm Thomas Joiner and Amos Atkerson.
JESSE JOINER to ? 30 May 1781. Bdsm Jesse Joiner and John Whitley.
JOHN RHODES to ? 26 Aug 1782. Bdsm John Rhodes and Samuel Lee.
JOHN KEARNI to ELIZABETH WHITTINGTON 25 Jul 1783. Bdsm John Kearni and Aaron Vinson.
ALEXANDER GRAY to ANN LIGHTFOOT 10 Feb 1783. Bdsm Alexander Gray and Joseph Boon.
JOHN EARP to LUCRETIA CASSE 27 Sep 1787. Bdsm William Casse.
REUBEN BARBER TO EDY SPIGHTS 8 Apr 1783. Bdsm Reuben Barber.
GEORGE BARBER to NANCY JOHNSON 5 Jan 1788. Bdsm George Barber and Reuben Barber.

JOHNSTON COUNTY MARRIAGES

SIMON WRIGHT TO ANN WILKS 4 Mar 1785. Bdsm John Wright and William Stevens.

ASA ARRSTON to LUCRETIA WHITINGTON 27 Feb 1787. Bdsm Asa Arrston and Richard Whitington.

STEPHEN LEE to KEZIAH LEE 4 Dec 1782. Bdsm Stephen Lee and James Lee.

WILLIAM SANDERS to MARY BRYAN 8 Sep 1785. Bdsm William Sanders and William Bryan.

JOHN SNIPES to ION HILLINGSMITH 6 Jul 1785. Bdsm John Snipes and Samuel Baldwin.

JOHN STANSILL, JR. to ZILPHA GRICE 29 Aug 1785. Bdsm John Stansill Jr. and Benjamin Oneal.

ISAAC INGRAM to WINIFRED LEE 28 Mar 1786. Bdsm Isaac Ingram and James Lee.

ZADOK STALLINGS to ANNE AVERA 12 Apr 1785. Bdsm Zadok Stallings and Jacob Stallings.

ABRAHAM SMITH to SARAH ROPER 17 Jan 1787. Bdsm Abraham Smith and John Eason.

HUGH SHAW TO MARY JERNIGAN 10 Mar 1784. Bdsm Hugh Shaw and Joseph Iven.

JAMES SPICER to PEYSILIA PRICE ? 30 Mar 1784. Bdsm James Spicer and Joseph Spicer.

JAMES PRICE to SUSANNA ROGERS 17 Feb 1787. Bdsm Thomas Price and Edward Price.

JOHN DODD to MARTHA JOHNSON 13 Dec 1788. Bdsm John Dodd and William Youngblood.

JOHN FISH to PHREBE TOMLINSON 13 Oct 1787. Bdsm John Fish and Edmond Tomlinson.

NATHANIEL SNIPES to MARGARET BRIDGERS 5 Sep 1789. Bdsm Nathaniel Snipes.

THOMAS POYNER to ELIZABETH GUION ? 9 Sep 1787. Bdsm Thomas Poyner and Jerem Powell.

WILLIAM ONEIL to ELIZABETH HOCUTT 2 Nov 1789. Bdsm William Oneil and William Richardson.

JOHN RHODES to ? 26 Aug 1782. Bdsm John Rhodes and Samuel Lee.

RICHARD FURLEY to MARY PEAL 25 Aug 1788. Bdsm Richard Furley and William Ward.

JOHN HINTON to CHARLOTTE CARTER 21 Dec 1789. Bdsm John Hinton and William Hinton.

JACOB WOODALL to PHREBE GOWER 16 Dec 1789. Bdsm Jacob Woodall and Absalom Woodall.

HEROD I. WILLIAMS to FATHY BREWER 15 Apr 1788. Bdsm Herod I. Williams and Jesse Wooten.

JOHN TAYLOR to DEANMIAH BAILEY 6 Mar 1789. Bdsm John Taylor and William Bailey.

JOHN LEAREY to MARY AVERA 2 Feb 1789. Bdsm Aaron Vinson.

ABSALOM WOODALL to CATY PARRISH 24 Dec 1788. Bdsm Absalom Woodall and Ryal Jennings.

JOHN WOOD to DORCAS JOHNSON 23 Dec 1789. Bdsm Etheldred Johnson.

WILLIAM BALLENGER to SUSANNA STEPHENS 3 May 1788. Bdsm William Ballenger and John Ballenger.

HARRIS CLARK to LYDIA GOWER 14 Nov 1789. Bdsm Harris Clark and

MARRIAGE BONDS

James Carrell.
LEWIS MARTIN to LUCRECY AVERA 9 Jul 1788. Bdsm John Eason and Lewis Avera.
WILLIAM RIVERS to ELIZABETH POOL 20 Dec 1788. Bdsm William Rivers and Richard Rivers.
ISOM JOHNSON to POLLY STEPHENS 17 Dec 1788. Bdsm Isom Johnson and Martin Johnson.
ARTHUR DAVIS to ELIZABETH PATTERSON 12 Sep 1788. Bdsm John Harps.
ISAAC ATKINS to ANN PENNY 31 Jan 1789. Bdsm Isaac Atkins.
JAMES WOODALL to MARY JENNINGS 28 Jan 1789. Bdsm James Woodall and Ryal Jennings.
WILLIS MONK to CELIA POOL 18 Jun 1788. Bdsm Willis Monk and Simon Watson.
HARBARD ROBERTSON, JR to EDITH HINTON 13 Apr 1789. Bdsm Harbard Robertson, Jr. and George Hinton.
MATTHEW HARRIS to MILDRED BROWN 20 Mar 1788. Bdsm Matthew Harris and John Hillingsworth.
JOHN PAGE to MARY JOHNSON 29 Oct 1788. Bdsm John Page and Thomas Page.
HENRY LEWIS to RUTH BARBEY 26 Mar 1789. Bdsm David Lewis.
CLAYTON LOWELL to SARAH ADAMS 6 Mar 1788. Bdsm Clayton Lowell and Howell Adams.
JOSIAH BAGGET to EDITH JOINER 28 Nov 1789. Bdsm James Langdon.
SIMON PRICE to PHEREBY WOODARD 25 Nov 1788. Bdsm Simon Price and Henry Hayles.
BENJAMIN HATCHER to ANNE WILKERSON 26 Feb 1789. Bdsm Benjamin Hatcher and Benjamin Wilkerson.
SAMUEL ONEIL to PHEREBY BAILEY 27 Aug 1788. Bdsm William Oneil.
ISOM BAILEY to ELIZABETH PARNOLD 24 Feb 1789. Bdsm Samuel Oneil and Arthur Bailey.
HARDY PARKER to PHEREBY BARBEY 25 Feb 1789. Bdsm Hardy Parker and Joseph Irvin.
AARON GODWIN to LISBA BRYAN 22 Aug 1789. Bdsm William Bryan.
JAMES CLIFTON to SUSANNA LEWIS 19 Nov 1788. Bdsm William Clifton.
WILLIAM MESSER to POLLEY BARBER 2 Apr 1787. Bdsm Phina Barber.
BENJAMIN MOTT to ESTHER GOWER 31 Aug 1784. Bdsm Benjamin Mott and Solomon Staton.
DUNCAN MORREY to ? 2 Nov 1784. Bdsm, Duncan Morrey and John Barefoot.
STEPHEN VANN to MARY VINSON 15 May 17? Bdsm Stephen Vann and Arthur Bryan.
AUGNELIA NAIRR to ? BAILEY 15 Nov 1782. Bdsm Augnelia Nairr and William Holleman.
HENRY DAVIS to ELIZABETH EDWARD 20 Apr 1798. Bdsm Henry Davis and Philip Raiford.
ARTHUR BAILEY to FANNY PARKER 27 May 1789. Bdsm William Holliman.
BENJAMIN SIMS to ANNE TYNER 21 Aug 1788. Bdsm William Stevens.
JOHN KILLNGSWORTH to LEVERLEY HARPER ? 1788. Bdsm John Killingsworth and Freeman Killingsworth.
NEEDHAM FLOWERS to ELIZABETH BAVADRIL 28 Mar 1789. Bdsm Needham Flowers and William Blunt.
WILLIAM BRIDGERS to JANE SMITH 16 Apr 1788. Bdsm William Bridgers.

JOHNSTON COUNTY MARRIAGES

JOHN DINMORE to CHARITY BRIDGERS 11 Mar 11 1788. Bdsm Drury Bryan and John Fuller.

RANDOLPH MOORE to ELIZABETH STANSEL 18 Jun 1783. Bdsm Randolph Moore and Amos Atkerson.

JOHN WILSON to PATTY DAVIS 14 Sep 1782. Bdsm John Wilson and Jacob Davis.

WILSON NELSON to SARAH WALL 5 Aug 1784. Bdsm Wilson Nelson and Jesse Wall.

YOUNG BRIDGERS to CLARRY NORRISS 7 Jun 1789. Bdsm Young Bridgers and John Norriss.

WILLIAM MUSSLEWHITE to MARGARET STORKTON 11 Mar 1780. Bdsm William Musslewhite and Edmond Griffin.

LEVAN WATSON to PRUELLA ADAMS 21 Nov 1785. Bdsm Levan Watson and William Fish.

MECAJAH PRICE to PENELOPIA GARDNER 1 Mar 1787. Bdsm Mecajah Price and Daniel Dees.

NEHEMIAH SMITH to LEVANA AVERA 9 Jan 1787. Bdsm Nehemiah Smith and Nahor Norriss.

DAVID WALKER to PHENELAH SILKS 9 Oct 1785. Bdsm David Walker and Clement Armstrong.

JOHN HAYLES to CYNTHIA THOMAS 14 Dec 1785. Bdsm John Hayles.

DRURY MUSSELENWHITE to ANNIE CASSE 1 Dec 1782. Bdsm Drury Musslenhwhite and Matthew Raper.

MOSES JOHNSON to SUSANNA CLERK 6 Dec 1784. Bdsm Moses Johnson and Thomas Tomlinson.

EDWARD PRICE to DUDINIAH LEVERY 17 Feb 1789. Bdsm Leonard Price and Thomas Price.

JAMES WISE to RUTH WARREN 6 Feb 1780. Bdsm James Wise and Richard Warren Esq.

ELKENY WILKERSON to PATIENCE ROGERS 27 Dec 1782. Bdsm Elkeny Wilkerson and Charles Wilkerson.

SOLOMON WILLOUGHBY to MARTHA CLARKE 1 Jan 1785. Bdsm Solomon Willoughby and James Hardcastle.

GEORGE WARREN to MARY BLACKMAN 15 May 1783. Bdsm George Warren and Richard Warren.

SIHON WRIGHT to ANN WILKS 4 Mar 1785. Bdsm Sihon Wright and William Stevens.

THOMAS UNDERWOOD to SARAH THORNTON 10 Mar 1783. Bdsm Thomas Underwood and John Whitley.

THOMAS WISE to HESTER SIMS 13 Dec 1785. Bdsm Benjamin Sims.

PETER WATKINS to DELIAH GRICE 25 May 1789. Bdsm Stephen Grice and Thomas Woodward.

WILLIAM WALTHAL to POLLY RUSSELL ? Bdsm Charles Hood.

DAVID PEACOCK to CHARLOTTE BRYAN 26 Feb 1789. Bdsm John Bryan.

JOHN DRIVER to ZELPHA POPE 8 Dec 17? Bdsm William Hobbs.

WILLIAM ATKINSON to ELIZABETH HARRISON ? Bdsm Josiah Holder.

PHILIP JOHNSON to NAMMY GILES 26 Feb 1792. Bdsm William Giles.

PHILIP SWANSON to SARAH PARRISH 12 Nov 1792. Bdsm Philip Swanson and Uriah Johnson.

JAMES LOVE to NANCY CARLILES 21 Jan 1791. Bdsm James Love and Hardy Bryan.

JAMES LANGDON to WINNIFRED BRADDY 24 May 1791. Bdsm James Langdon

MARRIAGE BONDS

and William Braddy.
CLAYTON SMITH to JAMAEY BAILEY 1 Mar 1795. Bdsm John Dixon and John Thomas.
HENRY DAVIS to ELIZABETH EDWARD 20 Apr 1798. Bdsm Henry Davis and Philip Raiford.
WILLIAM WALTON to SALLY AVERA 21 Apr 1798. Bdsm Aventon Avera.
JOHN THOMPSON to BARBARA CAPPS 19 May 1798. Bdsm Barnaby Bulls.
JOHN HINNANT to MARY HOCUTT 4 Mar 179. Bdsm Robert Gulley.
WILLIE TINER to CARTHINA JORNIGAN 12 Apr 1799. Bdsm Willie Tiner and Jesse Tiner.
JAMES WOODALL to MARY ALLEN 26 Jan 1792. Bdsm James Woodall and Absalom Woodall.
NATHAN STANSILL to NANNEY PENDER 27 Feb 1799. Bdsm Frederick Holmes.
REUBEN SANDERS to KEREN SMITH 6 Nov 1793. Bdsm Hardy Bryan and Reuben Sanders.
WILLIAM BRASWELL to NAMMY HUMPHRIES 19 May 1798. Bdsm William Braswell and Robert Gulley, Jr.
TRAVIS PATE to ANN TOMLINSON 28 Nov 1791. Bdsm Travis Pate and John Williams.
ISAAC KEEN to JUDITH KIRBY 25 Feb 1799. Bdsm Jesse Kirby.
KINDRED CARTER to LEVEY ETHRIDGE 1 Aug 1797. Bdsm Kindred Carter and Peter Williams.
WILLIAM EARP to ALSOBETH ONEIL 15 Feb 1792. Bdsm James Shaw, Jr.
ISAAC FURR to JUDITH KIRBY 25 Feb 1799. Bdsm Jesse Kirby.
ELIJAH BAKER to ROSEY SOLOMON ? Bdsm William Mandley.
ISAAC SMITH to SARAH ONEIL 26 Jul 1798. Bdsm Isaac Smith and Samuel Godwin.
HUGH CRAVY to KISSEY NONSWORTHY 29 Apr 1797. Bdsm John Williams.
KINCAID TYLES to PENNY STRICKLAND 28 Feb 1798. Bdsm Samuel Wilder.
ISAAC KINDALL TO MARY PRITCHET 10 Jul 1790. Bdsm Isaac Kindall and John Noms.
LOVELL IVEY to FANNY MORGAN 28 Dec 1796. Bdsm Absalom Woodall.
JAMES ROSE to JERUSAH McGLAWHON 18 Dec 1798. Bdsm Joseph Langston and James Rose.
ROBERT MASSINGILL to SALLY SELLARS 15 Aug 1798. Bdsm Equila Mace.
HENRY STEVENSON to DELILAH DANIEL 23 May 1798. Bdsm Henry Stevenson and James Johnson.
STEPHEN PACE to LUCY WALKER 8 Mar 8 1799. Bdsm Stephen Pace and Major Walker.
JOHN JONES to SARAH MATTHEWS 6 Aug 1798. Bdsm John Jones and John Carrell.
HENRY BRYAN to UTLEY PENNY 7 May 1798. Bdsm James Penny.
ETHELDRED MASSINGILL to ESTHER BLACKMAN 22 Dec 1794. Bdsm John Blackman.
JOHN POOL to ANNY AVERA 1 Mar 1794. Bdsm John Pool and Hardy Bryan.
HENRY AARON to CHRISTIAN DURHAM 23 Oct 1797. Bdsm Aaron Smith.
WILLIS HINTON to SALLY HALLINGS 15 Jan 1798. Bdsm Joseph Brown.
FREDERICK BRUI to ZILPAH ALTMAN 26 Nov 1799. Bdsm Nathan Altman.
JOHN LEE to MOURNING ALTMAN 25 Oct 1783. Bdsm John Lee and Dixon Fail.
ARCHIBALD PEPLES to SARAH RENN 16 Jun 1790. Bdsm Archibard Peples

JOHNSTON COUNTY MARRIAGES

and Jeremiah Powell.
BRYANT GREEN to LUCY SMITH 20 Nov 1798. Bdsm Sion Green.
NATHANIEL GILES to MARY ANN BRIDGERS 1 Jun 1794. Bdsm Nathaniel Giles and Hardy Bryan.
BURWELL BARBER to LYDIA JONES 27 Dec 1796. Bdsm Burwell Barber and Thomas Barber.
WILLIAM LEWIS to PATTY WRIGHT 24 Jul 1798. Bdsm William Lewis and William Williams.
BENJAMIN WOODARD to POLLEY DAVIS 27 Feb 1798. Bdsm Benjamin Woodard and Jacob Edwards.
JACOB STEVENS to ELIZABETH BOON 3 May 1793. Bdsm Joseph Boon.
ISAAC INGRAM to FRANCES COLLINS 6 Feb 1799. Bdsm Isaac Ingram and William Ingram.
JAMES TALTON to SARAH ALMOND 8 Feb 1798. Bdsm William Talton.
ROLAND WILKINSON to SENETH YELVERTON 12 Dec 1792. Bdsm Roland Wilkinson and Reuben Wilkinson.
ENOCH WHITLEY to ELIZABETH GULLEY 20 Dec 1792. Bdsm Enoch Whitley and Nathan Gulley.
GABRINE PARKER to OLIVE MOORE 29 Nov 1798. Bdsm Joseph Richardson.
HENRY PARNOLD to NANCY STARLING 27 Feb 1792. Bdsm Arthur Bailey Johnson.
CHARLIE LITTLETON to ELPSAHA ARMSTRONG 1 Mar 1796. Bdsm Henry Stevens.
JAMES ODOM to BETSEY HEARNE 24 Sep 1798. Bdsm Mason Hearne.
REDDER JOHNSON to ELLENDER FLOWERS 31 Jan 1797. Bdsm Redder Johnson and Joseph Deloach.
JOHN HINTON to ELIZABETH HINTON 1 Mar 1796. Bdsm Matthew Sturdivant.
THOMAS AVERA to PATIENCE AVERA 24 Jan 1797. Bdsm Thomas Avera and Etheldred Smith.
ZADOCK WATSON to BADEATH JOHNSON 30 Jul 1792. Bdsm Zadock Watson and James Faulk.
HOPKINS LEE to TABITHA LEE 16 Mar 1792. Bdsm Robert Lee.
JOHN KITTINGSWORTH to PATTY GULLEY 2 Oct 1798. Bdsm John Kittingsworth and Shadrock Eason.
CHARLIE RYALS to ALSEY BAGGET 8 Sep 1792. Bdsm Charlie Ryals and Edward Penny.
JOHN JARRELL to AMELIA HINNANT 1 Jan 1797. Bdsm John Jarrell.
THOMAS ATKINSON to PATIENCE ODOM 27 Feb 1798. Bdsm John Atkinson.
ISIAH CARTER to MARY YOUNGBLOOD 9 Aug 1790. Bdsm Isiah Carter and William Youngblood.
CHARLES WOODELE to MOIDON LEARCY? 21 Jan 1797. Bdsm Richard Holt.
JEREMIAH LEE to ELIZABETH AVERA 1 Jan 1790. Bdsm Jeremiah Lee.
THOMAS CARRELL to ? 20 May 1797. Bdsm Robert Whittington.
ROLAND WILLIAMS to NANCY RER 25 Feb 1792. Bdsm Thomas Leach.
SAMPSON ROGERS to POLLY WATKINS 27 Nov 1798. Bdsm Daniel Rogers, Jr.
WILLIAM GRIMES to FRANCES ADAMS 11 Jun 1792. Bdsm William Grimes and Howell Adams.
BENJAMIN EDWARDS to SARBY TINER 1 Oct 1793. Bdsm Benjamin Edwards and Drury Musslewhite.
JOSEPH BROWN to PHEREBY SMITH 4 Jun 1793. Bdsm Joseph Brown and

MARRIAGE BONDS

Abner Sauls.
JACOB WALKER to LEVERY GARDNER 1 Nov 1790. Bdsm John Moore.
JOHN WILDER to KATHRIN KITTINGSWORTH 27 Feb 1798. Bdsm Samuel Wilder, Jr.
RUEBEN JORDAN to OLIVE RICHARDSON 30 Nov 1790. Bdsm Rueben Jordan and Applewhite Richardson.
JOSEPH BROWN to POLLY SNIPES 25 May 1792. Bdsm Robert Gulley, Sr.
JACOB FLOWERS, JR. TO PHEREBY JOHNSON 8 Apr 1798. Ddsm Jacob Flowers, Jr. and Henry Flowers.
BARNEY INGRAM to EDITH ALTMAN 24 Jan 1797. Bdsm William Lee.
SAMUEL STRICKLAND to SARAH HOWELL 30 Nov 1794. Bdsm Samuel Strickland and Applewhite Richardson.
WARREN ONEIL to SALLY RICHARDSON 1 Oct 1799. Bdsm Warren Oneil and James Gregory.
MATTHEW PARKER, JR. to MARY ODOM 27 Aug 1793. Bdsm Hardy Parker.
JESSE CREECH to MARGARET WORLEY 28 Nov 1798. Bdsm William Worley.
THOMAS EDWARDS to NANCY PRICE 8 Sep 1796. Bdsm Thomas Pierce.
BRITAIN LOCKHART, JR. to MARY VINSON 22 Feb 1797. Bdsm Osborn Lockhart.
MEAD GULLEY to AVIE ATKINSON 31 Mar 1796. Bdsm Amos Atkinson.
DANIEL ROGERS to LYDIA GARNER 23 Nov 1797. Bdsm Robert Rogers.
SAMUEL AVERA to SARAH VINSON 30 Jan 1794. Bdsm Samuel Avera and Henry Gray.
WILLIAM WILSON to ELIZABETH W? 22 Mar 1794. Bdsm John Moore.
LEWIS GOWER to JANE OVERBY 26 Nov 1796. Bdsm William Gower.
CULLEN WILDER to WELLY BRANNON 1 Oct 1790. Bdsm Cullen Wilder and William Brannon.
ELISHA GARNER to SALLY BROWN 1 Oct 1799. Bdsm Elisha Garner and Daniel Rogers.
SANDER AVERA to POLLY OLIVER 23 Nov 1797. Bdsm William Jones.
ISOM RYALS to PATTY ROWLINE 30 Aug 1796. Bdsm Edmond Tomlinson.
LINSEY ROBERTS to BEADY NINV? 10 Sep 1793. Bdsm Linsey Roberts and James Langford.
HENRY PROCTOR to AMY LEE 2 Apr 1798. Bdsm James Carrell.
WILLIAM JONES to WINIFRED AVERA 26 Jan 1793. Bdsm William Jones and Zadok Stallings.
SHERAD EARP TO EDITH ATKINSON 16 Apr 1798. Bdsm Sherod Earp and Icabod Blackman.
STEPHEN PARKER to RACHEL JOHNSON 2 Oct 1798. Bdsm Matthew Parker.
EDMOND TOMLINSON to DELIAH MCKAY 26 Mar 1794. Bdsm Nahor Norris.
JESSE WALL to MARY PENNY 2 Mar 1796. Bdsm Robert Gulley, Jr.
WILLIAM RYALS to EDITH CHILES 20 Nov 1790. Bdsm William Ryals and Isom Oneil.
SAMUEL GODWIN, JR. to POLLY DUIK 28 Feb 1797. Bdsm Samuel Godwin, Jr.
WILLIE GARNER to SARAH COCKRELL 12 Dec 1797. Bdsm Willie Garner and William Garner.
J. W. LEAREY to BETSEY SELLARS 23 Jan 1798. Bdsm Jenkins Farmer.
VINSON WEST to LEVINA HAYSE 18 Jan 1798. Bdsm Vinson West and Adam Alexander.
AZEL CLIFTON to JANY POOL 8 Dec 1796. Bdsm Azel Clifton and Britain Suggs.

JOHNSTON COUNTY MARRIAGES

JOHN STEVEN to PHEREBY FAILE 7 Apr 1792. Bdsm Thomas Faile.
DRURY MEDLEN to SARAH JOHNSON 1 Feb 1793. Bdsm Isaac Jones.
EDWARD ETHELDRED to CLARA PROCTOR 1 Jan 1798. Bdsm Edward Etheldred.
ROBERT GULLEY to SALLY BRIDGERS 2 Jan 1798. Bdsm Joseph Brown.
THOMAS JOINER to SARAH BAILEY 31 May 1797. Bdsm Frederick Holmes.
LABON WATSON to SALLY WATSON 24 Feb 1795. Bdsm Labon Watson and David Watson.
AARON SMITH to WINIFRED VINSON 12 Jan 1798. Bdsm Daniel Averyt.
THOMAS BARBER to BETSY LANGDON 8 Apr 1799. Bdsm Thomas Barber and Burwell Barber.
NATHAN ALLEN to APSABETH BALLENGER 22 Mar 1791. Bdsm Nathan Allen and William Ballenger.
BRASWELL NARON to TEMPY PARKER 1 Oct 1799. Bdsm Joseph Broughton.
JESSE PENNY to MILLEY BROADSTREET 20 Apr 1792. Bdsm Jesse Penny and Edward Stevens.
PETER WILLIAMS to LYDIA CARTER 1 Nov 1794. Bdsm Peter Williams and Irvin Carter.
LEWIS ROLIN to RODA BAGGET 10 Feb 1797. Bdsm Charles Ryals.
WILLIAM BROADSTREET to BETSY FURLEY 31 Aug 179. Bdsm David Evans.
JOSEPH BOON, JR. to HESTER STRICKLAND 28 May 1794. Bdsm William Musslewhite.
TOBIAS PAGE to POLLY TOMLINSON 11 Sep 1794. Bdsm Tobias Page and Isham Johnson.
JOHN F. ELLINGTON to ADER CARTER 27 Aug 1798. Bdsm John F. Ellington and Kindred Carter.
JOHN DIVIN to ? 28 May 1794. Bdsm Henry Stevens.
JAMES PARKER to PATIENCE JARRELL 18 Aug 1794. Bdsm Matthew Parker.
TIMOTHY WALTON to NANCY LEACH 2 Jan 1792. Bdsm Timothy Walton and Elliot Sanders.
BRIDGERS ONEIL to POLLY HINTON ? Aug 1798. Bdsm Simon Price.
JENKINS FARMER to SUSANNAH HADLEY 20 Aug 1798. Bdsm William Farmer.
NOAH JOHNSON to DRENNY MERBLINS? 1 Feb 1793. Bdsm Isaac Jones.
RYAN JOHNSON to JANE CARRELL 28 Oct 1794. Bdsm Ryan Johnson and Joel Johnson.
BURWELL JONES to JUDITH SMITH 8 Aug 1794. Bdsm Charles Copeland.
MATTHEW JONES to SALLY LEACH 1 Oct 1793. Bdsm Matthew Jones and James Ogburn.
JOHN KILLINGSWORTH to SARAH BLACKMAN 9 Nov 1793. Bdsm John Killingsworth and William Hobby.
GREEN HILL to SALLY LEE 21 Aug 1799. Bdsm Green Hill and John Carrell.
LEWIS ADAMS to SUSANNAH MORGAN 1 Dec 1799. Bdsm Lewis Adams and John Morgan.
NICHOLAS THOMPSON to BETSY HAYS 11 Jan 1793. Bdsm Elijah Thompson.
SAMUEL WILDER to MARY GREEN 26 Aug 1794. Bdsm Joseph Irvin.
MICAJAH WOODARD to CHLOE LILES 26 Aug 1794. Bdsm Micajah Liles.
JOHN WOODARD to SARAH HOCUTT 30 Nov 1794. Bdsm William Hocutt.
ISHAM BAUCOM to ALEY PENNY 11 Jun 1798. Bdsm Samuel Smith.
WILLIAM PEEBLES to REBECCA JOHNSTON 17 Feb 1792. Bdsm Moses Johnston.
JOHN WALL to POLLEY GULLEY 2 Jan 1798. Bdsm John Wall and William

MARRIAGE BONDS

Wall.
GEORGE HINTON to LILIPAH JOHNSON 8 Dec 1793. Bdsm George Hinton and Peter Williams.
EDWARD ETHRIDGE to CLARKY PROCTOR 1 Jan 1798. Bdsm Jacob Woodall.
WILLIAM HONEYCUTT to BETSY HONEYCUTT 28 May 1794. Bdsm Moses Johnson.
WILLIAM SHAW to ELIZABETH WILDER 31 Dec 1792. Bdsm William Shaw and Edward Lee.
JACOB RENFROW to MARTHA SIMMS 11 Nov 1794. Bdsm Stephen Grice.
JONATHAN EARP to DOROTHY WILDER 15 Feb 1797. Bdsm Burwell Earp.
HENRY FLOWERS to ELIZABETH MARSHALL 18 Jul 1797. Bdsm Henry Flowers and John Coats.
THOMAS COREY to RHODA WILSON 31 Dec 1799. Bdsm John Wilson.
JUSTIS PARRISH to AMY FLUELLER 30 May 1797. Bdsm Justis Parrish and John Jones.
AARON JOHNSON to PATSY ONEIL 1 Mar 1796. Bdsm Willie Watkins.
HENRY JORDAN to MARY STEVENS 30 May 1797. Bdsm William Brown Hocutt.
RUEBEN CARTER to PENELOPIA PRICE 2 Feb 1799. Bdsm Hardy Barber and John Bailey.
CORNELIUS LYNETT to CYNTHIA WHITLEY 27 Feb 1779. Bdsm Needham Whitley.
JONAS MANN to MARY SIMS 17 Nov 1794. Bdsm Jonas Mann and William Braswell.
OLATHANIEL TRAYWICK to SARAH EASON 6 May 1797. Bdsm George Traywick.
ARCHIBALD VINSON to RUTH SMITH 31 Mar 1797. Bdsm William Bryan.
NATHAN WILKERSON to SWEETEN PARNOLD 1 Mar 1796. Bdsm Benjamin Wilkerson.
UZ GREGORY to SALLY MAY 21 May 1796. Bdsm Uz Gregory and Little Berry May.
JOHN DEAN to JANE STRICKLAND 1 Mar 1796. Bdsm Joseph Langston.
JACOB FERRELL to SIDDY JOHNSON 20 Feb 1797. Bdsm Jacob Ferrell and Plyer Barber.
WILLIAM JOHNSON to CLAREY GALE 27 Feb 1797. Bdsm Charles Copeland.
WILLIAM CARRELL to PIETY FLUELLER 18 Mar 1797. Bdsm Abraham Perry.
NATHAN BATTAN to ELIZABETH ADKERSON 12 Oct 1796. Bdsm John Battan.
JOHN McHONDIKES to PENNY LEE 2 Dec 1792. Bdsm Henry Stevens.
WILLIAM HATCHER to CHRISTEAN GANNER 1 Mar 1796. Bdsm Thomas Cockrell.
PATON VINSON to NANCY HARPER 2 Mar 1796. Bdsm Drury Vinson.
NEEDHAM SNIPES to PHEREBEE TURNER 10 Mar 1796. Bdsm Needham Snipes and Philip Johnson.
SAMUEL COCKRELL to PATTY HATCHER 17 Jan 1797. Bdsm Benjamin Hatcher and John Vinson.
NATHAN STANSILL to CLARY TAYLOR 26 Feb 1797. Bdsm John Stansill.
BENJAMIN LEATS to ELIZABETH CRAWFORD 2 Mar 1797. Bdsm Willis Cole.
JESSE HOLLIMAN to POLLY JONES 2 Jul 1796. Bdsm William Hackney.
JOHN ROGERS to POLLY KELLY 11 May 1797. Bdsm Robert Rogers and Daniel Rogers.
JAMES SMITH to JANE LEE 14 Oct 1797. Bdsm Samuel Lee, Jr.
JESSE STEPHEN to POLLY GRAVES 2 Jul 1796. Bdsm William Hackney.

JOHNSTON COUNTY MARRIAGES

WILLIAM PEARCE to BETSY HATCHER 31 Oct 1800. Bdsm Levi Pearce and Robert Gulley.
OSBORN LOCKHART to LUCY THOMAS 8 Nov 1793. Bdsm James Lockhart.
JOHN PARNELL to PEGGY CLEMMONS 25 Mar 1797. Bdsm John Parnell and Jethro Bulls.
SAMUEL HARRELL to POLLY FARMER 2 Apr 1798. Bdsm William Farmer and Samuel Harrell.
JOHN GULLEY to ANN BROWN 25 Dec 1779. Bdsm John Gulley and John Watson.
WILLIAM ALLEN to RACHEL JONES 7 Nov 1794. Bdsm William Allen and Jacob Woodall.
JOSEPH RICHARDSON to MARTHA HACKNEY 30 May 178. Bdsm Robert Gulley, Jr. and Joseph Richardson.
JAMES CHAMBERS to ZILPAH JERNIGAN 25 Nov 1799. Bdsm John Stevens.
JOSIAH HOLDER to MILDRED HOLLIMAN 27 Nov 1798. Bdsm James Holder.
JOSIAH ATKINS to FRANCES PENNY 28 Dec 1799. Bdsm Ellak Sanders and Henry Penny.
PETER BALLARD to SARAH WILLIAMS 19 Oct 1796. Bdsm Peter Ballard and William Hackney.
EDMUND HOWELL to PHEREBY STRICKLAND 10 Aug 1791 Bdsm Uriah Strickland and William Worley.
RYAL PRICE to ELIZABETH OLIVER 18 Aug 1798. Bdsm Ryal Price and John Price.
JAMES OGBURN to EDITH YOUNGBLOOD 8 May 1796. Bdsm James Ogburn and Thomas Youngblood.
GEORGE BLACKBURN to MARY JONES 18 May 1798. Bdsm George Blackburn and Isaac Jones.
GEORGE WIMBERLY to PHEREBY HINTON 11 Feb 1798. Bdsm George Wimberly and George G. Hinton.
NATHAN STRICKLAND to ELIZABETH HARRELL 28 May 1793. Bdsm Nathan Strickland and John Strickland.
LEWIS BRYAN to ? ETHELDRED 7 Feb 1790. Bdsm William Hackney.
JAMES HOULDEN to PENELOPIA PRICE 20 Feb 1792. Bdsm James Houlden and Joseph Irwin.
WILLIAM BLACKMAN to NANCY JERNIGAN 19 Dec 1792. Bdsm William Blackman and Ichabod Blackman.
NATHAN POWELL to NANCY INGRAM 16 Jun 1790. Bdsm Nathan Powell and Jeremiah Powell.
JOHN HERRING to DORCAS STRICKLAND 28 May 1799. Bdsm Joshua Creech.
HENRY DUNCAN to KEZIAH AVERYT 20 Mar 20 1792. Bdsm Henry Duncan and William Durham.
EDMUND DEES to MARY WHITINGTON 16 Feb 1790. Bdsm Phaddy Whitington.
WILLIAM BRYAN to AMELIA VINSON 21 Aug 1793. Bdsm John Eason and Hugh Whitaker.
ARCHIBALD FLUELLER to NANCY PARRISH 7 Dec 1790. Bdsm Archibald Flueller and Ludom Smith.
E. STALLINGS to ELIZABETH NEWSOM 21 Jan 1790. Bdsm Isaac Stallings.
HEZEKIAH JENNING to SARAH JOHNSON 28 Aug 1790. Bdsm Richard Rivers.
OWEN BARBER to ELIZABETH JORDAN 4 Oct 1791. Bdsm Owen Barber and George Barber.
WILLIAM STEVENS to MARY SASSER 28 Aug 1792. Bdsm William Stevens and John Atkinson.

MARRIAGE BONDS

ROBERT WATKINS to CELAH BRYAN 11 Jan 1790. Bdsm Robert Watkins and Barnaby Lane.
RICHARD PILKINTON to MARY ANN DAVIS 11 Oct 1791. Bdsm Joshua Creech.
JAMES POMON to EDITH GREEN 20 Dec 1791. Bdsm James Promon and Andrew Collins.
WILLIAM PILKINTON to SARAH EDWARDS 26 Mar 1791. Bdsm Richard Pilkinton.
WILLIAM STEVENS to PHEREBY STEVENS 1 Jun 1790. Bdsm William Stevens.
JOSEPH IRWIN to ANN SHORE 21 Mar 1793. Bdsm Joseph Irwin and John Watson.
WILLIAM HINTON to TEMPERANCE POPE 25 Nov 1793. Bdsm John Petty Cobb.
LEWIS COLLINS to ABIGAIL FISH 4 Apr 1792. Bdsm Lewis Collins and John Fish.
WANCEY ATKINSON to NANCY MOORE 9 Aug 1793. Bdsm Robert Gulley.
THOMAS OLIVER to ELIZABETH POOL 13 Aug 1795. Bdsm Isaac Stallings.
ARTHUR TALTON to UNITY PEARCE 21 May 1791. Bdsm Arthur Talton and William Talton.
JOHN GREEN to WELTHY MOORE 28 Feb 1791. Bdsm John Green and Alexander Avera.
JAMES HOLLIMAN to NANCY NARIN 8 Nov 1791. Bdsm John Holder.
THOMAS COLLINS to CHARLOTTE DAVIS 6 Apr 1791. Bdsm William Bulls and Nathan Powell.
SAMUEL MITCHENER to FRANCES NORRISS 28 Jan 1790. Bdsm Samuel Mitchener and John Bryant.
WILLIAM MARSHALL to NANCY NORRISS 3 May 1790. Bdsm William Blunt.
WILLIAM WRIGHT to ELIZABETH ONEAL 13 ? 1790. Bdsm William Wright and Arthur Price.
DANIEL ROGERS to BETSY GARNER 27 Nov 1792. Bdsm Daniel Rogers and William Smith.
WILLIAM CARRELL to SARAH STEVENS 8 Feb 1790. Bdsm John Carrell and James Carrell.
THOMAS EATMAN to CELAH BAILEY 1 Mar 1794. Bdsm John Thomas and John Driver.
WILLIAM HOBBY to ELIZABETH AVERYT 3 Feb 1790. Bdsm William Hobby and Henry Blurton.
LITTLE BERRY MAY to PATTY GREGORY 14 Jun 1790. Bdsm Thomas Price, Edward Price and Little Berry May.
URIAS COLLINS to SALLY FISH 8 Jan 1791. Bdsm Urias Collins and John Fish.
BENNETT BLACKMAN to NANCY STEVENS 27 Feb 1793. Bdsm Henry Stevens.
ZACHARIAH STEVENS to SUSANNAH RIVERS 19 Jan 1791. Bdsm Richard Rivers.
JOHN STEAVNER to PHEREBY FAILE 18 Apr 1792. Bdsm Thomas Faile.
JARRETT THOMPSON to SUSANNAH CHAMBERS 19 Sep 1791. Bdsm Michael Reynolds.
HENRY KING to SARAH WILLIAMS 29 Apr 1790. Bdsm Henry King and Josiah Blackman.
JACOB EDWARDS to ELIZABETH PILKINTON 23 Jun 1790. Bdsm Jacob Edwards and Jethro Bulls.

JOHNSTON COUNTY MARRIAGES

LEROY BRANNON to REBEKAH COLE 4 Oct 1791. Bdsm Leroy Brannon and William Brannon.
AMOS WATKINS to LUCY SWAN 14 Oct 1799. Bdsm James Kirby and Amos Watkins.
FRANCIS HARRELL to MARY LEACH 25 Feb 1794. Bdsm Francis Harrell and Joseph Langston.
JESSE EDWARDS to PATTY PENDER 10 Aug 1798. Bdsm Jeremiah Gurley.
JOSEPH BROUGHTON to MARY STANSILL 28 Mar 1796. Bdsm Frederick Holliman.
ENOS SCARSBOROUGH to LEVEY WARD 19 Nov 1796. Bdsm Hugh Cravy and David Drake.
JACOB STEVENS to PATIENCE PEARCE 22 May 1797. Bdsm Jacob Stevens and John Stevens.
WILLIAM ROBERTS to BETSY REAVES 12 Oct 1793. Bdsm William Roberts and Thomas Roberts.
GEORGE MINOR to SALLY WHITINGTON 22 Nov 1799. Bdsm Richard Whitington and Isaac Johnson.
WILLIAM BROWN HOCUT to ALVEY ONEIL 5 Apr 1795. Bdsm William B. Hocut and Benjamin Hill.
WILLIS ATKINSON to EDITH AVERA 4 Mar 1797. Bdsm Robert Gulley.
ALLEN JOHNSON to PEGGY WHITINGTON 30 Sep 1795. Bdsm John Stevenson and James Langsdon.
GEORGE PARRISH to CATHRIN BRYAN 1 Aug 1792. Bdsm George Parrish and James Woodall.
JOSEPH HODGES to SARAH ALLEN 21 Apr 1791. Bdsm Joseph Hodges and Bryant Adams.
DRURY BRYAN to PATIENCE NOWELL 30 May 1790. Bdsm Drury Bryan and William Durham.
HENRY OLIVER to WIMMY INGRAM 13 Nov 1799. Bdsm Henry Oliver and William Powers.
JESSE McCLINTON to FEREBE McCONIC? 29 May 1793. Bdsm Henry Gray.
JOHN TINNER to POLLY AVERA 22 Dec 1796. Bdsm Zadock Stallings.
ABNER HILL to CHARLOTTE ADKINSON 2 Nov 1792. Bdsm Abner Hill and James Holder.
JOHN BLACKMAN to RACHEL KILLINGWORTH 4 Jan 1792. Bdsm Ichabod Blackman.
REDDUCK WATSON to MILLY WATSON 27 Feb 1792. Bdsm Redduck Watson and David Watson.
TOBIAS HOLLIMAN to PRUDENCE HOLDER 29 May 1793. Bdsm Hardy Parker.
GEORGE GULLEY to ZILPAH BARNES 1 Nov 1795. Bdsm John Ellis.
JAMES ROSN, JR to LEVINA VINSON 13 Feb 1792. Bdsm James Rosn, Jr. and Hardy Bryan.
ELIJAH ELLIS to PATIENCE COLLINS 20 Jul 1791. Bdsm Elijah Ellis and George Collins.
CHARLES RUSSEL to PHEBY BARBER 21 Mar 1791. Bdsm Charles Russel and William Giles.
NATHAN ATKINSON to NANCY MOORE 29 May 1793. Bdsm Henry Gray.
HENRY MITCHELL to POLLY AVERA 4 Sep 1792. Bdsm Henry Mitchell.
MOSES NEWSOME to ANN SCOTT 4 Apr 1792. Bdsm John Dement.
DAVID STRAPKERS? to AMY JOHNSON 13 Mar 1793. Bdsm Urias Johnson.
WILLIAM TEAL to RACHEL BULLS 6 Apr 1791. Bdsm William Bulls and Nathan Powell.

MARRIAGE BONDS

BIN PRICE to PRUDENCE HOLDER 29 Feb 1792. Bdsm William Hackney.
WILLIAM SHAW to KATHERINE SHAW 15 Feb 1792. Bdsm William Shaw and James Shaw.
JOHN SANDERS to MIMMIE JONES 14 Mar 1797. Bdsm Nahor Norriss.
JACOB HINTON to SALLY STALLINGS 1 Jan 1792. Bdsm Zadock Stallings.
HENRY HILLIARD to PRISCILLA SIMS 5 Apr 1791. Bdsm Henry Hilliard and Noel Renfrow.
RICHARD PRINCE to MOLLY RAINS 9 Aug 1791. Bdsm Richard Prince and John Snipes, Jr.
JESSE PITTMAN to POLLY KILLINGSWORTH 26 Feb 1813. Bdsm John Sanders, Jr. and David Holliman.
JAMES STANLEY to LELAH BLACKMAN 9 May 1809. Bdsm Jesse Stanley.
JOHN COOK to BETSY PARISH 16 Mar 1803. Bdsm George Parish.
JESSY BRITT, JR. to NANCY NORRIS 21 Apr 1792. Bdsm Isaac Kindrall.
WILLIAM POWELL to SARAH PEARCE 12 Aug 1808. Bdsm Enos Powell.
DAVID MOODY to PATSY EDWARDS 29 Sep 1808. Bdsm John William.
RODERICK McCLOUD to CADY GODWIN 24 May 1808. Bdsm Samuel Lee, Jr.
ZACHARIAH LEE to MARY HOBBY 14 Aug 1801. Bdsm Peter Johnson.
RICHARD BYRD to JERUSHA DELOACH 13 Oct 1806. Bdsm John Byrd.
THOMAS BLENSON to SUSANNAH FERRELL 1 Mar 1809. Bdsm Theo Pool.
JESSE WALL to POLLY DEVOLT 20 Jan 1809. Bdsm Jacob Brooks.
DAVID WATSON to REDDY ROE 22 Oct 1808. Bdsm William Gray.
WARREN HOUSE to DELILAH CARROLL 28 Feb 1809. Bdsm Benjamin Carroll.
SETH BALKAM to SALLY ELLIOT 17 Nov 1808. Bdsm Seth Balkam and Ichabod Balkam.
FRANCIS CLARK to RUTH POWELL 7 Dec 1808. Bdsm Jacob Powell.
JOSEPH THOMAS to POLLY SMITH 24 Feb 1808. Bdsm Simon Pearce.
DRURY LYLES to WINIFRED HIGH 23 Oct 1801. Bdsm Drury Lyles and Seth Holliman.
GEORGE GOODRICH to ELIZABETH WALSTON 19 Apr 1809. Bdsm Elijah Baker and George Goodrich.
JOHN FARMER to ELIZABETH BALLENGER 22 Apr 1809. Bdsm John Farmer and Allen Ballenger.
STARLING TEMPLES to NAOMI MASSINGILL 20 May 1808. Bdsm George Massengill.
DAVID SMITH to SALLY INGRAM 28 Apr 1805. Bdsm Bryan Smith.
DAVID BRASWELL to BETSEY ADAMS 13 Jan 18? Bdsm David Braswell.
BENJAMIN HOLMES to CELAH PEACOCK 22 Feb 1808. Bdsm John Stansell.
ALLEN S. BALLENGER to SUSANNAH FARMER ? Bdsm Allen Ballenger and John Farmer.
SIMON STEVENS to KEZIAH KILGO 2 Jan 1808. Bdsm Berry Wooten.
JAMES AYCOCK to CHARITY WILKERSON 29 Mar 1808. Bdsm Charles Wilkerson.
HENRY RAINS to BEDIE JORDAN 2 Jan 1808. Bdsm Berry Wooten.
JOHN FELLOWS to POLLY GERMILLON 28 Dec 1807. Bdsm John Stevens.
EDMOND BLACKMAN to MOURNEN MASSENGILL 4 Jan 1808. Bdsm William Blackman.
ISHAM ONEAL, JR. to SAVEL HILL 28 Nov 1809. Bdsm Isham Oneal Jr. and Lindrick Oneal.
WILLIAM WHITLEY to NANCY POPE 23 Dec 1807. Bdsm Kedar Whitley.
ARCHIBALD PARNOLD to PENNY FEDDER 4 Feb 1808. Bdsm Henry Parnold.
ASA CRUMPLER to NANCY ONEAL 12 Nov 1808. Bdsm William Crumpler and

JOHNSTON COUNTY MARRIAGES

Asa Crumpler.
STEPHEN COCKRELL to ANNE WATSON 23 Dec 1807. Bdsm Willis Garner.
JOHN PILKERTON to PHEREBY CAPS 13 Jan 1808. Bdsm Barnaby Bulls.
LEVY HARRELL to BETSY HOCUTT 24 Feb 1809. Bdsm Willis Cole.
JOHN JONIER to SARAH PEARCE 25 Oct 1808. Bdsm William Hinnant.
NEEDHAM ROBERTSON to PATIENCE RICHARDSON 13 Jan 1808. Bdsm Noah Nicholas.
ADIN ADAMS to SALLY RYALS 23 Dec 1805. Bdsm Jacob Woodall and Needham Robertson.
NEEDHAM FUTRELL to CATHY SHARP 29 Nov 1808. Bdsm Lovard Pearce and Samuel Pearce.
WILLIAM ROBERTS to POLLY MASSENGILL 28 Dec 1808. Bdsm Samuel Strickland.
SAMUEL RICHARDSON to CELAH HACKNEY 23 Dec 1807. Bdsm John High.
HENRY HAILS TO ZELPHA WOODELL 29 Nov 1808. Bdsm Chatman Hails.
HARDY HOLMES to ELIZABETH OGNIM? 24 Aug 1808. Bdsm Samuel Lee Jr.
PERRY SMITH to CATHRAN FROST 28 Nov 1809. Bdsm Stephen Brown.
WILLIAM CLEMMY to PHEREBY LEE 25 Nov 1807. Bdsm Samuel Lee.
BENJAMIN CREECH to SALLY CREECH 13 Feb 1808. Bdsm Joshua Creech Jr.
ASA LEARCEY to ELIZABETH JOHNSON 27 Feb 1802. Bdsm Asa Learcey and John Learcey.
EDMOND CRUMPLER to DELILAH HODGES 17 Jan 1809. Bdsm William Hinnant, Sr.
JESSE SNIPES to SALLY ROBERTS 27 Aug 1802. Bdsm Jesse Snipes and Edward Price.
JOHN LEARCY to BETSY LANGSTON 12 Nov 1806. Bdsm Thomas Barber.
WILLIAM FAIL to ELIZAETH BRYAN 23 Jan 1804. Bdsm William Fail and Jeremiah Lee.
DAVID JOHNSON to DELITHA SASSETON 18 Jan 1803. Bdsm Allen Johnson.
HILLIARD DEES to SALLY SMITH 20 Mar 1802. Bdsm Hilliard Dees and Matthew Handy.
FREDERICK ONEIL to BEDITH HORTON 28 Feb 1804. Bdsm Samuel Oneil.
STANSILL MOORE to PATSY BARNES 3 Jan 1810. Bdsm Stansill Moore and Elias Barnes.
THOMAS WINBURN to PATSY POPE 23 Apr 1810. Bdsm William Hinton.
WILLIAM LASHLEY to BETSY JOHNSON 8 Feb 1810. Bdsm Harry Johnson.
JOHN AUSTON to SALLY YOUNGBLOOD 6 Apr 1803. Bdsm John Auston.
NATHAN STRICKLAND to EDITH SMITH 29 Feb 1804. Bdsm Samuel Lee, Jr.
THOMAS DOUGLAS to EDITH THOMPSON 29 Feb 1804. Bdsm Samuel Lee, Jr.
WILLIAM DODD, JR to DEDEMIAH PRICE 29 Jul 1804. Bdsm William Dodd, Jr. and Thomas Price.
WILLIAM HINNANT to LEVEY SMITH 8 Feb 1824. Bdsm William Hinnant and Needham Hinnant.
ALEXANDER JERNIGAN to ? 25 Nov 1803. Bdsm Alexander Jernigan and Deal D. Collins.
SAMUEL HOALT to SALLY JOHNSON 28 May 1802. Bdsm Samuel Lee, Jr.
WILLIS WATSON to BETSY BULLS 4 Jun 1807. Bdsm Willis Watson and Ellich Sanders.
JONATHAN BRITT to VICY BROWN 10 Jul 1807. Bdsm Willis Nelms.
GIDDEON ALLEN to ELIZABETH RUSSELL 2 Mar 1807. Bdsm Giddeon Allen and John Farmer.
PEYTON ALFORD to LEVEY HINTON 28 May 1802. Bdsm Blake Brady.

MARRIAGE BONDS

HENRY STEVENS to BETSY BASS 23 Apr 1807. Bdsm Henry Stevens and John Stevens.
JAMES DURHAM to CELAH AVERA 22 Jun 1805. Bdsm Harriss Tomlinson.
PETER DUPREE to SALLY JOHNSON 18 Apr 1806. Bdsm Jonathan Johnson.
JAMES HETH to PRISCALLA HORN 15 Feb 1807. Bdsm Stephen Grice.
JOHN COOK to BETSY PARRISH 16 Mar 1803. Bdsm George Parrish.
WILLIAM FARRAR to SARAH TINER 1 Mar 1804. Bdsm James Tiner.
ELISHA REDDER to AGGY WRIGHT 5 Dec 1810. Bdsm Rigdon Johnson.
WILLIS WATSON to RACHEL HERRING 28 Jan 1802. Bdsm Matthias Handy and Willis Watson.
THOMAS AVERA to JUDITH JONES 23 Dec 1804. Bdsm William Jones and Brigdon Johnson.
JOHN ATKINS to IRENE JOHNSON 19 Sep 1802. Bdsm Henry Johnson.
JOHN HART to BETSY GURLEY 27 Feb 1805. Bdsm Samson Edmond.
WILLIAM HATCHER to CHARITY McCLEMEY 10 Jan 1804. Bdsm Benjamin Hatcher.
IRVIN WILDER to WIMEY AVERA 28 Mar 1804. Bdsm John Wilder and Irvin Wilder.
GEORGE BARBER to ? 20 Jan 1807. Bdsm George Barber and Owen Barber.
DEMPSEY AVERA to BETSY BYRD 17 Sep 1807. Bdsm Redder Byrd.
WILLIAM KENNEDY to ETTER SMITH 12 Sep 1807. Bdsm Alexander Penny.
HENRY HINTON to POLLY SANDERS 30 Apr 1807. Bdsm Rueben Sanders.
SOLOMON FUTERAL to RACHEL WATSON 28 Aug 1809. Bdsm Etheldred Futeral.
CHARLES STEVENS to ELIZABETH INGRAM 14 May 1805. Bdsm Matthew Handy.
JAMES BEAD to CHARLOTTE JAMES 22 Oct 1807. Bdsm James Bead and David Stevens.
TELL WILDER to ESTHER AVERA 14 Nov 1803. Bdsm David Wilder.
DAVID TINNER to JANE BRIDGERS 27 Oct 1803. Bdsm David Tinner and William Tinner.
SAMUEL BROWN to SALLY WILSON 10 Jul 1802. Bdsm Henry Hobby.
JOHN BRANNON to EDNEY ELLIS 29 Aug 1809. Bdsm German Ellis.
JAMES ADAMS to EDNY HOBBY 21 Dec 1800. Bdsm Master Woodall and William Allen.
ALEXANDER SMITH, JR. TO PEGGY AVERA 16 Feb 1803. Bdsm William Ryals, Jr.
JOHN ROPER to ELIZABETH PEARCE 28 Jan 1804. Bdsm John Roper and John Sanders, Jr.
JACOB PEACOCK to SALLY HOLMES 25 Aug 1806. Bdsm Jacob Peacock and Frederick Holmes.
WILLIAM TUCKER to SALLY MEREDITH 9 Nov 1807. Bdsm Daniel Sauls and John Kelly.
ARNOLD BAILEY to BETSY ONEIL 27 Mar 1806. Bdsm Benjamin Oneil.
THOMAS TAYLOR to CHARLOTTE SPIVEY 12 Apr 1805. Bdsm Simon Pearce.
SIMON PEARCE, JR to POLLY RAINS 22 Sep 1807. Bdsm John Rains.
WILLIAM POOL to RHODA PEARCE 5 Apr 1807. Bdsm Samuel Pearce.
SILAS ONEIL to MARY GREGGEL 22 Nov 1805. Bdsm Harland Gilman.
THOMAS YOUNG to BETSEY GARNER 2 Dec 1809. Bdsm Thomas Page.
DRURY VINSON to ANNE DURHAM 2 Dec 1804. Bdsm Samuel Avera.
MILES LANGLEY to SARAH GANNER 25 May 1807. Bdsm Elisha Ganner.
WILLIAM FOLK to SARAH PEETEVITT 13 Oct 1803. Bdsm Thomas Folk.

JOHNSTON COUNTY MARRIAGES

WILLIAM BEARD to MARY ANN ROSE 2 Mar 1803. Bdsm Joseph Hearne.
KEDAR AVERA to SALLY JOHNSON 8 Oct 1807. Bdsm John Tiner.
ICHABOD BALKAM to NANCY SASSER 23 May 1807. Bdsm Icahabod Balkam and Jacob Stevens.
JACOB TINER to CATY BENSON 28 May 1805. Bdsm William Holt.
ZACHARIAH LEE to SALLY JOHNSON 6 Sep 1807. Bdsm Samuel Johnson.
JOHN RAIFORD to CHERRY HONEYCUTT 28 Aug 1805. Bdsm John Raiford and Philip Raiford.
ETHELDRED EVANS to NANCY COLLINS 5 Mar 1806. Bdsm James Peden.
ALEXANDER THOMAS to POLLY MURPHY 22 Nar 1805. Bdsm Elisha Thomas.
REUBEN SMITH to CREACEY GODWIN 26 May 1807. Bdsm John Byrd.
JAMES McCALESS to LUSANNA DURHAM 29 Mar 1802. Bdsm James McCaless and Willis Watson.
MICHAEL FLOWERS to MARY KEEN 27 May 1807. Bdsm Stephen Grice.
JOHN BOYET to CATY WILDER 30 Sep 1807. Bdsm John Boyet and John Killingsworth.
JOHN PULLEY to POLLY RAINS 20 Oct 1807. Bdsm John Pulley and W. Watson.
ELIAS PRICE to DELILAH NARRON 12 Oct 1807. Bdsm Allen Richardson.
BRITAIN PAGE to NANCY GARNER 9 Sep 1809. Bdsm Thomas Page.
JAMES TALTON to NANCY SPIVY 21 Mar 1807. Bdsm James Talton and Reuben Wilkinson.
WILLIAM JOHNSON to BURCHETT LEE 23 Sep 1807. Bdsm William Johnson and Samuel Johnson.
WILLIAM JONES to AMY BARBER to 9 Jan 1805. Bdsm William Jones and Burwell Barber.
CHARLES FULGHAM to ? ? Bdsm Joseph Fulgham and Charles Wellons.
DAVID MOODY to PATTY EDWARDS 29 Sep 1808. Bdsm John Williams.
GEORGE HILLIARD to ALEY SNIPES 24 Feb 1809. Bdsm Matthew Jones.
JOHN LEE to POLLY NONSWORTHY 3 Jun 1806. Bdsm John Lee and Henry Champion.
JOHN PARRISH to BETSY FERRELL 28 Nov 1807. Bdsm John Parrish and John Ellis.
JOHN CAUDLE to ELIZABETH TOLER 26 Dec 1804. Bdsm Robert Toler.
JAMES GODWIN to SALLY STEVENS 9 Oct 1807. Bdsm Jacob Beaman.
JOSEPH LANGSTON to BERSHEBA JORDAN 16 Oct 1804. Bdsm James Rose.
MITCHELL CARRELL to SALLY CARRELL 3 Dec 1805. Bdsm Benjamin Carrell.
INGRAM LEE to MARTHA BRASWELL 26 Dec 1804. Bdsm Levy Braswell.
JOHN WILLIAMS to POLLY ALLEN 13 Sep 1804. Bdsm John Sanders, Jr.
SAMUEL NONSWORTHY to ELIZABETH HINTON 12 Jul 1802. Bdsm Samuel Nonsworthy and Matthew Handy.
DIXON JORDAN to JUDITH MANOR 26 Sep 1803. Bdsm Mammeduke Strickland.
JOSEPH LANGSTON to "SUKEY" BAKER 20 Nov 1802. Bdsm Joseph Langston and Francis Harrell.
JACOB MATTHEWS to SARAH FARMER 3 May 1800. Bdsm Jacob Matthews and Jenkins Farmer.
ROBERT TOLAR to MARY HOLLAND 9 Mar 1802. Bdsm Robert Tolar and Samuel Nonsworthy.
WILLIAM POWERS to BETSY OLIVER 10 Feb 1805. Bdsm William Powers and Isaac Stallings.

MARRIAGE BONDS

FRANCIS LOTHROP to LANEY BRASWELL 29 Mar 1803. Bdsm Francis Lothrop and Abraham Webb.
JESSE BAILEY to LYTHIA BLANKETSHIP 2 Apr 1800. Bdsm Jesse Bailey and Micajah Bailey.
JESSE PITTMAN to MILLY JONES 22 Mar 1807. Bdsm Jesse Pittman and Charles Wilkerson.
STEPHEN PERRY to ELIZABETH ONEIL ? Bdsm Stephen Perry and Charles Stevens.
JACOB HARRELL to POLLY WHITTEN 1 Dec 1802. Bdsm Jacob Harrell and Francis Harrell.
ABRAHAM GWIN to CATHARINE CRAWFORD 27 Nov 1802. Bdsm Abraham Gwin and John Learcy.
BENJAMIN BRYAN to POLLY STEVENS 8 Jun 1807. Bdsm Benjamin Bryan and Samuel Smith.
JOHN DOWDEN to BETSY DURHAM 7 May 1802. Bdsm John Dowden and Young Bridgers.
BENJAMIN EASON to POLLY KEAL 26 Dec 1801. Bdsm Benjamin Eason and Henry Horne.
RHODHAM DOUGLAS to PATTY HARRELL 20 Nov 1802. Bdsm Rhodham Douglas and Francis Harrell.
SAMUEL MITCHINER to PATSY LOCKHART 8 Sep 1802. Bdsm Samuel Mitchiner and John Stevens.
LARRY BRYAN to SALLY HINTON 26 Dec 1801. Bdsm Larry Bryan and Willis Watson.
ROYAL PRICE to NANCY BATEMAN 29 Dec 1800. Bdsm Royal Price and William Harris.
SAMUEL ONEIL to KIDDY HINTON 18 Feb 1802. Bdsm Samuel Oneil and Silas Oneil.
WILLIS NELMS to BETSY BROWN 28 Mar 1803. Bdsm Willis Nelms.
JESSE JOHNSTON to MOANING PARKER 3 Apr 1802. Bdsm Jesse Johnston and Jesse Pearce.
NICHOLAS FAULK to RHODA HARMAN 8 Apr 1802. Bdsm Nicholas Faulk and Etheldred Futrell.
WILLIAM HINTON to LYDIA HINTON 24 Dec 1801. Bdsm William Hinton and Larry Bryan.
WILLIAM POPE to ANNE DEW 24 Jan 1803. Bdsm Edward Lee.
PEARCE HOOD to BENETER TAYLOR 6 Jun 1801. Bdsm Pearce Hood and William Davis.
JOHN LANGIER to PEGGY MUSSLEWHITE 27 Apr 1802. Bdsm John Langier and John A. Smith.
HENRY AVERA to CELIA THORP 13 Oct 1802. Bdsm Henry Avera and David Avera.
WILLIAM WORLEY to NANCY EDWARDS 20 Jan 1805. Bdsm William Worley and Joseph Edwards.
DRURY VINSON to NANCY BROWN 18 Oct 1802. Bdsm Drury Vinson and S. Brown.
JOHN PRICE to NANCY VASS 8 Apr 1809. Bdsm William Phillips.
THOMAS RICHARDSON to MILBANY HEATH 11 Jul 1802. Bdsm Thomas Richardson and William Hinnant.
LEVI BAILEY to BEADY DUIK 9 Oct 1801. Bdsm Levi Bailey and Thomas Eatman.
RICHARD SMITH to CADY TINNER 18 Feb 1805. Bdsm Richard Smith and

JOHNSTON COUNTY MARRIAGES

Alexander Penny.
ISAAC ROPER to ELIZABETH VINSON 13 Mar 1802. Bdsm Isaac Roper and Levin Moses.
ELISHA THOMAS to EDITH LOCKHART 7 Sep 1802. Bdsm Elisha Thomas and Stephen Lockhart.
THOMAS LOCKHART to WIMMEY THOMAS 18 Apr 1801. Bdsm Thomas Lockhart and Osborn Lockhart.
SIMON COCKRELL to DICY GANNER 21 Mar 1803. Bdsm Simon Cockrell and Willis Ganner.
EPHRAMIN FERRELL, JR. to BETSY PARRISH 9 Dec 1800. Bdsm Ephramin Ferrell, Jr. and John Ellis.
WILLIAM POPE to POLLY FISHER 14 Feb 1807. Bdsm William Pope and Jonathan Pullen.
WILLIAM COATS to LILAY STEVENSON 18 Jan 1806. Bdsm William Coats and Benjamin Blunt.
JOHN EVANS to DILLEY RAINS 2 Mar 1801. Bdsm David Evans and John Evans.
ASA PEARCE to BETSY DAVIS 20 Mar 1802. Bdsm Asa Pearce and Isaac Jarrell.
NEWIT PEEDIN to POLLY SPICER 21 Sep 1804. Bdsm Amos Peedin.
AVENTON AVERA to ? 16 Nov 1800. Bdsm Aventon Avera and Jonas Frost.
WILLIAM ONEIL to RINI HINTON 1 Dec 1801. Bdsm Bryant Richardson.
ISAAC CHAMPION to NANCY TAYLOR 3 Jun 1801. Bdsm Henry Champion and John Lee.
THOMAS S. ASHE to DELIAH STEVENS 14 Nov 1801. Bdsm Thomas S. Ashe and John Carrell.
DRURY BARBER to EDITH WOODALL 13 Jan 1810. Bdsm George Barber.
LEWIS JERNIGAN, JR to FRANCES DOUGLASS 13 Jan 1801. Bdsm Benjamin Philips.
RODHAM POWERS to "SUSY" SNIPES 14 Mar 1805. Bdsm Isom Stevens.
HOLM STURDIVANT to ESTHER PENNY 28 Feb 1801. Bdsm Alexander Penny and Ellick Sanders.
RICHARD BYRD, JR to BETSY HAISTIP 11 Dec 1815. Bdsm John Byrd.
MOSES NICHOLAS to NANCY CAR 26 Feb 1806. Bdsm Samuel H. Car.
SOLOMON PARNOLD to SARAH TOMLIN 26 May 1801. Bdsm Burwell Johnson.
JOHN POOL, JR. to NANCY BRITT 20 Apr 1805. Bdsm John Pool, Jr. and Benjamin Farmer.
GEORGE LONG to ELIZABETH BULLOCK 9 Dec 1805. Bdsm David Joy, Jr.
EDWARD LEE to NANCY FAIL 25 Feb 1806. Bdsm Jermeiah Lee.
OSBORN HOWELL to NANCY STRICKLAND 25 Sep 1810. Bdsm Edmond Howell.
BENJAMIN FLOWERS to SLIMEY HORN 24 Feb 1801. Bdsm Stephen Grice.
JOHN CARRELL to ALEY FERRELL 21 Jul 1801. Bdsm John Sanders and Ellick Sanders.
JOSHUA JOHNSON, JR. to ANNA HOBBY 8 Jan 1810. Bdsm John Lee Jr.
ETHELDRED HOLT to ELIZABETH WELLONS 15 Oct 1804. Bdsm Etheldred Holt and William Hinnant.
WEST WOODWARD to BETSY SMITH 29 Sep 1803. Bdsm John Smith.
LEWIS M. MOORE to RACHEL BRETT 19 Feb 1805. Bdsm Lewis M. Moore and Thomas Tobson.
GEORGE LASSITER to ELIZABETH JOHNSON 29 Feb 1804. Bdsm Jacob Flowers.
JOHN HARPER to ANNE WIGGS 13 Mar 1801. Bdsm John Harper and

MARRIAGE BONDS

Benjamin Rose.
WILLIAM FRANKLIN to SALLY RIVERS 31 Dec 1805. Bdsm John Smith, Jr.
PEYTON JOY to VINY AVERA 27 Nov 1804. Bdsm Peyton Joy and David Joy, Jr.
JOSEPH E. RHODES to POLLY BUCK 9 Aug 1804. Bdsm Isaac Willams.
JOHN LEE to GRACY CLARK 11 May 1801. Bdsm John Lee and Henry Proctor.
DAVID BEAMAN to SILVY GODWIN 12 Nov 1800. Bdsm James Carrell.
JONAS FROST TO POLLY McCULLERS 5 Feb 1801. Bdsm Samuel Smith.
JOHN ARTHUR BRYAN TO ELIZA SMITH 25 Nov 1801. Bdsm John Arthur Bryan and William Bryan.
CORNELIUS LOVET TO SALLY FAIL 1 Feb 1802. Bdsm Francis Harrell.
WILLIAM PENNY to SALLY PENNY 9 Mar 1805. Bdsm Philip Johnson.
JONATHAN BUSBY to CHRISTIAN SMITH 14 Jun 1805. Bdsm Abner Smith.
JOSEPH E. RHODES to POLLY BUCK 9 Aug 1804. Bdsm Isaac Williams.
DICKSON SPIVEY to "SCARBY" SLAUGHTER 1 Oct 1804. Bdsm Cullen Talton.
BLAKE BRADY to LUCY CARTER 14 Oct 1801. Bdsm Blake Brady and Robert Gulley.
DAVID AVERA to REBEKAH THORP 15 May 1802. Bdsm Henry Avera.
JOHN WILSON to SALLY HOBBY 11 Sep 1802. Bdsm John Wilson and John Briggs.
JOHN RICHARDSON to POLLY HOYLES 24 Feb 1809. Bdsm John Richardson and Jacob Flaser.
JOHN STEVENS to ELIZABETH ALLEN 11 Oct 1804. Bdsm John Stevens and John A. Smith.
BRITAIN SNIPES to ALEY MARTIN 30 Aug 1800. Bdsm Britain Snipes and Joseph Brown.
SAMUEL WALTON to CYNTHIA AVERA 18 Nov 1800. Bdsm Samuel Walton and Etheldred Smith.
KINCHIN FARMER to SARAH WATTS 21 Dec 1805. Bdsm John Farmer, Sr.
WILLIAM COCKRELL to THINY BAGLEY 1 Mar 1802. Bdsm Willis Garner.
HARDY BAILEY to "MICHEY" HOLLIMAN 30 Nov 1802. Bdsm Harbard Gilman.
JAMES ONEAL to ELIZABETH RICHARDSON 25 Nov 1856. Bdsm Allen Richardson.
THOMAS PRICE to SARAH DODD 4 Jun 1800. Bdsm Penud Penny.
JOHN SCOTT to SILVEY IVY 2 Sep 1806. Bdsm John Scott and Ellick Sanders.
DAVID THORNTON to NANCY INGRAM 20 Jan 1806. Bdsm David Thornton and Samuel Lee, Jr.
JACOB BEAMAM to WINIFRED LANGDON 2 Mar 1806. Bdsm James Carrell.
SAMUEL ONEAL to ESTHER PRICE 14 Oct 1806. Bdsm Allen Richardson.
ICHABOD YOUNGBLOOD to BETSY PRICE 16 Dec 1820. Bdsm Thomas Folsom.
JOHN SPITT to CRESY GODWIN 8 Nov 1808. Bdsm Thomas Taylor and Jonathan Stansell.
DEMPSEY GREEN to LEWEY SMITH 26 Jan 1800. Bdsm William Bryan, Jr.
ALEXANDER AVERYT, JR. to ELIZABETH VINSON 31 Jan 1800. Bdsm Alexander Averyt, Jr.
INGRAM LEE to MARTHA BRASWELL 26 Dec 1804. Bdsm Levy Braswell.
STARLING SHORT TO POLLY SMITH 3 Sep 1806. Bdsm William Johnson.
BEADING JOHNSTON to CELIAH WALL 5 May 1810. Bdsm Larry Bryan.
ALLEN JERNIGAN to CLARY TOLER 22 Dec 1806. Bdsm Willis Tiner.

JOHNSTON COUNTY MARRIAGES

WILLIAM HARRELL to KATY BASS 24 May 1803. Bdsm William Harrell and Francis Harrel.
HENRY SHARP TO KEZIAH GURLEY 21 May 1801. Bdsm Jeremiah Gurley.
JOHN MASSEY to DICY KILLINGSWORTH 12 Oct 1801. Bdsm John Massy and Maniss Gurley.
HENRY HOBBY to NANCY WILSON 7 Jan 1801. Bdsm John Wilson.
JOSEPH HINTON to ESTHER HINTON 23 Dec 1807. Bdsm William Hinton.
NOEL WEST to WINIFRED JOHNSTON 19 Dec 1806. Bdsm John Wood.
SILAS GODWIN to ELIZABETH STEVENS 8 Sep 1804. Bdsm James Carrell.
BASHAM LILES to LUCY MORGAN 11 Nov 1806. Bdsm David Ivy, Jr.
LEON HILL to "STRANGE" LEE 21 Oct 1807. Bdsm Leon Hill and Green Hill.
JOHN CRAWLEY to WINIFERD LANE 19 Feb 1800. Bdsm John Crawley and Jonathan Farmer.
AMOS BATTEN to EDITH WATSON 28 Aug 1810. Bdsm John Gerrall.
BATTLING G. HOBBS to EDITH WILLIAMS 30 Nov 1804. Bdsm John Williams.
AARON SMITH to WINIFRED VINSON 12 Jan 1798. Bdsm Daniel Averyt.
JAMES MANOR to POLLY JOHNSON 21 Oct 1802. Bdsm Willie Johnson.
DRURY MEDLIN to SARAH JOHNSON 21 Feb 1793. Bdsm Isaac Jones.
SAMUEL WALTON to CYNTHIA AVERA 18 Nov 1800. Bdsm Samuel Walton and Etheldred Smith.
ZACHARIAH PRICE to LYDIA SHARP 18 Feb 1800. Bdsm Zachariah Price and John Sims.
MATTHEW SMITH to EDITH LYNCH 26 May 1801. Bdsm Joseph Langston.
EDMOND TOMLINSON to SALLY COATS 25 Jul 1809. Bdsm Harris Tomlinson.
BRAMMISTER GRIZZLER to SALLY PUGH 6 Feb 1810. Bdsm Jesse Bailey.
JEREMIAH HAISTIP to RACHEL MITCHELL 20 Sep 1805. Bdsm Jermiah Haistip and Isaac Beaman.
AARON SMITH to FEREBY POOL 31 Jan 1809. Bdsm John Smith, Jr.
THOMAS MASSE to WINIFORD NONSWORTHY 15 Aug 1808. Bdsm Thomas Barber.
? BEDDON to MILDRED SOWELL 2 Jun 1804. Bdsm Joel Clifton.
JOHN RICHARDSON to POLLY HOYLES 24 Sep 1809. Bdsm John Richardson and Jacob Flowers.
JOHN STEVENS to ELIZABETH ALLEN 11 Oct 1804. Bdsm John Stevens and John A. Smith.
BRITAIN SNIPES to ALLEY MARTIN 30 Aug 1800. Bdsm Britain Snipes and Joseph Brown.
JACOB SIMS to CHARLOTTE JERNIGAN 24 May 1803. Bdsm Edward Sims.
JOHN AVERA TO FANNY WILDER 18 Jan 1802. Bdsm John Avera and Young Bridgers.
FREDERICK TOLE TO RHODA JINSEE 24 Aug 1807. Bdsm Frances Harrell and Samuel Lee, Jr.
JAMES CARR to CYNTHIA BRITT 8 Aug 1809. Bdsm Samuel Willoughley.
BENTON BIRD to SUKEY RICHARDSON 20 May 1800. Bdsm John Chamley.
WILLIAM THOMPSON to FERBY ROBERTS 20 Aug 1808. Bdsm Needham Warren. and William Thompson.
JOHN STEVENS, JR. TO ELIZABETH ALLEN 11 Oct 1804. Bdsm John Stevens, Jr. and John A. Smith.
JOHN WALLACE TO "SIRENTY" STANLEY 16 May 1809. Bdsm John Avera.
WILLIAM PRICE to WINIFRED PARCH 24 Jun 1809. Bdsm William Teal.

MARRIAGE BONDS

JESSE ELLINGTON to BETSY BRANNON 25 Aug ? Bdsm Samuel Willoughley.
MATTHEW COLLINS to PENNY EARP 12 Aug 1803. Bdsm Matthew Jones, Jr.
SAMUEL JOHNSON to CHARLOTTE JOHNSON 15 Jan 1803. Bdsm Isaac Johnson, Jr.
EDMOND GODWIN to CELAH RICHARDSON 3 Dec 1802. Bdsm Willis Watson.
WORSHAM ELLINGTON to ELIZABETH A. TUCKER 2 Feb 1807. Bdsm Worsham Ellington and Pennington Tucker.
MATTHEW WOODWARD to LEATHY SMITH 29 Sep 1803. Bdsm John Smith.
SHADERICK INGRAM to POLLY DELOACH 3 Oct 1803. Bdsm Samuel Deloach Jr.
SIR WILLIAM WHITFIELD to BETSY WIMBERLY 27 Dec 1808. Bdsm Willis Watson and Ellick Sanders.
RICHARD YALLMAY to SARAH PORTER 18 Jan 1804. Bdsm Josiah Baggett.
WILLIAM SAVING to CELAH COCKRELL 27 Nov 1810. Bdsm Simon Cockrell.
KINARD ONEIL to CULIA HAYLES 21 Feb 1810. Bdsm Moses Oneil.
FREDERICK WILLIAMS to POLLY GOWER 24 Sep 1802. Bdsm Frederick Williams and John Matthews.
JONAS MACE TO ELIZABETH NEWSOM 26 Oct 1808. Bdsm James Mace and Equilla Mace.
JOHN PEACOCK to "UNITY" PEARCE 21 Sep 1806. Bdsm William Hinnant.
DAVID IVY, JR to RACHEL JONES 9 Aug 1805. Bdsm David Ivy Jr. and David Ivy, Sr.
HENRY JONES to SALLY SMITH 4 Sep 1806. Bdsm Henry Jones and Reuben Sanders.
HENRY BRYAN to EDITH EASON 8 Mar 1808. Bdsm William Sasser and Needham Bryan.
SAMUEL McCLEMMY to ELIZABETH NOLIS 29 Mar 1805. Bdsm Samuel Lee, Jr.
ALFRED MEDIN to ADY SMITH 18 Sep 1806. Bdsm William Johnson.
NATHAN BEAMAN to BETSY WRIGHT 24 Jul 1805. Bdsm Nathan Beaman and Bartley Stevens.
WILLIAM CARRELL to SARAH PENNY 29 Jul 1806. Bdsm John Carrell and Edwin Smith.
JOHN BRADY to MARY TINNER 19 Feb 1804. Bdsm Joseph Boon.
WILLIAM LYNCH to POLLY LUSS 19 Aug 1809. Bdsm William Jones.
EZEKIEL CREACH to BETSY INGRAM 4 Mar 1809. Bdsm Ezekiel Creach and Joshua Creach.
JACOB HOOKS to CELAH NOBY 26 Aug 1806. Bdsm William Williams.
PETER PEARSON to ELIZABETH STEVENS 24 Mar 1807. Bdsm Simon Pearce.
BENJAMIN CARREL to NANCY FERRELL 16 Dec 1806. Bdsm Benjamin Carrell and Drury Johnson.
JONATHAN HOLDER to PIETY HACKNEY 12 Oct 1810. Bdsm Jonathan Holder and Tobias Holliman.
HARROD THORNTON to ZILPHIA BLACKMAN 24 Aug 1803. Bdsm Samuel Lee.
HARDY RICHARDSON to BEADY GODWIN 14 Oct 1803. Bdsm Daniel Eavins.
FREDERICK GURLEY to PATIENCE TINER 24 Feb 1801. Bdsm Frederick Gurley and William Capps.
CHARLES HOOD to SALLY ELLINGTON 30 May 1800. Bdsm Maleke Hinton.
EDMOND DEES to BETSY BRASWELL 15 Nov 1803. Bdsm David Braswell.
MARTIN WOODALL to JUDITH GILES ? Bdsm Martin Woodall and Jacob Woodall.
JAMES SILLS to POLLY LEE 24 Dec 1809. Bdsm Harris Tomlinson.

JOHNSTON COUNTY MARRIAGES

WILLIAM RENFROWE to MARY PELT 15 Feb 1805. Bdsm Stephen Grice.
KEDAR BRANNON to ELIZABETH WILDER 8 Oct 1802. Bdsm Kedar Brannon and Cullen Wilder.
ZACHARIAH GOWER to NANCY WILLIAMS 15 Sep 1822. Bdsm William Gower.
WILLIAM KELLY to ALSEY EASON 24 Mar 1813. Bdsm Abner Smith.
JONATHAN GURLEY to RENE BAILEY 28 Dec 1809. Bdsm Morris Gurley.
WILLIAM B. HOCUT to CREACY ONEIL 24 Jan 1806. Bdsm William B. Hocut and John Hinnant.
ARCHIBALD PARNELL to ANN CAPS 15 Jan 1806. Bdsm John Eason.
LEWIS BUCK to POLLY INGRAM 30 Jan 1808. Bdsm Joshua Creech.
HENRY RAINS to HANNAH HAWKINS SMITH 12 Apr 1800. Bdsm Henry Rains and Simon Pearce.
JOHN EASON to FARANRICH EASON 11 Oct 1803. Bdsm Benjamin Eason.
HENRY DENBY to DELANEY STEVENS 19 Sep 1800. Bdsm Henry Denby and James Denby.
JOHN ROGERS to CELAH KELLY 19 Jan 1804. Bdsm John Kelly, Jr.
SAMUEL BATTEN to JIMNIA STARLING 8 Oct 1802. Bdsm Samuel Batten and John Batten.
GEORGE STARLING to ANNE HAINES 28 Feb 1810. Bdsm Samuel Batten.
ARTHUR GURLEY to POLLY PEEDIN 24 Jul 1803. Bdsm Etheldred Holt.
HARRIS TOMLINSON to EDITH LOCKHART 29 Sep 1802. Bdsm John Sanders.
FREDERICK BRYAN to ELIZABETH WOODARD 28 Nov 1809. Bdsm Frederick Bryan and West Woodard.
MOSES BOYETT to POLLY STEVENS 28 Feb 1810. Bdsm Benjamin Stevens.
LEVI REAVERS to BETSY NORRISS 23 Aug 1802. Bdsm Ellick Sanders and Edwin Smith.
JAMES VINSON to ELIZABETH BARNES 16 Apr 1810. Bdsm James Vinson.
KEDAR PEARCE to RHODA WADDELL 27 Aug 1805. Bdsm Philip Pearce.
JOHN SMITH, JR. to BETSY RIVERS 18 Feb 1804. Bdsm John Smith, Jr. and Redden Johnson.
RICHARDSON JOHNSON to POLLY STALLINGS 5 Jan 1810. Bdsm Kedar Avera.
ADAMS ALEXANDER to MARY ANN CAREL 1 Aug 1803. Bdsm Adams Alexander and John Arthur Bryan.
ALFRED JOHNSON to CORNELIA INGRAM 16 Oct 1815. Bdsm Obed Johnson and Barnaby Ingram.
DANIEL GOWER to ALSY INGRAM 29 Apr 1809. Bdsm Willis Watson and Allen Ballenger.
SAMUEL STRICKLAND to SALLY THOMPSON 20 Aug 1803. Bdsm John Herring.
BRYAN GREEN to MILLY WELCH 24 Feb 1801. Bdsm Samuel Wilder, Jr.
OLIVER RAINS to ELIZABETH PEARCE 6 Feb 1804. Bdsm John Rains.
WILLIE JONES to PENNY H. JONES 24 Dec 1809. Bdsm Ellick Sanders and Robert H. Helme.
SOLOMON WHITINGTON to SALLY SASSETON 28 Nov 1806. Bdsm William Wilder.
JAMES MANOR to POLLY JOHNSON 21 Oct 1802. Bdsm Willie Johnson and Henry Johnson.
HARTWELL IVY to POARTOCK PARRISH 11 Aug 1809. Bdsm Hartwell Ivy and Rivers Ivy.
WILLIAM ALLEN to BETSY BUCKS 12 Mar 1803. Bdsm John Stevens and William Allen.
ASA YELVINGTON to SARAH HORN 25 Feb 1806. Bdsm Tegnal Pugh.
HENRY HOSEA to FEREBY LEARCY 29 Mar 1809. Bdsm Everett Renfrowe.

MARRIAGE BONDS

ALLEN WATSON to DICY PARRISH 27 Dec 1805. Bdsm Isham Watson.
BENNETT DODDE to WINIFRED BRITT 27 Dec 1805. Bdsm Jonathan Britt.
JAMES TINNER to HISY DODD 13 Jan 1808. Bdsm Brigdon Johnson.
MOSES BOYETT to POLLY STEVENS 2 Feb 1810. Bdsm Benjamin Stevens.
GEAPLER STARLING to ANNA HARREN 28 Feb 1810. Bdsm Samuel Batten.
ROBERT RAIFORD to PRISCILLA SHARP 27 Feb 1806. Bdsm Jeremiah Gurley.
ISOM ONEIL to ANN PEARCE 14 Oct 1800. Bdsm Moses Oneil and John Pearce.
JAMES ONEAL to ELIZABETH RICHARDSON 25 Nov 1806. Bdsm Allen Richardson.
THOMAS MELSER to WINIFRED NONSWORTHY 15 Aug 1808. Bdsm Thomas Barber.
GIDDEON ALLEN to ESTHER JOHNSON 25 Feb 1800. Bdsm Giddeon Allen and James Woodall.
JOEL HERRING to EDITH FULGHAM 2 Nov 1802. Bdsm John Learcy.
SAMUEL BROWN to SALLY WILSON 25 Jul 1802. Bdsm Samuel Brown and Hardy Bryan.
BRYAN HOOD to ELIZABETH WILLOUGHLEY 18 Aug 1810. Bdsm Samuel Willoughley.
JOSEPH BLACKMAN to POLLY STANDLEY 4 Jan 1802. Bdsm Etheldred Massingill.
CHARLES STEVENS to EDITH FARMER 14 Oct 1805. Bdsm William Guy.
REDDEN JOHNSON to MERIBETH SOWELL 2 Jun 1804. Bdsm Joel Clifton.
JAMES LEWIS to SARAH CRAWFORD 15 Dec 1804. Bdsm William Giles.
ZACHARIAH GOWER to "THINY" MASSINGELL 24 Jul 1804. Bdsm William Roberts.
ALEXANDER GODWIN to MARY HOLLEMAN 25 Feb 1806. Bdsm Alexander Godwin and Stephen Grice.
JOHN GILES to BETSY JOHNSON 25 Jan 1808. Bdsm Philip Johnson.
CADEN WILLOBY to SUSANNAH MOODY 8 Dec 1805. Bdsm Caden Willoby and James Moody.
MATTHEW WILDER to MILLA ONEAL ? Aug 1815. Bdsm Matthew Wilder and Hardy Avera.
JOHN PEARSON to PENNY TAYLOR 26 Feb 1806. Bdsm Simon Pearce.
NEEDHAM CAPPS to MARTHA DAVIS 24 Feb 1807. Bdsm William Capps.
AMBROSE INGRAM to SALLY NORRISS 16 Dec 1806. Bdsm Ambrose Ingram and Barnaby Ingram.
MECHAJAL EDWARDS to POLLY SPENCER 22 Nov 1805. Bdsm Stephen Edwards.
CULLEN TALTON to LEWEY CLARK 7 Jun 1806. Bdsm Jonathan Talton.
ICHABOD BAULKAM to DELANIE JARRELL 22 May 1806. Bdsm Ichabod Baulkam and Isaac Jarrel.
BRIDGERS BATTEN to SUSAN LYNET 24 Jun 1808. Bdsm Johnson Busbee.
JOHN RAINS to ELIZABETH PEPLES 1 Apr 1806. Bdsm John Rains and Jarot Peples.
BENJAMIN HUGHES to RACHEL TINER 19 Sep 1806. Bdsm Jeremiah Gurley.
MOSES GARNER to MARY COCKRELL 25 Aug 1805. Bdsm Moses Garner and John Brown.
HENRY SMITH to DORCAS JOHNSON 1 Apr 1806. Bdsm Ambrose Ingram.
DEAL COLLINS to NANNY PEEDIN 30 Sep 1805. Bdsm Deal Collins and Robert Gulley.

JOHNSTON COUNTY MARRIAGES

MYNCK BARNES to POLLY LEACH 25 Feb 1805. Bdsm Mynck Barnes and Matthew Jones.
JESSE PENNY to SALLY LUSS 12 Jan 1807. Bdsm Philip Johnson.
WILLIAM STANLEY to POLLY WEBB 9 Aug 1809. Bdsm Elijah Baker.
WILLIAM CARTER to RACHEL FROST 25 Jul 1805. Bdsm James Durham.
BURWELL COATS to POLLY BAREFOOT 27 Nov 1805. Bdsm Jaob Lee.
BARNABY BUSBY to POLLY WILLIAMS 24 Dec 1806. Bdsm Henry Johnson, Sr.
WILLIAM PHILIPS to NANCY CAUDLE 29 Apr 1806. Bdsm William Philips and John Caudle.
WARREN PATTERSON to THEANEY EASON 23 Mar 1805. Bdsm Warren Patterson and Levy Barnes.
JONATHAN TALTON to POLLY TAYLOR 15 Jul 1809. Bdsm Needham Talton.
ELI CLARK to EDITH POWELL 24 Mar 1806. Bdsm John Stevens.
NATHANIEL JONES to POLLY BAVRY 7 Jan 1806. Bdsm Nathaniel Jones and John Leach.
LEWIS WILBURN to MARY GARLAND 13 Feb 1804. Bdsm Sampson Rogers and John Sanders.
JESSE STANLEY to ANNE BAKER 13 Jul 1802. Bdsm Jesse Stanley and William Stanley.
LEWIS TEAL to EANEY LANFORD 19 Apr 1807. Bdsm Barnaby Bull.
WILLIAM WOOTEN to WINIFRED ONEAL 6 Oct 1809. Bdsm William B. Hocutt.
ABRAHAM BATTEN to RUTH STARLING 8 Oct 1802. Bdsm Abraham Batten and John Batten.
ELIAS GODWIN to NANCY WATKINS 30 May 1810. Bdsm Willie Watkins.
JAMES RICHARDSON to ALEY WOODWARD 9 Aug 1805. Bdsm Joseph Richardson.
SODWICK ONEIL to BETSY WILDER 5 Jan 1807. Bdsm Thomas Oneil.
ELISHA EASON to EDITH AVERA 9 Jun 1804. Bdsm Benjamin Eason.
RICHARD WARREN to POLLY FURLEY 23 Aug 1808. Bdsm Needham Warren.
BRITAIN SMITH to SALLY BULLS 16 Jul 1808. Bdsm Thomas Avera.
HAMMON CAUDLE to SALLY MASSENGILL 13 Nov 1808. Bdsm Jonathan Caudle.
BENJAMIN HOCUTT to NANCY HOLOMAN 26 Sep 1809. Bdsm James Woodward.
ASA BRYAN, JR. to SUSANNAH LEE 15 Mar 1809. Bdsm Henry Lee.
JAMES BRYAN to NANCY GREEN 23 Feb 1808. Bdsm Sir Green.
JOHN PENNY to BETSY COOPER 6 Oct 1809. Bdsm Benjamin Smith.
ZACHARIAH COLLINS to WELTHY BEAMAN 8 Oct 1802. Bdsm Zachariah Collins and Isaac Beaman.
DANIEL BUSBY to SALLY HARDY 24 Dec 1806. Bdsm Daniel Busby and Benjamin Caudle.
WILLIAM W. BRYAN to PATSY McCULLARS 7 Nov 1805. Bdsm Needham Bryan.
EVERETT BAILEY to HAILEY DRAUGHAM 13 Aug 1809. Bdsm Jesse Bailey.
ELAM SMITH to CYNTHIA GRICE 28 Mar 1809. Bdsm Elam Smith and Britain Deloach.
HENRY POOL to REBECAH WELLONS 22 Jun 1809. Bdsm Henry Pool and Zachariah Wellons.
HARDY REVEL to ELIZABETH HINNANT 11 Sep 1808. Bdsm William Hinnant Jr.
JOHN WHITLEY to ESTHER BULLS 15 May 1806. Bdsm Willis Watson.
WILLIAM HAILS to TABITHA COOPER 19 Feb 1810. Bdsm Thomas Lockhart.

MARRIAGE BONDS

ELI PEARCE to PEGGY WATKINS 23 May 1809. Bdsm Philip Raiford and Truman Hillingsworth.
DANIEL SMITH to SALLY INGRAM 28 Apr 1808. Bdsm Bryan Smith.
JONATHAN SHEPHERD to POLLY DODD 10 Feb 1811. Bdsm Thomas Price.
JOHN FELLOWS to POLLY GAMALIAN 28 Dec 1817. Bdsm Reuben Sauders.
IZERIAH EARP to CHARITY WIMBERLY 6 Oct 1809. Bdsm Charles Hood.
MILES LANGLEY to CRECY ? 25 Mar 1816. Bdsm Miles Langley and Thomas Atkins.
OBED JOHNSON to CORDELIA JOHNSON 6 Oct 1810. Bdsm Obed Johnson and Barnaby Ingram.
ASA JERNIGAN to SALLY SMITH 7 Nov 1814. Bdsm William H. Bulls, Jr.
MECAJAH MYDELL to NANCY BROOKS 27 Oct 1814. Bdsm John C. Guy.
WILLIAM WILDER to "RETER" GREEN 16 Apr 1813. Bdsm William Wilder.
NATHANIEL K. HOLLINGSWORTH to REBEKAH ROSE 28 Dec 1816. Bdsm Nathaniel K. Hollingsworth and Nathan Thornton.
CARRELL JOHNSON to AMY BRITT 5 Jul 1815. Bdsm Benjamin Carrell.
JAMES JOHNSON to HANNAH PATE 11 Feb 1812. Bdsm James Johnson and Jacob Johnson.
AARON MASSINGILL to SCELY HILL 24 Feb 1810. Bdsm Aaron Massingill and Peter Lee.
HENRY HORN to BEEDY BAILEY 23 Dec 1817. Bdsm Henry Horn and Warren Bailey.
WILLIAM HOBBS to ZILPHA PRICE 26 Mar 1816. Bdsm William Hobbs and John Richardson.
WARREN JOHNSON to EDNY JOHNSON 23 Mar 1819. Bdsm Benjamin Carrell and Jesse Wood, Jr.
THOMAS JONES to SUSANNAH FARMER 7 Jun 1814. Bdsm Thomas Price.
JAMES HARMON to SALLY BAILEY 30 Apr 1812. Bdsm James Harmon and Daniel Dees.
SAMUEL MEGEL to NANCY BRENT 21 Apr 1816. Bdsm Samuel Megel and Eden Rhodes.
IRA HAYLES to SUSAN GREEN 21 Dec 1816. Bdsm Ira Hayles and Elam Lockhart.
JAMES JOHNSON to LUCY LASSETER 9 Aug 1811. Bdsm James Johnson and John Coats.
JONATHAN HOLDER to CATHERINE WILDER 19 Mar 1814. Bdsm John Avera.
JOHN JOINER to ZILPHA WILDER 27 Aug 1811. Bdsm William Hinnant, Jr.
LOVET LEE to BETSY HILL 28 Aug 1815. Bdsm John Lee.
JAMES CORBET to AVEY MASSINGILL 23 Apr 1815. Bdsm James Corbet and George Massingill.
JOHN McLEOD to BETSY HINTON 3 Feb 1814. Bdsm John McCleod and Alexander Dickerson.
JOHN BARNES to SALLY PERKINS 27 Feb 1805. Bdsm John Barnes and H. Sasser.
WILLIAM KELLY to ALSEY EASON 24 Mar 1813. Bdsm Abner Smith.
HENRY LEE to MARY COATS 17 Jan 1815. Bdsm Edward Lee, Jr.
JOSEPH HEARN to BETHINIA THORNTON 24 Mar 1812. Bdsm Joseph Hearn and John Sanders, Jr.
ISIAH HAYLES to CALLY HOLLIMAN 24 Jan 1815. Bdsm Isiah Hayles and Matthew Hayles.
EPHRAIM EVANS to BETSY LEE 11 Jan 1812. Bdsm John Evans.
WILLIAM KENT to ZILLA PARKER 9 Jan 1815. Bdsm Iredell Williams.

JOHNSTON COUNTY MARRIAGES

BENJAMIN HADLEY to NANCY GURLEY 18 Jul 1814. Bdsm Thomas Jones.
EDWARD JONES to THARED GARRELL 1 Apr 1817. Bdsm Edward Jones and Willis Garrell.
WILLIAM HOOD to SUSANNAH "WIGS" 22 Jul 1816. Bdsm William Hood and Jesse Whitley.
JONATHAN HOBBY to THINY PATTERSON 11 Aug 1811. Bdsm Thomas Tolson.
JOHN KEEN to JERUSHA BLACKMAN 18 Mar 1815. Bdsm John Keen and George Keen.
BRYAN LYNCH to SALLY FARVER 23 Nov 1813. Bdsm Bryan Lynch and David Sauls.
HENRY BELL to BETSY KITTINGSWORTH 14 Dec 1811. Bdsm Henry Bell and Freeman Kittingsworth.
JACOB JOHNSON to CREASEY DURHAM 18 Jul 1816. Bdsm Jacob Johnson and John Whittinger.
JOHN GULLEY to MARY C. GREEN 4 Dec 1811. Bdsm John Gulley and Lewis Sasser.
JOHN COOPER to CYNTHIA HAYLES 7 Aug 1817. Bdsm John Cooper and Elam Lockhart.
JAMES BROWN to SUSANNAH HAYLES 14 Apr 1813. Bdsm Wilson Brasham.
ROBERT BROADSTREET to LYDIA CARTWRIGHT 12 Aug 1816. Bdsm Noah Nichols.
MATTHEW JOHNSON to SUSANNA DURHAM 18 Feb 1814. Bdsm William Johnson.
JAMES JACKSON to NANCY BEARFOOT 29 May 1811. Bdsm James Smith.
DAVID LEE to EDITH LEE 17 Oct 1811. Bdsm William Johns.
WHITMILL JOHNSON to ELIZABETH MESSER 19 Jan 1812. Bdsm Whitmill Johnson and William Messer.
GEORGE KEEN to MILBY GODWIN 1 Mar 1814. Bdsm Isaac Keen.
JESSE JOINER to ELIZABETH DUIK ? Jan 1812. Bdsm James Duik.
GREEN HILL to POLLY DOXEY 6 Jan 1818. Bdsm Green Hill and Nathan Strickland.
CHARLES CARTER to POLLY CAVENDER 23 Jan 1811. Bdsm Charles Carter and John Carter.
BRITTAIN LANGDON to PEGGY CARRELL 7 Nov 1815. Bdsm Brittain Langdon and Thomas Barber.
WEST JOHNSON to BRIMMITER WOOD 3 Aug 1815. Bdsm Samuel Johnson.
JOHN JIMMET to BETSY STALLINGS 28 Aug 1817. Bdsm Herbert Gilman.
JOSEPH INGRAM to NANCY POWELL 8 Jan 1813. Bdsm William Sasser.
WILLIAM INGRAM to BARTHMA LEE 26 Nov 1816. Bdsm Samuel Lee, Jr. and William Ingram.
JONATHAN LEE to ABESEBETH LEE 5 Dec 1818. Bdsm Loverd Eldridge, Jr.
LOVERD INGRAM to MARTHA LEE 28 May 1816. Bdsm James Lee and Loverd Ingram.
DUNCAN JOHNSON to CLOE NARRON 8 Jan 1819. Bdsm Duncan Johnson and Griffin Lewis.
THOMAS KIRBY to TEMPERANCE BOYETT 31 Dec 1818. Bdsm Henry Sasser.
ROBERT McKINNCE to ZILPAH B. SMITH 8 Jul 1813. Bdsm Edmond Blackman.
JOHN JELKS to ABESEBETH BRIDGERS 4 Jul 1818. Bdsm Thomas A. Brown.
WILLIAM ONEAL TO POLLY HOLMES 24 Feb 1819. Bdsm Joshua Musgrave.
ALLEN JONES to ELIZABETH HOLLMAN 19 Jan 1813. Bdsm James Smith.
JOHN WOODWARD to BETSY JORDAN 28 Aug 1816. Bdsm Tobias Holliman.

MARRIAGE BONDS

JORDAN JACKSON to LETHA SMITH 1 Mar 1815. Bdsm B. Ingram and Jordan Jackson.
HENRY JORDAN to ELIZABETH WOOD 11 Apr 1814. Bdsm John Jordan.
WILLIAM HINTON to BETSY BRYAN 1 Nov 1817. Bdsm William Hinton and James Stallings.
STEPHEN HINNANT to NANCY GARRALD 14 Jan 1817. Bdsm Stephen Hinnant and Theophilius Bagley.
ASA MEDDYETT to MARY THORP 20 May 1818. Bdsm Asa Meddyett and Willis N. White.
JAMES HARRISON to PHEREBY TOMLINSON 26 Jun 1819. Bdsm James Harrison and Thomas Tomlinson.
LEWIS JACKSON to PATSY KNOWL 28 Feb 1814. Bdsm William Bryan.
BENJAMIN JOINER, JR to MELBRY SILKS 16 Dec 1815. Bdsm Benjamin Joiner, Jr. and John Rhodes Jr.
FREDERICK HARPER to ? 1 Mar 1815. Bdsm Solomon Whitington.
LITTLETON JOHNSON to SIDDY ALLEN 3 Feb 1819. Bdsm Littleton Johnson and William Johnson.
BURWELL JONES to TEMPERANCE FERRELL 22 Aug 1818. Bdsm Burwell Jones and John Beal.
LEWIS BRYAN to AMY JOHNSON 12 Jan 1815. Bdsm John Johnson.
DAVID BRIDGERS to EDITH CRAWFORD 27 May 1815. Bdsm David Bridgers and Etheldred Holt.
JOHN BOON to LITHY DODD 30 Oct 1815. Bdsm John Boon and Peter Ivy.
ENOCH HAYLES to DELANY VICK 11 Jan 1816. Bdsm John Joiner.
SAM HILL to POLLY LANGDON 24 Mar 1812. Bdsm Etheldred Bell.
JESSE SNIPES to CEACY ROBERTS 7 Feb 1811. Bdsm Edmond Howell.
THEOPHILUS BARBER to SALLY BARBER 19 Dec 1814. Bdsm Rueben Barber.
FREDERICK ANDERSON to EDITH NORRISS 20 Dec 1817. Bdsm Frederick Anderson and John Avera.
BRYAN LYNCH to BETSY STEVENS 15 Feb 1817. Bdsm Bryan Lynch and John C. Guy.
SETH JOHNSON to EDITH STEPHENSON 2 Mar 1812. Bdsm Redder Byrd.
ALLEN HODGE to NANCY COLLINS 21 Mar 1817. Bdsm Allen Hodge and Willey Garrell.
ISHAM HARVILLE to PEGGY DAVIDSON 2 Jun 1812. Bdsm Isham Harville and Moses Harville.
JOSEPH HARPER to POLLY BISHOP 29 Nov 1814. Bdsm Joseph Harper and Asa Bishop.
WHITLEY STEVENS to BETSY KILLINGSWORTH 3 Jan 1816. Bdsm Whitley Stevens and William Raiford.
WILLIAM VINCENT to WINIFRED AVERYTT 30 Jan 1814. Bdsm William Vincent and Jonathan Averytt.
HARROT JOHNSON to BERTY FINCH 9 Feb 1814. Bdsm Wily Johnson.
JOHN W. JOHNSON to SALLY WILDER 29 Nov 1817. Bdsm Solomon Whitington.
NATHAN BRYAN to NANCY DANIEL 21 Mar 1815. Bdsm Nathan Bryan.
ARCHIBALD WIGGINS to ELIZABETH WALLIS 22 Feb 1819. Bdsm Archibald Wiggins and Hardy Adams.
REUBEN WILDER to OLIVE WILDER 29 Jul 1817. Bdsm Thomas Brannon and Rueben Wilder.
WILLIAM TUCKER to MILLY WILDER 6 Feb 1816. Bdsm William Tucker.
MAURICE GURLEY to ELIZABETH GURLEY 26 Aug 1812. Bdsm Maurice Gurley

JOHNSTON COUNTY MARRIAGES

and Robert Raiford.
JAMES GREGORY to ANN COOPER 12 Dec 1812. Bdsm John Parrish.
DAVID GEORGE to WINIFRED LEE 24 Mar 1813. Bdsm David George.
ENOS GARRALD to BIDIE STARLIN 10 Apr 1816. Bdsm Simon Batten and Enos Garrald.
ELISHA DAVIS to POLLY CRAFFORD 28 Sep 1812. Bdsm Daniel Ward.
THOMAS SIMPKINS to WINIFRED JOHNSON 12 Feb 1814. Bdsm Thomas Price.
JOSHUA CORBET to POLLY BLACKMAN 21 Dec 1815. Bdsm Joshua Corbet and John Owens.
ROBERT GURLEY to NANCY GREEN 25 Sep 1816. Bdsm Robert Gurley and James Davis.
JAMES GATLIN to PHEREBE HOBBY 1 Mar 1816. Bdsm Thomas Barber and John Sanders, Jr.
JAMES WOODALL, JR. to POLLY JOHNSON 10 Jul 1819. Bdsm James Woodall, Jr. and Absalom Woodall.
JOHN BUTCHER to PATIENCE PEEDIN 17 Feb 1814. Bdsm John Peedin.
REDDAM BRITT to RACHEL FROST 20 Jan 1813. Bdsm Bennett Dodd.
WILLIE ONEAL to POLLY HOLMES 24 Feb 1819. Bdsm Joshua Musgrave.
EDWARD PRICE to EDITH PARRISH 20 Jun 1825. Bdsm John Duncan.
WILLIAM CARTER to APPY OLIVER 2 Jun 1818. Bdsm David Thompson.
THOMAS FINLEY to PATIENCE BRADY 24 Feb 1819. Bdsm Thomas Finley and Etheldred Holt.
EDWIN BRANTLY to SUSANNAH CORBETT 25 May 1819. Bdsm Samuel Lee, Jr.
JESSE STARLING to WINIFRED GUY 27 Aug 1822. Bdsm Jesse Starling and Henry Parnell.
THOMAS STETWELL to NELLY RAINS WORLEY 23 Aug 1819. Bdsm John Rains.
ETHELDRED FUTRELL, JR to POLLY GURLEY 28 Sep 1819. Bdsm Etheldred Futrell, Jr.
HENRY CAPPS to CHILLY THOMPSON 21 Dec 1818. Bdsm Henry Capps and Henry Guy.
URIAS BAUCOM to BETSY LEE 29 Sep 1815. Bdsm Bennett Baucom.
BERRY WILKINSON to BEEDY ONEAL 27 Nov 1815. Bdsm William Hinnant Esq. and Berry Wilkinson.
EDMUND BAGLEY to LATY MISBURN 6 Oct 1815. Bdsm Edmund Bagley and Theophilus Bagley.
GEORGE BYRD to PENNY RETTER 8 Mar 1818. Bdsm George Byrd and Benjamin Martin.
ARTHUR DAUGHTERY to NANCY TINER 1 Feb 1816. Bdsm Arthur Daughtery and Henry Daughtery.
MILES BAREFOOT to MEADY ALLEN 18 Apr 1817. Bdsm Miles Barefoot and John Barefoot.
HARDY BELL to PATSY POOL 9 Jul 1818. Bdsm Baldy Sanders.
CARMEL CAUDELL to SALLY LEE ? Bdsm Harmon Caudell.
BARNABY BULLS to HARRIET EADOM 11 Mar 1819. Bdsm Willie N. White.
WILLIAM WILLIS BODDIE to TRANQUILLA SANDERS 2 Jan 1818. Bdsm John Boddie.
DEMPSEY BOON to LOTTY STEVENS 26 Jan 1818. Bdsm Harrison Tomlinson and Harris Clark.
THOMAS DAVIS to JANE ROE ? Bdsm Henry Sasser.
MATTHEW WOODWARD to PHEREBE BRYAN 14 Aug 1818. Bdsm Allen Richardson.
JESSE TINER to SALLY WYATT 26 Nov 1812. Bdsm Jesse Tiner.

34

MARRIAGE BONDS

WILLIAM TEAL to PATIENCE DAUGHTERY 24 Feb 1819. Bdsm Isaiah Massey and William Teal.
RICHARD DAUGHTERY to REBECCA CREACH ? Bdsm Needham Warren.
WARREN WOODWARD to SALLY HAMILTON 10 Apr 1816. Bdsm Warren Woodward and William Guy.
WINDSOM WATKINS to PHEREBY HARPER 24 Oct 1818. Bdsm Windsom Watkins and W. F. Williams.
PEARCE WATKINS to PATSY PEARCE 20 Jan 1817. Bdsm Pearce Watkins and Loverd Pearce.
HARRISS WATSON to PENNY PRIVETT 13 Nov 1818. Bdsm Harris Watson and William Watson.
ELIJAH THOMPSON to NANCY BRASWELL 21 Dec 1814. Bdsm Elijah Thompson and Samuel Strickland.
CHARLES BENSON to ELIZABETH CAPPS 28 Sep 1812. Bdsm William Capps.
WILLIAM WHITINGTON to SALLY EASON 5 Dec 1815. Bdsm Etheldred Bell.
WILLIAM WATSON to NANCY BRYAN 23 Oct 1815. Bdsm William Watson and Willis Watson.
JOHN B. WATSON to MARY COOPER 21 Aug 1817. Bdsm John B. Watson and Nathan V. Boddie.
ROSSEN MORLY to BETSY COLLINS 27 Jan 1810. Bdsm Cornelius Lynch.
STEPHEN WATSON to BETSY WATSON 10 Mar 1812. Bdsm Jesse Sillivant.
ABSALOM BARBER to SUSAN JOHNSTON 6 Sep 1817. Bdsm Absalom Barber and Plyer Barber.
RICHARD CORBET to SARAH BRANTLY 25 May 1819. Bdsm Samuel Lee, Jr.
JOHN WHITLEY, JR. to ESTHER BULLS 24 Jan 1814. Bdsm Alfred Whitley.
WILKERSON FUTRELL to POLLY MASSEY 8 Oct 1817. Bdsm Wilkerson Futrell and Isaiah Massey.
WILLIAM HOOK to LUCY MASSINGELL 5 SEP 1811. Bdsm James Stanley.
WILLIAM McGLAWHON to CATY KEEN 23 May 1814. Bdsm Allen L. Ballenger.
JOHN EATMAN to "ZARDY" TRISDELL 29 SEP 1812. Bdsm Solomon Johnson.
MOSES EASON to ANNY HAYLE 12 Aug 1814. Bdsm Jeremiah Parnold and Moses Eason.
JESSE STAFFORD to PATSY FOREHAND 28 Dec 1813. Bdsm Lewis Forehand.
CHARLES WELLONS to NANCY GODWIN 18 Nov 1815. Bdsm Thomas Sasser and Charles Wellons.
MOSES BARNETT to POLLY STEVENS 28 Feb 1810. Bdsm Benjamin Stevens.
EDWARD CARLILE to SUSAN HALL 11 Nov 1816. Bdsm Edward Carlile and Kinch Whitley.
DAVID EVANS to ZILPHIA LEE 14 Jun 1817. Bdsm William Wood.
JOEL BRYAN to DELIAH EATMAN 23 Jan 1811. Bdsm Joel Byan and Robert Lewis.
JOSEPH EDWARDS to LERCY BRASWELL 19 Mar 1815. Bdsm Joseph Edwards and Elijah Thompson.
JOHN BEARFOOT to BETSY SMITH 26 Dec 1815. Bdsm Miles Bearfoot.
REUBEN DODD to TABITHA YOUNGBLOOD 7 Oct 1815. Bdsm John Parrish.
JOHN COCKRELL to POLLY FOLK 4 Jun 1816. Bdsm John Cockrell and Samuel Cockrell.
RICHARD DRAMHAM to NICY POPE 27 Mar 1815. Bdsm Jesse Adams.
JEREMIAH CAPPS to POLLY EDWARDS 11 Mar 1815. Bdsm Jeremiah Capps and William Bulls, Jr.
HUTSON EARP to SALLY EARP 13 Nov 1816. Bdsm John G. Gulley.

JOHNSTON COUNTY MARRIAGES

CHARLES BATTEN to ELIZABETH BULLOCK 9 Nov 1816. Bdsm Charles Batten and Peyton Vinson.
JAMES WOODALL to MILDRED SPIED 18 Nov 1815. Bdsm James Woodall and John Woodall.
JEREMIAH PARNOLD to CATY STEVENS 28 May 1816. Bdsm Micajah Wilkinson.
JESSE THOMAS to POLLY STAFFORD 11 Apr 1813. Bdsm Jesse Thomas and Joseph Thomas.
WILLIAM JOHNSON to CELAH WATSON 29 Jul 1810. Bdsm Isam Watson.
JOSEPH WRIGHT to SALLY PATE 2 Sep 1815. Bdsm Allen Tomlinson.
MARTIN WIGGS to MARTHA ELLIS 24 May 1814. Bdsm James Rose.
JONATHAN WHITENTON to SALLY ALLEN 25 Mar 1816. Bdsm James Whitenton.
JOHN SMITH to POLLY AUSTON 24 Nov 1819. Bdsm John Auston.
NATHANIEL FUTERAL to NANCY DEANS 4 Jul 1812. Bdsm Nathaniel Futeral and Josiah Hinnant, Jr.
WILLIAM DAVIS to SALLY DAVIS 5 Mar 1816. Bdsm William Davis and Henry Capps.
JEREMIAH CAPPS to ZILPHA MASSEY 11 Jan 1816. Bdsm Isiah Massey.
WILLIAM WILDER to POLLY RICHARDSON 29 Jul 1818. Bdsm William Wilder and Etheldred Bell.
WILLIAM WATSON to PATIENCE WILLIAMSON 25 May 1818. Bdsm Henry Sasser.
WILLIAM WARREN to "ELIAS" TALTON 27 Nov 1812. Bdsm P. Raiford.
ADDISON VINSON, JR. to SARAH BAINES 16 Apr 1818. Bdsm Addison Vinson, Jr. and John Vinson, Jr.
JOSEPH WOODWARD to PATIENCE DAUGHTERY 13 Feb 1813. Bdsm Joseph Woodward and John Pearce.
RENFROW LASSITER to CATY WILDER 12 Mar 1818. Bdsm Hillary Wilder.
JEREMIAH JOHNSON to CRECY WILDAIR 24 Jul 1817. Bdsm Redding Byrd.
JOHN WINDHAM to POLLY CARTER 20 Jul 1814. Bdsm John Windham and F. T. Walton.
A. POWELL to "SUKEY" GUY ? Bdsm M. Gorman.
JAMES GRICE to PRISCILLA "MOONAHAM" 31 Dec 1812. Bdsm Josiah Hinnant.
WILLIAM COATS to ANNA BLACKMAN 29 Dec 1812. Bdsm Jeremiah Blackman.
JOHN L. GUY to PATSY GULLEY ? Bdsm John L. Guy and Asa Midyett.
DAVID THOMPSON to SALLY McCULLERS 10 Nov 1818. Bdsm David Thompson and Roy Helme.
JESSE A. TALTON to LYDIA LEWIS 9 Sep 1817. Bdsm James Clark .
LEWIS POWERS to NANCY DODD 22 Aug 1812. Bdsm Jesse Powers and Lewis Powers.
BRIGHT BYRD to GRACY GODWIN 20 Mar 18? Bdsm Benjamin Stevens.
JOHN CRUMPLER to OLIVE ONEAL 14 Jan 1817. Bdsm William Crumpler.
WILLIE FERRELL TO EDITH RENTFROW 27 Feb 1816. Bdsm Willie Ferrell.
WILLIS GAY TO CREACY FAULK ? Bdsm William Batten.
BENJAMIN BELL to REBECKAH JOHNSON 8 Feb 1815. Bdsm D. Bell.
WILLIAM EDWARDS to PENNY PARKER 25 Nov 1817. Bdsm William Edwards and John Carter.
BENJAMIN EASON TO BETHANY SNIPES 15 Jul 1817. Bdsm Benjamin Eason and John C. Guy.
WILLIAM EASON to BETSY BROUGHTON 2 Jan 1819. Bdsm Jonathan

MARRIAGE BONDS

Stansill.
MATTHEW HINTON TO BETSY JONES 27 Sep 1816. Bdsm Matthew Hinton and Wilson Busbee.
THOMAS EDWARDS to ELIZABETH PEEDIN 16 Jul 1814. Bdsm Thomas Edwards and James Peedin.
JOHN STEVENS to ELIZABETH ALLEN 11 Oct 1804. Bdsm John Stevens and John A. Smith.
BRITAIN SNIPES to ALEY MARTIN 30 Aug 1800. Bdsm Britain Snipes and Joseph Brown.
READING JOHNSTON to CELIAH WALL 21 May 1810. Bdsm Larry Bryan.
ALLEN JERNIGAN to CLARY TOLER 22 Dec 1806. Bdsm Allen Jernigan and Willis Rivers.
WILLIAM HARRELL to CATY BASS 24 May 1803. Bdsm Frances Harrell.
JOHN FERREL to ELIZABETH JONES 26 Oct 1816. Bdsm John Ferrell and Reuben Dodd.
HENRY SIMMON to POLLY SMITH 6 Aug 1818. Bdsm Henry Simmon and William Smith, Jr.
WILLIAM SPENCER to PEGGY MASSEY 15 Mar 1819. Bdsm Isiah Massey
ALEXANDER LANDERS to BETSY MASSENGILL 2 Feb 1819. Bdsm Etheldred Bell.
JOHN STANSILL to POLLY WORLEY 9 Sep 1818. Bdsm Stephen Barnes.
RICHARD ROLLINS to POLLY BRADY 9 Aug 1816. Bdsm Richard Rollins and Jesse Wellons.
JAMES PRICE to ALEY BLACKMAN 28 Dec 1816. Bdsm James Price and Nathan Johnson.
WILLIAM PARSONS to "CRUZZY" BROGDEN 24 Aug 1818. Bdsm Loverd Ethridge and William Parsons.
MARK ROSE to SALLY KEEN 26 Feb 1816. Bdsm Henry Lasser.
JARROT STEVENS to OLIVE JOHNSON 27 Feb 1816. Bdsm David Stevens.
ELISHA PITTMAN to POLLY BOLTEN 18 Apr 1818. Bdsm Elisah Pittman and John Bolten.
AMOS PEEDIN to POLLY EDWARDS 11 Aug 1815. Bdsm Philip Johnson.
NATHAN PRICE to RACHEL RAIFORD 28 Aug 1817. Bdsm Nathan Price and William B. Hocut.
SIMON POPE to PATSEY COLE 17 May 1817. Bdsm William Todd.
ICHABOD PRICE to "CULEY" JOHNSON 4 Nov 1814. Bdsm Ichabod Price and Jacob Bryan.
STEPHEN PETTIS to EDITH MESSER 23 May 1814. Bdsm Thomas Barber.
WILLIAM RIVERS to MARY ANN HINTON 18 Apr 1813. Bdsm William Rivers.
HARDY AVERA to ELIZABETH CARRELL 10 May 1814. Bdsm Noah Nichols.
WILLIAM STRICKLAND to LANY CREECH 20 May 1813. Bdsm Joshua Creech.
GEORGE BRYD to SUSAN BYRD 13 Mar 1812. Bdsm Benjamin Stevens.
BENJAMIN JONES to NANCY CAPPE 24 May 1813. Bdsm Edward Stevens.
REDDICK HENS TO GILLY AVERA 5 Jan 1813. Bdsm Abner Smith.
OSBURN HOWELL to LOTTY STRICKLAND 29 Dec 1812. Bdsm Osburn Howell and Edmond Howell.
RICHARD STALLINGS to POLLY TIMPKINS 12 Mar 1814. Bdsm Richard Stallings and Joseph Brown.
WILLIS HINTON to POLLY HART 20 Sep 1811. Bdsm John Kelly.
WILLIAM JONES to RUTHY PENNY 6 Oct 1811. Bdsm Cader Avera.
JONES DAVIS to SALLY GREEN 30 Oct 1813. Bdsm John L. Guy.
JAMES HILLIARD to ZILPHA FINLEY 28 Sep 1819. Bdsm William Penny.

JOHNSTON COUNTY MARRIAGES

BARNABY DUNN to MARGARET MASSINGILL 17 Dec 1819. Bdsm Barnaby Dunn and John Keen.
RICE PRICE to CYNTHIA PRICE 7 Jan 1812. Bdsm Bird Price.
THOMAS BRANNON to MARY WILDER 14 Sep 1816. Bdsm Thomas Brannon and Kedan Brannon.
WILLIAM WOODALL to EDITH BARBER 6 May 1819. Bdsm William Woodall.
WILLIS N. WHITE to MARY EASON 16 Sep 1819. Bdsm Willis N. White.
LABON GRIFFIN to EDNEY THOMAS 15 Jul 1819. Bdsm Labon Griffin and Jonathan Britt.
SIMON BRYAN to LOTTY BRYAN 9 Jun 1819. Bdsm William Fail.
THEOPHILUS BAGLEY to CATHERINE GESBORN 18 Oct 1815. Bdsm Theophilus Bagley and Hilbird Starling.
WARREN BAILEY to ELIZABETH ONEAL 29 Nov 181?. Bdsm Arthur Bailey.
ELIJAH BAKER to SALLY JOHNSON 15 Mar 1813. Bdsm George Keen.
HENRY GUY and OLIVE EASON 25 Feb 1817. Bdsm Henry Guy and Allen T. Ballenger.
CARY ATKINSON to MILLY HINTON 25 Apr 1818. Bdsm William Oneal and Cary Atkinson.
JOHN ATKINSON to PHEREBY ALTMAN 14 Feb 1818. Bdsm Etheldred Holt.
NATHAN ATKINSON to NANCY EASON 1 Mar 1815. Bdsm Nathan Atkinson and Elam Smith.
LUKE ARTEST to MARTILLA BELL 18 Oct 1815. Bdsm Jacob Powell and Luke Artest.
LEWIS WHITFIELD to PATSEY BRYAN 9 Nov 1816. Bdsm Lewis Michiner.
MEREDITH WEBB to CREECY MOORE 22 Aug 1811. Bdsm James Webb.
MARMADUKE WILLIAMS to POLLY WARREN ?. Bdsm E. Starling.
JONATHAN WHITINGTON to CLARY GREEN 13 July 1813. Bdsm William Whitington.
WILLIAM WOOD to ZILPHA EVANS 26 Dec 1815. Bdsm John Johnson.
JOHN RHODES to SARAH MOORE 3 Jan 1816. Bdsm King Viann.
JAMES STRICKLAND to CELAH HORN 31 Jul 1815. Bdsm James Strickland and John C. Guy.
WILLIAM OLIVER to WINIFRED "TELL" 28 Jan 1815. Bdsm Asa Oliver.
WILLIAM SERVING to ZILPHA PRICE 12 Mar 1818. Bdsm William Serving and Thomas Lockhart, Jr.
RICHARD STEVENS to LIZZIE JOHNSON 23 Jul 1818. Bdsm Richard Stevens and J. Simms.
JOSEPH SHAW to PHEREBY NEWBY 16 Dec 1817. Bdsm John Nowell and Joseph Shaw.
JAMES STALLINGS to "ULRICA" BRYAN 2 Apr 1818. Bdsm James Stallings and Isaac Stallings.
JEREMIAH SIMS to ELLY STEVENS 6 May 1818. Bdsm Jeremiah Sims and Hartwell Ivy.
EZEKIEL STALLINGS to ELIZABETH WILDER 11 Apr 1818. Bdsm Jesse Creech.
HARRY BARBER to "LUSEY" BARBER 4 May 1816. Bdsm Harry Barber and Plyer Barber.
BARNA BURNETT to SALLY POWELL 23 May 1813. Bdsm David Freeman.
JOHN BROADWELL to "ANEY" GULLY 25 Nov 1811. Bdsm John Broadwell and Noah Nichols.
DAVID H. BRYAN to WINIFRED McCULLERS 7 Oct 1816. Bdsm David H. Bryan and Roy Helme.

MARRIAGE BONDS

ELISHA STANLY to PRISCILLA DUNN 11 Sept 1811. Bdsm John Carter.
STEPHEN BROWN to LANCY STRICKLAND 17 Aug 1814. Bdsm Stephen Brown and John Avera.
FREDERICK BRYAN to SALLY GULLY 30 Mar 1814. Bdsm James Bryan.
DAVID WATKINS to "TANY" SELLARS 26 Feb 1812. Bdsm James Bryan.
DAVID BELL to PHEBE THORP 29 Sep 1812. Bdsm Etheldred Bell.
MARK BIMDIE to POLLY GODWIN 23 Sep 1817. Bdsm Mark Bimdie and William Bryan.
WILLIAM W. HOPKINS to SALLY BOON 16 June 1812. Bdsm David Lanceford.
WILLIAM MORGAN to EDITH JOHNSON 14 Nov 1818. Bdsm William Johnson and William Morgan.
BENJAMIN MOORE to POLLY WEBB 27 Aug 1816. Bdsm Benjamin Moore and Hardy Adams.
MARK NOWELL to "VICY" JORDAN 24 Jun 1817. Bdsm Mark Nowell and Henry Jordan.
EDMUND JOHNSON to "WILSY" JOHNSON 7 May 1819. Bdsm Benjamin Carrel.
BENNETT NUTT to "LEUCY" SMITH 11 Feb 1815. Bdsm Bennett Nutt and Benjamin Smith.
ROBERT H. HELME to PHEREBA McCULLERS 11 Nov 1817. Bdsm Robert H. Helme and Braswell Bridgers.
JOSEPH WOODWARD to SALLY HATCHER 19 Mar 1811. Bdsm Benjamin Hatcher.
BRIDGERS PARCH to WINIFRED DODD 17 Nov 1818. Bdsm Bridgers Parch and James Grigery.
WILLIAM WILSON to SARAH HICKS 16 Sept 1818. Bdsm William Wilson and Etheldred Holt.
EDWARD WADELL to REBECCA BALLARD 7 Oct 1818. Bdsm Edward Ballard.
MOSES LLOYD HILL to TRANQUILLA GULLY 1 Apr 1819. Bdms Moses Lloyd Hill and Thomas Lockhart.
REDICK BARNES to POLLY BRETT 30 Sept 1819. Bdsm William Penny.
SOLOMON STEPHENSON to CRECY JOHNSON 10 Feb 1817. Bdsm Solomon Stephenson and Barnaby Johnson.
MARTIN PRICE to CEELY PRICE 3 Nov 1816. Bdsm Dixon Price.
JOHN WELLONS to ANNA MEDYETT 19 Sept 1817. Bdsm James Wellons.
HEZEKIAH CAPELAND to PATSY BOON 8 Jan 1813. Bdsm Wiliam Honeycut.
DANIEL LASHLEY to NANCY HOLT 30 July 1815. Bdsm Henry Smith.
"CAMMELL" CAUDELL to POLLY HARPER 2 Dec 1819. Bdsm Henry Guy.
HENRY BARTLETT to REBECKAH MASSENGILL 27 Dec 1819. Bdsm Henry Bartlett and John Keen.
STEPHEN TOLER to CATTY BRENT 23 Nov 1819. Bdsm Stephen Toler and Benjamin Dunn.
LEMMEL PEEBLES to CHERRY PARKER 17 Nov 1818. Bdsm Lemmuel Peebles and John Lee, Jr.
RYALS ELDRIDGE to JANE MASSENGILL 22 Mar 1813. Bdsm Ryals Elkridge and Martin Hall.
FRANCES HARRELL to SOUTHEY JOINER 23 Nov 1819. Bdsm Frances Harrell and Thomas Allen.
WILLIAM SHAW to POLLY NOWELL 9 Oct 1818. Bdsm George Todd.
SAMPSON EDWARDS to SALLY BRASWELL 29 Sept 1812. Bdsm Benjamin Edwards.
JAMES SELLERS to ELIZABETH COLLINS 13 Aug 1819. Bdsm Etheldred

JOHNSTON COUNTY MARRIAGES

Holt.
ABSALOM WOODALL to PHEBA JOHNSON 28 Jul 181? Bdsm Absalom Woodall and Allen Johnson, Sr.
WILLIE ATKINSON to APPY WHITLEY 23 Apr 1816. Bdsm Willie Atkinson and Etheldred Holt.
BRYAN ADAMS to BEDLY JOHNSON 29 Sept 1813. Bdsm Jesse Adams.
OWEN THORNTON to JOHANNAH BRYAN 12 Oct 1811. Bdsm Owen Thornton and Harrold Thornton.
JOHN BROGDEN to REBECCA THORNTON Sep 1820. Bdsm William Pajon and John Brogden.
JOHN HOBBY to POLLY TEMPLER 11 Feb 1814 Bdsm Littleton Johnson.
HARDY BATTEN to "PECY" STARLING 9 Jun 1813. Bdsm Abraham Batten.
APPLEWHITE RICHARDSON to "WILLY" HOUDLER 22 Nov 1819. Bdsm Applewhite Richardson and Simon Pope.
JONATHAN DRIVER to WINIFRED PRICE 22 Nov 1819. Bdsm John Driver.
ALSEY BUSBEE to POLLY SAULS 15 Nov 1812. Bdsm Willis Jones.
WILLIS JONES to LOTTIE STEPHENSON 13 May 1811. Bdsm Rueben Landers and Hardy Jones.
SAMUEL CROCKER to CHARITY CRUMPLER 25 Jul 1816. Bdsm Samuel Crocker and Solomn Futrell.
TOBIAS GODWIN to CREACY RICHARDSON 7 Jan 1811. Bdsm Tobias Godwin and Hardy Richardson.
JOHN BARBER to BETSY WOODALL 19 Jan 1816. Bdsm Terry Barber and John Barber.
SAMUEL BATTEN to BARBARA STARLING 20 Jan 1816. Bdsm Samuel Batten and John Batten.
JOHN KELLY to TABITHA SIMPKINS 13 Feb 1811. Bdsm Kedar Avera.
WILLIAM EVERYTT to ? 23 Feb 1818. Bdsm George Massengill.
LEWIS BRASWELL to SALLY BRIDGERS 29 Dec 1815. Bdsm Lewis Braswell and Joseph Edwards.
JESSE EDWARDS to "PHEREBY" HALL 1 Sept 1813. Bdsm Amos Peedin.
NATHANIEL DUNN to POLLY POOL 26 Mar 1813. Bdsm Richard Johnson.
AMOS BATTEN to MARY CORBET 18 May 1812. Bdsm Amos Batten.
JOHN WILLIAMS to NANCY PATE 1 May 1812. Bdsm John Williams and Bolling G. Hobbs
HARDY AVERA to POLLY RIVERS 20 Oct 1810. Bdsm Hardy Avera and Ellick Sanders.
JAMES GOODRICH to SALLY "CROFORD" 14 Jan 1811. Bdsm John Wallace.
ALLEN JOHNSON to EDITH BARNES 21 Aug 1814. Bdsm Willie Johnson.
BOLLING G. HOBBS to AGATHA H. SPEED 22 May 1813. Bdsm Bolling G. Hobbs and Hardy Sanders.
JACOB MERCER to ZELPHA PAGE 23 Aug 1813. Bdsm William Smith.
ROBERT H. HELME to NANCY GUY 6 Jan 1811. Bdsm Robert H. Helme and William M. Hopkins.
JESSE SILMAN to PRISCILLA WATSON 16 Jan 1811. Bdsm Henry Sasser.
DIXON DAVIS to "MOURNING" POPE 1 July 1818. Bdsm Dixon Davis and Etheldred Holt.
JOHN DAVIS to MORNING PILKINGTON 25 Feb 1812. Bdsm Jeremiah Gurley.
ELISHA TISDALE to POLLY ONEAL 5 Sept 1818. Bdsm Isham Oneal.
TOBIAS BIMS to ANNY LEE 25 Feb 1811. Bdsm Lewis Lee and John Avera.
OZWELL LANGLEY to OLIVE "SWEARINGGAME" 26 Mar 1811. Bdsm Phillip Raiford.

MARRIAGE BONDS

WILLIAM LASSITER to "LEWEY" STEVENSON 6 Jan 1813. Bdsm Solomon Whitington.
BARNABA LOVET to CALLY CELLARS 17 Feb 1816. Bdsm Barnaba Lovet and John B. Watson.
JOSIAH ADAMS to BETSY GEORGE 16 November 1813. Bdsm Josiah Adams and Reuben Sanders.
WILLIAM HOALT to DIANNA WELLONS 21 Jan 1811. Bdsm Charles Wellons.
JOHN HARPER to WINIFRED FLOWERS 24 May 1819. Bdsm Solomon Whittington.
EDIN RHODES to BETSY BRENT 27 Aug 1819. Bdsm Edin Rhodes and Josuha Daniel.
EVERIGHT P. STEVENS to RHODA HOULDER 28 Dec 1819. Bdsm Jacob Stevens.
ASA WEAVER to BETSEY WEAVER 16 Aug 1820. Bdsm Lewis Fail.
ELISHA BEDDIN to BETSY DOWDY 6 Aug 1820. Bdsm John Lee.
AMOS JOHNSON to SALLY JOHNSON 25 Mar 1817. Bdsm Amos Johnson and John Leach.
BRIGHT JERNIGAN to ELIZABETH WATSON 2 May 1816. Bdsm Bright Jernigan and Thomas Rice.
JOHN A. BROWN to SARAH LOCKHART 19 Jan 1820. Bdsm John A. Brown and Simon T. Sanders.
WILLIAM NOWELL to MARTHA EARP 23 Oct 1819. Bdsm John Nowell.
MATTHEW JONES to BETSY TURNER 26 May 1815. Bdsm Cader Avera.
ELIJAH PITMAN to ORPAH PUGH 19 Oct 1819. Bdsm Elijah Pitman and Micajah Wilkinson.
PETER PARISH to EDITH STEVENSON 16 Nov 1819. Bdsm Garrot Stevenson.
BENJAMIN NICHOLS to "FEREBY" BOYET 28 Aug 1811. Bdsm Henry Sasser.
JOHN HATCHER to SUSANNAH WATKINS 25 Feb 1815. Bdsm Robert Gulley.
JASPER HOWELL to WINIFRED DENKINS 11 Apr 1819. Bdsm Bold Robin Hood.
ASA HARREL to BETSY GOODRICH 25 Mar 1811. Bdsm Willis Cole.
EZEKIEL HILLIARD to JANE WILDER 20 Dec 1816. Bdsm Ezekial Hilliard and Griffin Holloman.
AMOS JOHNSON to SALLY TOMLINSON 23 Aug 1819. Bdsm Amos Johnson and Solomon Whitington.
THOMAS LOCKHART, JR. to TEMPERANCE EASON 11 Dec 1817. Bdsm Thomas Lockhart, Jr. and William H. Guy.
JOSEPH FARMER to POLLY NELMS 3 Aug 1819. Bdsm Joseph Farmer and William H. Guy.
WILLIAM H. BULLS to SALLY POWELL 3 Apr 1819. Bdsm William H. Bulls and Charles Stevens.
WILLIAM G. MERCER to NANCY DOXY 15 Aug 1811. Bdsm William W. Hopkins.
WILLIAM KINGRY to JANE "LUSTENE" 25 Dec 1819. Bdsm William Kingry and John "Avery".
THOMAS PRICE to TEMPERANCE PRICE 24 Aug 1819. Bdsm Henry Lewis.
MOSES HARVILLE to POLLY SIMS 25 May 1812. Bdsm James Adams.
JOSEPH INGRAM, JR. to ELIZA BOON 29 Apr 181?. Bdsm Joseph Ingram, Jr. and William H. Guy.
JORDAN ROSE to ALSEY KEEN 19 Nov 1819. Bdsm Jordan Rose and H. Sasser.
ISAAC BEASLEY to PHEREBY ROBERTS Jul 1819. Bdsm Isaac Beasley and

JOHNSTON COUNTY MARRIAGES

Henry Johnson.
WILLIAM WHITMORE to SUSANA MARTIN 3 Apr 1819. Bdms Rigdon Suggs.
JOEL CROCKER to SPENCY TAYLOR 24 Jul 1829. Bdsm Samuel Crocker.
JOSIAH HINNANT to BETHENA GULLEY 11 Feb 1815. Bdsm Josiah Hinnant and William Hinnant.
LEWIS STANLEY to MILLY JOINER 17 Dec 1876. Bdsm Lewis Stanley and John Owen.
STEPHEN ONEAL to NANCY RICHARDSON 11 Jan 1817. Bdsm Stephen Oneal and Benjamin Hocut.
JESSE WOODWARD to EDNEY HOLLEMAN 1 Jan 1818. Bdsm Jesse Woodward and James Richardson.
WESTLEY WELLONS to ELIZABETH PEARCE 3 Nov 1812. Bdsm Kedar Pearce.
IREDELL WILLIAMS to GILLY PARKER ? 1816. Bdsm Berry Lewis and Iredell Williams.
JOHN WHITINGTON to AMY MESSER 22 Apr 1815. Bdsm Whitwell Johnson.
LEWIS TINER to CELAH MEDDYATT 7 Mar 1815. Bdsm Micajah Meddyatt.
WILLIAM TURNER to EDITH SMITH 9 Oct 1812. Bdsm David Turner.
JAMES TURNER to EDITH SMITH 2 Feb 1814. Bdsm Philip Johnson.
STEPHEN TOLLER to POLLY GULLY 28 Sept 1818. Bdsm Stephen Toller and William Holt.
THOMAS TOMLINSON to SARAH PENNY 17 Apr 181?. Bdsm Thomas Tomlinson and Harriss Tomlinson.
HINTON VINSON to PATSEY BRYAN 7 Feb 1817. Bdsm Hinton Vinson and Noah Nichols.
LEWIS THOMPSON to "KERN" STRICKLAND 4 Aug 1815. Bdsm William Thompson.
LARRY WILKINSON to EDITH STANCILL 31 Dec 1819. Bdsm Benjamin Hatcher.
ENOS GARRALD to BEDIE STARLING 10 Apr 1816. Bdsm Enos Garrald.
DIXON PRICE to SALLY TALTON 6 Dec 1817. Bdsm Dixon Price and Daniel Deese.
ELISHA PEEDIN to LALEY CAPPS 15 Jul 1815. Bdsm Henry Peedin.
NATHAN SKINNER to NANCY BENNET 25 Feb 1817. Bdsm Nathan Skinner and Henry Stevens.
THOMAS RICE to PATSY TURNER 11 Sep 1817. Bdsm Thomas Rice and John Sanders, Jr.
WILLIAM CARTER to NANCY WELLONS 12 Dec 1816. Bdsm William Carter and Neil Brice.
JOHN PEEDIN to EDITH CAPPS 26 Aug 1814. Bdsm Lemmuel Pearce.
WILSON BARLOW to BARSHEBA LEE 8 Mar 1816. Bdsm Wilson Barlow and Henry Lee.
HUDSON REAVES to ELIZABETH HOLLOMAN 17 June 1817. Bdsm Hudson Reaves and Henry Parnold.
WILLIAM JOHNSON to SALLY HORN 17 Sept 1814. Bdsm Solomon Johnson.
NICHOLAS LYNCH to NANCY DAVIS 25 June 1814. Bdsm Charles Stevens.
SIMON PEARCE to PHEREBY TAYLOR 15 Apr 1811. Bdsm Ivy Watkins and Simon Pearce.
JOHNSON PARISH to PATSEY STEVENS 11 Mar 1815. Bdsm Johnson Parish and Britain Langdon.
JOSIAH BLACKWELL to ANZY MITCHELL 13 Oct 1815. Bdsm Jesse Grice.
WILLIAM JACKSON to NANCY HOLLAND 26 July 1820. Bdsm William Jackson and John Jackson.

MARRIAGE BONDS

JAMES LEE to POLLY DURHAM 27 Sept 1819. Bdsm Kedar Lee and James Lee.
LEVY YELVINGTON to PATIENCE HINNANT 28 Oct 1820. Bdsm Levy Yelvington and Nathaniel Futrell.
JAMES PRICE to NANCY JOHNSON 18 May 1815. Bdsm James Price and John McLeod.
LABON GRIFFIN to SUSANNA CARRELL 16 Jan 1811. Bdsm Benjamin Carrell.
JAMES RENTFROW to POLLY THORN 9 Oct 1818. Bdsm Jesse Sullivan.
GARRY PITTMAN to PATSY "FIVASH" 12 Aug 1816. Bdsm Harry Pittman and Elisha Pittman.
RUEBEN BARBER to ELIZABETH BARBER 14 Feb 1814. Bdsm Rueben Barber and Etheldred Bell.
BRITAIN CARRELL to BETSY AUSTIN 1 Aug 1820. Bdsm Britain Carrell and John Carrell.
WILLIAM MARTIN to PATSY BARBER 4 Mar 1811. Bdsm Benjamin Martin.
BRASWELL BRIDGERS to ELIZABETH STALLINGS 1 Oct 1814. Bdsm John Stevens Jr.
SAMUEL BEAMAN to SALLY LANGDON 31 Jul 1811. Bdms Thomas Barber.
LITTLE BERRY BROWN to BETSY SIMPKINS 2 Feb 1820 Bdsm Little Berry Brown and Joseph Brown.
JOHN SASSER to "DELANY" HALL 20 Apr 1816. Bdsm John Sasser and Enos Garrald.
GREEN H. SCOTT to POLLY HINTON 28 Oct 1811 Bdsm Green H. Scott and Jonathan Britt.
WILLIAM S. SPIVEY to POLLY LANGLEY 22 Apr 1810. Bdsm William Spivey and Isaac Langley.
JAMES FLUELLERS to CLARY OSTON 13 Nov 1814. Bdsm Martin Overby.
JOHN ROBERD to ELIZABETH BODDERY 4 Dec 1815. Bdsm Ephraim Overby.
WILLIAM PERRY to BETTY COOPER 25 Aug 1812. Bdsm Jesse Wall.
WILLIAM POOL to SALLY JOHNSON 10 Mar 1812. Bdsm Penud Penny.
JOSIAH RENTFROW to POLLY GODWIN 11 Apr 1811. Bdsm Brammister Grizzel.
JOHN RAPER to BETSY SASSER 11 Feb 1814. Bdsm John Sasser.
NEWIT PEEDIN to SALLY TINER 8 Apr 1811. Bdsm James Peedin.
ISAAC RAIFORD to "CIVIL" RAIFORD 19 May 1817. Bdsm Isaac Raiford and Philip Raiford.
JOHN STALLINGS to NANCY ONEIL 30 Dec 1812. Bdsm Aaron Solomon.
HENRY SASSER to NANCY KIRBY 25 Feb 1812. Bdsm Ichabod Balkcom.
SIM PRICE to PENNY HAYLES 1 Mar 1814. Bdsm Thomas Lockhart.
BRITAIN SMITH to MARTHA PRICE 8 Dc 1813. Bdsm John Smith.
ROBERT SPEED to NANCY RYALS 29 Sept 1812. Bdsm Jesse Adams.
BANNISTER HARPER to PATSY BARBER 7 Nov 1818. Bdsm Bannister Harper and William W. Jones.
EDWARD PRICE to EDITH PARKER 6 Oct 1815. Bdsm Edward Price and Micajah Oneal.
BRITAIN SCOTT to NANCY RAINES 4 Jul 1817. Bdsm Britain Scott and Jessy Whitley.
EATON SAULS to SALLY POOL 30 Mar 1818. Bdsm Eaton Sauls and William Jones.
JAMES POOL to PATSEY THORP 21 Dec 1813. Bdsm Hardy Pool.
ELISHA WOODWARD to NANCY EARP 7 Jan 1819. Bdsm Elisha Woodward and

JOHNSTON COUNTY MARRIAGES

Tobias Holliman.
ASA ROE to SALLY EDWARDS 22 Mar 1817. Bdsm Asa Roe and James Peedin.
JOEL ELLINGTON to BETSY HOCUT 26 Nov 1816. Bdsm Joel Ellington and Allen Richardson.
JAMES ROBERTS to NANCY BODIARY 5 May 1816. Bdsm James Roberts and Britain Roberts.
DICKSON PHILLIPS to EDITH OLIVER 16 Apr 1814. Bdsm William Phillips.
WILLIAM WIGGINS to WEALTHY BARTLEY 12 Aug 1814. Bdsm Jesse Stanley and William Wiggins.
THOMAS TEDDER to CELIA HOLLOMAN 8 Nov 1816. Bdsm Thomas Tedder and Reuben Dodd.
JOHN ROBERTS to POLLY SNIPES 6 Feb 1816. Bdsm John Roberts and Meed Gully.
SIM HILL to SALLY STEVENS 17 Aug 1813. Bdsm Gideon Warner.
EDMOND PATE to PEGGY JOHNSON 18 Jan 1814. Bdsm John Williams.
THOMAS RICE to CLOE BULLS 14 Dec 1814. Bdsm Thomas Rice and John Eason, Jr.
BURT STEVENS to PENCY VILLIA JONES ? Bdsm Burt Stevens and Alexander Smith Jr.
JAMES HINTON to BETSEY HINTON 23 ? 1815. Bdsm Daniel Sauls.
ERASMUS STINSON to PATIENCE FORD 18 Dec 1813. Bdsm Erasmus Stinson.
HAMILTON PHILLIPS to SARAH FAULK 9 Sep 1812. Bdsm Dixon Phillips.
GREEN ADAMS to OLIVE MAINORD 26 Sep 1814. Bdsm William Wilder and Green Adams.
ELISHA STARLIN to PRISSY PARKER 21 Sep 1816 Bdsm Elisha Starlin and Abraham Batten.
WILLIAM RYALS to LOTTY PORTER 13 Jan 1819 Bdsm William Ryals and James Ryals.
JOHN RHODES to CHARLOTTE BRUNT 14 Sep 1814. Bdsm Allen L. Ballenger.
ALLEN PRICE to PATSY EDWARDS 25 May 1812. Bdsm Joseph Boon.
BENJAMIN HATCHER to POLLY WATKINS 24 Jun 1813. Bdsm Sampson Rogers.
DEMPSEY SPELL to ZILPHA HORN 11 Oct 1815. Bdsm Dempsey Spell and Lewis Caudell.
LABON GREEN to "RELEY" GREEN 23 Feb 1819 Bdsm Willie Green.
ISAAC WILLIAMS to SUSAN LEE 7 Dec 1816. Bdsm John Sanders Jr.
DAVID PARISH to BETSY JOHNSON 25 Nov 1819. Bdsm Joel Clifton and David Parish.
JOHN HILL to ELIZABETH ELDRIDGE 14 Sep 1818. Bdsm John Hill and Labon Green.
SHEROD BER to JANE MASSINGILL 21 Oct 1815. Bdsm Zachariah Gower.
WILLIAM FARROR to CATHARINE TURLEY 19 Mar 1816. Bdsm Thomas Turley.
URIAH PEACOCK to ZILPHA HAYLES 5 Nov 1815. Bdsm Uriah Peacock and John A. Smith.
BENJAMIN SIMPKINS to RACHEL BLACKMAN 25 Mar 1814. Bdsm Jeremiah Blackman.
JOHN STANLEY to "SEALY" CORBET 2 Jan 1816. Bdsm James Stanley.
JOHN STEPHENSON to SARAH PLEASANT 30 Dec 1816. Bdsm John Stephenson and James Whittington.
MARTIN OVERBY to SARAH FLUELLER 9 Aug 1811. Bdsm William Roberts.

MARRIAGE BONDS

WILLIAM ODOM to REBECKAH HILL 28 Mar 1814. Bdsm Isaac Williams.
REDDICK SPELL to ELIZABETH WORLEY 18 Nov 1811. Bdsm Reddick Spell and Hilbert Starling.
EDWIN SMITH to ELIZABETH McCULLERS 15 Mar 1811. Bdsm William W. Bryan.
GILMAN K. L. POOL to POLLY POOL 7 Mar 1812. Bdsm Gilman K. L. Pool and Hardy Pool.
ASA OLIVER to NANCY WISE 7 Jan 1812. Bdsm William Oliver.
BRITAIN HONEYCUT to CANDISS COURDELL 25 Aug 1813. Bdsm Britain Honeycut and William Honeycut.
HARDY POOL to NANCY THORP 12 Oct 1816. Bdsm Hardy Pool and N. L. Brice.
ZACHARIAH WELLONS to ELIZA LOCKHART 5 Feb 1817. Bdsm Zachariah Wellons and Bryan Smith.
LEMMUEL PEARCE to NANCY BULLS 29 Jun 1813. Bdsm John Stevens, Jr.
JAMES. D. WOODALL to SARAH HILL 7 Nov 1816. Bdsm James D. Woodall and Peyton Ivy.
JOHN NARRON to MILLY PRICE 22 Nov 1819. Bdsm William Johnson.
JOSEPH I. SUMMER to WINIFRED RIVERS 12 Aug 1814. Bdsm William Rivers and Joseph I. Summer.
ALEXANDER SMITH to SARAH TALTON 24 Mar 1812. Bdsm Larkin Smith.
JOSHUA DANIEL to NANCY CORBET 29 Mar 1814. Bdsm Lewis Sasser.
WILLIS WOODARD to EDITH PHILLIPS 13 Nov 1812. Bdsm Warren Woodard
HARDY WATFORD to SUSANNA PRICE 3 Dec 1818. Bdsm Moses Jordan.
MOSES WALLIS to ELIZABETH GRIFFIN 21 Apr 1816. Bdsm Moses Wallis and Abraham Webb.
HARDY DAUGHTERY to ELIZABETH RHODES ? Bdsm Needham Warren.
JOHN WHITLEY to SALLY GREEN 11 Dec 1816. Bdsm John Whitley and Enoch Whitley.
MICHAJAH WILKINSON to MATILDA JERALD 13 Jul 1815. Bdsm Micajah Wilkinson and Elisha Pitman.
WILLIAM WHITTINGTON to ELIZABETH BARBER 28 Sep 1813. Bdsm John Barber.
KINCHEN BUSBEE to NANCY RUSSEL 17 Nov 1823. Bdsm Ransom Busbee.
BRYANT WHITLEY to NANCY THOMAS 23 Dec 1824. Bdsm Willie Whitley.
ALLEN MORGAN to CRECY OLIVER 29 Mar 1825. Bdsm Kinchen Q. Adams.
AMOS ATKINSON to JULIA PRICE 9 Mar 1822. Bdsm Amos Atkinson and Elam Lockhart.
JOHN C. MONTAGUE to ELIZA DEES 14 Dec 1824. Bdsm William H. Guy.
HENRY JORDAN to EDITH HOULDER 26 Dec 1823. Bdsm Mark Nowell.
GIDION PARNOLD to ELIZABETH BROWN 27 Dec 1823. Bdsm Jesse Starling.
MARK JOHNSON to SALLY EVANS 29 Nov 1823. Bdsm Noel West.
MOSES BISHOP to LUCY ROSE 1 Mar 1825. Bdsm Council J. Beard.
REDDIN RAIFORD to ELIZA OLIVER 21 Oct 1823. Bdsm Reddin Raiford and Levi Oliver.
CLEM BAKER to POLLY WALSTON 10 Mar 1824. Bdsm James Baker.
WILLIE PILKINGTON to SALLY POE 29 Nov 1823. Bdsm Willie Pilkington and Allen Price.
JAMES STALLINGS to NANCY CREECH 29 Apr 1824. Bdsm John Spencer.
WILLIE GERRALD to PATSEY GERRALD 5 Jun 1824. Bdsm Henry M. Stevens.
THOMAS L. BAGSDALE to DELANY HINTON 5 Jul 1824. Bdsm William Hinton.

JOHNSTON COUNTY MARRIAGES

HENRY HAMBLETON to "LECRECY" OLIVER 4 May 1824. Bdsm Reddick Warren.
THOMAS HADLEY to MILLICENT RICHARDSON 5 May 1824. Bdsm Thomas Hadley.
MAJOR GRIFFIN to ELIZABETH GULLY 2 May 1824. Bdsm James Minnchel.
COGDELL MASSY to POLLY HOLLOWELL 10 Oct 1823. Bdsm William Spencer.
EDWARD BRYAN to ELISBRA BRYAN 29 Dec 1824. Bdsm Lunnon Byran.
WILLIE JACKSON to POLLY PEARCE 11 Jun 1824. Bdsm Thomas Holland.
TEEL BALANCE to ZILPHA GARNER 8 May 1824. Bdsn Teel Balance and John Rams.
WILLIAM ROBERTS to "CHILLY" HOWELL 9 Jun 1825. Bdsm William Strickland.
ROBERT BRADDY to "DIZY" STRICKLAND 27 Dec 1824. Bdsm Levi Strickland.
ADIM ROBERTS to SOPHIA STEVENS 20 May 1824. Bdsm Adim Roberts and Bythan Bryan.
JESSE KIRBY to MORNING "FIBIASH" 15 Aug 1823. Bdsm Henry Sasser.
THOMAS BELL to SALLY POWELL 25 May 1824. Bdsm Nicholas Lee.
BARNABY PHILLIPS to SALLY GULLY 11 Sep 1824. Bdsm Dickson Phillips.
ASA HOLLOMAN to WINIFORD HOLLOMAN 21 Dec 1824. Bdsm Gideon Price.
ELIJAH STANLY to NANCY DUNN 19 Dec 1823. Bdsm Ezekiel Creech.
HENRY POPE to POLLY LEE 28 Dec 1823. Bdsm Henry Pope and John Tiner.
NATHAN A. MORGAN to PENELOPE BARBER 5 Feb 1825. Bdsm Young Morgan.
AARON PRESCOTT to BETSEY SNIPES 12 Mar 1822. Bdsm Aaron Prescott and Nathan Braddy.
JOHN WILLIS to "RILEY" PRICE 15 Aug 1825. Bdsm John D. Talton.
LABON GRIFFIN to SALLY FLOWERS 18 Dec 1824 Bdsm Labon Griffin and William W. Bryan.
ADIN EASON to SALLY BRANNON 12 Aug 1825. Bdsm William Hayles.
JOEL PITMAN to WINIFRED WILDER 4 Jun 1825. Bdsm Levi Yelvington.
JOHN SHEPHERD to ANNA BARBER 15 Aug 1823. Bdsm Nicholas Rose.
CHARLES MASSY to ZILPHA STALLINGS 29 Apr 1824. Bdsm Callin Stallings.
BARZILLA BLACKMAN to SARAH "RANSER" 1 Jan 1824. Bdsm Starling W. Temple.
JOSEPH DAVISON to NANCY LEE 5 Jan 1824. Bdsm Samuel Lee, Jr.
JAMES R. ALLEN to WINIFRED ADAMS 2 Nov 1829. Bdsm Thomas Lee.
JOSHUA SUGG to MARTHA MARTIN 7 Oct 1829. Bdsm John H. Martin.
HENRY FLOWERS to ALICE INGRAM 18 Dec 1824. Bdsm William Powell.
ARTHUR JOHNSON to NANCY WOODWARD 21 Dec 1824. Bdsm Jonathan Woodward.
BARDAM HOLLOMON to PATSY HOLLOMON 28 Jan 1824. Bdsm Garry Hollomon.
DAVID WATFORD to PATSY PRICE 12 Feb 1824. Bdsm Hardy Watford.
EDWIN E. PEARCE to MANDY SNIPES 24 Feb 1824. Bdsm Edwin E. Pearce and Allen L. Ballenger.
ISAAC STALLINGS to SALLY JENKINS 30 Apr 1825. Bdsm Edwin Spivy.
WILLIAM ROBERTSON to MORNING HOULDER 9 Dec 1824. Bdsm William Robertson and John T. Hayles.
ROBERT DAUGHTERY to SALLY BRADDY 30 Nov 1824. Bdsm William Teal.
ARISON AUSTON to BETSY ROBERTS 14 Jan 1829. Bdsm Elisha Harrison.
BANKS CADELL to NANCY JOHNSON 6 Dec 1828. Bdsm Bright Byrd.

MARRIAGE BONDS

THOMAS O. HINTON to MARTHA JONES 29 Nov 1828. Bdsm John McCleod.
ALLEN BRANNON to LOTTY JONES 13 Nov 1828. Bdsm William Brannon.
THOMAS COBBS to SARAH HOPKINS 2 Dec 1824. Bdsm John Cobbs and Benjamin A. Barham.
MECAJAH EDWARDS to ELIZABETH "STUCKEY" 13 Aug 1824. Bdsm Jesse Whitley.
ISAAC HINTON to MATILDA HINTON 15 Aug 1823. Bdsm Isaac Stallings.
COMSILL BEARD to NANCY STEVENS 22 Mar 1823. Bdsm David Stevens.
ALEXANDER JOHNSON to ALLY COLTON 9 Oct 1824. Bdsm Noel West.
JOHN PHILLIPS to MARY THOMSON 4 Oct 1824. Bdsm John Phillips and Loverd Pearce.
RICHARD HOGG to EATTY EATMAN 25 Nov 1824. Bdsm Russel Sillivent.
JACOB BARNES to MORNING HINNANT 27 Feb 1827. Bdsm Jacob Barnes.
MATTHEW PARKER to ELIZABETH HINNANT 15 Oct 1829. Bdsm Matthew Parker and Josiah Hinnant.
LEVY ODOM to ZILPHA LAMB 13 Jun 1829. Bdsm Jacob Odom.
JAMES JOHNSON to PHEREBY SMITH 23 Sep 1828. Bdsm Alexander Johnson.
JOHN AUSTON to "LUVENSY" JOHNSON 13 Jun 1826. Bdsm Alsey Auston.
WILLIAM SAULS to ELIZABETH YOUNG 11 Feb 1825. Bdsm James Hilliard
ELIAS RICHARDSON to SARAH PEARCE 28 May 1826. Bdsm Jonathan Hinnant.
MOSES PARNOLD to WELTHY PARNOLD 26 Mar 1826. Bdsm Young Morgan.
CALEB PENNY to POLLY TURNER 3 Nov 1823. Bdsm Harry Penny.
RICHARD JOHNSON to FANNY JOHNSON 18 Nov 1823. Bdsm Richard Stevens and Reuben Gower.
THOMAS C. CLIFTON to JOANNA LEE 20 Nov 1826. Bdsm John Lee.
EZEKIEL YOUNG to MARTHA TOMLINSON 2 Apr 1828. Bdsm Birnice H. Tomlinson.
BUD JONES to SUSANNA TAYLOR 22 Mar 1827. Bdsm Reddin Taunt.
JOHN ADAMS to MARGARET JOHNSON 20 Jan 1827. Bdsm Allen Johnson.
HENRY W. EASON to SUSAN WILLIAMS 15 Jul 1828. Bdsm Henry Eason and Samuel Mitchiner.
WILLIAM CARRELL to HOLLY GIBBS 12 Apr 1828. Bdsm Ivy Richardson.
SAVAGE LITTLETON to EMILY PARKER 31 Jan 1828. Bdsm Savage Littleton and Robert H. Helme.
RIGDON DEES to PENELOPE "CORE" 3 Feb 1827. Bdsm B. Robin Hood, Jr.
BENJAMIN DOWDY to ALEY EASON 26 Jan 1828. Bdsm Andrew Bass.
WILLIAM PEEDIN to PATSY CORKE 11 Sep 1827. Bdsm John Rams.
GEORGE BARBER, JR. to CASSANDANA TOMLINSON 2 Feb 1827. Bdsm George Barber, Jr. and Thomas Lockhart, Jr.
JAMES BINN to BEEDY ONEAL to 27 Nov 1821. Bdsm William Oneal.
ROBERT N. GULLY to ELIZABETH WALL 5 Oct 1827. Bdsm John S. Powell.
WHITLEY MESSER to THIANA JOHNSON 17 Oct 1827. Bdsm John Messer.
JOEL LITTLETON to PIETY PITMAN 7 Aug 1827. Bdsm Savage Littleton.
SION PAGE to ELIZA BURRIETT 24 Jul 1827. Bdsm Holmes Hardy.
JOSIAH HOULDER, JR. to ? HOCUTT 14 Jul 1827. Bdsm Drury Snipes.
ELIJAH L. CHAMPANE to OLIVE BYRD 18 Jul 1827. Bdsm Elijah Champane and John Byrd.
ELISHA HOLLAND to BETSY HOLLAND 26 Mar 1822. Bdsm Enos Holland and George Mitchell.
MATTHEW GILES to SALLY THORNTON 13 Nov 1827. Bdsm James K. Barber.
BRIDGERS WATSON to MILLY STARLING 24 May 1825. Bdsm Etheldred

JOHNSTON COUNTY MARRIAGES

Futrell.
KINEAN POWELL to BETSY ADAMS 18 Sep 1827. Bdsm Cudney Adams.
ELAM LOCKHART to NELLY HARDY 27 Nov 1827. Bdsm Elam Lockhart and Edwin Spivy.
ASA HARRELL to "LIANY" BROADSTREET 24 May 1825. Bdsm Adin Powell.
MERRILL RYALS to BRAZZILLA WORDALL 16 Jun 1821. Bdsm Lemuel Peebles.
OLIM SASSER to NANCY SCOTT 23 Nov 1824. Bdsm Charles Crawford.
BENNET BOON to NANCY ONEAL 24 May 1823. Bdsm John Manor and Bennet Boon.
WILLIAM BYRD to NANCY JOHNSON 18 May 1821. Bdsm Robert Stevens.
HERITT MANERY to CHARITY BAILY 19 Aug 1828. Bdsm William R. Privett.
WILLIAM INGRAM to NANCY JOHNSON 20 Jan 1823. Bdsm Nicholas Lee.
BRASWELL BRIDGERS to JANE JENKINS 3 May 1825. Bdsm Thomas D. Bridgers.
RICHARD AVERA to CHARLOTTA JONES 28 Nov 1822. Bdsm William Coats.
THOMAS JOHNSON to "AON" ALLEN 11 Oct 1822. Bdsm Benjamin Bell.
JAMES PEEDIN to LELIA MASSY 24 Oct 1825. Bdsm Wilkerson Futrell.
RICHARD BRINT to NANCY INGRAM 6 Feb 1827. Bdsm Richard C. Terry.
RICHARD PEARCE to "CLARKY" PEARCE 4 Apr 1826. Bdsm Simon A. Pearce.
DAVID HOWELL to CALLY STRICKLAND 21 Sep 1826. Bdsm Reddick Warren.
CONDARY ONEAL to LEASY BAILEY 6 Oct 1826. Bdsm Condary Oneal and Mecajah Oneal.
JOHN BAKER to ANN JOHNSON 4 Oct 1826. Bdsm Clement Baker.
DAVID BRYAN to ELIZABETH SMITH 8 Jul 1826. Bdsm David Tomson.
JAMES FELICK to EMILY G. HINTER 31 Jul 1822. Bdsm Roy Helme.
BENJAMIN STEVENS to PEGGY CROSS 26 Nov 1822. Bdsm James Godwin.
ASA B. MEDYETT to ELIZABETH HINTON 9 Oct 1825. Bdsm Asa B. Medyett and Allen S. Ballenger.
WILLIAM BRANNON, JR. to "CULY" PRICE 21 Jul 1822. Bdsm William Brannon, Jr. and Willie Brannon.
WILLIAM HOLLAND to CYNTHIA GARNER ? Feb 1823. Bdsm Simon Cockrell and William Holland.
HENRY RAINES to NANCY RAIFORD 27 Feb 1821. Bdsm Philip Raiford and Jesse Whitley.
LITTLETON CAPPS to ZILPHIA PRICE 12 May 1827. Bdsm Bright Jernigan.
JOHN B. CLIFTON to "THITORSON" BARBER 12 Apr 1827. Bdsm Joel Clifton.
WILLIAM B. WALL to MARY ANN HINTON 10 Jan 1827. Bdsm Robert N. Gully.
JAMES PEEDIN to NANCY RAIFORD 26 May 1826. Bdsm Needham Warren.
JOHN BEAL to EDNEY ELLIS 19 Jun 1826. Bdsm John Ellis.
JOHN NARRON to "NAMMY" WATKINS 22 Mar 1827. Bdsm Burwell Johnson.
JOSIAH HINNANT to CALLY HINNANT 1 Nov 1827. Bdsm Josiah Hinnant and Reuben Wilkinson.
JOHN WHITLEY, JR. to NANCY WILDER 11 Apr 1825. Bdsm Richard Taylor.
JASON LASSITER to THENA H. COTTON 11 Apr 1825. Bdsm James Lassiter.
BUD SMITH to PENNY JOHNSON 20 Apr 1828. Bdsm Noel West.
GUIDEON PRICE to PATIENCE PARKER 5 Apr 1825. Bdsm Powell Parker.
ROBERT SNEED to MARY ELDRIDGE 25 Nov 1828. Bdsm Richard Washington.
WILLIAM BROWN to BETSY BATTEN 13 Sep 1826. Bdsm William Brown and

MARRIAGE BONDS

John Brown.
OSBORN HOLT to PATSY HOBBY 9 Jan 1828. Bdsm John Holt.
CALVIN WILKERSON to NANCY COCKRELL 2 Jan 1828. Bdsm Levy Yelvington.
JOHN MASSEY to "LOUSEE" CREECH 10 Aug 1827. Bdsm William Massey, Jr.
NICHOLS LEE to POLLY ALLEN 12 Feb 1827. Bdsm Isaac Lee.
HENRY ROSE to NANCY EDWARDS 3 Dec 1827. Bdsm James Peedin.
JAMES PARISH to ELIZABETH JONES 8 Dec 1827. Bdsm William W. Jones.
JACOB EDWARDS to APSABETH CREECH 4 Jan 1827. Bdsm Joshua Creech Jr.
ELISHA LASSITER to BEEDY CARRELL 9 Jan 1827. Bdsm James Lassiter.
EDWIN RAINS to SALLY REVEL 8 Jan 1828. Bdsm Isaac Boothe.
BERYEAK HORN to BETSY "LARVIR" 15 Dec 1827. Bdsm Edwin Spivy.
JOHN PEARCE to JANE WHITTINGTON 31 Jan 1828. Bdsm John Pearce and Lemmuel Peebles.
ADIN POWELL to MARY WILLIAMS 5 Jan 1828. Bdsm Harmon Cordle.
JOHN BYRD to NANCY JONES 29 Sep 1829. Bdsm Thomas Jones.
SAMUEL SELLARS to MARY HOCUT 31 Dec 1827. Bdsm Ivy Richardson.
ALLEN PAGE to POLLY LEE 27 Sep 1820. Bdsm Plyer Barber.
WILLIAM GILES to NANCY STANSILL 23 Jan 1826. Bdsm Bryant Adams.
WILLIAM BENNET to SALLY STEVENS 26 Aug 1828. Bdsm Bold R. Hood.
JOHN HOLMES to SALLY GILES 9 Aug 1828. Bdsm James Ivy.
JOHN DRAUGHORN to PUDISY WOOD 29 Aug 1828. Bdsm Etheldred Futrell.
JOHN GILES to ELIZA PETTIS 28 Jun 1828. Bdsm James K. Barber.
ALFRED BUSBEE to BETSY ELLINGTON 19 May 1828. Bdsm Lewis Jenkins.
NEEDHAM BRYAN to SALLY JONES 23 May 1828. Bdsm James Jones.
JASON YELVINGTON to REBECCA BARNES 14 Jul 1828. Bdsm Levi Yelvington.
WARREN COLLINS to POLLY SELLERS 26 Mar 1822. Bdsm Samuel Strickland.
WILLIAM SASSER to MARION GERRALD 18 Aug 1828. Bdsm William Sasser and John Sasser.
NEEDHAM WHITLEY to ZILPHA WILLIAMSON 22 Jan 1828. Bdsm William Green.
BERRY JOHNSON to NANCY COLE 20 May 1822. Bdsm Allen Richardson.
JOHN ATKINSON, JR. to PATSY ROBERTS 24 Jul 1820. Bdsm John Atkinson, Jr. and Bright Jernigan.
AQUILLA NARRON to ELIZABETH BAILEY 11 Oct 1822. Bdsm Josiah Holliman.
JOEL HORN to ZILPHA RICHARDSON 24 Sep 1822. Bdsm Stephen Barnes.
SAMUEL LEE YOUNG to BETSY INGRAM 20 Mar 1821. Bdsm Edward Lee, Jr.
EPHRAIM LOVE to TILPHA KEEN 25 Feb 1822. Bdsm Hardy Hinnant.
ALLEN PAGE to POLLY LEE 27 Sep 1820. Bdsm Pyler Barber.
ALSEY PACE to ZILPHA HALL 21 Sep 1820. Bdsm James Carrell.
WARREN MASSINGALE to LUCY MASSINGALE 17 Dec 1825. Bdsm Warren Massingale and Noel West.
LEWIS OLIVER to POLLY STRICKLAND 24 Sep 1822. Bdsm Stephen Oliver.
RAMS LEE to NANCY WOOD 16 Sep 1819. Bdsm Rams Lee and Kedar Lee.
BRYAN ALLEN to SUSANNA WOOD 29 May 1821. Bdsm Bryan Allen and John Morgan.
LITTLETON WATSON to OLEA KEEN 27 Aug 1821. Bdsm Garry Grice.
HARDY BRITT to LOTTY PENNY 21 Jan 1823. Bdsm Nathaniel Johnson.

JOHNSTON COUNTY MARRIAGES

JOEL DUNN to BETSY HARRELL 28 Aug 1821. Bdsm Francis Harrell.
BENNET WALL to SALLY MURPHREY 1 Feb 1823. Bdsm Aaron Wall and Bennet Wall.
JOHN ATKINSON to MARTHA WATSON 27 Aug 1821. Bdsm Garry Grice.
BENJAMIN WORLEY to SALLY BRITT 28 Feb 1820. Bdsm Needham Warren and Benjamin Worley.
DAVID LANGLEY to NANCY LEGON 26 May 1829. Bdsm William Pridgin.
ADAM BANKS to SUSAN LEACH 22 Jun 1829. Bdsm Simon Smith.
WILLIAM WILLIAMS to BETSY ADAMS 29 Aug 1826. Bdsm Gideon Woodall.
CHERBY RODGERS to PEGGY BOWLER 17 Jul 1829. Bdsm James Jones.
JAMES LASSITER to LUCY LOCKHART 27 Nov 1827. Bdsm William Lassiter.
WILLIAM LEE to PHEREBE FAIL 27 Nov 1827. Bdsm Edward Lee.
JOHN MAINARD to POLLY HOWARD 10 Feb 1828. Bdsm Green Adams.
ALFORD ADAMS to ZILPHA GATLIN 29 May 1827. Bdsm John Dixon.
JACOB DAUGHTERY to CELIA EDWARD 27 Mar 1827. Bdsm William Brown.
JACOB WOODALL to PENNY LASSITER 29 Aug 1826. Bdsm Gideon Woodall.
EVERETT DUNCAN to PATIENCE AVERYT 8 Dec 1826. Bdsm George Duncan.
JAMES HILLIARD to CLOE PENNY 29 Sep 1827. Bdsm Thomas D. Bridgers.
BRYAN ONEIL to PHEREBE POOL 9 Dec 1826. Bdsm Reuben Sanders.
JONATHAN WALL to PHEREBY MURPHREY 23 Nov 1824. Bdsm Aaron Wall.
HARDY DURHAM to BETSY PENNY 2 Mar 1827. Bdsm Bird Youngblood.
JOSIAH SASSER to SALLY BEARD 13 Dec 1825. Bdsm Josiah Sasser and James Felick.
WILLIE JONES to ALEY HICKS 25 Feb 1823. Bdsm Allen Young.
ALEXANDER COLLINS to AGATHA WHITTINGTON 16 Feb 1823. Bdsm William Whittington.
NATHAN PORTER to ELIZABETH IVEY 16 Nov 1822. Bdsm William Ryals.
DAVID STACTROCK to BETSY SANDERS 15 May 1827. Bdsm John Sanders.
WILLIAM JOHNSON to BETSY HARRISON 5 Dec 1826. Bdsm Nathaniel Johnson.
ROBERSON KENT to CINITH BINV 23 May 1826. Bdsm Jonathan Hinnant.
WILLIAM BATTEN TO ELIZABETH FAULK 24 Dec 1827 Bdsm John Sasser.
JOHNSON MEDLIN to TEMPY FERRELL 24 Dec 1826. Bdsm James Jones.
JOHN ROSE to "MILLY" JOHNSON 12 Feb 1830. Bdsm Warren Johnson.
JACOB WALKER to "SALEY" BATTEN 22 Jan 1822. Bdsm Jacob Walker and John Brown.
BENJAMIN MOORE to LUCY ADAMS 24 Mar 1830. Bdsm Bryan Allen.
JOSIAH GARNER to CATTY CROCKER 9 Sep 1827. Bdsm James Crocker.
GIDEON ALLEN to CHARITY GEORGE 24 Mar 1823. Bdsm Barzella Blackman.
WILLIAM JAMES PEEDIN to NANCY CREECH 17 Mar 1827. Bdsm Newit Peedin.
JAMES ALLEN to ELIZABETH RHODES to 28 Jun 1823. Bdsm James Allen and John Allen.
JAMES RAIFORD to ESTHER WHITLEY 13 Dec 1827. Bdsm Benjamin Stevens.
JAROLD JOHNSON to LEANNA COLTON 2 Jan 1826. Bdsm Nathan T. Allen.
JOHN LEE to DOROTHY SMITH 22 May 1826. Bdsm Calvin Jernigan and John Lee.
ROBERT MASSINGILL to SALLY LEE 1 Jan 1826. Bdsm Starling W. Temple.
THOMAS OLIVER to ANCY WATSON 24 Aug 1829. Bdsm Solomon Futrell.
WILLIS HAYES to NANCY PORTER 24 Jan 1826. Bdsm Lazarus Matthews.
HARRY LANE to NARCISSY GUY 6 Jan 1826. Bdsm Harry Lane and John Sanders, Jr.

MARRIAGE BONDS

JOSIAH GAME to EDNEY RAINS 4 Nov 1823. Bdsm Josiah Game and Samuel Game.
ALSEY AUSTON to DRUSILLA TOMLINSON 15 Apr 1820. Bdsm William Bryan and Alsey Auston.
JESSE HINNANT to NANCY SELLIVANT 28 Nov 1824. Bdsm Jesse Sellivant.
JOSHUA HOOD to BETSY COLE 26 Feb 1830. Bdsm Bold Robin Hood.
JAMES PEEDIN to BETSY PILKINTON 24 Feb 1827. Bdsm Climck Pilkinton.
IREDELL WATKINS to FANNY BALLANCE 31 May 1823. Bdsm Iredell Watkins and Cullen Talton.
HOWELL HASTINGS to EDITH EDWARDS 28 Nov 1826. Bdsm John H. Rose.
JAMES H. SMITH to NANCY BRYAN 8 Aug 1825. Bdsm James H. Smith and A. Smith.
EATON PORDI to PATIENCE BATTEN 26 ? Bdsm Dickson Price.
DAVID BROWN to CLARY WINDBORN 31 May 1822. Bdsm David Brown and Alsey High.
SAMUEL LEE to ANN HARRELL 26 Nov 1822. Bdsm Francis Harrell.
EDWARD STEVENS to DRUSILLA HOWARD 18 Sep 1822. Bdsm Absalom P. Woodall.
MARTIN WALL to ALEY CARRELL 7 Sep 1823. Bdsm Martin Wall and Reuben Sanders.
MATTHEW CAPPS to SALLY PARNOLD 16 May 1825. Bdsm Dixon Davis.
JOHN HARRELL to NANCY BENSON 27 Feb 1827. Bdsm John Phillips.
LEE BROWN to ANN PARKER 28 Feb 1825. Bdsm Nicholas Rose.
WILLIAM GREEN to "KIDDY" E. WIN ? 1827. Bdsm Aaron Wall.
BURWELL HOWELL to BETSY BRADY 27 May 1824. Bdsm Lewis Thomson.
DIXON PEARCE to POLLY GODWIN 7 Feb 1827. Bdsm Dixon Pearce.
GEORGE GULLY to "WILLY" WILDER 15 Oct 1825. Bdsm Aaron Wall.
BALDY SANDERS to DELIAH SANDERS 21 Mar 1822. Bdsm Baldy Sanders and John Eason.
JAMES STEVENS to SARAH COLE 15 Oct 1825. Bdsm Josiah Cole.
ARRISON AUSTIN to ANIRILLA TOMLINSON 20 Oct 1824. Bdsm Alsey Austin.
LEWIS McCULLEN to MARGARET WILSON 27 May 1823. Bdsm Bold Robin Hood.
CALEB PENNY to LIZZY AVERYT 23 Oct 1824. Bdsm Harry Penny.
CURTIS HOLLAND to NANCY HOLLAND 1 May 1823. Bdsm William Jackson.
STEPHEN LEE to EDITH BLACKMAN 13 Oct 1821. Bdsm Stephen Lee and Jeremiah Blackman.
STEPHEN PRICE to SALLY GREEN 1 Mar 1825. Bdsm Jonathan Holliman.
WILLIE HOLLIMAN to BETSY GREEN 28 May 1823. Bdsm John Cooper.
JAMES SPENCE to NANCY PATE 1 Jan 1825. Bdsm Elisha Spence.
JOSIAH COLE to NANCY DUNN 28 Feb 1825. Bdsm Nicholas Rose.
JONATHAN WOODARD to JUDY B. JOHNSON 29 Jul 1822. Bdsm Solomon Johnson.
PERRY WALL to ALEY JOHNSON 27 Aug 1822. Bdsm John Brown.
ATHA LEE to CYNTHIA POWELL 27 Aug 1822. Bdsm Atha Lee and Noel West.
WILLIAM JOHNSON to PATSY JOHNSON 24 Jan 1823. Bdsm Reuben Johnson.
HARDY PILKINTON to SALLY COCKRELL 29 Mar 1825. Bdsm Hardy Pilkinton and Handy Peedin.
HARDY JOHNSON to VINCY MORRIS 30 Dec 1826. Bdsm Thomas Hicks.
JOHN DRIVER to CLARY DEANS 28 Aug 1822. Bdsm John Driver and John

JOHNSTON COUNTY MARRIAGES

Windborn.
HINTON VINSON to PHEREBY ALLEN 1 May 1823. Bdsm Hinton Vinson and Simon T. Sanders.
CLEMENT WOODALL to SALLY MESSER 26 Feb 1822. Bdsm James A. Woodall.
JOHN MITCHELL to NANCY "STUEKY" 3 Jun 1827. Bdsm Isaac Boothe.
WILLIAM POOL to MARY GARNER 27 Nov 1826. Bdsm Simon Cockrell.
AARON GODWIN to FEREBY LEE 28 Nov 1826. Bdsm Noel West.
ICHABOD PRICE to MILLY NARRON 6 Dec 1826. Bdsm Willie Price.
WILLIS SASSER to POLLY RAIFORD 10 Nov 1826. Bdsm Allen C. Sasser.
BRYANT MESSER to JANE SHAW 27 Dec 1826. Bdsm John Messer.
ISAAC LEE to POLLY FAIL 12 Mar 1827. Bdsm William Lee.
JOSEPH WHEELER to FANNY JOHNSON 26 Sep 1827. Bdsm Henry Jordan.
BENNET JONES to POLLY HOLT 21 Nov 1826. Bdsm William W. Jones.
ROBERT BRYAN to "SARALL" WOODARD 23 Dec 1826. Bdsm Larkin Holloman.
ADIN STRICKLAND to BETSY STRICKLAND 20 Mar 1827. Bdsm Reddick Warren.
ALFRED LEE to SALLY WEST 21 Jan 1828. Bdsm Kedar Lee.
JAMES HOLLOMON to KERN BEDINGFIELD 25 Sep 1827. Bdsm James Carrell.
THOMAS DAUGHTERY to PATSY RAGAN 3 Mar 1827. Bdsm Thomas Daughtery and Barna Bulls.
ELISHA LEE to BETSY CAPPS 2 Mar 1827. Bdsm William Ingram.
MICHAEL INGRAM to REBECCA STEVENS 7 Mar 1827. Bdsm Reddick Warren.
WILLIAM ONEAL, JR to HARRIET RICHARDSON 20 Jan 1827. Bdsm William Oneal, Sr.
BARTY JOHNSON to EDITH WILKINSON 13 Mar 1828. Bdsm Hardy Baily.
SAMUEL A. BRYAN to JULIA LOCKHART 10 Mar 1828. Bdsm Edwin Spivey.
HILLIARD BAILY to NICY BAILY 5 Mar 1828. Bdsm Hilliard Baily and Robert H. Helme.
BENJAMIN WALSTON to ELIZABETH LEE 16 Feb 1828. Bdsm Clement Baker.
GEORGE W. WHITFIELD to CATHARINE HART 4 Feb 1828. Bdsm Wimberly Hinton.
WIMBERLY HINTON to EDITH HINTON 26 Sep 1822. Bdsm Hugh Lee.
ELI STRICKLAND to SUSAN ONEAL 5 Mar 1828. Bdsm Richard Oneal.
TIMOTHY WALTON to ELIZABETH JONES 26 Jun 1822. Bdsm William A. Walton.
RIGDON SUGG to "SYLVEAR" MARTIN 28 Feb 1825. Bdsm Lazarus Matthews.
BERRY HOLLOMAN to PATIENCE PARKER 16 Mar 1826. Bdsm Thomas D. Bridgers.
DANIEL CRAWFORD to WINIFRED THOMSON 18 Mar 1826. Bdsm Nicholas Thomson.
ELISHA SPENCE to NANCY WOOD 25 Nov 1823. Bdsm Elisha Spence and William W. Nichols.
WILLIAM HIGH to PATSY RICHARDSON 26 Nov 1823. Bdsm Calvin Richardson.
DRURY JOHNSON to ANNA OVERBY 17 Mar 1825. Bdsm Gideon Gower.
SOLOMON STEVENS to NANCY LANGDON 18 Dec 1822. Bdsm Simon Parish.
CHARLES WILKERSON to ALICE BREWER 26 May 1822. Bdsm Hardy Baily.
JOHN SMITH to WINIFRED GILMAN 24 Sep 1821. Bdsm Jesse Holliman.
JESSE WATSON to SALLY HINNANT 16 Sep 1820. Bdsm Jesse Sellivant.
JOSIAH NICHOLS to NANCY HOCUT 11 Jan 1823. Bdsm Gibson Martin.
JOHN COATS, JR to "CARDIS" COLLINS 17 Apr 1822. Bdsm John Coats, Sr.

MARRIAGE BONDS

JOHN MOONAHAM to FRANCIS TANT 28 Feb 1823. Bdsm John Moonaham and William Moonaham.
JESSE BAILEY to ALSEY TISDELL 15 Mar 1821. Bdsm Jesse Bailey and Burwell Johnson.
JOHN WALKER to CARION WOODALL 28 May 1821. Bdsm Absalom Woodall.
THOMAS MESSER to POLLY SELLS 9 Sep 1821. Bdsm Thomas Messer and William W. Sanders.
WILLIAM HONEYCUTT to ABBY "CORDDE" 12 Apr 1821. Bdsm William Honeycutt and Jonathan White.
JOSEPH H. HINTON to TEMPY ANN GRICE 11 May 1825. Bdsm Phillip Johnson.
THOMAS ALLEN to ESTHER LEE 20 Nov 1821. Bdsm William S. Whittington.
BYTHAN BRYAN to JULIA C. SMITH 11 Jun 1821. Bdsm Bythan Bryan and David Thompson.
WILLIAM PARISH to EDITH LANGDON 25 Jul 1821. Bdsm David Parish.
CHARLES STEVENS to BETSY FARMER 25 Sep 1821. Bdsm Adin Powell.
LOVERD SPIVEY to LIZY AVERA 20 Jul 1821. Bdsm Isaac Stallings and Loverd Spivey.
SHADRECK LASSITER to LUCY JOHNSON 10 Sep 1825. Bdsm James Lassiter.
JAMES WOODALL to SALLY BARBER 10 Aug 1821. Bdsm Plyer Barber.
ERVIN GREEN to NANCY GREEN 28 May ? . Bdsm John Cooper.
JAMES CROCKER to "RUTHA" GAY 5 Dec 1822. Bdsm James Crocker and Exum Futrell.
BERRY HOLLIMAN to "DRUMY" NARON 10 Mar 1822. Bdsm Thomas Brown.
GEORGE McCULLEN to SALLY DUPREE 6 Jan 1823. Bdsm George McCullen and Bythan Bryan.
JESSE OVERBY to BETSY ERRANT 11 Jan 1820. Bdsm Joseph Edwards.
JESSE HOLLEMAN to BETSY HOLLAND 28 Mar 1820. Bdsm Charles Crawford.
JOHN PACE to EDNY BATTEN 22 Dec 1821. Bdsm John Pace and Levy Yelvington.
SAMUEL STRICKLAND to DELILAH POPE 15 Mar 1821. Bdsm Samuel Strickland and Henry Jordan.
HENRY COOPER to HARRIET HINTON 20 Apr 1820. Bdsm William Russell.
JOHN SPENCER to POLLY STALLINGS 24 Mar 1821. Bdsm John Spencer and William Spencer.
ZACHARIAH SIMS to "SYNDARLEIGH" PAGE 7 Oct 1820. Bdsm Zachariah Sims and James G. Woodall.
SAMUEL LEE to NANCY GEORGE 28 Nov 1820. Bdsm Samuel Lee and Loverd Eldridge.
JONATHAN WHITE to NANCY CORDELL 1 Mar 1820. Bdsm Jonathan White and David Parish.
JOHN FELLOWS to MARY BELL 3 Jan 1820. Bdsm John Fellows and David Bell.
LEVY OLIVER to BARSHEBA RAIFORD 4 Jan 1820. Bdsm Levy Oliver and William M. Carter.
JOHN VINSON, JR to SARAH ALLEN 21 Nov 1822. Bdsm John Vinson, Jr and Hinton Vinson.
WILSON BUTTS to ZILPHIA PUGH 21 Sep 1820. Bdsm John Farmer.
BENJAMIN S. BROOKS to NANCY BEEL 13 Dec 1820. Bdsm Benjamin S. Brooks and John W. Brooks.
WILLIAM PUGH to RHODA THOMAS 27 Nov 1820. Bdsm Russell Sellivant.

JOHNSTON COUNTY MARRIAGES

MOSES RHODES to PHEREBE LEE 25 Jan 1820. Bdsm Brian Lee and Moses Rhodes.
WILLIAM BROWN to FANNY WARREN 10 Jun 1820. Bdsm Reddick Warren.
PHILLIP RAIFORD to ELIZABETH RAMS 27 Feb 1821. Bdsm Phillip Raiford and Jesse Whitley.
JEREMIAH BLACKMAN to WINIFRED GEORGE 4 Mar 1823. Bdsm Barzella Blackman.
ISAAC INGRAM to TABITHA BLACKMAN 3 Jan 1822. Bdsm Isaac Ingram and Jeremiah Blackman.
JESSE HORNE to NANNY BOYT 1 Nov 1820. Bdsm Jesse Horne and James Strickland.
BENJAMIN SELLERS to SALLY TAYLOR 5 Aug 1820. Bdsm Adin Powell.
JOHN BLACKMAN to CATY LEE 18 Jan 1821. Bdsm John Blackman and Barzella Blackman.
JACOB WOODALL to THENA MASSENGILL 9 May 1825. Bdsm Jacob Woodall and James Woodall.
JAMES GREEN to DORCAS JONES 21 Feb 1820. Bdsm Nathan Atkinson and James Green.
JEREMIAH EVANS to "CEELA" CRAWFORD 1 Nov 1822. Bdsm Alexander Sanders and Jeremiah Evans.
HARMON CAUDELL to POLLY WARREN 13 Oct 1828. Bdsm Isaac Wise.
EXUM FUTRELL to RHODY POOL 10 Feb 1821. Bdsm Exman Futrell and Nathaniel Futrell.
JAMES PARKER to SARAH TALTON ? 1820. Bdsm James Parker and Abraham Batten.
JOHN DUPREE to SALLY PETTIS 11 Jan 1820. Bdsm John Dupree and William Welch.
GILBERT DRIVER to EDITH HALL 1 Mar 1820. Bdsm John Driver and Gilbert Driver.
LEMMUEL LEE to NANCY ALFORD 2 Apr 1823. Bdsm Lemmuel Lee and John Lee.
JAMES ELLIS to PATSY POWELL 17 Dec 1825. Bdsm Isaac Hutchins.
BRYAN JONES to CALLY BOYLE 9 Dec 1822. Bdsm Bryan Jones and John Spencer.
WILLIAM WIMDEON to SALLY VINSON 1 Feb 1826. Bdsm John Sanders.
ELISHA REDING to LUCY HINNANT 4 Oct 1825. Bdsm James Hilliard.
GIDEON GARNER to "SINDY" SNIPES 19 Jul 1826. Bdsm Drury Johnson.
LEWIS CRUISE to SALLY HORN 7 Jul 1820. Bdsm Deal Collins.
GEORGE MASSENGILL to POLLY COTTON 12 Sep 1820. Bdsm George Massengill.
DAVID CARRELL to POLLY MATTHEWS 29 Aug 1820. Bdsm Briton Langdon.
WILLIAM WELLONS to ELIZABETH ROBERTS 11 Sep 1820. Bdsm James Wellons and William Wellons.
JAMES WELLONS to CYNTHIA SANDERS 13 Feb 1821. Bdsm James Wellons and William N. White.
WILLIAM GREEN to CAROLINE BROADSTREET 27 Sep 1820. Bdsm Josiah Holliman.
TERRY BARBER to POLLY WOODALL 27 Feb 1821. Bdsm Terry Barber and Young Morgan.
WILLIAM WHITLEY to CELAH HOLDER 1 Mar 1820. Bdsm William Whitley and John Sanders, Jr.
JOHN B. ALLEN to "CANDIS" STALLINGS 2 Apr 1823. Bdsm Nathan Allen

MARRIAGE BONDS

and John B. Allen.
JOHN RICHARDSON to PENNY PRICE 23 May 1820. Bdsm John Richardson and Hillery Wilder.
HENRY RETTER to POLLY PETTIS 30 Jan 1821. Bdsm Henry Whitmor.
MECAJAH MEDDYETT to NICY BROOKS 12 Feb 1821. Bdsm Mecajah Meddyett.
JAMES EASON to LOTTY MOORE 19 Oct 1822. Bdsm James Eason.
FREDERICK MITCHELL to BETSY THOMAS 4 May 1822. Bdsm Frederick Mitchell and Needham Warren.
JAMES HICKS to PENELOPE BOYETT 14 Jul 1824. Bdsm Stephen Hicks.
JAMES LEE to ELLINDER INGRAM 24 Dec 1821. Bdsm James Lee and Samuel Lee (younger).
JOSIAH SASSER to SALLY BEARD 26 Sep 1826. Bdsm Boykins Lee.
JOHN EASON to BETSY WILLIAMS 22 Jan 1827. Bdsm John Eason and Thomas Lockhart, Jr.
GIDEON WOODALL to MARY LASSITER 26 Sep 1826. Bdsm James Lassiter.
GEORGE W. LIMSDON? to NANCY BUSBEE 18 Feb ?. Bdsm Herberd Robertson.
THOMAS PAGE to CANDIS HONEYCUT 23 Mar 1826. Bdsm William White.
SOLOMON PARNOLD to VINEY EASON 13 Apr 1821. Bdsm Henry Parnold and Solomon Parnold.
WILLIAM RUSSELL to ELIZABETH STEVENS 18 Jan 1820. Bdsm William Russell and William Wilder.
DAVID LEE to ANNA LEE 5 May 1821. Bdsm Kedar Lee.
WILLIS COBB to MARTHA LEE 29 Nov 1825. Bdsm Nicholas Rose.
WILLIS HINTON to POLLY DELOACH 2 Jul ? Bdsm Edwin Spivey.
JOSEPH FARMER to MARY MITCHINER 7 Aug 1821. Bdsm Joseph Farmer and Thomas Lockhart, Jr.
NATHAN BRADY to CYNTHIA ROBERTS 8 Feb 1820. Bdsm James Roberts.
RUSSELL SELLIVANT to ISABEL PUGH 22 Feb 1820. Bdsm Jesse Bailey.
HEROD THORNTON to PHEREBE CLEMMY 23 May 1820. Bdsm Samuel Lee.
MATTHEW HICKS to PENNY TURLEY 14 May 1823. Bdsm Matthew Hicks and Clem N. Shaw.
CALVIN SMITH to DOLLY CARRELL 17 Mar 1820. Bdsm Levi Ferrell.
DANIEL HARPER to MARY HARPER 28 Nov 1820. Bdsm Absalom Harper.
DAVID ADAMS to LUCY GRIMES 30 Aug 1820. Bdsm David Adams and Charles Stevens.
WILLIAM BRADY, Jr to ELIZABETH HARRELL 24 May 1820. Bdsm John Atkinson and Etheldred Holt.
BURWELL JOHNSON to SUSAN NARON 12 Jan 1822. Bdsm Burwell Johnson and George Barber, Jr.
MARTIN HARPER to NANCY BAILEY 28 Feb 1820. Bdsm Garry Grice.
THOMAS DAVIS to NANCY SASSER 28 Nov 1823. Bdsm Thomas Davis and Stephen Barnes.
JOHN HINTON to SALLY COOPER 29 Feb 1820. Bdsm Joseph Hinton.
BERRY EARP to PATSY LEE 15 Jan 1822. Bdsm Berry Earp and Moses Jordan.
PETER LEE to AMY CAUDLE 4 Sep 1821. Bdsm Aaron Massingill and Peter Lee.
MOSES GARNER to ANNA BAILEY 13 May 1821. Bdsm Moses Garner and Levi Garner.
WILLIAM RILEY PRIVET to MILLY BAILEY 18 Oct 1821. Bdsm William Riley Privet and Nathan Thomas.

JOHNSTON COUNTY MARRIAGES

AVERA WALTON to CYNTHIA PATE 9 Oct 1821. Bdsm Joseph Wright and Avera Walton.
CHARLES STEWART to SALLY WOODALL 29 Oct 1821. Bdsm Charles Stewart and Terry Barber.
JOHN STEVENSON to SOLLY "COPPER" 18 Oct 1824. Bdsm Harris Tomlinson.
DEMPSEY GREEN to SALLY "JEFFERS" 24 May 1820. Bdsm Reding Green.
WILLIAM MESSER to NANCY WOODALL 13 Jun 1821. Bdsm John Messer.
YOUNG CARTER to SALLY "LARVER" 16 Dec 1829. Bdsm William Penny.
BARNABY LOVETT to EDNEY BROADSTREET 27 Nov 1821. Bdsm William Hinton.
JESSE KENNEDY to DORCAS PETTIS 25 Dec 1821. Bdsm George Byrd Jr. and Jesse Kennedy.
ETHELDRED FUTRELL, JR. to EDNEY GERRALD 2 Jul 1821. Bdsm Etheldred Futrell, Jr. and Thomas Price.
LITTLETON JOHNSON to NANCY LEE 13 May 1821. Bdsm William Johnson and Littleton Johnson.
WILLIAM GAY to BETSY SPENCER 15 Jan 1821. Bdsm Elisha Starling and William Gay.
EDMOND HONEYCUT to POLLY JOHNSON 6 May 1820. Bdsm David Parish.
DRURY SNIPES to UNITY HOUDLER 6 Aug 1822. Bdsm Drury Snipes and John S. Whitley.
JESSIE DAVIS to ZILPHIA BOYETT 28 Feb 1820. Bdsm S. Barnes.
WILLIAM MUSSLEWHITE to PATSY OVERBY 4 Dec 1821. Bdsm William Musslewhite and William Tule.
THOMAS BROWN to SARAH HATCHER 23 Dec 1822. Bdsm Benjamin Hatcher and Thomas Brown.
LOVERD ELDRIDGE to MARY WILLIAMS 24 Jun 1822. Bdsm Loverd Eldridge and W. W. White.
RICHARD TURLEY to ELIZA FARRAR 29 Jun 1822. Bdsm Richard Turley and Thomas Turley.
JAMES KELLY to ELIZABETH BELL 3 Jul 1822. Bdsm James Kelly and James Murphey.
YOUNG MORGAN to HEDDY OLIVER 2 Mar 1822. Bdsm Young Morgan and Henry Lane.
EXUM WELLONS to EDITH GODWIN 14 Aug 1822. Bdsm Jesse A. Talton and Exum Wellons.
WILLIAM CAPPS JR. to POLLY DEANS 18 Mar 1822. Bdsm William Capps, Jr. and William Capps, Sr.
THOMAS BAILEY to SUSAN DAVIS 22 Jan 1822. Bdsm Thomas Bailey and James Peedin.
ELI GODWIN to SARAH ATKINSON 2 Jan 1823. Bdsm Eli Godwin and Stephen Barnes.
WILLIAM POWELL to SARAH INGRAM 14 May 1821. Bdsm William Powell and John B. Allen.
DAVID STEPHENSON to ANN CLIFTON 24 Feb 1824. Bdsm Simon P. Parrish.
JESSE WELLONS to NANCY JOHNSON 29 Nov 1823. Bdsm James Wellons.
DAVID STARLING to NANCY JOHNSON 31 Jan 1824. Bdsm David Starling and Exum Wellons.
JOHN PEARCE to CHARITY WATKINS 10 Oct 183. Bdsm Loverd Pearce.
HENRY PARNOLD to EDITH STARLING 8 Apr 1824. Bdsm Abner Smith.
WILLIE WATFORD to "WILLEY" LESSERD 6 Aug 1824. Bdsm John

MARRIAGE BONDS

Richardson.
HUGH LEE to PATSY HOLLOMAN 9 Feb 1824. Bdsn Kindred C. Ellington.
JAMES KING to EDITH JOHNSON 22 Jan 1822. Bdsm James King and Edward Stevens.
GARRY HOLLOMAN to RHODA HOLLOMAN 28 Aug 1822. Bdsm Garry Holloman and John Holloman.
JAMES VINSON to BETSY BRIDGERS 12 Feb 1822. Bdsm James Vinson and Abner Vinson.
WILLIE GREEN to PENNY ONEAL 24 Dec 1822. Bdsm Willie Green and John C. Gully.
JESSE GREEN to POLLY PRICE 28 Jan 1825. Bdsm Josiah Holloman.
WILLIAM WOODALL to "PENCY" JOHNSON 21 Jan 1825. Bdsm James Woodall.
PLEASANT BATTEN to BETSY GAY 28 Jan 1825. Bdsm Charles Wellons and Jaob Smith.
JOHN MORRIS to ELIZABETH BEAL 27 Jan 1825. Bdsm John Beal.
JAOB SMITH to MARY JOHNSON 26 Jan 1825. Bdsm Allen T. Ballenger.
WILLIAM HARRELL to ANNA LAUHORN 12 Aug 1825. Bdsm Nichols Rose.
TURNER YOUNG to NANCY ELLINGTON 7 Aug 1825. Bdsm Hardy Watford.
POWELL PARKER to CYNTHIA PARKER 7 Feb 1825. Bdsm Willie Jones.
JOSEPH FARMER to SARAH FROST 19 Jan 1825. Bdsm David H. Bryan.
CLEMENT SHAW to BETSY EARP 25 Jan 1825. Bdsm Lucas Hayles.
FREDERICK JOHNSON to "PARRIZADY" PARRISH 15 Feb 1825. Bdsm David Parrish.
MECAJAH THOMAS to PATSY LONG 25 Jun 1825. Bdsm John W. McLeod.
THOMAS BRIDGERS to FANNY WILDER 17 Mar 1821. Bdsm Braswell Bridgers.
McKINNE OLIVER to LOTTY RAIFORD 30 Aug 1821. Bdsm Levi Oliver.
SAMUEL GAME to ZELPHIA RAINS 18 Jan 1821. Bdsm Samuel Game and Robert Raiford.
BERRY WOODWARD to TEMPERANCE WILDER 23 Aug 1825. Bdsm Reuben Wilder.
REUBEN CARRELL to MARGARET MATTHEWS 25 Apr 1826. Bdsm David Carrell.
HENRY HAMBLETON to EDITH WOODWARD 4 Jan 1826. Bdsm Thomas Edwards.
JOHN CREECH to BETSY GIMETT 13 Nov 1825. Bdsm Ezekiel Creech.
STARLING BATTEN to CELIA BROWN 15 Nov 1825. Bdsm Jonathan Sellivant.
EDWARDS PEEDIN to DRUSILLA FUTRELL 29 Oct 1825. Bdsm Handy Peedin.
WILLIE WHITLEY to BETSY WILLIAMSON 25 May 1824. Bdsm Aaron Wall.
JEREMIAH STRICKLAND to "RETCY" PRICE 10 Oct 1825. Bdsm Samuel Strickland.
DANIEL WHITLEY to SARAH WOOTEN 26 Dec 1825. Bdsm Daniel Whitley and Thomas Lockhart, Jr.
JAMES WATKINS to MOLLY KIRBY 3 Ja 1826. Bdsm Jesse Kirby.
BERRY WOODWARD to CARY TUCKER 10 May 1825. Bdsm Irvin Wilder.
REDDIN WEBB to BETSY BLACKWELL 29 Nov 1825. Bdsm James Ivey.
WILLIAM STANLEY, JR to NANCY WEBB 4 Jan 1826. Bdsm William Stanley, Sr.
THOMAS DUNN to SUSANNA HARRELL 23 Feb 1824. Bdsm Nicholas Rose.
KEDAR BLACKMAN to ABSABETH WOOD 26 Sep 1826. Bdsm Loverd Eldridge.
RANSOM SANDERS to JEMMIA I. SANDERS 27 Jul 1824. Bdsm Ransom Sanders and William McCullers.

JOHNSTON COUNTY MARRIAGES

JAMES K. BARBER to CHARITY WOODALL 27 Dec 1821. Bdsm James K. Barber and Reuben Barber.
JEREMIAH PARNELL to NANCY STRICKLAND 22 Jul 1824. Bdsm Reddick Warren.
JOHN SMITH to EDITH BRYAN 10 Oct 1823. Bdsm Simon Bryan.
JEREMIAH CAPPS to DILEAH BAKER 10 Oct 1823. Bdsm Nicholas Rose.
BOLING G. AVERA to CHARITY W. BROOKS 21 Dec 1822. Bdsm Boling G. Avera and Edwin Spivey.
WILLIAM ASHLEY to NANCY STEVENS 7 Jan 1822. Bdsm William Ashley and Jonathan Britt.
JAMES BATTEN to SALLY GARNER 22 Jan 1824. Bdsm Jonathan Sellivant.
CHARLES FOWLER to PATSEY HOLLOMAN 27 Feb 1824. Bdsm Charles Fowler and Patrick Fowler.
THOMAS COCKRELL to PATEY GARNER 10 Jan 1825. Bdsm Simon Cockrell.
GREEN JORDAN to MIDDY MATTHEWS 5 Jan 1825. Bdsm Solomon Whitington.
JOSEPH JERNIGAN to "COLIN" ADAMS 22 Feb 1830. Bdsm Simon Bryan.
"CHRISTER" CHRISTIFER to SALLY BOON 3 Nov 1829. Bdsm John Lee Haywood.
JOHN BARBER to PENNY WOODALL 23 Nov 1830. Bdsm Reuben Barber.
ATLIS GRIFFIN to BEDDY HOLT 29 Aug 1828. Bdsm Owen Barber.
ANDERSON COOL to BETSY BEDINGFIELD 24 Nov 1829. Bdsm John Bedingfield.
JOSEPH HILL to ELIZABETH JOHNSON 2 Sep 1825. Bdsm Peter Lee.
ALLEN CAPPS to ELIZABETH PARNOLD 7 Sep 1825. Bdsm Dixon Davis.
SIDNEY ADAMS to LOUIZE GARLAND 6 Apr 1826. Bdsm Hinton Vinson.
SIMON LEE to "LOVY" JERNIGAN 25 Apr 1828. Bdsm Simon Bryan.
WILLIE RENTFROW to ATHY EVANS 9 Oct 1828. Bdsm Jesse Sellivant.
WILLIE JEFFRYS to PATSY HOLLOMAN 3 Sep 1825. Bdsm Russell Sellivant.
CALVIN SYMPKINS to ELIZABTH HINTON 24 Sep 1825. Bdsm Edwin Spivey.
GEORGE BOYETT to "CUZZY" WATSON 25 Dec 1827. Bdsm Isaac Boyett.
LARRY HOLLIMAN to "DUNNY" NARRON 30 Aug 1827. Bdsm Allen Jones.
BLAKE ATKINSON to PENELOPE SMITH 28 Jul 1824. Bdsm James Holloman.
WILLIAM NELMS to POLLY LARNER 5 Oct 1825. Bdsm Ryal W. Frost.
JOHN COLLIER to POLLY PEARCE 7 Feb 1828. Bdsm John Collier and David Thomson.
BENNET CREECH to LYDIA WALL 11 Jan 1825. Bdsm Joshua Creech, Jr.
JOHN PETTIS to BETSY GARNER 8 Feb 1825. Bdsm Matthew Barber.
WILLIAM WILDER to NANCY GREEN 14 May 1825. Bdsm William Green.
JESSE WOODARD to "REDLEY" ADAMS 27 Feb 1826. Bdsm James Adams.
JONATHAN SELLAVANT to ANNY BATTEN 28 Nov 1821. Bdsm Jonathan Sellavant and Willie Gerald.
JOHN CLIFTON to POLLY HINTON 31 Mar 1823. Bdsm Hardy Avera.
HANDY PEEDIN to KEZIAH JOHNSON 31 Jul 1824. Bdsm Hardy Pilkinton and Major Griffin.
RICHARD HOLT to JEMIMA MASON 10 Oct 1823. Bdsm John Holt.
EDMOND DOZIER to SALLY AVERA 11 Jan 1826. Bdsm Banister Harper.
ALSEY EATMAN to ELIZABETH RICHARDSON 24 Apr 1826. Bdsm Calvin Richardson.
BERRY HINNANT to ELIZABETH EARP 28 Jan 1825. Bdsm William Nowell.
JOSIAH ALLEN to WINIFRED INGRAM 30 ? 1821. Bdsm Josiah Allen and James Allen.

MARRIAGE BONDS

JAMES BAKER to POLLY MASSENGILL 25 Mar ? Bdsm Noel West.
WILLIAM NELMS to POLLY DELOACH 24 May 1825. Bdsm Ryal W. Frost.
RICHMOND NARON to DILNY BAILY 14 Jan 1825. Bdsm Calvin Lee.
JONATHAN MURPHREE to POLLY GREEN 23 Sep 1828. Bdsm Bryan Whitley.
GASTON LOCKHART to RACHEL STEVENS 21 Apr 1825. Bdsm John B. Allen.
THOMAS LEE to BETSY ALLEN 22 Jan 1822. Bdsm Thomas Lee and William Ingram.
JAMES TIMMELL to ELIZABETH TALTON 29 Nov 1825. Bdsm Willie Garrald.
NEEDHAM PRICE to NANCY LANDERS 27 Dec 1830. Bdsm Bennet A. Boddir.
BRYAN LEWIS to SALLY WOOD 23 Sep 1828. Bdsm Bryan Lewis and Jesse Whitley.
REUBEN WILDER to CATHERINE HOLDER 7 Jan 1826. Bdsm Reuben Wilder and Samuel Mitchiner.
JOHN BROUGHTON to PATSY BOYETT 8 Feb 1825. Bdsm Thomas Rice.
JONATHAN FAIL to LUCY FIELD 26 Mar 1828. Bdsm Francis Harrell.
JOSEPH JOHNSON to VINEY REDDING 9 Feb 1830. Bdsm Isaac Penny.
CEBORN CARRELL to NANCY ELLEN ? 15 Mar 1830. Bdsm Ceborn Carrell and Carrell Johnson.
AARON WALL to ZILPHA GULLY 11 Mar 1826. Bdsm Aaron Wall and David Thomson.
CALLEN STALLINGS to POLLY MASSEY 17 Jan 1825. Bdsm Callen Stallings and Allen Ballenger.
BRIGHT RYALS to SUSAN CREECH 26 Sep 1826. Bdsm John Allen.
JOHN F. ELLINGTON to CHRISTIAN AVERA 3 Jan 1831. Bdsm Joseph Clifton.
SAMUEL CANNON to WIMMY JONES 13 Feb 1827. Bdsm Benjamin Hatcher.
ELIJAH LASSITER to POLLY TOMLINSON 28 Mar 1826. Bdsm Thomas Barber.
JAMES OLIVER to EDITH JOHNSON 22 Jul 1825. Bdsm James Oliver and Robert H. Helme.
STEPHEN JOINER to BETSY PITMAN 20 Dec 1825. Bdm Thomas Cockrell.
CARON BRANNON to MILLY GREEN 26 Sep 1826. Bdsm William Hinton.
JONATHAN HEARN to EMILY CARTER 24 Dec 1825. Bdsm Bythan Bryan.
ELIJAH LEE to PEGGY YOUNG 28 Mar 1826. Bdsm Elijah Lee and Peter Lee.
WILLIAM EASON to SALLY BROUGHTON 28 Mar 1826. Bdsm Jesse Eason.
LEVI STRICKLAND to WINIFRED BRADDY 2 Mar 1824. Bdsm Abner Braddy.
RIGHT MOORE to ELIZABTH PUGH 23 Mar 1824. Bdsm Josiah Houlder.
BARNABA HAMILTON to EDITH ANN FAIL 1 Sep 1837. Bdsm Crawford Futrell.
DANIEL GURLY to ALTARA JOHNSON 21 Aug 1837. Bdsm Plyer Barber.
FRANKLIN PHILLIPS to ZILPHIA STRICKLAND 10 Dec 1834. Bdsm Jacob Yelvington.
CRAWFORD FUTRELL to MARIAH DAVIS 10 Jan 1837. Bdsm James Davis.
AUGUSTUS PARISH to EDITH ELLINGTON 30 Dec 1835. Bdsm Lovett Spivey.
SAMUEL DURHAM to BETSY STALLINGS 6 Nov 1835. Bdsm James Youngblood.
FRANCIS YOUNG to LUCY OGBURN 20 Oct 1835. Bdsm Thomas Durham.
JAMES BARBER to EDITH AVERYETT 10 Apr 1827. Bdsm Burwell Barber.
JESSE WHEELER to "BULANY" JOHNSON 11 Apr 1827. Bdsm Joseph Wheeler.
JAMES TOMLINSON to MARY BRIDGERS 27 Sep 1836. Bdsm Jackson A. Leach.
DAVID THOMSON to MRS. PHEREBY HELME 9 Jan 1837. Bdsm David Thomson and Thomas Rice.

JOHNSTON COUNTY MARRIAGES

STEPHEN BROWN to LAURA PEARCE 28 Sep 1831. Bdsm Edwin Jones.
DAVID PRICE to SUSAN WALLACE 11 Jan 1837. Bdsm Moses Wallace.
EDIN JACKSON to BUNY SMITH 27 Sep 1836. Bdsm Zachariah Pope.
MARTIN LANGLEY to THANEY DAVIS 25 Jan 1837. Bdsm Henry H. Davis.
ROBERTSON RAPER to CLARA MOORE 16 Jul 1840. Bdsm Garry Sellavent.
JOHN T. HATCHER to AILSY EARP 15 Sep 1840. Bdsm Robert Hatcher.
LEMUEL HOCUT to LUCY LEGAN 9 Jan 1841. Bdsm William Moody.
DEVERUX D. THOMSON to LUCY EDWARDS 18 Dec 1840. Bdsm Elijah Thomson.
KINDRICK BEASLY to "EMY" BRYAN 6 Aug 1835. Bdsm Heron Holmes.
JACOB STEVENS to PATIENCE PEARCE 22 May 1797. Bdsm Jacob Stevens.
DANIEL ROBERTS to DRUSILLA HUGHES 6 Nov 1840. Bdsm Upton Carrell.
SAMUEL BATTEN to BARBARA STARLING 25 Jan 1816. Bdsm Samuel Batten.
RANSOM TINER to MARY ANN ALLEN 1 Aug 1840. Bdsm James H. Corbet.
AMOS COATS to POLLY LILLINGTON 1 Feb 1840. Bdsm William H. Coats.
DAVID STRICKLAND to SOPHIA STEVENS 30 Sep 1834. Bdsm David H. Bryan.
HARDY HOOKS to PATIENCE PEARCE 27 Dec 1830. Bdsm Henry M. Stevens.
ELIAS LANGSTON to JANE LEWIS 24 May 1836. Bdsm Joel Flowers.
MATTHEW WILDER to MARTHA AVERA 22 Apr 1826. Bdsm Solomon Lockhart.
JOHN WILLIS to MATILDA SIMPKINS 21 Jun 1836. Bdsm John G. Gully.
THOMAS T. HOLLIOWELL to SOPHIA HOLT 5 Oct 1833. Bdsm Jesse Holt.
CAMPBELL LASSITER to SUSAN LEE 7 Aug 1833. Bdsm Campbell Lassiter and Stephenson Godwin.
CALVIN GRICE to JOANNA EVANS 6 Sep 1837. Bdsm Gideon Allen.
WILLIE JOHNSON to PHEREBY SAULS 28 Sep 1835. Bdsm Willie Johnson and Reuben T. Sanders.
ALDRIDGE MESSER to ELIZABETH KENEDY 11 Mar 1835. Bdsm John Messer.
MYRACH JOHNSON to SUSAN BAREFOOT 13 Dec 1840. Bdsm Thomas Barefoot.
BLACKMAN COATS to POLLY TEMPLES 24 Mar 1840. Bdsm Barzella Blackman.
JAMES STEWART to HARRIET WOODALL 9 Dec 1840. Bdsm James G. Woodall.
JOSEPH ROBERTS to MARY FUTRELL 26 Nov 1840. Bdsm John P. Williams.
HENRY M. JETER to ELENA V. BLACKMAN 2 Nov 1839. Bdsm Christopher Christophers.
CALVIN STURIDVANT to MARTHA BAMCUMB 3 Jan 1836. Bdsm Thomas Busbee.
ABSALOM WARD to RHODA WATKINS 24 Feb 1835. Bdsm Tegal Balance.
EDWARD PRICE to POLLY FERRELL 9 Apr 1836. Bdsm Willis Turner.
JONATHAN DRIVER to GINCY PRICE 17 Apr 1840. Bdsm Thomas Price.
WILLIAM PARISH to TEMPERANCE STEVENS 1 Dec 1840. Bdsm Isham Parish.
ELBERT ROBERTS to POLLY ALLEN 4 May 1836. Bdsm Henry Stallings.
REUBEN T. SANDERS to ELIZA C. BOON 30 Mar 1832. Bdsm Reuben T. Sanders and John Watson.
ISAAC BODERY to EDITH HAMELTON 26 Feb 1833. Bdsm John Atkinson.
JOHN BEDINGFIELD to LUCY M. HINTON 13 Nov 1833. Bdsm William P. Johnson.
JAMES DENNIS to CAROLINE HELME 24 Sep 1833. Bdsm David Thomson.
ALFRED PARTIN to JANE HOWARD 31 Dec 1835. Bdsm Joseph P. Howard.
STARLING MASSINGALE to SALLY REAVES 4 Jan 1837. Bdsm Needham Massingale.
YOUNG RYALS to SUSAN CANADA 28 May 1833. Bdsm Right Byrd.
GEORGE DUNN to SALLY BLACKMAN 24 Nov 1833. Bdsm Cary Johnson.

MARRIAGE BONDS

WILLIE GURLEY to LYDIA GURLEY 26 Feb 1833. Bdsm Francis Bridgers.
JONATHAN LOVE to EDITH LEE 17 Nov 1834. Bdsm John Evans.
WILLIAM OLIVER to JOANNAH CREECH 22 Mar 1834. Bdsm Stephen Oliver.
NEWSOM EDWARDS to MOURNING DAVIS 12 Apr 1834. Bdsm Isaac Starling.
CAREY JOHNSON to POLLY WEST 10 Jan 1835. Bdsm Reuben Johnson.
BLANERY CARR to APPY WHITLEY 3 Jun 1834. Bdsm John C. Montague.
WILLIAM JONES to SALLY SIMPKINS 13 Jan 1835. Bdsm Calvin Simpkins.
JOSIAH BROWN to POLLY HORN 24 Dec 1834. Bdsm John Batten.
JAMES DURDEN to NANCY GODWIN 22 Dec 1834. Bdsm Willie Godwin.
JOHN BLACKMAN to NANCY AVERA 18 Feb 1835. Bdsm Samuel Lee.
KINCHEN CRUMPLER to BETSY JOINER 18 Feb 1835. Bdsm Thomas Davis.
JAMES TINER to WINIFRED THOMSON 8 Jun 1835. Bdsm Lewis Thomson.
BURWELL JONES to ELIZABETH CLIFTON 4 Apr 1835. Bdsm William Jones.
SAMUEL STRICKLAND to SUSAN STANLY 18 Jul 1835. Bdsm Elijah Baker.
CULLEN BARFIELD to MARY WESTBROOK 17 Jul 1835. Bdsm John Eason.
EDWIN McCULLERS to SOPHRINA WARREN 28 May 1835. Bdsm William McCullers.
HENRY H. KENNEDY to "PENSY" WHITINGTON 24 Mar 1835. Bdsm William S. Whitington.
FERNIFOLD HALL to ZILPHA GRICE 11 May 1833. Bdsm Ethedred Holt.
CHARLES WELLONS to BETHANEY JONES 12 Mar 1834. Bdsm James A. Furnell.
HENRY C. ENNIS to EDNEY DURHAM 22 Aug 1837. Bdsm Edwin Boykins.
VINE H. ADAMS to LUANNA JOHNSON 22 Feb 1836. Bdsm Vine H. Adams and Harry Johnson.
JONATHAN STRICKLAND to MARY DARCIL 23 Feb 1836. Bdsm Young Eldridge.
WILLIAM BENSON to LOUISA TYNER ? 1837. Bdsm John Jackson.
ELBERT ROBERTS to SALLY MITCHELL 17 Jan 1837. Bdsm William Brown.
GREEN HOLLAND to ELIZABETH GARNER 15 Feb 1830. Bdsm Asa Garner.
CARTER PEACOCK to NANCY RAINS 11 Feb 1836. Bdsm William Rains.
ATLAS TURNER to EDITH SIMPKINS 22 Mar 1836. Bdsm William Jones.
JOHN P. PEARCE to PIETY GODWIN 26 Mar 1834. Bdsm James A. Turnell.
JAMES AVERYT to NANCY LANE 29 Sep 1830. Bdsm Henry Duncan.
JOSEPH PRICE to "STRAWDRY" BATTEN 26 Aug 1836. Bdsm Solomon Lockhart.
JAMES STRICKLAND to ELIZABETH B. WALL 25 Oct 1836. Bdsm Robert N. Gully.
MATTHEW BATTEN to ELIZABETH BATTEN 25 Jul 1835. Bdsm John Batten.
WILLIAM H. STEVENS to ELIZABETH S. ALLEN 20 Dec 1834. Bdsm William A. Bass.
JOHN COLE to JANE MacCLAMS 29 Mar 1834. Bdsm Jonathan Fail.
ELISHA WALLACE to REBECCA ADAMS 24 Feb 1835. Bdsm Lewis Blackman.
AHAB ALLEN to REDLY JOHNSON 4 Jul 1834. Bdsm Elisha Harrison.
SAMUEL S. GULLY to JANE FELICK 9 Oct 1833. Bdsm John Lee Haywood.
ALSEY JOHNSON to DELIAH JOHNSTON 24 Feb 1835. Bdsm Edward Price.
JAMES STANLY to NICEY ADAMS 28 Mar 1833. Bdsm George Dunn.
JOHN ODOM to NANCY LOVE 4 Jul 1834. Bdsm Jesse Hinnant.
GIDEON ALLEN to REDLY JOHNSON 12 Apr 1833. Bdsm James Allen.
CULLEN BLACKMAN to ERDENA V. BOON 27 Sep 1831. Bdsm William H. Watson.
JOHN WINDHAM to SARAH STEVENSON 21 Feb 1833. Bdsm Joseph Carter.

JOHNSTON COUNTY MARRIAGES

BRYAN HOOD to EDITH JOHNSON 10 May 1834. Bdsm James Hinnant.
CANNON CARMADY to PATSEY JOHNSON 20 Jan 1835. Bdsm James Carrell.
JOHN CROCKER to CELIA NAHORN 20 Oct 1834. Bdsm Josiah Guy.
GIDEON ALLEN to ALEY BRYAN 24 Sep 1833. Bdsm John Peacock.
HENRY WOODARD to SALLY MASSEY 23 Feb 1835. Bdsm Henry Woodard.
GEORGE STEPHENSON to PENNY WOODALL 14 Feb 1835. Bdsm Moore Stephenson.
ISAAC BARBER to POLLY CAUDLE 14 Jan 1835. Bdsm Reuben Barber.
GIDEON BARBER to RETTY JONES 2 Feb 1835. Bdsm Nathaniel Barber.
MATTHEW DODD to EMILY FLOWERS 7 Feb 18? Bdsm Bryan Harper.
PHILLIP JONES to MARY BENSON 27 Sep 1837. Bdsm William Brown.
JACK A. LEACH to MARTHA WHITLEY 19 Sep 1837. Bdsm William A. Walton.
HARRY THOMSON to MILLY COLLINS 2 Mar 1835. Bdsm Lewis Thomson.
JAMES PEEDIN to SALLY STARLING 26 Sep 1837. Bdsm Ezekiel Stevens.
BARNABA GREEN to ELINOR EVANS 21 Jan 1835. Bdsm Silas Webb.
STEPHEN CLARK to PEGGY EVANS 23 May 1833. Bdsm Henry Lee.
WILLIAM ARNOLD to LUCINDA MASSINGILL 11 Oct 1832. Bdsm Crawford Mitchell.
SIMON WATKINS to BEDY FLOWERS 28 May 1833. Bdsm Gaston Lockhart.
JAMES F. LEACH to ELIZABETH W. SANDERS 19 Jul 1833. Bdsm Matthew McCullers.
ALEXANDER STANSELL to CELIA BARBER 20 Jan 1835. Bdsm James G. Woodall.
SAMUEL M. TURLEY to "LULY" ELLIS 11 Jan 1834. Bdsm John G. Gully.
JACOB JOHNSON to RACHEL BIRD 26 Dec 1840. Bdsm Isaac Johnson.
JAMES A. DEBNAM to ADELINE WILLIAMS 5 Mar 1840. Bdsm Edward Debnam.
ASA WARD, JR. to PATSEY RICHARDSON 26 Jan 1840. Bdsm Asa Ward, Jr.
WILLIAM DURHAM to BEDY MOORE 11 Nov 1833. Bdsm William Johnson.
JONATHAN HEARN to EDNY DODD 21 Dec 1833. Bdsm Young Bridgers.
BENJAMIN DEBERY to CRECY HOCUT 11 Jan 1834. Bdsm Burwell Earp.
LEMUEL BURCKET to SUSAN SHEPPERD 22 Feb 1836. Bdsm Robert W. Sneed.
WILLIAMSON HINNANT to CALLY HINNANT 25 Feb 1833. Bdsm Jesse Hinnant.
WHITLEY GRANTHAM to POLLY ROSE 23 May 1837. Bdsm Thomas Toler.
WILLIAM BUNTING to MARTHA HIGH 3 Sep 1833. Bdsm Mark B. Richardson.
THOMAS EASON to HARRIET GULLY 11 May 1834. Bdsm Edwin S. McCullers.
SEAMWELL R. WEBB to ANNA BEASLEY ? Bdsm Seamwell R. Webb and Jesse Beasley.
JOHN ELLIS to LEACY FERRELL 21 Mar 1834. Bdsm James R. Ellis.
WILLIAM FISH to MATILDA GRIMES 23 Feb 1836. Bdsm John W. Johnson.
JOHN BATTEN to BETSY GARNER 7 Sep 1833. Bdsm Samuel Batten.
RANSOM ENNIS to SALLY GRIMES 23 Feb 1836. Bdsm John W. Johnson.
BRITTON LANGDON to WINIFRED JORDAN 5 Aug 1836. Bdsm Benjamin Martin.
NICHOLS JORDAN to NANCY JORDAN 4 Jul 1836. Bdsm Plyer Barber.
WILLIAM HILLIARD to NANCY HOCUT 22 Oct 1840. Bdsm Matthew Avera.
BENJAMIN CARRELL to SUSAN DICKENS 10 Sep 1840. Bdsm Josiah Hollimon.
BENJAMIN HUGHS to NANCY OLIVER 3 Aug 1839. Bdsm Willam J. Peedin.
JOHN LUSBY to EDITH EDWARDS 22 Aug 1836. Bdsm Bryan Smith.
THADDEUS WHITLEY to S. E. FELLOW 23 Sep 1840. Bdsm William H.

MARRIAGE BONDS

Hastings.
ABRAM DIXON to LOUISA ADAMS 28 Jan 1841. Bdsm Crawford Futrell.
GEORGE PRICE to POLLY AVERY 2 Nov 1840. Bdsm Elisha Harrison.
WILLIAM WOOD to PHEREBE BAREFOOT 16 Sep 1840. Bdsm James T. Jackson.
JAMES TALTON to SALLY TALTON 1 Sep 1840. Bdsm John H. Rains.
JAMES WALLIS to THENA CROCKER 8 Oct 1840. Bdsm Young Bridgers.
NEEDHAM STEVENS to "EMILY" STEVENS 24 Mar 1830. Bdsm Henry Stevens.
SILAS HORN to WINIFRED JOHNSON 24 Sep 1834. Bdsm Warren Johnson.
NEEDHAM ENNIS to ELIZABETH GRIMES 3 Feb 1834. Bdsm Needham Ennis and Ransom Ennis.
BLAKE ATKINSON to POLLY EASON 29 May 1831. Bdsm Blake Atkinson and William Earp.
WESTBROOK LEE to ESTHER SMITH 28 Feb 1837. Bdsm Joel Lee.
BLACKMAN LEE to MARY BLACKMAN 28 Feb 1837. Bdsm Ivey Lee.
WILLIS TURNER to MARY BEDINGFIELD 8 Nov 1836. Bdsm Edward Price.
ELIJAH OWEN to TERESA STOKES 18 Dec 1835. Bdsm Sterling Temples.
MATTHEW McCULLERS to SALLY FARMER 6 Jan 1834. Bdsm Thomas Eason.
REDDICK MORRIS to ALLEY GRANTHAM 28 Mar 1837. Bdsm Thomas Toler.
DUNCAN McPHERSON to EDITH BROADSTREET 4 Oct 1830. Bdsm Jordan Cowell.
RANSOM HINTON to BETSY WILDER 19 Oct 1830. Bdsm Ransom Hinton and Ransom Sanders.
FERNIFOLD GREEN to MARY MURPHREY 20 Oct 1831. Bdsm Lewis W. Jenkins.
WILLIE HINTON to CALLY WILDER 5 Aug 1831. Bdsm Ransom Hinton.
RANSOM RICHARDSON to LUCINDA ONEAL 2 Oct 1833. Bdsm Richardson Oneal.
ISAAC JOHNSON to LUCY HONEYCUT 28 Feb 1837. Bdsm John W. Johnson.
SAMUEL MALABY to REBECCA TUCKER 17 Sep 1834. Bdsm William Green.
MERRIT FERRELL to WINIFRED TURNER 22 Apr 1837. Bdsm Gaston Parrish.
JOHN C. AVERA to SARAH PENNY 24 Jan 1834. Bdsm Needham Bryan.
WILLOUGHBY HALL to NANCY EATMON 23 May ? Bdsm Benajah Horn.
WILLIS COLE to MARY FLOWERS 29 Feb 1836. Bdsm Alexander H. Thornton.
BRYAN PEACOCK to POLLY RAMS 19 Jan 1836. Bdsm John H. Adams.
SAMUEL WOODARD to NANCY RIVENBARK 23 May ? Bdsm William Benson.
NATHAN PARSONS to ELIZABETH MUNDEN 19 Jan 1836. Bdsm John C. Montague.
SAMPSON EDWARDS to MARY EDWARDS 16 Aug 1836. Bdsm William Peedin, Jr.
ISAAC MATTHEWS to SARAH MARTIN 24 Dec 1836. Bdsm Haywood Martin.
ISAAC STERLING to LOUISA OLIVER 27 Aug 1836. Bdsm Henry O. Stallings.
SIMEON CARRELL to SARAH HALL 18 Jul 1836. Bdsm Richard H. White.
WILLIAM ADAMS to NANCY "MAELEMORE" 25 Jun 1836. Bdsm Sidney Adams.
LUNEFORD RICHARDSON to LAURINDA VINSON 13 Dec 1836. Bdsm William H. Watson.
JOSIAH BRANNON to HARRIET WILDER 7 Mar 1834. Bdsm Isham Wilder.
JOHN ATKINSON to BETSY LYNCH 29 Nov 1832. Bdsm James K. Raiford.
JOSEPH CLIFTON to MASON PARRISH 28 Dec 1832. Bdsm Loverd Spivey.
BENJAMIN BROUGHTON to MARY BAGWELL 20 Feb 1834. Bdsm Steven

JOHNSTON COUNTY MARRIAGES

Broughton.
HUTSON BAILEY to PIETY ONEAL 1 May 1834. Bdsm Warren Bailey.
JOEL SMITH to RACHEL WATSON 25 Feb 1836. Bdsm Reddick Warren.
WILLIS FERRELL to OLIVE BRAMMON 18 Jul 1832. Bdsm Isaac Stallings.
RIGHT A. ADAMS to THENY INGRAM 25 Feb 1834. Bdsm Right H. Adams and Right A. Adams.
FRUMAN SCHOMBLY to "RELDY" ONEAL 26 Aug 1834. Bdsm Hinton Bailey.
ROBERT DUNN to ELIZABETH COLE 22 Mar 1830. Bdsm Nicholas Rose.
RIGDON JOHNSON to EMILY JOHNSON 22 Mar 1832. Bdsm Edmond Johnson.
LEWIS W. JENKINS to BETSY RIVERS 7 Sep 1831. Bdsm Harry Avera.
JAMES JONES to ULRICA STALLINGS 8 Mar 1832. Bdsm Needham Bryan.
JACKSON STEVENSON to ISABEL CAUDELL 8 Jun 1832. Bdsm Moore Stephenson.
WILLIAM GARNER to ELIZABETH GARNER 11 Mar 1834. Bdsm James Garner.
HARDY EASON to MARY SHAW 8 Feb 1834. Bdsm Bythan Bryan.
WESTLY HODGE to LOUIZA THOMAS 8 Mar 1834. Bdsm Westly Hodge.
THOMAS THORNTON to NANCY JORDAN 1 Dec 1831. Bdsm John Eason.
WILLIAM CARRELL, JR. to PIETY HOBBY 30 Nov 1831. Bdsm Elisha Harrison.
HARRISON JONES to EMILY WELSH 25 Jul 1832. Bdsm Benjamin Jones.
BRYAN HOCUT to NANCY WILDER 14 Oct 1832. Bdsm George Gully.
MOORE STEPHENSON to ZILLA COATS 3 Nov 1832. Bdsm Joshua Stephenson.
ISAAC JOHNSON to JENNY STEVENSON 28 Jul 1832. Bdsm David Parish.
ALLEN JOHNSON, JR to PENNY ALLEN 23 Dec 1833. Bdsm Allen Johnson, Sr.
LEWIS HENRY PHILLIPS to EMILY BOND 25 Oct 1833. Bdsm Lewis Henry Phillips and Allen Ballenger.
SOLOMON WATSON to HEPSEBAH JANE HINNANT 14 Jan 1834. Bdsm Hardy Pilkinton.
REUBEN WILKINSON to "RELDY" PARNELL 27 Nov 1833. Bdsm John Jackson.
THOMAS BARBER to ELIZABETH WILLIAMS 8 Jan 1834. Bdsm Terry Barber.
JOSEPH INGRAM to REBECCAH THOMSON 23 Dec 1833. Bdsm Needham G. Bryan.
HARRY BARBER to ELIZABETH BARBER 8 Jan 1834. Bdsm Terry Barber.
EATON PORCH to NELLY PRICE 29 May 1832. Bdsm Thomas Bridgers.
ISHAM WILDER to CASANDA WISE 14 Oct 1832. Bdsm George S. Gulley.
ZACHARIAH HARRISON to BETSY AVERA 1 Oct 1832. Bdsm Abram G. Borden.
OSBORN JOHNSON to JENCY ETHRIDGE 26 Aug 1832. Bdsm Thomas Ethridge.
GASTON PARRISH to THETUS FERRELL 21 Feb 1833. Bdsm Loverd Spivey.
JESSE HORN to NANCY JOHNSON 28 Nov 1831. Bdsm Jesse Hinnant.
BENNET GODWIN to MARTHA MATTHEWS 8 Jan 1834. Bdsm Terry Barber.
JAMES HINNANT to CYNTHIA BARNY 1 Mar 1831. Bdsm Jonathan Woodard.
THEOPHILUS DODD to REBECCA ONEAL 20 Feb 1832. Bdsm Theophilus Dodd and Ransom Sanders.
STEPHEN HICKS to EMILY HORN 22 Feb 1836. Bdsm Benejah Horn.
REDDICK ADAMS to POLLY AVERA 16 May 1833. Bdsm Young Bridgers.
ALVIN AUSTIN to CYNTHIA COATS 14 Apr 1837. Bdsm Samuel M. Utley.
ALSY PACE to CASSANDRA DEAN 6 Mar 1837. Bdsm Hiram Chambler.
WILLIE DEANS to ALLAMA BROADSTREET 4 Jul 1836. Bdsm Josiah Houlder.
ALVAN JOHNSON to BETSY DUNCAN 28 Mar 1836. Bdsm Ambrose Lee.
JAMES JOHNSON to HARRIET STEVENS 28 Apr 1836. Bdsm Allen Johnson.
ERASMUS WOODARD to JULIA IVY 21 Oct 1835. Bdsm Needham Oliver.

MARRIAGE BONDS

CURTIS PARNELL to POLLY INGRAM 16 Mar 1835. Bdsm Barnaba Hamilton.
CURTIS H. WELLONS to HARRIET KING 4 Feb 1839. Bdsm Dixon Pearce.
WHITFIELD WOOD to PATSY TART 27 Mar 1832. Bdsm Asa Thomson.
LARKIN PEARCE to SALLY PEARCE 26 Feb 1836. Bdsm George W. Griffin.
ALSEY PERRY to EDITH STALLINGS 28 Dec 1831. Bdsm Thomas Rice.
HENRY GURLEY to POLLY JONES 27 Oct 1835. Bdsm John Montague.
MATTHEW M. MURPHREY to SALLY JOHNSON 1 Aug 1835. Bdsm Fernifold Green.
HENRY RAINS to "WILLY" GERRALD 1 Feb 1836. Bdsm William Rains.
NATHAN T. ALLEN to MARY JANE ADAMS 17 Mar 1832. Bdsm Joseph J. Adams.
JOHN B. TURNER to SOPHIA G. POWELL 27 Sep 1831. Bdsm William H. Watson.
SAMUEL G. SMITH to NANCY BRYAN 27 Jul 1833. Bdsm Samuel G. Smith.
ROBERT W. STEVENS to SUSANNAH BARBER 29 Mar 1837. Bdsm Haywood Martin.
JETHRO YELVINGTON to ELIZABETH N. TALTON 2 Apr 1833. Bdsm Samuel A. Bryan.
HENRY BELL to HELEN MARIAH CLARK 18 Feb 1837. Bdsm Benj. Walston.
BRIGHT JERNIGAN to JERUSHA LINDSEY 28 Sep 1830. Bdsm Bright Jernigan and Baldy Sanders.
WILLIAM M. ADAMS to WINIFRED ALLEN 24 Nov 1840. Bdsm David Adams.
SAMUEL S. TURNER to EDITH MITCHINER 22 Jul 1835. Bdsm Britain S. Utley.
JOHN LEE to BETHANA JONES 1 Apr 1837. Bdsm Peter Lee.
ELIJAH PARKER to SALLY BAREFOOT 23 Feb 1836. Bdsm John C. Hood.
EDWIN OVERBY to PENNY BARBER 2 Sep 1837. Bdsm William Robertson.
BENJAMIN DAUGHTRY to APEY FURLEY 26 Jan 1837. Bdsm Crawford Futrell.
JOSIAH JOHNSON to SUSAN PHILLIPS 7 Mar 1835. Bdsm Elias Barnes.
JAMES HODGES to CYNTHIA WHITTINGTON 24 Nov 1835. Bdsm James G. Woodall.
WILLIE GODWIN to HARRIET FLOWERS 18 Feb 1836. Bdsm Elijah Godwin.
JOHN TINER to ELIZABETH MIMDEN 16 Apr 1836. Bdsm Berry Price.
AARON WALLACE to NANCY STANLEY 8 Mar 1837. Bdsm Barnaba Dunn.
BERRY PRICE to SMITHY WALLACE 15 Sep 1834. Bdsm Thomas Lockhart.
DAVID JOHNSON to PHEREBE BYRD 27 Sep 1836. Bdsm John W. Johnson.
JESSE HINNANT to ELIZABETH HAWKINS 9 Dec 1835. Bdsm William Hayles.
JESSE STANCIL to RHODY PRICE 10 Dec 1835. Bdsm Hudson Reaves.
JOSEPH GURLEY to ELIZABETH THOMAS 27 Oct 1835. Bdsm John C. Montague.
TERRY BARBER to ANNE MORGAN 15 Feb 1836. Bdsm John Barber.
RAIFORD WILLIAMSON to CHARLOTTE PEARCE 6 Feb 1836. Bdsm Allen S. Ballenger.
JAMES MAMMERY to PHEREBE BAILEY 27 Mar 1836. Bdsm John Mammery.
JACOB JOHNSON to ELIZABETH POPE 24 Mar 1835. Bdsm Hillary Wilder.
JONATHAN POOL to POLLY ELLINGTON 22 Dec 1834. Bdsm Hardy Pool.
BRASWELL RENTFROE to POLLY WILLIAMSON 3 Jun 1836. Bdsm Nelson Kent.
HILLIMAN STRICKLAND to PATIENCE PRICE 27 Sep 1836. Bdsm Applewhite Richardson.
WILLIAM SANDERS to LOUENSA AVERA 7 Sep 1835. Bdsm William Sanders and Thomas Price.

JOHNSTON COUNTY MARRIAGES

JOHN B. EVANS to CAROLINE RHODES 4 Jan 1836. Bdsm Ambrose Lee.
GEORGE JERNIGAN to SALLY BASS 23 Jan 1836. Bdsm William B. Allen.
JOHN YOUNG to CYNTHIA BRYAN 13 Mar 1838. Bdsm Thomas Young.
WRIGHT STRICKLAND to SUSAN TAILOR 23 May 1836. Bdsm Julius A. Stevens.
GOLDY BURK to SALLY HATCHCOCK 9 Feb 1837. Bdsm William B. Allen.
MATTHEW DOUGHDY to SUSAN CREECH 24 Sep 1833. Bdsm William Baker.
ELISHA HARRISON to JANE BRIDGERS 27 Mar 1833. Bdsm Allen S. Ballinger.
BENJAMIN PARKER to BETSY RENTFROW 7 Jan 1837. Bdsm Jesse Parker.
WILLIAM H. GUY to SUSAN McCULLERS 24 SEP 1833. Bdsm David Thomson.
THOMAS FARMER to ELIZABETH FERRELL 26 Jul 1837. Bdsm William G. Parrish.
BLACKMAN BALANCE to MARTHA WARD 4 Apr 1837. Bdsm Absalom Ward.
BENJAMIN EDWARDS to EXALINE MORLEY 13 Apr 1837. Bdsm Needham Morley.
JENNET HOLLAND to ELIZABETH LOVE 8 Apr 1837. Bdsm Bryan A. May.
JOHN EARP to FRANCES EASON 21 Apr 1837. Bdsm William Earp.
LEVY STEVENS to SARAH CARRELL 28 Jun 1836. Bdsm Haywood Martin.
ISAREL HOULDER to SALLY NICHOLS 18 Jun 1836. Bdsm Clem Baker.
SAMUEL LEE, JR. to PATSY J. BRITT 16 Jun 1837. Bdsm Samuel Lee, Jr. and J. H. Youngblood.
ELDRIDGE BARHORN to MARIA AVERA 9 Apr 1833. Bdsm Elias Harrison.
HINSON LOVE to CLARY TURLEY 28 Sep 1836. Bdm Needham Bryan.
WILLIAM ETHRIDGE to ELIZABETH SANDERS 22 Dec 1836. Bdsm S. M. Utley.
JAMES NORRIS to JANE HOLMES 5 Aug 1831. Bdsm Plyer Barber.
JOSEPH SASSER to LUCY HOLLINGSWORTH 12 Jun 1837. Bdsm Julius Stevens.
HENRY PENNY to MARTHA SMITH 13 Jul 1837. Bdsm Henry W. Johnson.
WILLIAM EARP to PATHERLY ATKINSON 18 Aug 1837. Bdsm Robert Bryan.
WILLIAM BLINSON to LUCY STEVENS 29 Aug 1836. Bdsm Henry Penny.
ASA GARNER to NANCY PRICE 5 Sep 1836. Bdsm James Stallings.
ALSEY EARP to MARTHA ONEAL 29 Jul 1836. Bdsm Alsey Earp and Thomas Rivers.
WILLIAM MASON to CELIA WOODWARD 9 May 1836. Bdsm William Oneal.
HENRY DEAN to "GINCY" CARRELL 9 May 1836. Bdsm Simon Carrell.
SAMUEL WOODY to "ACCULY" WARM 4 Jul 1836. Bdsm Stephen Hicks.
THOMAS COLE to ELIZABETH FAIL 28 Feb 1832. Bdsm William Reaves.
JONATHAN COCKRELL to WILLY CREECH 26 Apr ? Bdsm Levy Yelvington.
ELBERT ROBERTS to POLLY ALLEN 5 May 1836. Bdsm Joseph Gurley.
JONATHAN T. WALL to POLLY HAYLES 12 Mar 1836. Bdsm Hutson Earp.
RICHARD BLACKMAN to SUSAN TEMPLE 7 Jan 1835. Bdsm Robert Massengill.
JOSEPH J. MATTHEWS to RHODA CARRELL 14 Jul 1832. Bdsm Robert Whitman.
SAMUEL BUTLER to MILLEY ROSE 27 Mar 1832. Bdsm Needham Richardson.
STEPHEN BROUGHTON to "WILLY" STALLINGS 19 Mar 1833. Bdsm Jesse Broughton.
NATHAN STRICKLAND to REBECCA LEE 20 Apr 1833. Bdsm Robert W. Sneed.
HOPSON ONEAL to "LANY" ONEAL 2 Aug 1833. Bdsm Benjamin Hocut.
JARROT B. WALL to SALLY HINNANT 28 Sep 1835. Bdsm Robert N. Gully.

MARRIAGE BONDS

LEWIS STRICKLAND to ELIZABETH THORNTON 5 Sep 1833. Bdsm Harry Ingram.
HARRY AVERA to BETSY DURHAM 26 Feb 1835. Bdsm Matthew Avera.
DEMPSEY WATSON to EDITH POPE 25 Feb 1835. Bdsm Stephen Hicks.
MATTHEW BASS to SALLY WARD 3 Sep 1836. Bdsm Richard Pearce.
WILLIAM G. RAMS to GILLY ONEAL 22 Mar 1836. Bdsm Hopkins Oneal.
WILLIAM R. PEACOCK to ELINOR EVANS 7 Jan 1836. Bdsm Jonathan Evans.
NEEDHAM STEVENS to ELIZABETH MITCHINER 11 Jan 1836. Bdsm Samuel Turner.
THOMAS SURLS to PENNY JOHNSON 13 Jan 1836. Bdm John Wood.
JOHN PEACOCK to WINIFRED ALLEN 26 Dec 1835. Bdm William H. Adams.
JESSE DAVIS to AMY CRAFFORD 25 Oct 1835. Bdsm David Parish.
WILLIAM TOMLINSON to SARAH HORN 15 Feb 1835. Bdsm William Tomlinson.
IRVIN PARNOLD to ANNE GERRALD 29 Oct 1835. Bdm Enos Gerrald.
JOHN S. COGDELL to SALLY C. STEVENS 29 Mar 1836. Bdsm Julius A. Stevens.
WILLIAM PEACOCK to NANCY ROBERSON 18 Jul 1836. Bdsm Bryan Peacock.
QUINTON KELLY to NICY JONES 6 Sep 1836. Bdsm William Jones.
THOMAS F. GRICE to ELIZA JANE HINTON 16 Aug 1836. Bdsm Fernifold Green.
JESSE H. BARBER to LANEY MASSINGALE 10 Aug 1835. Bdsm John Barber.
CALVIN STRICKLAND to ANNE ONEAL 14 Sep 1835. Bdsm John Bryan.
ISAAC GEORGE to SARAH FAIL 28 Aug 1837. Bdsm Aaron Lee.
HARRY JOHNSON to SUSAN ADAMS 9 Oct 1835. Bdsm Joel Lee.
HERON JOHNSON to LEWENEY DARDEN 29 Mar 1836. Bdsm John W. Johnson.
JOEL B. CLIFTON to SUSAN LUNCEFORD 24 Dec 1833. Bdsm Joseph Clifton.
WILLIAM A. BASS to CHILLY INGRAM 25 Aug 1835. Bdsm William H. Stevens.
RANSOM TAYLOR to ESTHER NOWELL 7 Dec 1835. Bdsm Thomas Turley.
CALVIN DEAN to REBECCA EDWARDS 16 Jul 1836. Bdsm Alsey Earp.
WESLEY MASSEY to ZILPHIE E. PHILLIPS 26 Oct 1835. Bdsm Charles Massey.
SIMON STEVENS to EMILY SCOTT 4 Dec 1832. Bdsm Joseph Matthews.
JESSE FUTRELL to PATIENCE JOINER 20 Mar 1833. Bdsm Solomon Futrell.
JOHN MURFHREY to PHEREBY WALL 23 Aug 1831. Bdsm Bennet Wall.
JOHN BROWN to BEDY GARNER 25 Dec 1835. Bdsm James Garner.
BENNET WEBB to LECY ELLIS 31 Oct 1835. Bdsm Henry Green.
SOLOMON PEARSON to MARY SASSER 23 Feb 1836. Bdsm Benjamin W. Raiford.
ETHELRED NICHOLS to CINITH HARRELL 9 Dec 1837. Bdsm John Worley.
HENRY W. JOHNSON to ELIZA SMITH 14 Mar 1838. Bdsm William W. Johnson.
RUFFIN HOULDER to TEMPERANCE A. WHITLEY 2 Nov 1837. Bdsm J. William Wilder.
THOMAS TART, JR. to "PURNY" JANE SMITH 28 May 1838. Bdsm Joel Lee.
EDWARD DEBNAM to NANCY J. BULLS 14 Aug 1838. Bdsm William Debnam.
BENJAMIN MARTIN to MARY BYRD 16 Oct 1837. Bdsm Haywood Martin.
WILLIAM BRYAN to "RAINEY" STRICKLAND 19 Jan 1838. Bdsm Hudson Bailey.
HARDY POOL to MARY BAUCOM 27 Dec 1837. Bdsm Jonathan Pool.

JOHNSTON COUNTY MARRIAGES

DELPHA SASSER to JAMES ROSE 27 Sep 1837. Bdsm Jesse Hinnant.
BENJAMIN H. SMITH to ELIZABETH YOUNGBLOOD 1 Jan 1838. Bdsm James R. Ellis.
LOWELLEN LITTLE to MARY OLIVER 31 Jan 1840. Bdsm William Peedin.
WILLIAM WILLIAMS to SALLY ANN DUNN 15 Aug 1839. Bdsm Augustus W. Stevens.
JAMES COBB to NANCY AVERA 19 Dec 1837. Bdsm Elvin Bryan.
WILLIAM LEE to ELIZABETH ANN WALL 15 Dec 1838. Bdsm Samuel Wall.
ABNER TELFAIR? to JULIA A. BOON 17 Nov 1838. Bdsm William Morning.
JAMES JOHNSON to "AIRY" PARISH 30 Jan 1839. Bdsm George Stephenson.
LEWIS STANLY to CRECY KEAN 1 Dec 1837. Bdsm Silas Webb.
CARON PENNY to REBECCA DAVIS 21 Dec 1837. Bdsm Silas Webb.
JOSEPH LANGSTON to RACHEL FAIL 26 Nov ? Bdsm Thomas Toler.
KINBARD GOTMAN to PIETY GRICE 5 Apr 1840. Bdsm Auston Hatcher.
DAVID HATCHCOCK to ABISHA CLARK 30 Dec 1837. Bdsm Henry Massengale.
HENRY A. CLIFTON to ELIZABETH KERN 12 Jan 1839. Bdsm Joel Clifton.
ELI GARDNER to DICY YELVINGTON 26 Mar 1839. Bdsm Thomas Bagley.
JOHN McLEAN to LOUISA LEACH 2 Feb 1839. Bdsm Levy Jones.
JOHN SASSER to KEZIA STALLINGS 24 Nov 1838. Bdsm Alsey Perry.
CARRELL LANGDON to NANCY BYRD 6 May 1838. Bdsm Haywood Martin.
JOHN DIXON to TEMPE MATTHEW 25 Dec 1838. Bdsm Abram Dixon.
JOHN FLOWERS to TEMPE FLOWERS 1 Dec 1838. Bdsm Stephen Godwin.
JOHN CARRELL to WINIFRED FERRELL 26 Feb 1839. Bdsm Needham Bryan.
WILLIAM ELLIS to ALTNA PARISH 15 Jan 1839. Bdsm Samuel Turley.
BERTIE RICHARDSON to HARRIET EARP 2 Jan 1838. Bdsm Sampson Morgan.
URIAH D. COLLINS to AQUILLA JOHNSON 8 Jan 1839. Bdsm D. G. Collins.
WILLIAM McCLIM to NANCY TART 26 Jan 1839. Bdsm Jesse Weaver.
MATTHEW T. GULLEY to NANCY EARP 3 Jan 1838. Bdsm James William Wilder.
ROBERT D. HINNANT to "ULEY" TALTON 9 Jan 1839. Bdsm Jethro Yelvington.
LABON EATMAN to TEMPERANCE HOGG 14 Aug 1838. Bdsm Sampson Morgan.
NEEDHAM EDWARDS to POLLY BRASSELL 6 Feb 1838. Bdsm John Edwards.
BRYAN HARPER to NANCY JONES 18 Feb 1839. Bdsm Elisha Harrison.
THOMAS LOCKHART to EDITH THORP 4 Dec 1838. Bdsm Matthew Avera.
STEPHEN HAMMONTREE to CIVIL LUCAS 13 Apr 1839. Bdsm Peter Hammontree.
STEPHEN EDWARDS to BETSY THOMSON 20 Nov 1838. Bdsm Sampson Edwards.
LARRY HINNANT to WIMMY CREECH 26 Feb 1839. Bdsm Nelson Kent.
ELISHA STARLING to MARGARET MILLINER 17 Jan 1839. Bdsm James Peedin, Sr.
JAMES HATCHER to POLLY GARNER 5 Dec 1839. Bdsm John Hatcher.
MONROE GURLEY to HARRIET LYNCH 6 Jan 1840. Bdsm Ezekiel Stevens.
HANDY W. WEST to TRANQUILLA JOHNSON 18 May 1839. Bdsm Noel West.
JAMES R. ELLIS to MARTHA POOL 27 Feb 1839. Bdsm Samuel M. Turley.
WILLIAM GARNER to CYNTHIA SMITH 26 Mar 1839. Bdsm John W. Johnson.
WILLIAM E. EDWARDS to AMANDA M. JONES 8 May 1839. Bdsm N. H. Blackwood.
JENKINS A. STEVENS to REBECCA A. BULLS 4 Aug 1838. Bdsm Alexander Thornton.
SAMUEL WHITAKER to LYDIA STALLINGS 15 Jun 1837. Bdsm Isaac

MARRIAGE BONDS

Stallings.
LEWIS THOMSON to SOPHIA RHODES 7 Apr 1840. Bdsm John P. Williams.
JOSEPH J. ADAMS to ELIZABETH LEE 26 Mar 1839. Bdsm Josiah Adams.
WILLIAM HOLLIMON to POLLY DAVIS 22 Jan 1840. Bdsm John Harrell.
WILLIAM BARNES to MARY COX 14 Mar 1840. Bdsm Robert N. Gulley.
DAVID LUNCEFORD to SUSAN ALLEN 6 Jun 1839. Bdsm Allen L. Ballenger.
ALSEY STOLT to POLLY STANSIL 25 Dec 1837. Bdsm Godfrey Stansil.
BARNA GRANTHAM to "SIDNEY" STEVENS 26 Nov 1839. Bdsm Thomas Toler.
LEMUEL JONES to CALLY SPENCER 11 Feb 11 1840. Bdsm Curtis Holland.
THOMAS H. LEGON to RILDA HOCUT 22 Jan 1840. Bdsm Benajah Horne.
ROBERT OLIVER to MALEARD WELLONS 11 Feb 1840. Bdsm McKinne Oliver.
WILLIAMSON STEVENS to EMILY TRAWICH 27 Feb 1838. Bdsm Benjamin Whitley.
THOMAS McCLAM to JANE BAREFOOT 24 Feb 1838. Bdsm Hardy Barefoot.
JULUIS G. SLOCOMB to LOUISA BOON 9 Apr 1838. Bdsm K. N. Husted.
WILLIAM TARLET to WINIFRED SMITH 17 Mar 1838. Bdsm Harry Johnson.
HENRY O. STALLINGS to AQUILLA HUGHS 6 Oct 1838. Bdsm Needham Oliver.
JOSHUA CREECH to NANCY EDWARDS 3 Aug 1838. Bdsm John Massey.
BARTLEY HARPER to SALLY CORDELL 3 Aug 1838. Bdsm John Cordell.
DANIEL GURLEY to EDITH PHILLIPS 10 Feb 1838. Bdsm Henry Hamilton.
URIAH TYNER to TRANQUILLA GRIFFIN 21 Dec 1839. Bdsm William Wimdeon.
JOSIAH COATS to EDNA HOBBY 7 Nov 1837. Bdsm Starling Massingale.
KEDAR CREECH to CATHARINE CREECH 19 Nov 1839. Bdsm William J. Peedin.
PHARAOH RICHARDSON to MARY VINSON 23 Nov 1839. Bdsm William H. Morning.
JOHN WHITE to TEMPERANCE UTLEY 26 Oct 1839. Bdsm William B. Sanders.
IREDELL PEARCE to BETHANY WILLIAMSON 25 Feb 1840. Bdsm Thomas Durham.
WILLIS TAYLOR to TEMPE HOWLEY 25 Nov 1839. Bdsm Robertson Raper.
HENDERSON STRICKLAND to PATSY ONEAL 9 Nov 1838. Bdsm Hillaird Strickland.
LOVERD LANGLEY to CHARLOTTE TOLER 9 Nov 1838. Bdsm John Jackson.
GODFRED STANSIL to "RANEY" GODWIN 7 Sep 1838. Bdsm John G. Stansil.
WILLIAM EDWARDS to DISEY GERRALD 12 Oct 1838. Bdsm Sampson Edwards.
AMOS HAYES to NANCY STANSELL 24 Aug 1840. Bdsm Quincy Watson.
JOSIAH HOLLIMAN to AILY NARRON 25 Jun 1838. Bdsm Edwin Boykins.
WARREN BAILEY, JR. to POLLY NARRON 25 Sep 1838. Bdsm Theophilius Dodd.
KIMBREL EATMON to NANCY BAILEY 11 Oct 1837. Bdsm Austen Hatcher.
THOMAS EDWARDS to SALLY JACKSON 27 oct 1838. Bdsm Reddick Warren.
RANSOM H. TEMPLES to NANCY ALLEN 1 Nov 1837. Bdsm Starling W. Temple.
HENRY GREEN to WINIFRED PORCH 20 Mar ?. Bdsm Solomon Lockhart.
HARDY PRIDGEN to BETSY PEACOCK 31 Jan 1838. Bdsm Arthur Thomson.
NEEDHAM MORLEY to SALLY HICKS 17 Jan 1838. Bdsm Jesse Overby.
ISAAC BOYETT to BETSY WATSON 27 Sep 1837. Bdsm Jesse Hinnant.
ROBERT HATCHER to PIETY BAILEY 17 Oct 1837. Bdsm John T. Hatcher.
BRIDGERS PARROT to MORNING CROCKER 13 Sep 1838. Bdsm Mark Freeman.

JOHNSTON COUNTY MARRIAGES

RANSOM TAYLOR to NANCY LEE 16 Jun 1838. Bdsm John Lee.
SAMUEL STANSELL to PATSEY RENTFROW 20 Jul 1838. Bdsm Austin Hatcher.
YOUNG BARBER to REBECCA JORDAN 9 Jan 1838. Bdsm Daniel Gurley.
ALEXANDER DUNCAN to "SORIND" DURHAM 15 Jan 1838. Bdsm George W. Duncan.
HIRAM CHAMBERLEE to PATIENCE STRICKLAND 16 Dec 1837. Bdsm Freeman Chamberlee.
SILAS WEBB to LOUISA CREECH 13 Jan 1837. Bdsm William Stanly, Jr.
ELIAS BARNES to EDNA BEEL 15 Dec 1838. Bdsm William Ellis.
JAMES RAINER to BERSEBA HOLMES 2 Nov 1837. Bdsm James G. Rainer.
MERRITT JOHNSON to MARY HOLLAND 20 Sep 1837. Bdsm Alsey Johnson.
WILLIAM LANGLEY to SALLY LANGLEY 16 Mar 1838. Bdsm Miles Langley.
BENJAMIN WOODARD to EMMA PHILLIPS 29 Feb 1838. Bdsm Henry Woodard.
HENRY SASSER to PATSY BAGLEY 3 Mar 1838. Bdsm Clark Gerrald.
ELI CREECH to SALLY DAUGHTRY 24 Sep 1839. Bdsm Reddick Warren.
ALFRED ALLEN to LEACY JOHNSON 10 Sep 1839. Bdsm Alfred Johnson.
JOSHUA DAVIS to SYLVIA WARD 4 Apr 1838. Bdsm Henry M. Stevens.
HENRY H. LEE to BETSY ANN EVANS 21 Sep 1838. Bdsm John H. Lee.
REVELL JONES to MARGARET CREECH 2 Nov 1839. Bdsm Roy Jones.
ALEXANDER HONEYCUT to DILLA PARISH 17 Sep 1839. Bdsm Johnson Parish.
ROBERT HOOD to DICY GRANTHAM 28 Aug 1839. Bdsm Thomas Toler.
JOHN A. ADAMS to CIVIL L. REAVES 28 Aug 1839. Bdsm Thomas Bagley.
EDMUND JOHNSON to ELIZABETH LASSITER 24 Sep 1839. Bdsm Alfred Lassiter.
JAMES BRADDY to CATHARINE FARROW 24 Jul 1838. Bdsm Matthew Avera.
VINE EDWARDS to PATSEY PEEDIN 31 Aug 1840. Bdsm Vinson Edwards.
KEARNEY EASON to "COZZY" GODWIN 25 May 1840. Bdsm Lemmuel Jones.
JOHN H. LEE to SALLY STANDLEY 25 Sep 1839. Bdsm John Strickland.
JAMES GREEN to SARAH PEARCE 23 Jun 1838. Bdsm Allen Brammon.
THOMAS BYRD to REBECCA SANDERS 7 Nov 1838. Bdsm John Cordell.
HENRY G. EDWARDS to ELIZABETH ANN JERNIGAN 29 Jul 1840. Bdsm John Edwards.
PRESTON KELLY to NANCY BROWN 29 Apr 1840. Bdsm William Pool.
THOMAS DURHAM to ZILPHIA PEARCE 26 Mar 1839. Bdsm James Durham.
BENJAMIN STEVENS to KERN THOMSON 17 Apr 1839. Bdsm Benjamin Stevens.
EDWIN BRYAN to JANE E. JONES 5 Nov 1838. Bdsm Edwin Bryan.
SIMON BARBER to CASANDRA BARBER 6 Aug 1838. Bdsm Needham Bryan.
NATHAN FLOWERS to NANCY BRUNT 25 Mar 1839. Bdsm Thomas Toler.
HAYWOOD WHITLEY to ESTHER JERNIGAN 16 Oct 1839. Bdsm Haywood W. Whitley.
GEORGE W. LIMSDEN to MARIA FAIL 2 Dec 1839. Bdsm John McLeod.
JAMES ROBERTS TO NICY MILLINER 24 Nov 1838. Bdsm Elbert Roberts.
AUGUSTUS W. STEVENS to SARAH BRYAN 16 Dec 1839. Bdsm Thomas Stevens.
JAMES PENNY to MARY JANE WOOD 11 Jun 1840. Bdsm Caleb Penny.
WILLIAM D. WOOD to MARY PENNY 7 Aug 1840. Bdsm Willie Johnson.
GARRY SYLLAVENT to PATIENCE ODOM 9 Mar 1838. Bdsm Jesse Hinnant.
BENAJAH HOLLAND to AMANDA JOHNSON 17 Jun 1838. Bdsm Ransom Johnson.

MARRIAGE BONDS

JOHN GREGORY to REBECCA MARIA BRITT 29 May 1838. Bdsm Samuel Lee.
BRITAIN RYALS to SARAH CROSS 27 Feb 1838. Bdsm Merrel Ryals.
ISHAM McLANE to PHEREBE TART 11 Jan 1848. Bdsm William McLane and Isham McLane.
JOHN C. VINCENT to EMILY W. EASON 8 May 1848. Bdsm John C. Vincent and A. A. McDugald.
SIR WILLIAM INGRAM to FANNY DOWDY 20 May 1849. Bdsm Sir William Ingram and Needham Ingram.
SOLOMON PEARSON to JULIA ANN TALTON 31 Dec 1844. Bdsm Solomon Pearson.
MANLY ONEAL to REBECCA HARE 22 Nov 1848. Bdsm Manly Oneal and Stephen Stancell.
NEEDHAM BARNES to CATHARINE AVERA 28 Feb 1849. Bdsm Needham Barnes and Isaac Munden.
JACOB BARNES to PENNY WATSON 24 Mar 1849. Bdsm Jacob Kirby and Robert Raper.
E. P. STEVENS to ELIZABETH STANCELL 20 Jun 1849. Bdsm Stephen Stancell.
JOHN LEE to ANN E. LASSITER 25 Jan 1850. Bdsm John Lee and William G. Adams.
HARRY DURHAM to MARTHA SHAW 23 May 1844. Bdsm Harry Durham and Duncan McPherson.
JOHN WOODARD to DELANEY EDWARDS 18 Mar 1839. Bdsm Jesse Holt.
ALEXANDER LAMLERS to PHEREBE JOHNSON 2 Mar 1839. Bdsm Robert T. Massengill.
HENRY OLIVER to "HULDY" WOODARD 24 Apr 1838. Bdsm Jesse Holt.
FERNIFOLD MILLINER to AILSEY LYNCH 13 Mar 1839. Bdsm James Roberts.
LEWIS POOL to ELIZABETH TALTON 25 Dec 1837. Bdsm Lovett Spivy.
BISHOP HICKS to WILLY BRYAN 23 Jan 1839. Bdsm Stephen Hicks.
REDDIN JOINER to ELIZABETH WILDER 26 Nov 1838. Bdsm John Whitley, Jr.
JOSEFUS MOORE to RUTHY SIMPSON 11 Feb 1850. Bdsm Thomas Price.
GASTIN BAILY to MARY BAILY 21 Feb 1850. Bdsm Mabry Hinnant.
JAMES STALLINGS to ELIZABETH JONES 15 Dec 1847. Bdsm James Stallings and William H. McCullers.
JOSEPH E. ALLEN to BIDY WHITTENTON 6 Apr 1844. Bdsm Joseph E. Allen and Nicholas Lee.
JESSE CREECH to POLLY WALL 9 Apr 1847. Bdsm Jesse Creech and Standford Creech.
STEPHEN PARKER to PATSY PEEBLES 11 Sep 1845. Bdsm Jesse Parker and Stephen Parker.
GEORGE BARBER to TEMPY ANN BLENKET 27 Feb 1849. Bdsm George Barber and William W. Morgan.
WILLIAM A. BRADY to ELIZABETH DAVIS 31 Dec 1847. Bdsm William A. Brady and Green Hill.
HARRY JOHNSON to SARAH LEE 29 Jan 1848. Bdsm Harry Johnson and George Stephenson.
NICHOLAS STENLEY to ELIZABETH POPE 23 Nov 1847. Bdsm Nicholas Stenley and George Dunn.
ROBERT WATSON to SALLY ANN PEEDIN 16 Feb 1848. Bdsm Robert Watson and Garry Crumpler.
BUD FEWTRELL to "CHOSA" BOYETT 13 Jan 1848. Bdsm Bud Fewtrell and

JOHNSTON COUNTY MARRIAGES

Howel Yelvington.
PETER R. TEMPLE to MARY WOODALL 8 Jan 1840. Bdsm Peter R. Temple an R. H. Blackman.
WILLIAM H. PITMAN to SALLY WATKINS 5 Jan 1850. Bdsm William H. Pitman and Thomas Pitman.
DUNCAN JOHNSON to "CISSALEY" LOVE 5 Apr 1844. Bdsm Duncan Johnson and William Johnson.
THOMAS H. THORNTON to RHOBRA L. HAYS 27 Feb 1844. Bdsm Thomas H. Thornton and Daniel Salmon.
HENRY S. GREEN to MARY H. GURLEY 25 May 1847. Bdsm Henry S. Green and John H. Bryan.
HENRY C. JOHNSON to DELITHA JOHNSON 30 May 1849. Bdsm Robert W. Stevens.
REUBEN GOWER to ELINOR LOCKOBOY 4 Jul 1849. Bdsm Reuben Gower and George Kean.
RANSOM CARRELL to LUCINDA STEVENSON 10 Aug 1849. Bdsm Ransom Carrell and Dallas Carrell.
JAMES R. JONES to BERLIN JORDAN 17 Aug 1849. Bdsm James R. Jones and David Turner.
WILLIAM MOODY to JUANNA HOCUT 6 Jul 1849. Bdsm William Moody and Lunceford Bailey.
WILLIAM HOLLIMON to CAROLINE STALLINGS 21 Nov 1848. Bdsm Ransom Hollimon and William Hollimon.
JAMES H. THOMAS to MARIAH STANLY 9 Sep 1848. Bdsm James H. Thomas and William Stanly.
MALACHI WALL to MARY GIMMET 11 Jul 1849. Bdsm Malachi Wall and John Murphrey.
TOBIAS ROSE to SALLY PARRISH 3 Jun 1849. Bdsm Tobias Rose and Henry Bagley.
HAYWOOD CREECH to WINIFRED OLIVER 27 Jan 1849. Bdsm Haywood Creech and Larkin Creech.
DANIEL SMITH to LUGENIA CROSS 5 Dec 1848. Bdsm Daniel Smith and William H. Morning.
FREDERICK GRANTHAM to SARAH ANN THORNTON 31 Jan 1849. Bdsm Frederick Grantham and John H. Daniel.
VINE A. IVEY to NICY WOODALL 13 Dec 1848. Bdsm Vine A. Ivey and William W. Morgan.
HENRY STARLING to CERNONTHA PAIR 26 Feb 1844. Bdsm Henry Starling and James Hinnant.
DUNCAN McPHERSON to MARY JANE GURLY 26 Dec 1846. Bdsm Duncan McPhereson and William H. Morning.
JAMES AUSTIN to PATIENCE BARNES 17 Nov 1849. Bdsm James Austin and Ransom Bridgers.
JAMES MOORE to LUCY RENTFROW 18 Jan 1850. Bdsm G. W. Godwin and James Moore.
DAVID H. BRIDGERS to NANCY PAMENTER 10 Oct 1849. Bdsm David H. Bridgers and Lewis Williams.
GEORGE KEAN to SARAH LASTER 6 Feb 1850. Bdsm George Kean and Nathan L. Allen.
ZEROBABEL WHEELER to ELIZABETH DUN 14 Dec 1847. Bdsm Zerobabel Wheeler and Mark Wheeler.
JESSE STEWART to SALLY McLANE 21 Dec 1847. Bdsm Jesse Stewart and

MARRIAGE BONDS

William A. Stewart.
JAMES JEFFREYS to MILLY ATKINSON 13 May 1847. Bdsm James Jeffreys and Ruffin Jeffreys.
WILLIAM NORRIS to WINIFRED HONEYCUT 1 Jan 1849. Bdsm William Norris and Robert W. Stevens.
W. F. S. ALSTON to EMILY N. CLIFTON 25 Aug 1847. Bdsm W. F. S. Alston and Needham Stevens.
OLIVER RAINS to "MONTED" SASSER 24 Aug 1847. Bdsm Oliver Rains and Henry Rains.
WESTLY LABORN to SMITHEY HAGAN 12 Jun 1847. Bdsm Westly Laborn and Exum Holland.
KINEDTON G. PHILLIPS to EVLINA PITMAN 28 Jul 1847. Bdsm Kinedton G. Phillips and Turner Joiner.
ASHLY R. OLIVER to CATHERAN A. BOSWETH 5 Aug 1847. Bdsm Ashly R. Oliver and Willie Holt.
BARDIN PEARCE to TIBITHY HOWELL 8 Jul 1847. Bdsm Bardin Pearce and Richmond Pearce.
JEREMIAH PLEASANT to PENNY STEVENSON 24 May 1847. Bdsm Jeremiah Pleasant and Robert W. Stevens.
WILLIAM N. ROSE to PHEREBE LEE 22 Dec 1847. Bdsm William N. Rose and Sir William Blackman.
JAMES A. HACKNEY to MARY J. CRISTMAN 24 Apr 1847. Bdsm James A. Hackney and Bryan B. Hinnant.
THOMAS HOLLAND to KESIAH JOHNSTON 23 Jul 1847. Bdsm Stephen Johnston.
HILLIARD HORN to HAWKINS STANCELL 21 Jul 1847. Bdsm Staton Johnston.
WILLIAM PEARCE to "RANY" HINNANT 14 May 1849. Bdsm William Pearce and Macle Talton.
WILLIE S. BOON to BARSHEBA RICHARDSON 27 Jul 1846. Bdsm Willie S. Boon and David H. Holland.
K. B. WHITLEY to MARTHA HEATH 23 Jun 1849. Bdsm K. B. Whitley and Bryan Smith.
LARKIN SPIVEY to RELDY TALTON 22 Jan 1849. Bdsm Larkin Spivey and Jimmett Holland.
HENDERSON GODWIN to ? 12 Jun 1844. Bdsm Henderson Godwin and David H. Holland.
JOSEPH A. LEE to MARTHA E. LEE 4 Jun 1847. Bdsm Joseph A. Lee and John Lee.
WILLIAM CHAMBLEE to MARTHA HARDY 23 Jul 1847. Bdsm Stephen Johnston.
EVERETT D. WHITLEY to CATHERINE RICHARDSON 6 Jun 1848. Bdsm Everett D. Whitley and Josiah H. Whitley.
MATTHEW PARKER to VETRINA WELLONS 12 Jun 1849. Bdsm Matthew Parker and Henry Bagley.
JOSEPH A. INGRAM to JULIA C. MORGAN 7 Mar 1844. Bdsm Joseph A. Ingram and Bevely O. Ballgener.
JOHN H. DANIEL to MARTHA J. ROSE 3 Apr 1844. Bdsm John H. Daniel and David Smith.
DANIEL GARDNER to MARTHA EARP 16 Dec 1847. Bdsm Daniel Gardner and H. H. Hobbs.
CHARLES M. LEE to "CURDISS" TURLEY 14 Dec 1847. Bdsm Charles M. Lee

JOHNSTON COUNTY MARRIAGES

and James R. Jones.
JOHN EARP to EDNEY GODWIN 9 Dec 1847. Bdsm John Earp and Bryan Sanders.
WILLIAM HALL to SALLY RYALS 23 Nov 1847. Bdsm William Hall and Robert W. Stevens.
ERASMUS KIRBY to ZILPHIA PEEL 30 Aug 1847. Bdsm Erasmus Kirby and Stanley Kirby.
WILLIAM GOWER to HARRIET HOLT 18 Nov 1847. Bdsm William Gower and Baldy Sanders.
WILLIAM STARLING to SUSAN BLACKMAN 13 Dec 1848. Bdsm William Starling and William Guy.
LEMMUEL DIXON to LUCY H. JOHNSON 20 Jan 1849. Bdsm Lemmuel Dixon and Robert W. Stevens.
ROBERT McLANE to BETSY JERNIGAN 13 Dec 1848. Bdsm Robert McLane and William McLane.
K.M.C. WILLIAMSON to SARAH McKIMMEL 16 Jun 1849. Bdms K.M.C. Williamson and Edwin Boykins.
WILLIAM H. MORNING to PHEBE T. BABOCK 1 Jun 1848. Bdsm William H. Morning and Edwin Boykins.
CASWELL HOOD to MARTHA CANBERT 5 May 1848. Bdsm James Byrd and Caswell Hood.
ALVIN CREECH to EDNEY BAGLEY 28 Dec 1846. Bdsm Robert Edwards and Alvin Creech.
GEORGE BRASSEL to CINTHIA GARNER 28 Jan 1848. Bdsm George Brassel.
GIDEON STANLEY to PHEOBEE POPE 18 Aug 1846. Bdsm Gideon Stanley and William Stanley.
JOHN E. ALLEN to ELIZABETH AVERA 22 Nov 1848. Bdsm John E. Allen and William R. Lee.
BRYANT H. NORRIS to SUSAN C. JORDAN 20 Apr 1849. Bdsm Bryant H. Norris and Robert W. Stevens.
JOHN GODWIN to ELIZABETH SMITH 11 Nov 1849. Bdsm John Godwin and Joel Lee.
JAMES H. JONES to ELIZABETH SMITH 3 Nov 1847. Bdsm James H. Jones and Willie Jones.
JOSEPH FARMER to MARIAH PHILLIPS 10 Apr 1844. Bdsm Joseph Farmer and A. J. Lloyd.
HENRY SILIVENT to ELIZABETH BROUGHTON 20 Sep 1849. Bdsm Henry Silivent and S. P. Horton.
ELIJAH REED to PHEREBY STANDEN 14 Nov 1849. Bdsm Elijah Reed and Willie Holt.
HENRY EDWARDS to ZILPHA STARLING 5 Oct 1849. Bdsm Edwin Boykins.
JOSIAH HINNANT, JR. to AILSEY FAIL 12 Mar 1849. Bdsm Josiah Hinnant, Jr. and Elihugh Jones.
JAMES HOLLAND to MARY CARTER 27 Jan 1847. Bdsm James Holland.
WILLIAM LUCUS to BETSY RYALS 21 Oct 1847. Bdsm William Lucus and Young Barber.
HERRON CREECH to LUVENSIA SELLARS 1 Mar 1849. Bdsm Herron Creech and William Brown.
ISAAC W. JONES to AMANDA CABLE 31 May 1847. Bdsm Isaac W. Jones and Henry I. Bell.
JOHN LEE to CANDIS CLIFTON 11 Jun 1844. Bdsm John Lee and Aeriel P. Clifton.

MARRIAGE BONDS

HENRY GERHEARDT to EMILY ? 15 Mar 1841. Bdsm Duncan McPherson.
HARDY BARBER to ? 21 Apr 1842. Bdsm Hardy Barber and Bailie Barber.
EMMEON WOODALL to HARRIET MACE 9 Dec 1841. Bdsm William Woodall and John Barber.
SOLOMON DAUGHTRY to PATSEY CAPPS 3 Jan 1842. Bdsm Kedar Creech.
JOHN PEEDIN to AXCY SPENCER 5 Feb 1842. Bdsm Newit Peedin.
JOEL JOINER, JR. to ISABELLA STRICKLAND 27 Dec 1841. Bdsm W. B. Stevens.
MAJOR HANDY to ELIZABETH BELL 7 Aug 1846. Bdsm Major Handy and Abram Dixon.
EDWARD STEVENSON to LOUISA HOLLAND 2 Sep 1846. Bdsm Jesse Stevenson.
HENRY MILLINER to MARY FUTRELL 27 Feb 1841. Bdsm Jacob A. Stevens.
JACOB BRASWELL to SALLY SPENCER 23 Dec 1841. Bdsm Arthur Woodard.
HENRY JOHNSON to LYDIA JOHNSON 28 Dec 1841. Bdsm Henry Johnson and A. W. Stevens.
BENNET YELVINGTON to NELLY RAINS 14 Dec 1841. Bdsm Levy Yelvington.
BURWELL EARP to NANCY TRAYWAY 24 Feb 1846. Bdsm Burwell Earp and Wyatt Earp.
JAMES HONEYCUT to BETHANY PARISH 7 Dec 1841. Bdsm Justes Parish.
JAMES H. BUNCH to CAROLINE WILLIAMS 17 Dec 1841. Bdsm Samuel P. Horton.
JOHN A. LOVE to SARAH JOHNSON 26 Dec 1841. Bdsm John A. Love and Samuel Johnson.
WESLEY FOWLER to "JULY" CARRELL 22 Jan 1846. Bdsm Wesley Fowler and Ephraim A. Smith.
WILLIAM RAPER to ? 28 Feb 1843. Bdsm William Raper and Silas Lamb.
NATHAN RHODES to PATSEY JONES 4 Aug 1840. Bdsm Burwell Barber Jr.
WILLIAM J. SCOTT of Sampson County to DICY EVANS 8 Nov 1843. Bdsm William J. Scott and Evans Chance.
WILLIAM H. McCULLERS to SALINA HINTON 18 Sep 1843. Bdsm W. T. Jones.
PEOLA BARBER to Miss ELIZABETH GURLEY 26 Oct 1843. Bdsm Peola Barber and Hardy Barber.
HENRY MOORE to CEELIA ANN BEASLY 20 Oct 1843. Bdsm Henry Moore and Simeon Woodall.
EZEKIEL CREECH to POLLY COLLINS 25 Dec 1841. Bdsm Joshua Creech.
WILLIAM DRIVER to TEMPE TODD 9 Jan 1840. Bdsm Monroe Todd.
SIMON AYCOCK, JR. to MARY RIVEL 25 Jan 1843. Bdsm William H. Aycock.
HAYWOOD BAKER to BETHANIA INGRAM 15 Nov 1849. Bdsm Haywood Baker and George Keen.
CALVIN LAMB to NANCY BARBER 20 Dec 1842. Bdsm Isaac Boyett.
BERTIE WOODARD to POLLY BAILEY 7 Aug 1840. Bdsm Warren W. Bailey.
WILLIAM H. COATS to MARTHA PENNY 20 Jul 1846. Bdsm William H. Coats and James Tomlinson.
SANDY JOHNSON to ELIZABETH ? 4 Jul 1846. Bdsm Abram Dixon and Sandy Johnson.
JACOB DAVIS to REBECCA HOLLINGSWORTH 20 Oct 1843. Bdsm Jacob Davis and Furney Langster.
WILLIAM VINSON to JANE FORD 27 Dec 1849. Bdsm William Vinson and John Ford.

JOHNSTON COUNTY MARRIAGES

THOMAS HOLLAND to MARIA EARP 2 Dec 1845. Bdsm Thomas Holland and Elbert Austin.
DAVID GRICE to CEELA JOHNSON 11 Feb 1840. Bdsm William Johnson.
ALBERT J. POOL to SALLY BAMDAM 1 Jan 1846. Bdsm Albert J. Pool and Caswell A. Smith.
JOEL CLIFTON to SALLY IVEANS 23 Aug 1842. Bdsm Henry A. Clifton.
JESSE R. THOMSON to HARRIET SPENCER 8 Jan 1842. Bdsm Daverick D. Thomson.
THOMAS PITMAN to CHARITY PITMAN 5 Jan 1846. Bdsm Thomas Pitman and Bryan R. Hinnant.
JOHN H. RAINS to CATHARINE HOWELL 27 Sep 1842. Bdsm John H. Rains.
GUILFORD HAYLES to AMANDA GODWIN 16 Apr ? . Bdsm Guilford Hayles and L. Richardson.
WILLIAM H. PARTIN to SARAH OGBURN 11 Apr 1842. Bdsm William H. Partin and Washington Partin.
ELI SASSER to PEGGY ANN GAME 5 Mar 1846. Bdsm Eli Sasser and Raiford Gurley.
THOMAS EDWARDS to SALLY SNIPES 25 Mar 1841. Bdsm William Brown.
MATTHEW HALL to SINTHA CARRELL 31 Mar 1842. Bdsm Matthew Hall and Thomas Ligon.
BENNET B. STRICKLAND to CAROLINE ALLEN 8 Apr 1842. Bdsm Bennet B. Strickland and Sir William Stanley.
NATHAN TART to AMY BAREFOOT 21 Mar 1842. Bdsm Nathan Tart and William Tart.
ROBERT BATTEN to MARTHA STANCELL 24 Oct 1849. Bdsm Robert Batten and Jesse Creech.
SHADRACK B. LASSITER to MARTHA HARDY 20 Oct 1849. Bdsm Shadrack B. Lassiter and William Lassiter.
BAYLEY R. LEE to TEMPY C. BARBER 3 Oct 1848. Bdsm Bayley R. Lee and Ransom Lee.
LOYED WEST to MARTHA MORGAN 16 Oct 1846. Bdsm Loyed West and Zacharich Tiner.
JAMES EASON to HAWKINS BARBER 28 Nov 1849. Bdsm James Eason and Benjamin Stewart.
CALVIN JERNIGAN to EADY LEE 26 Dec 1841. Bdsm Calvin Jernigan and Absalom Barber, Sr.
ELIJAH H. PHILLIPS to WINIFRED H. CAPPS 14 Jan 1850. Bdsm Elijah H. Phillips and Elijah Capps.
BARTLEY PACE to ZILPHA BATTEN 15 Jan 1850. Bdsm Bartley Pace and Henry Starling.
RANSOM BRIDGERS to ADELINE BARBER 23 Oct 1849. Bdsm Ransom Bridgers and William H. Buckman.
N. R. WHITLEY to MARTHA RICHARDSON 27 Nov 1849. Bdsm N. R. Whitley and William Hilliard.
ELBERT AUSTIN to "RILDY" BARNES 7 Oct 1846. Bdsm Elbert Austin and James Roberts.
EZEKIEL CREECH to NANCY FAIL 28 Sep 1846. Bdsm Sylvester Jones and Ezekiel Creech.
STEPHEN RENTFROW to PRITSEY HASE 18 Jan 1842. Bdsm Stephen Rentfrow and Perry Rentfrow.
JAMES YOUNGBLOOD to MIRIAM LANCEFORD 27 Aug 1840. Bdsm H. H. Youngblood.

MARRIAGE BONDS

PERRY RENTFROW to LUCINDA HAWKINS ATKINSON 29 Dec 1841. Bdsm Thomas Christianbury.

JAMES RICHARDSON to NELLY TALTON 19 Sep 1841. Bdsm James Richardson and Henry Sasser.

JOHN H. BRYAN to LUCY E. WALL 29 Sep 1846. Bdsm John H. Bryan and David Adams.

GEORGE EASON to JANE PRICE 29 Sep 1841. Bdsm Avera Eason.

LEVI RADFORD to AMY EDWARDS 29 Sep 1846. Bdsm Levi Radford and Willie Holt.

ROBERT H. MASSENGILL to S. BAKER 25 Oct 1849. Bdsm Robert H. Massengill and R. H. Temple.

JOHN S. BOYKINS to GLATHA H. KENT 26 Nov 1845. Bdsm John S. Boykins and Mabry Hinnant.

JOHN CARTER to RILDA PEARCE 21 Nov 1845. Bdsm John Carter and Stanley Kirby.

RAIFORD GURLEY to CHERRY HOWELL 2 Apr ? Bdsm Raiford Gurley and William H. Toler.

ELIJAH ATKINSON to PENELOPE YELVINGTON 25 Nov 1845. Bdsm Elijah Atkinson and Levi Yelvington.

WILLIAM K. CRAWFORD to SARRAH EDWARDS 27 Feb 1846. Bdsm William K. Crawford.

WILLIAM ATKINSON to MARTHA GODWIN 23 Feb 1846. Bdsm William Atkinson and Richardson Oneil.

ISRAEL MATTHEWS to PENNY DIXON 6 Jan 1846. Bdsm Israel Matthews and William R. Lee.

WILLIE WATSON to HARRIET BOYETT 2 Jan 1846. Bdsm Willie Watson and Stanley Kirby.

HILLIARD STRICKLAND to NANCY RICHARDSON 24 Feb 1842. Bdsm A. J. Taylor.

CHARLES HOLLAND to TEMPY HOLLAND 7 Jan 1847. Bdsm Eason Holland.

LEWIS BYRD to SUSETTA JONES 20 Jan 1846. Bdsm James Jones and Lewis Byrd.

QUINTON KELLY to PHEREBY M. BOON 27 Dec 1841. Bdsm John W. Boon.

WILLIAM ONEAL, JR. to SALLY HARE 9 Feb 1842. Bdsm Nathan Oneal.

THOMAS JONES to PATSY JOHNSON 19 Jan 1842. Bdsm John Cordele.

HENRY POOL to NANCY ELLIS 12 Feb ? Bdsm Samuel M. Turley.

BRITTON BARBER to SUSAN JONES 9 Feb 1841. Bdsm Larkin Barber.

JOHN W. JOHNSON to MARY JANE REAVES 19 Jan 1842. Bdsm John W. Johnson and R. Green.

THOMAS BLACKWELL to EVELINE HATCHCOCK 14 Dec 1841. Bdsm Isaac L. George.

STEPHEN HINNANT to HARRIET BAGLEY Oct 1842. Bdsm James Faulk.

ATLAS J. R. RHODES to SPICY WEST 6 Oct 1846. Bdsm Atlas J. R. Rhodes and George Keen.

ROBERT MASSENGILL to MARTHA FLOWERS 7 Jan 1846. Bdsm Bartlett Hamper.

WILLIE BRAXTEN to PATIENCE PEARCE 9 SEP 1846. Bdsm Willie Braxten and James H. Hinnant.

JACKSON WILLIAMS to CHARLOTTE OGBURN 17 Jan 1840. Bdsm Thomas Barber.

JOHN CORBET to CATHARINE BARNES 7 Oct 1846. Bdm John Corbet and Ransom Hinton.

JOHNSTON COUNTY MARRIAGES

JAMES C. JORDAN to RODY PARRISH 10 Oct 1846. Bdsm James C. Jordan and Carrell Langdon.
JOHN H. RAINS to CATHARINE HOWELL 27 Sep 1842. Bdsm John H. Rains and Willie Holt.
JOHN W. STANLEY to CHARLOTTE STRICKLAND 13 Oct 1842. Bdsm Sir William Stanley.
WILLIAM HINTON PRICE to NANCY WILDER 5 Jan 1843. Bdsm William Hinton Price and Matthew Wilder.
SIMON P. LEE to CHARLOTTE EVANS 2 Aug 1842. Bdsm Simon P. Lee and Elijah B. Johnson.
JOHNSON PARRISH to HARRIET PARRISH 5 Aug 1842. Bdsm Johnson Parrish and Ransom Parrish.
JAMES HOLLAND to MARY CARTER 27 Jan 1847. Bdsm James Holland and Bryant Holland.
NELSON D. PARE to EMILY RICHARDSON 27 Nov 1843. Bdsm Nelson D. Pare and Edward Debnam.
JOHN B. HIGH to ELIZABETH J. ATKINSON 27 Nov 1843. Bdsm John B. High and Benjamin J. Glover.
JAMES HINNANT to REBECCA RAPER 21 Dec 1846. Bdsm James Hinnant and Joseph Raper.
GEORGE DENNING to MARY WOODARD 26 Jan 1847. Bdsm George Denning and Abram Dixon.
LEWIS STANLY to "RIDLEY" KEAN 4 Nov 1846. Bdsm Lewis Stanly and Gideon Kean.
RAIFORD R. MEHAMS to ? 26 Nov 1844. Bdsm Thomas Cole.
CHARLES WEST to CHARLOTTE MARTIN 26 Feb 1844. Bdsm Charles West and Robert W. Stevens.
OSBERN STEVENSON to M. PLEASANT 4 May 1847. Bdsm Osbern Stevenson and Solomon Stevenson.
ASHLEY BLACKMAN to JUDITH BEASLEY 20 May 1847. Bdsm Ashley Blackman and Harry Blackman.
WILLIAM W. BATTEN to LOUIZA BATTEN 1 Jan 1847. Bdsm William W. Batten and Pleasant Batten.
JOEL TISDALE to ELIZABETH BAYLEY 22 Feb 1847. Bdsm Joel Tisdale and Richardson Oneal.
CHARLES JOLLY to MARTHA WHEALLER 17 Jul 1844. Bdsm Charles Jolly and Richardson Oneal.
WILLIAM D. WOOD to MARY JOHNSON 23 Feb 1847. Bdsm William D. Wood and John Daniel.
THOMAS R. ROSE to MARY ALLEN 12 Jul 1847. Bdsm Thomas R. Rose and Ransom G. Allen.
LARKIN PEARCE to MARY ANN CORBETT 21 Dec 1846. Bdsm Larkin Pearce and William H. Oneal.
REUBEN WILDER to NANCY WHITLEY 26 Aug 1847. Bdsm Reuben Wilder and William T. Robertson.
WILLIAM WOODARD to ELIZA MOORE 15 Feb 1847. Bdsm William Woodard and Williamson Hinnant.
JOHN WADDELL to EMILY BIRD 25 Jan 1847. Bdsm John Waddell and Elbert A. Bryan.
HENRY H. HAYLES to PATSY PEARCE 24 Aug 1847. Bdsm Henry H. Hayles and John A. Allen.
HENRY RAPER to ANNY JOHNSON 21 Nov 1848. Bdsm Henry Raper and Perry

MARRIAGE BONDS

Rentfrow.
WESTBROOK LANGSTON to PATIENCE ANN BRITT 28 Feb 1844. Bdsm Westbrook Langston and Joel Joyner, Jr.
JOHN MASON to SUSAN PRICE 19 Sep 1846. Bdsm John Mason and Richardson Oneal.
NEEDHAM VINSON to CAROLINE EVANS 27 Apr 1846. Bdsm Needham Vinson and Young Bridgers.
NEEDHAM G. MASSENGILL to SALLY TEMPLE 17 Dec 1846. Bdsm George Keen.
ELY STRICKLAND to CORNELIA ONEAL 4 Nov 1844. Bdsm Ely Strickland and Larkin Lee.
JOHN WARRICK to ZILPHA JONES 29 Aug 1843. Bdsm Mecajah Cox.
SAMUEL M. JONES to ELIZABETH PARISH 1 May 1849. Bdsm Samuel M. Jones and Zachariah Jones.
MOSES WALLACE to BERTHA PRICE 25 Jan 1849. Bdsm Moses Wallace and Ashley Price.
HARROD PERRY to AUGUSTA C. PHILLIPS 4 Jun 1846. Bdsm Harrod Perry and James R. Pearce.
MABRY RENTFROW to "SENEY" ATKINSON 28 Aug 1844. Bdsm Jesse Parker.
JAMES HERITAGE to ELIZABETH JOHNSON 14 Mar 1843. Bdsm James Heritage and Kirby Johnson.
RANSOM RYALS to ELIZABETH DIXON 28 May 1844. Bdsm Robert W. Stevens.
WILLIAM WALKER to NANCY LEE 11 Jul 1844. Bdsm William Walker and William Price.
JAMES H. DURHAM to MARTHA BRIDGERS 17 Jul 1844. Bdsm James H. Durham and David Thomson.
WILLIS H. SANDERS to LUCINDA SMITH 19 Sep 1844. Bdsm Willis H. Sanders and William B. Sanders.
WILLIAM A. POWELL to MARTHA PENNY 16 Oct 1844. Bdsm William A. Powell and Augustus G. Jones.
GARRY JOHNSON to ELIZABETH BAILEY 9 Jan 1845. Bdsm Garry Johnson and Baldy G. Bailey.
FERDINAND ELLIS to POLLY ANN LUNSFORD 16 Oct 1844. Bdsm Ferdinand Ellis and John W. Ferrell.
HENDERSON GRAHAM to EASTER A. WHITLEY 5 Oct 1844. Bdsm Henderson Graham and Redick Warren.
BARNABA HOWELL to SARAH RAIFORD 9 Dec 1839. Bdsm Willie Howell.
WEST MASSEY to ? 4 Nov 1846. Bdsm West Massey and James Hinnant.
INGRAM LEE to SUSAN CAUDELL 22 Sep 1845. Bdsm Ingram Lee and Barzella Blackman.
ALFRED LASSITER to DIANNA JONES 28 Jan 1840. Bdsm William Lassiter.
JETHRO LEWIS to ZILPHA RENTFROW 15 Aug 1843. Bdsm Hinton M. Godwin.
GREEN KEMP to NANCY HOPKINS 29 Nov 1843. Bdsm Green Kemp and Wyatt Earp.
ARTHUR WILSON to MARY LEE 27 Feb 1844. Bdsm Arthur Wilson and William MacLeod.
BARDIN ROSE to MOLLY DAVIS 27 Feb 1844. Bdsm Bardin Rose and Pitts Kirby.
EDWIN ADAMS to MARIE HOLLAND 27 Jan 1844. Bdsm Edwin Adams and Jesse Holland.
DAVID LANCEFORD to EMILY HICKS 26 Sep 1843. Bdsm David Lanceford

JOHNSTON COUNTY MARRIAGES

and Thomas Lockhart.
GEORGE W. BOVEY to AMANTHA JOHNSON 1 Nov 1845. Bdsm George W. Bovey and William Johnson.
STEVENS G. THOMPSON to HARRIET NARION 27 Aug 1844. Bdsm Zadock Peacock.
DEMPSEY HAYS to FANNY BAREFOOT 25 Feb 1845. Bdsm Dempsey Hays and Thomas H. Thornton.
CHARLES J. BINGHAM to CASANDA LANGDON 21 Oct 1846. Bdsm Charles J. Bingham and John F. Sanders.
MATTHEW PEEBLES to EDITH EVANS 21 Oct 1846. Bdsm Matthew Peebles and Isaac Munden.
HENRY WIGGS to LINDA PEARCE 18 Nov 1842. Bdsm William Massey.
JOHN ELLIS to WIMMY BLACKMAN 4 Sep 1848. Bdsm William Thornton.
ALSEY JOHNSON to POLLY LEE 5 Nov 1842. Bdsm Alsey Johnson and Elijah Johnson.
HENRY L. CORDELL to SARAH ANN AVERA 6 Ob 1847. Bdsm Henry L. Cordell and Edwin Boykins.
ASHLEY PRICE to WELTHY ANN BARBER 31 Mar 1845. Bdsm Ashley Price and Warren Holland.
ASHLEY ATKINSON to NANCY WATSON 3 Dec 1849. Bdsm Ashley Atkinson and Elijah Atkinson.
LANSFORD LEE to "SMITHA" HOGG 3 Apr 1845. Bdsm Lansford Lee and Matthew Wall.
JAMES H. LEE to "LOUISER" AVERA 1 Mar 1848. Bdsm James H. Lee and George Kean.
EVERETT WADEL to SALLY LANGLEY 25 Mar 1845. Bdsm Everett Wadel and James Hinnant.
JOSEPH PITMAN to ELIZABETH RAPER 11 Mar 1845. Bdsm Joseph Pitman and Joseph Raper.
WILLIAM MITCHELL to EMILY EDWARDS 10 Jan 1846. Bdsm William Mitchell and Willie Holt.
ROBERT EDWARDS to APSABETH DAUGHTEREY 20 Dec 1845. Bdsm Robert Edwards and Benjamin B. Bronson.
EZIEKEL HOLLAND to JULIA A. WOODALL 16 Feb 1846. Bdsm Eziekel Holland and William H. Morning.
JAMES STEVENSON to CHARLOTTE LEE 3 or 4 Dec 1845. Bdsm James Stevenson and Josiah Evans.
GILBERT HAYLES to "LUIZER" STANSEL 9 May 1846. Bdsm Gilbert Hayles and Stephen Stansel.
JOHN PEEL to EDNY PRICE 7 Mar 1845. Bdsm John Peel and Perry Rentfrow.
JOHN H. RAINES to RINDY SPIVEY 13 Jan 1846. Bdsm John H. Raines and Dixon Spivey.
OWEN CONEGY to ANNY OLIVER 27 Oct 1845. Bdsm Owen Conegy and Barna Creech.
MERRIT RENTFROW to ZILPHA BARNES 20 Sep 1845. Bdsm Merrit Rentrfrow and Griffin M. Godwin.
JEREMIAH PITTMAN to ELIZABETH DAVIS 23 Dec 1844. Bdsm Levi Yelvington.
MATTHEW BATTEN to ABEDIENCE BROWN to 26 Feb 1844. Bdsm Matthew Batten and Jesse Parker.
JARRET WALLIS to NANCY CROCKER 4 Oct 1843. Bdsm Berry Price.

MARRIAGE BONDS

SOLOMON PEARSON to JULIA ANN TALTON 30 Dec 1844. Bdsm Solomon Pearce and Philip B. Raiford.
LITTLETON LEE to ELIZABETH H. CROCKER 11 May 1844. Bdsm Littleton Lee and Joseph Lee.
HENRY FARMER of Alabama to ELIZABETH SNEED 17 Nov 1842. Bdsm Henry Farmer and A. L. Ballenger.
GRIFFIN W. GODWIN to CHERRY RENTFROW 22 Nov 1844. Bdsm Griffin W. Godwin and Muntean M. Godwin.
THOMAS COATS to BEDY STEVENS 12 Jul 1845. Bdsm Thomas Coats and James T. Leach.
JOSEPH M. SMITH to JULIA INGRAM 24 Jul 1845. Bdsm John W. Ferrell.
ALLEN MORGAN to ANGELINE BARBER 26 Oct 184 Bdsm Allen Morgan and Peter R. Temple.
RUFFIN CARRELL to BETSY E. EVANS 23 Apr 1846. Bdsm Ruffin Carrell and Raiford Edwards.
GARRY CRUMPLER to ALSEY WATSON 13 Apr 1846. Bdsm Garry Crumpler and Ransom Holloman.
STEPHEN MORRIS to MARTHA ATKINSON 23 Oct 1845. Bdsm Stephen Morris and John Holt.
GEORGE W. HINNANT to JULIA FAIL 24 Mar 1842. Bdsm Theophilius Bagley.
JOHN MORGAN to PATSEY BLACKMAN 23 Oct 1845. Bdsm John Morgan and William Tart.
LEE HATCHER to LANY MOORE 8 Feb 1842. Bdsm James G. Raynor.
WILLIAM RICHARDSON to EMELINE EARP 20 Jan 1847. Bdsm William Richardson and Josiah Richardson.
WILLIAM BROADWELL to MARY ANN GULLY 19 Jan 1847. Bdsm William Broadwell and James B. Stallings.
LARRY GARDNER to EMELY SASSER 30 Jun 1846. Bdsm Larry Gardner and John Sasser.
DOCTOR C. JONES to PATSEY JOHNSON 31 Aug 1842. Bdsm Doctor C. Jones and Larkin Barber.
JOHN HARE to WILLY ONEAL 4 Oct 1842. Bdsm Henry Hayles.
JOSIAH JONES to JANE WILDER 2 Feb 1843. Bdsm Simon Jones.
THOMAS IVES to SUSAN AVERA 26 Oct 1842. Bdsm Thomas Ives and Hiram W. Husted.
HENRY INGRAM to JANE GREEN 15 Mar 1842. Bdsm Henry Ingram and G. W. Duncan.
AARON MASSENGILL to WILSEY HARPER 25 Mar 1846. Bdsm Robert W. Stevens and Aaron Massengill.
? STURDIVANT to ELEANOR LOCKHART 18 Mar 1840. Bdsm ? Sturdivant and David Thomson.
LOFTON ELLIS to PENNY POOL 23 Mar 1842. Bdsm Lofton Ellis and Samuel M. Turley.
JAMES S. WALTON to JANE E. BRIDGERS 15 Mar 1841. Bdsm Ransom Sanders.
DANIEL AYCOCK to ELIZABETH STANSEL 25 Oct 1844. Bdsm Daniel Aycock and Willie P. Stansel.
JOHN RAPER to NANCY MOORE 15 Sep 1845. Bdsm John Raper and Williamson Hinnant.
FESTUS MITCHINER to POLLY A. WILDER 11 Sep 1845. Bdsm Festus Mitchiner and John Mitchiner.

JOHNSTON COUNTY MARRIAGES

ALLEN BRANNON to PENNY EASON 11 Sep 1845. Bdsm Allen Brannon and Josiah Gay.
SIMEON WOODALL to MARY MOORE 20 Oct 1843. Bdsm Simeon Woodall and Alexander Stansell.
LEWIS WALLACE to "GANZADA" HUGHES 15 Aug 1845. Bdsm Lewis Wallace and Calvin Simpkins.
GERMAN G. JOHNSTON to ELIZABETH A. REAVES 23 Feb 1841. Bdsm Alfred Johnston.
OSBORN BAILY to "CRISY" EATMAN 23 Feb 1841. Bdsm Simon Godwin.
BRYAN S. SANDERS to MARY EARP 10 Mar 1847. Bdsm Bryan S. Sanders and Aaron Martin.
WILLIAM JOHNSTON to MARY RICHARDSON 20 Mar 1847. Bdsm William Johnston and John D. Howell.
AGRISSA MITCHINER to NANCY ANN ATKINSON 6 May 1847. Bdsm Agrissa Mitchiner and Henry H. Hobbs.
HARTNEY STRICKLAND to CATHARINE BAILEY 6 May 1847. Bdsm Hartney Strickland and Griffin Bailey.
HENRY HINNANT to MARTHA EDWARDS 24 Nov 1846. Bdsm Henry Hinnant and Josiah Hinnant.
JAMES ALVIN JONES to EMELINE C. BARBER 1 Feb 1847. Bdsm James Alvin Jones and Nathaniel B. Barber.
ZACHARIAH LANGDON to ELIZABETH JOHNSON 4 Feb 1847. Bdsm Zachariah Langdon and Caswell Langdon.
BERTY JOHNSON to RHODY STEVENS 8 Jul 1847. Bdsm Berty Johnson and Robert N. Gully.
MONTRAVILLE BIZZELL to FANNY M. EZZEL 19 Dec 1846. Bdsm Montraville Bizzell and Joel Joyner, Jr.
WILLIAM K. ONEAL to MARY E. ROBERTSON 8 Mar 1847. Bdsm William K. Oneal and Stephen Stansel.
MABRY HINNANT to SUSAN WIGGS 23 Feb 1847. Bdsm Noel Barnes.
ISHAM PARISH to SARAH STEVENS 23 Feb 1841. Bdsm James Lassiter.
MARTIN BALLANCE to LIZZY LUCAS 23 Feb 1841. Bdsm William F. Robertson.
BENJAMIN A. SMITH to CARON GOWER 10 Jun 1841. Bdsm William T. Robertson.
RANSOM BRANNON to NANCY JONES 24 Aug 1841. Bdsm Gray W. Thomas.
HENRY SMITH to NANCY INGRAM 24 Feb 1841. Bdsm Joel Lee.
MICHAEL THORNTON to MARTHA NOWLS 26 Apr 1841. Bdsm William Bundy.
HIRAM HOLMS to SUSAN CAROLINE THORNTON 8 Apr 1841. Bdsm Right Ryals.
WILLIAM ROBBARDS to SALLY GRIFFITH 28 Jul 1841. Bdsm Isaac Beasly.
BEN B. ROSE to LIZZY ELDRIDGE 10 May 1841. Bdsm Jeremiah L. George.
CLINTON WELLONS to NANCY DODD 19 Feb 1842. Bdsm Zachariah Jones.
GREEN JOHNSON to POLLY SMITH 7 Oct 1841. Bdsm Allen Nichols.
ZACHARIAH EDWARDS to ZERILLY PADEN 9 Mar 1842. Bdsm William H. Creech.
MATTHEWS McCULLERS to SARAH S. WARREN 9 May 1846. Bdsm Matthew McCullers and Willie T. Jones.
ALFORD JOHNSON to LYDIA M. REAVES 7 Aug 1846. Bdsm Alford Johnson and John B. Johnson.
HAYWOOD MARTIN to EMILY DIXON 1 Dec 1841. Bdsm Benjamin Godwin.
JOSIAH BATTEN to MARTHA STANSILL 1 Mar 1842. Bdsm Ransom Sanders.

MARRIAGE BONDS

ELIJAH P. JOHNSON to SALLY LEE 1 Mar 1842. Bdsm James Johnson.
ELLY JONES to PATSY FAIL 2 Mar 1841. Bdsm Needham Fail.
HENRY JOHNSON to FANNY WELSH 30 Mar 1842. Bdsm Henry Johnson and Haywood Martin.
JETHRO WOODARD to BETSY WOODARD 24 Aug 1841. Bdsm Jethro Woodard and Tobias Woodard.
WILLIAM H. CREECH to MARY RAPER 30 Sep 1841. Bdsm Kedar Creech.
JESSE STANLY, JR. to BARTSHEBA STANLEY 25 Aug 1841. Bdsm Silas Webb.
BENJAMIN J. GLOVER to MILLY ATKINSON 27 Sep 1841. Bdsm Perry Rentfrow.
HOWELL YELVINGTON to WILLEY BROWN 11 Oct 1841. Bdsm Joel Garner.
THOMAS WHITE to BEDY HALL 25 Aug 1841. Bdsm Bryan Pulley.
WILLIAM K. BENNET to ELIZABETH BULLS 3 Aug 1841. Bdsm William H. Morning.
JOHN W. BOON to ALICE KELLY 14 Aug 1841. Bdsm Robert W. Sanders.
RICHARD MANNING to MARY PORTER 25 Sep 1841. Bdsm William R. Lee.
JESSE STEPHENSON to LOTTY STEPHENSON 1 Oct 1841. Bdsm Allen Stephenson.
BRYANT WILLIAMS to BETSY E. INGRAM 28 Oct 1848. Bdsm Bryant Williams and B. C. Blackman.
GILLIS HALES to PATSY "STAND" 27 Oct 1848. Bdsm Gillis Hales and John T. Hatcher.
GREEN JORDAN to DILLEY HONEYCUT 3 Mar 1842. Bdsm Green Jordan and Hayward Martin.
STEPHEN BROWN to WILLY STARLING 17 Feb 1841. Bdsm Charles Hatcher and Stephen Brown.
JOEL GARNER to MARTHA YELVINGTON 6 Feb 1841. Bdsm Eli Garner.
WILLIAM M. BRADDY to ? 9 Jan 1841. Bdsm Cullen Strickland.
WILLIAM RAINES to TEMPLE JOYNER 21 Jan 1841. Bdsm Henry Raines.
A. W. RICHARDSON to CELIA WHITLEY 24 Jan 1841. Bdsm John Green.
SIR WILLIAM ALLEN to RIDLEY ALLEN 27 Jan 1841. Bdsm Alfred Johnson.
BRITTON THORNTON to MATILDA WORLEY 21 Jan 1841. Bdsm John P. Williams.
WILLIAM SALMON to ATHEY WALLACE 3 Feb 1847. Bdsm William Salmon and Robert Massengill.
EPHRAIM BATTEN to CYNTHIA EATMAN 4 Aug 1845. Bdsm Ephraim Batten and John Broadwell.
JOHN TART to SUSAN INGRAM 26 Feb 1844. Bdsm John Tart and Westbrook Lee.
ALVIN PEEDIN to NANCY ANN E. EDWARDS 22 May 1845. Bdsm Alvin Peedin and Newit Peedin.
JOHN WOODARD to MARIAH TINER 18 Jun 1845. Bdsm John Woodard, Joseph Woodard and Green H. Holland.
JOHN R. CARRELL to "LUETY" ARTUS 19 Apr 1845. Bdsm John R. Carrell and Isaac W. Stallings.
WILLIAM I. SMITH to "SIDDY" BEAL 26 Feb 1844. Bdsm William I. Smith and Needham Gulley.
ABEL ELLIS to RENEY DUNN 11 May 1845. Bdsm Abel Ellis and Henry Gwin.
ELISHA TISDALE to NANCY ONEAL 5 May 1845. Bdsm Elisha Tisdale and Everett P. Stevens.

JOHNSTON COUNTY MARRIAGES

LEVI BOOTH to POLLY EAVENS 12 May 1845. Bdsm Levi Booth and William James.
WILLIAM HASTINGS to LUCY ANN McCULLERS 19 Jan 1841. Bdsm William McCullers.
JOHN NARON to PATIENCE WATKINS 4 Jul 1842. Bdsm John Naron and Josiah Hollimon.
AMOS STEVENSON to SALLY PARRISH 5 Apr 1845. Bdsm Amos Stevenson and Ransom M. Stevenson.
WILLIAM STEWART to MARY JERNIGAN 26 Sep 1848. Bdsm William Stewart and John C. Hood.
B. C. BLACKMAN to ? 23 Aug 1847. Bdsm B. C. Blackman and Powell Blackman.
HENRY EDWARDS to ZILPHA STARLING 5 Oct 1849. Bdsm Henry Edwards and Reding Jenkins.
WILLIAM CREECH to NANCY SPENCER 21 Jan 1850. Bdsm William Creech and Robert Edwards.
SETH T. EAVEN to MARY JOHNSTON 8 Jul 1845. Bdsm Seth T. Eaven and Joel Clifton.
LEWIS CAPPS to SALLY HALL 19 Dec 1843. Bdsm William Capps.
EVERETT P. STEVENS to NICY STEVENS 18 Aug 1848. Bdsm William Oneal and Everett P. Stevens.
IREDELL PEACOCK to HARRIET BALLANCE 29 Feb 1848. Bdsm Iredell Peacock and G. H. Holland.
KEDAR JERNIGAN to LEWEY BRYAN 29 Feb 1848. Bdsm Kedar Jernigan and Benjamin F. Hudson.
PARKER OVERBY to RACHEL WADDELL 1 Nov 1848. Bdsm Parker Overby and William A. Jones.
WILLIAM SASSER to MARTHA WATSON 29 Jan 1848. Bdsm William Sasser and James Davis.
THOMAS DURHAM to NANCY GRISWOLD 27 Sep 1849. Bdsm Thomas Durham.
FORT T. PHILLIPS to ELIZABETH RAINS 11 Jan 1847. Bdsm Fort T. Phillips and William H. Hastings.
MORTIMER CULLON to RACHEL LOCKHART 7 Sep 1848. Bdsm Mortimer Cullon and William Henry Cullon.
AQUILLA SUGGS to MARY BARBER 19 Aug 1848. Bdsm Aquilla Suggs and Young A. Barber.
WILLIAM SAMPSON to MARY ANN RAIFORD 5 Oct 1848. Bdsm William Sampson and A. D. Wortham.
LARKIN BARBER to WILSEY MASSENGILL 25 Mar 1843. Bdsm Ashley Barber.
ROBBIN EDWARDS to ELIZABETH OLIVER 22 Aug 1843. Bdsm Robbin Edwards and William Oliver.
MERRIT WOODALL to HARRIET ALLEN 4 Aug 1843. Bdsm Robert W. Stevens.
THOMAS McGEE to PATSY BELL 4 Aug 1843. Bdsm Robert W. Stevens.
ALFORD LEE to ELIZABETH WALSTON 20 Apr 1843. Bdsm James H. Lee.
BYTHAN ALFORD to JOANNA BARNES 19 Aug 1843. Bdsm Bythan Alford and William S. Ballenger.
JOHN HOLMES to EASTHER WOODALL 27 Feb 1843. Bdsm John Holmes and Robert W. Stevens.
MARK WADE to "TEDY" MESSER 28 Mar 1843. Bdsm Robert W. Stevens.
SOLOMON DAUGHTRY to ESTHER CAPPS 31 Jul 1843. Bdsm Solomon Daughtry and John Massey.
WILLIAM B. GULLEY to PHEREBE KELLY 4 Oct 1849. Bdsm William B.

MARRIAGE BONDS

Gulley and A. G. Thornton.
JOSEPH WATSON to MARTHA KIRBY 27 Aug 1849. Bdsm Joseph Watson and Robert Raper.
DANIEL H. HOLLAND to SARAH AVERA 11 May 1843. Bdsm William H. Morning.
B. F. HUDSON to BETSY ELDRIDGE 27 Aug 1849. Bdsm B. F. Hudson and J. J. Hudson.
JAMES FEARRELL to CHERRY WATSON 1 Jul 1848. Bdsm James Fearrell and Reddin Newsom.
HENRY DIMKINS to MEZANEY COLLIER 23 Jan 1850. Bdsm Henry Dimkins and Godfrey Stansell.
WILLIAM PARNOLD to CLARKY PARNOLD 10 May 1843. Bdsm Ely Garner.
JESSE HOLLAND to "JEMBY" GODWIN 11 Mar 1843. Bdsm Wiley Godwin.
HENDERSON CROCKER to NANCY ANDREWS 25 Jul 1843. Bdsm Josiah Gay.
WHITLEY MESSER to SUSAN JOHNSTON 24 Jun 1843. Bdsm John Messer.
JOHN AVERA, JR. to ANN MARIAH BELL 9 Aug 1843. Bdsm James H. Durham.
ALFRED JOHNSON to CENY WHITTINGTON 21 Jun 1843. Bdsm Frederick Holmes.
DANIEL BON to "XEXEY" SASSER 26 Feb 1848. Bdsm Daniel Bon and Matthew Cullen.
JOHN JONES to CASSANDRA LASHLEY 10 Feb 1848. Bdsm John Jones and Benjamin Jones.
EDMUND JOHNSTON to SUSAN ALLEN 22 Feb 1848. Bdsm Edmund Johnston and Thomas Allen.
JOHN R. THOMSON to MARTHA J. PEEDIN 8 Jan 1849. Bdsm John R. Thomson.
WILLIAM CHURCHILL to CALLY PEARCE 24 Jun 1848. Bdsm William Churchill and Charles Howell.
SOLOMON LOCKHART to WINIFRED AVERA 25 Apr 1844. Bdsm Solomon Lockhart and Matthew Avera.
HARRIS H. WHITLEY to MARSELINE VINSON 9 Sep 1844. Bdsm Harris H. Whitley and Thomas T. Grice.
ZADOCK PEACOCK to NANCY HINNANT 26 Mar 1844. Bdsm Zadock Peacock and Stanford Creech.
JOSIAH BLACKMAN to BETSEY JERNIGAN 10 Jan 1849. Bdsm Josiah Blackman and George P. Rose.
J. W. PHILLIPS to CAROLINE PITMAN 20 Sep 1848. Bdsm Bryan R. Hinnant and J. W. Phillips.
BRYAN SMITH to MARY WHITLEY 16 Nov 1843. Bdsm Samuel S. Turner.
WILLIE JONES to DELLA HARRISON 13 Apr 1843. Bdsm James J. Farmer.
JAMES CORBET to CHELLY WIGGS 7 Nov 1848. Bdsm Lordrick A. Corbet and James Corbet.
NATHAN DEMING to SUSANNA MORGAN 23 Aug 1847. Bdsm Nathan Deming and Powell Blackman.
JESSE BEASLEY to FANNY MOORE 30 Sep 1841. Bdsm Jesse Beasley and J.I. Adams.
PETER W. WHITLEY to ZILLY WHITLEY 14 Nov 1843. Bdsm Peter W. Whitley and Jacob Johnson.
LYNN B. SANDERS to POLLY ANN SANDERS 22 Nov 1843. Bdsm Ashley Sanders.
AUGUSTUS JONES to HARRIET G. LOCKHART 6 Apr 1843. Bdsm James H.

JOHNSTON COUNTY MARRIAGES

Durham.
WILLIAM K. McCULLERS, JR. to MARY E. BELL 25 May 1843. Bdsm John D. Pate.
JACOB FLOWERS to PENNY COATS 14 Nov 184 Bdsm Jacob Flowers and William H. Coats.
FRANCIS LANGHON to ZILPHA WEAVER 28 Aug 184 Bdsm Francis Langhon and Powell Blackman.
THOMAS DURHAM to NANCY GRISWOLD 27 Sep 1849. Bdsm Thomas Durham and James Hinnant.
JAMES HOLT to ARABELLA CLARK 10 Jun 184 Bdsm James Holt and Richard Green.
JOHN MINDEN to PHEREBY JOHNSON 2 May 1843. Bdsm Hardy Barber.
JOHN DAUGHTRY to PATSY STRICKLAND 12 May 1848. Bdsm John Daughtry and George Daughtry.
JOHN MESSER to NANCY FLUELLER 2 Jun 1848. Bdsm John Messer and John B. Allen.
LEMMUEL BIRD to NANCY ENNIS 15 Aug 1848. Bdsm Lemmuel Bird and William H. Morgan.
NEEDHAM SNIPES to TEMPY A. WALL 8 Jan 1850. Bdsm Needham Snipes and Needham I. Whitley.
WILLIAM J. BARBER to SALLY THOMAS 3 May 1848. Bdsm Robert W. Stevens.
WILLIAM H. HAYLES to NANCY JORDAN 1 Jun 1843. Bdsm Elijah Todd.
RICHARD S. DUNN to PENELOPE RYALS 8 Dec 1849. Bdsm Richard S. Dunn and Robert W. Stevens.
ELIJAH A. CAPPS to REBECCA THOMSON 7 Jan 1850. Bdsm Elijah A. Capps and Elijah H. Phillips.
SANDY BARNETT to JULIA CRAWFORD 29 Dec 1849. Bdsm Sandy Barnett and Stephen Dawson.
WILLIAM JOHNSON to SALLY A.I. POPE 1 Nov 1848. Bdsm William Johnson and Stephen Johnson.
BUD JERNIGAN to SALLY A. ADAMS 1 Nov 1848. Bdsm Bud Jernigan and John C. Hood.
BARNEY B. HINNANT to NANCY ANN PEEDIN 1 Jan 1850. Bdsm Barney B. Hinnant and Thaddeus Whitley.
JOHN LASHLEY to SOPHIA TURNER 2 Jan 1850. Bdsm John Lashley and Henry Bell.
GEORGE POOL to EDNY GODWIN 12 Apr 1848. Bdsm George Pool and Jesse Parker.
JOHN B. BECKWITH to ANN G. THOMSON 22 Feb 1849. Bdsm John B. Beckwith and William H. Morning.
JOSIAH PRICE to ULRICA FERRELL 22 Oct 1848. Bdsm Josiah Price and Thomas L. Jordan.
LODWICK TOOL to SALLY LEE 28 Dec 1843. Bdsm Barna Gwin.
WILLIAM H. CAPPS to EMILY JANE RAINS 3 Jan 1843. Bdsm Elijah Capps.
JAMES BEASLY to POLLY JERNIGAN 29 Dec 1843. Bdsm Henry Moore.
JAMES PEEDIN (son of James Peedin) to LINSEY CROCKER 26 Dec 1843. Bdsm Willie Peedin.
ROBERT DENNING to POLLY TART 28 Mar 1848. Bdsm Robert Denning and Powell Blackman.
HARRISON PITTMAN to SMITHY EASON 19 Dec 1843. Bdsm Elisha Pittman.
SOLOMON WATSON to HARRIET HOOKS 25 Dec 1843. Bdsm Solomon Watson

MARRIAGE BONDS

and Bryant R. Hinnant.
ALLEN WEST to LUCY BAKER 28 Mar 1843. Bdsm Starling Massengill.
ALEXANDER J. LEE to SUSANNAH LEE 28 Apr 1842. Bdsm David B. Adams.
JAMES B. JOHNSON to EMILY COATS 23 Mar 1842. Bdsm William H. Coats.
WILLIAM GARNER to PATSEY BATTEN 14 Nov 1843. Bdsm William Garner and James Garner.
ISAAC INGRAM to BETSY LEE 8 Apr 1848. Bdsm Isaac Ingram and James H. Corbet.
GEORGE DUNCAN to LOUISA DURHAM 24 Oct 1848. Bdsm George Duncan and Henry Duncan.
STANFORD CREECH to MARTHA ELLEN HORN 11 Apr 1848. Bdsm Henry Hinnant and Stanford Creech.
STEPHEN H. WATLEY to CLARKEY RICHARDSON 9 Sep 1848. Bdsm Stephen H. Watley and Thomas H. Ligon.
JAMES STALLINGS to FANNY LEGON 9 Dec 1848. Bdsm James Stallings and Richmond Stallings.
JOHN W. BROWN to LUCINDA BATTEN 9 Dec 1848. Bdsm John W. Brown and Edwin Batten.
HENDERSON GARNER to JOANNY ATKINSON 21 Feb 1848. Bdsm Henderson Garner and Auston Hatcher.
THOMAS R. YOUNGBLOOD to CAROLINE LUNCEFORD 17 May 1848. Bdsm Thomas R. Youngblood and J. H. Youngblood.
BENJAMIN CARRELL to ELIZABETH PEEDIN 27 Dec 1848. Bdsm Benjamin Carrell and H. Pilkinton.
WILLIAM HOLLAND to MARTHA KIRBY 30 Dec 1847. Bdsm William Holland and Harris Rose.
NEEDHAM BARNES to CATHARINE H. AVERA 20 Mar 1849. Bdsm Needham Barnes and Sir B. Sanders.
ISHAM WILDER to WILTHY HOPKINS 20 Oct 1849. Bdsm Isham Wilder and Samuel W. Smith.
THOMAS L. VINCENT to SARAH A. E. EASON 25 Nov 1846. Bdsm Thomas L. Vincent and Needham Stevens.
STEPHEN BAGLEY to MARTHA J. JOYNER 22 May 1849. Bdsm Stephen Bagley and Minton M. Godwin.
ROBERT RAPER to NANCY WATSON 16 Jan 1849. Bdsm James H. Hinnant and Robert Raper.
ISAAC LAMB to PIETY PEELE 15 Feb 1849. Bdsm Isaac Lamb and Stephen Peele.
TURNER JOYNER to WINIFRED DUNCAN 14 Dec 1849. Bdsm Turner Joyner and Elbert A. Bryan.
CALVIN WREN to "PIETY" STEVENSON 13 Jan 1846. Bdsm Calvin Wren and Josiah Evans.
ISAIAH WIGGS to ANNY COOLEEN 22 Oct 1847. Bdsm Isaiah Wiggs and Stephen Bagley.
JOSIAH BRANNON to WILLEY JONES 26 Nov 1845. Bdsm Josiah Brannon and Jones Hinnant.
DAVID SMITH to KERON ANN SANDERS 8 Apr 1841. Bdsm David Smith and Bryan Smith.
WILLIAM B. THOMPSON to CLARY HOLLIMAN 18 Feb 1843. Bdsm Stephen Thompson.
HENRY HAMBLETON to PIETY EDWARDS 6 Sep 1842. Bdsm Henry Hambleton and Kedar Whitley.

JOHNSTON COUNTY MARRIAGES

BRYANT BARFIELD to ELEANOR ADAMS 31 Dec 1844. Bdsm Right A. Adams and Bryant Barfield.
RUFFIN COCKRELL to WILLY SILIVENT 1 Jan 1849. Bdsm Ruffin Cockrell and J. Oliver Rains.
JOHN B. HARPER to RHODA LANGDON 1 Nov 1848. Bdsm John B. Harper and Bartlet Harper.
DAVID B. ADAMS to REBENA DAVIS 16 Oct 1848. Bdsm David B. Adams and W. F. S. Alsten.
ARTHUR LANGLEY to POLLY COLLINS 17 Jan 1849. Bdsm Arthur Langley and Nicholas Thomson.
JOHN C. HOOD to CHARLOTTE PEACOCK 28 Nov 1848. Bdsm John C. Hood and W. S. Ballenger.
ASHLEY BARBER to NANCY MASSINGELL 14 Sep 1842. Bdsm Ashley Barber and Theophilus Barber.
ELBERT BRYAN to MARY ANN STALLINGS 25 Jan 1843. Bdsm Elijah Lancaster.
HARRY CROCKER to EMILY CLARK 28 Jan 1843. Bdsm James H. Durham.
HILLIARD PRICE to ISABEL BARBER 4 Oct 1842. Bdsm Solomon Lockhart.
WILLIS JOHNSON to PENNY STANLY 5 Aug 1842. Bdsm Willis Johnson and Starling Massingill.
JOHN BAKER to WINIFRED BLANEFORD 24 Jul 1844. Bdsm John Baker and John Stanly.
JOSHUA JOHNSON to EDITH INGRAM 2 May 1849. Bdsm Joshua Johnson and Willis T. Sanders.
WILLIAM CAPPS to CATHERINE CREECH 20 Jan 1847. Bdsm William Capps and Willie Holt.
ALLEN CAPPS to SALLY STRICKLAND 9 Dec 1846. Bdsm Allen Capps and John G. Gully.
JOHN DODD to ANGELINA JOHNSTON 4 Oct 1842. Bdsm Willie Dodd.
JOHN McLANE to ELIZABETH ANN YOUNG 29 Nov 1842. Bdsm Joel G. Hutson.
WRILEY NARON to GILLY BAILEY 29 Nov 1842. Bdsm Samuel W. Woody.
BENJAMIN WELLONS to SARAH BARNES 29 Mar 1849. Bdsm Benjamin Wellons, Ezekiel Rogers and K. M. C. Williamson.
NEEDHAM BROWN to EDITH ROBERTS 28 Apr 1849. Bdsm Needham Brown and Austen Hatcher.
JAMES A. WOODALL, JR. TO MARY DIXON 9 Sep 1847. Bdsm James A. Woodall, Jr. and William W. Morgan.
HENRY GERHEARDT to EMILY JANE CARTER 15 Mar 1842. Bdsm Henry Gerheardt.
THOMAS EGERTON to SARAH WOOTEN 9 Oct 1845. Bdsm Thomas Egerton and Thomas G. Hinnant.
JESSE ADAMS to HARRIET DUNN 4 Dec 1843. Bdsm Starling Massengill.
MARK COLLINS to ELIZABETH DODD 31 Jan 1846. Bdsm Mark Collins and Willie Dodd.
LOUIS LINDSEY to MARTHA GULLY 18 Sep 1847. Bdsm Louis Lindsey and Alvin Thornton.
CHARLES M. BUSBEE to MARY ANN WEBB 24 Jun 1844. Bdsm Charles M. Busbee and Reddin Webb.
BENJAMIN GODWIN to ELIZABETH H. BARBER 26 Nov 1842. Bdsm Simon Turner.
JAMES M. WHITLEY to NANCY RAIFORD 24 Aug 1842. Bdsm James M.

MARRIAGE BONDS

Whitley and T. Whitley.
NICKEY THOMPSON to SUSAN LEE 18 Aug 1845. Bdsm Nickey Thompson and Dempsey Grant.
JOHN EDWARDS to CAROLINE EDWARDS 22 Apr 1846. Bdsm John Edwards, William S. Ballenger and Bryan Sanders.
RIGDON WISE to CHRISTIAN LOCKANY 27 Mar 1848. Bdsm Rigdon Wise and N. B. Stevens.
WILLIE ALTMAN to SARAH C. TOLER 30 Jan 1849. Bdsm Willie Altman and Colie Toler.
HARRY BARNES to CINTHA DAVIS 3 May 1849. Bdsm Harry Barnes and Pitts Kirby.
WILLIAM POPE to ELIZABETH TEMPLE 25 Oct 1849. Bdsm William Pope and Barzella Blackman.
JAMES M. CORBET to MATTIE CROCKER 20 Apr 1849. Bdsm James M. Corbet and Lodrick Corbet.
JOHN POPE to AMY BALLANCE 17 Feb 1848. Bdsm John Pope and Iredell Peacock.
LARKIN CREECH to DELANY GEARALD 30 Apr 1849. Bdsm Larkin Creech and Alvin Creech.
JAMES K. CORBET to MARY ADAMS 13 Apr 1844. Bdsm James K. Corbet and Robert Massengill.
SANDERS EASON to MILLY PARNOLD 18 Mar 1844. Bdsm Sanders Eason and Solomon Parnold.
JAMES FERREL to JINCY RICHARDSON 28 Feb 1844. Bdsm James Ferrel and Calvin Richardson.
JOHN ADAMS to OLIEF BAILEY 25 Aug 1842. Bdsm John Adams and Gray W. Thomas.
BRYAN LYLES to MILLY PRICE 27 Feb 1849. Bdsm Bryan Lyles and Richardson Oneal.
JAMES HOLMS to MARY ANN BEASLY 25 Mar 1844. Bdsm James Holms and Heron Holms.
RANSOM M. STEVENSON to MATILDA HOLLAND 22 Oct 1841. Bdsm Ransom M. Stevenson and Amos Stevenson.
JEREMIAH L. GEORGE to MARY HUTSON 29 Feb 1849. Bdsm Jeremiah L. George and Sir William Blackman.
ELDRIDGE STEWART to DELANEY MATTHEWS 13 Jun 1846. Bdsm Eldridge Stewert and Robert W. Stevens.
JARRET T. JOHNSON to SUSAN JOHNSON 26 Nov 1842. Bdsm Moses A. Johnson.
SUTTON BYRD to MARGARET JOHNSON 23 Oct 1845. Bdsm Sutton Byrd and Isaac Johnston.
ELI MORGAN to MARIA SASSER 21 Jun 1845. Bdsm Eli Morgan and Jacob A. Stevens.
RANSOM HINTON to BETSY FLOID 20 Jan 1845. Bdsm Ranson Hinton and Aven Floid.
EPHRAIM O. BEASLEY to EDITH AVERYT 18 Dec 1845. Bdsm Ephraim O. Beasley and James Holmes.
RANSOM PARRISH to HARRIET JOHNSON 4 Feb 1846. Bdsm Ransom Parrish and McCoy Johnson.
ZACHARIAH HOULDER to NANCY CORBET 23 Aug 1845. Bdsm Zachariah Houlder and Allen Nicholas.
STEPHEN TEDER to ELIZABETH SIMPSON 16 Feb 1849. Bdsm Stephen Teder

and Harris Hawley.
ROBERT EDWARDS to TEMPY CREECH 21 Jan 1845. Bdsm Robert Edwards and Peleg Massey.
GIDDEON KEAN to SALLY ANN STANLY 3 Feb 1848. Bdsm Giddeon Kean and George Kean.
STEPHEN BOYKINS to SALLY GRISUE 30 Aug 1843. Bdsm Jesse Boykins.
DAVID D. PARISH to MARY ANN JONES 30 Jan 1849. Bdsm David D. Parish.
SIR WILLIAM STANLY to REBECCA STRICKLAND 17 Jan 1843. Bdsm John W. Stanly.
JOHN A. GRIFFIN to MARY WREN 11 May 1844. Bdsm John A. Griffin and Zachariah Tiner.
JACOB WOODARD to POLLY HAWLEY 26 Apr 1844. Bdsm Jacob Woodard and Garry Sillavant.
JOHN HOLT to EMILY WOODARD 30 Jan 1849. Bdsm John Holt and Elijah Capps.
JOSEPH HARE to LUCINDA STANSEL 23 Oct 1845. Bdsm Joseph Hare and John Hare.
JORDAN SANDERS to EMELINE MASSINGILL 5 May 1849. Bdsm Jordan Sanders and Allen Sanders.
ALBERT AYCOCK to JOANNY BAGLEY 11 Oct 1848. Bdsm James Faulk and Albert Aycock.
DAVID BELL to SARAH HARDY 2 Dec 1848. Bdsm David Bell and William Thornton.
HARRIS BOYKINS to MARY KENT 22 Apr 1844. Bdsm Harris Boykins and John S. Boykins.
STEPHEN BOYKINS to MILBRY KENT 19 Jan 1839. Bdsm Nelson Kent.
JAMES W. MORGAN to LUCY JOHNSON 1 Sep 1847. Bdsm Zachariah Tiner.
JOHN T. BATTIN to DOLLY BATTIN 30 Jan 1847. Bdsm James H. Battin and John T. Battin.
GIDEON WOODALL to TABITH DIXON 16 Feb 1848. Bdsm Gideon Woodall and Robert W. Stevens.
JOHN BAREFOOT to ELIZABETH LEE 25 Jan 1848. Bdsm John A. Barefoot and Willie Barefoot.
JOSEPH RAPER to SALLY WELLONS 16 Feb 1848. Bdsm Joseph Raper and Joshua Creech.
GEORGE BRASSEL to CINTHA GARNER 28 Jan 1848. Bdsm George Brassel and Jacob Brassel.
WILLIAM G. HALL to JANE LESSORD 29 Aug 1843. Bdsm Thomas H. Legon.
JOHN SASSER to BETSY SELLARS 9 Dec 1846. Bdsm John Sasser and William Holliman.
HARRIS ROSE to ZILPHA HOLLAND 8 Dec 1846. Bdsm Harris Rose and Josiah Hinnant.
PLYER BARBER to LUZANNA DUNCAN 15 Oct 1842. Bdsm Ruffin W. Tomlinson.
JOEL GREEN HUDSON to ALEY ALLEN 20 Oct 1842. Bdsm John L. Bryan.
MATTHEW WILDER to JANE AVERA 6 Feb 1843. Bdsm Matthew Wilder and George Price.
WILLIAM ADAMS to SALLY BLACKMAN 27 Apr 1847. Bdsm William Adams and Benjamin Moore.
STATON JOHNSON to PATIENCE BARNES 26 Oct 1846. Bdsm Staton Johnson and Stanly Kirby.

MARRIAGE BONDS

JOHN R. THOMSON to MARTHA J. PEEDIN 8 Jan 1849. Bdsm John R. Thomson and Devereaux Thomson.
JOSEPH WOODARD to ELVY EDWARDS 27 Sep 1847. Bdsm Joseph Woodard and Henry Hamilton.
CURTIS HODGE to SALLY HOBBS 3 Feb 1843. Bdsm Curtis Hodge.
WESTLY HARPER to CREACY ANN JONES 21 Nov 1842. Bdsm Ashley Barber.
HENRY WRIGHT STRICKLAND to ELIZABETH BAKER 24 Sep 1842. Bdsm Henry Wright Strickland and John Stanly.
THOMAS EDGERTON, JR. to ZILPHA PEARSON 14 Nov 1843. Bdsm Thomas Edgerton, Jr and Lazarus Pearson.
SIMON BARBER to JOSEPH ANN ADAMS 19 Oct 1849. Bdsm Simon Barber and William M. Morgan.
ALSEY SELLARS to CINTHA MILLINER 13 Jun 1846. Bdsm Alsey Sellers and Bryan Smith.
IRWIN SCOTT to LECY INGRAM 24 Jul 1844. Bdsm Irwin Scott and Nicholas Lee.
DEVEREAUX HARPER to JULIA BARBER 1 May 1847. Bdsm Devereaux Harper and John R. Harper.
HARRY JOHNSON to ELIZA THORNTON 23 Mar 1847. Bdsm Harry Johnson and James B. Bryan.
ACRIL P. CLIFTON to REDLEY JONES 1 Aug 184. Bdsm Acril P. Clifton and J. Clifton.
SOLOMON BARNES to NANCY E. SPENCE 26 Mar 1849. Bdsm Solomon Barnes and Joseph Barnes.
MOSES WEAVER to ELIZABETH HAYES 1 Nov 184. Bdsm Moses Weaver and Robert W. Stevens.
WILLIAM THORNTON to "MONY" BELLE 3 Feb 1846. Bdsm William Thornton.
BENNET BARNES to CELETY RENTFROW 27 Feb 1844. Bdsm Bennet Barnes and Mabry Rentfrow.
SAMUEL WALTON to JULIA PATE 24 Jan 1843. Bdsm Ruffin W. Tomlinson.
HARRY BLACKMAN to POLLY "AVERY" 26 Dec 1844. Bdsm Harry Blackman and George Keen.
ADEN BROWN to LENEY PITMAN 8 Nov 1845. Bdsm Stephen Brown.
GEORGE BARBER to COREAM BARBER 3 Apr 1846. Bdsm George Barber and Pyler Barber.
CALVIN R. WALLACE to MILLY CROCKER 15 Jan 1846. Bdsm Calvin R. Wallace and Daniel H. Price.
WILLIAM B. SANDERS to CANDICE E. STALLINGS 1 Jun 1846. Bdsm William B. Sanders and Robert Sanders.
WILLIAM J. ETHERIDGE to LUCY J. SANDERS 27 Feb 1844. Bdsm Thomas Bagley and William J. Etheridge.
HENRY H. LEE, JR. to ELIZABETH MASSENGILL 25 Aug 1848. Bdsm Henry H. Lee, Jr. and Robert Massengill.
JOHN G. STANSELL to RHODA JONES 1 Sep 1848. Bdsm John G. Stansell and John B. Beckwith.
JOHN ALFRED to POLLY ANN AVERA 27 Dec 18?. Bdsm John Alfred and James E. Barkam.
LOYED G. RIDGLEY to "RAVENA" HELME 7 Jan 1841. Bdsm Loyed G. Ridgley and William H. Morning.
JAMES H. THOMAS to MARIAH STANLY 21 Dec 1846. Bdsm George Kean and James H. Thomas.
JACKSON SNIPES to MARTHA WALL 6 Mar 1848. Bdsm Jackson Snipes and

JOHNSTON COUNTY MARRIAGES

William K. Lanester.
JESSE BROWN to ELIZABETH STEARLING 15 Mar 1848. Bdsm Jesse Brown and Thomas Brown.
JOHN C. HALLY to BETSY H. LANGHAM 23 Feb 1848. Bdsm Francis Langham and John C. Hally.
RUFFIN COCKRELL to SYLVA WATSON 9 Dec 1846. Bdsm Ruffin Cockrell and Ervin Cockrell.
JOSIAH STRICKLAND to SALLY HOLT 15 Jan 1847. Bdsm Josiah Strickland and Peleg Massey.
ELY SASSER to "ELIZER" GAME 20 Jan 1849. Bdsm Ely Sasser and Benajah Williams.
JOHN TART TO WINIFRED LEE 15 Mar 1849. Bdsm John Tart and Young J. Lee.
LOWANNA LEE to "NORCISA" LEGON 1 Feb 1848. Bdsm Lowanna Lee and Jacob B. Fulgham.
SAMUEL SMITH to PATIENCE CHAMBLEE 7 Feb 1848. Bdsm Samuel Smith and Bryan Hocut.
ELISHA STANLY to PENNY PEOPLES 20 May 1843. Bdsm Amos Johnson and Elisha Stanly.
McKOY JOHNSTON to SARAH JOHNSON 9 Feb 1848. Bdsm McKoy Johnston and Henry C. Johnson.
CALVIN WALLACE to AVEY PEOPLES 1 Feb 1848. Bdsm Calvin Wallace and Elisha Wallace.
JOHN CAUDLE to CAROLINE GREEN 26 Jul 18?. Bdsm John Caudle and Dudley Barber.
BRITTON STEPHENSON to NANCY ENNIS 28 Jul 18?. Bdsm Britton Stephenson and A. J. Leach.
SAPER HOLLAND to MARTHA PRICE 28 July 1850. Bdsm Saper Holland and Perren Price.
ROY THOMSON to SARAH LUIS 26 Jul 1850. Bdsm Roy Thomson.
ALBERT PARRISH to MILLY HARPER 8 Mar 1850. Bdsm Albert Parrish and David Parrish.
JOHN STRICKLAND to ABBY STANLY 11 Mar 1850. Bdsm John Strickland and John W. Stanly.
JAMES CREECH to MILLY WALL 16 Mar 1850. Bdsm James Creech and Ezekiel Creech, Jr.
WILLIE STRICKLAND to SALLY PERRY 19 Mar 1850. Bdsm Willie Hobbs and Josiah Strickland.
McCALLAN SMITH to MAZALLIAN SMITH 26 Mar 1850. Bdsm McCallan Smith and A. J. Leach.
JOHN SMITH to OBEDIENCE WHITLEY 20 Mar 1850. Bdsm John Smith and Ezekiel Rogers.
CASWELL LANGDON to ELIZABETH E. MATTHEWS 6 Apr 1850. Bdsm Caswell Langdon and Carrel Langdon.
GEORGE COLLINER to JOANNA OLIVER 9 Apr 1850. Bdsm George Colliner and William Creech.
NICHOLAS JORDEN to HEPSEY WILLIAM 16 Apr 1850. Bdsm Nicholas Jorden and William Peacock.
DANIEL STEWART to NANCY DIXON 16 Apr 1850. Bdsm Daniel Stewart and Robert W. Stevens.
BRYAN HARPER to RACHEL AVERA 16 Apr 1850. Bdsm Bryan Harper and A. G. Thornton.

MARRIAGE BONDS

JOHN STANLY to RANY WOODELL 16 Apr 1850. Bdsm John Stanly and Robert W. Stevens.
FREDERICK POOL to MARGARET GODWIN 16 Apr 1850. Bdsm Frederick Pool and Robert W. Stevens.
AZIEL BATTEN to CAROLIN BATTEN 22 Apr 1850. Bdsm Aziel Batten and John M. Bryan.
WILLIAM PENNY to ELIZABETH AVERA 30 Apr 1850. Bdsm William Penny and William H. Turner.
WILLIAM W. McCULLERS to MARY ANN JONES 4 May 1850. Bdsm William W. McCullers and James B. Stallings.
HENDERSON PITMAN to PIETY COCKRELL 7 May 1850. Bdsm Henderson Pitman and Thomas Pitman.
DIXON PEARCE to NANCY SMITH 10 May 1850. Bdsm Dixon Pearce and William D. Fail.
HARDY ADAMS to ELIZABETH BAKER 20 Mar 1850. Bdsm Hardy Adams and Alsey Adams.
DOCTOR L. CREECH to MARTHA RAPER 27 May 1850. Bdsm Doctor L. Creech and Jesse Parker.
BARNY LANE to ZELPHA BARNES 28 May 1850. Bdsm Barny Lane and Young N. Thornton.
WILLIAM B. WALL to PENNY JANE ELLEN GREEN 28 May 1850. Bdsm William B. Wall and Robert N. Gully.
McKINNE OLIVER to ELIZABETH SWING 25 May 1850. Bdsm McKinne Oliver and Willie Holt.
DAVID TRUMBULL to JANE W. FETCH 5 Jun 1850. Bdsm David Trumbull and William H. Morning.
SAMUEL B. LEGON to CELEY JOHNSTON 7 Jun 1850. Bdsm Samuel B. Legon and Stephen Johnston.
PROMULUS McCULLERS to MARY A. BALLENGER 6 Jun 1850. Bdsm Promulus McCullers and Willis J. Sanders.
THOMAS DENNING to SARAH JERNIGAN 8 Jun 1850. Bdsm Thomas Denning and Robert Denning.
ROBERT M. MASSINGILL to PENNY TEMPLE 8 Jun 1850. Bdsm Robert M. Massingill and N. G. Massingill.
HARDY ADAMS to ELIZABETH BAKER 20 May 1850. Bdsm Hardy Adams and Alsey Adams.
JAMES H. GREEN to ELIZABETH HINTON 20 Jun 1850. Bdsm James H. Green and Richard Green.
CALVIN JACKSON to HEPSABETH WADE 12 Jun 1850. Bdsm Calvin Jackson and Henry H. Hobbs.
LITTLETON STANLY to EDNY JOHNSON 26 Jun 1850. Bdsm Littleton Stanly and John W. Stanly.
MATTHEW RADFORD to AMANDA ROBERTS 20 Jun 1850. Bdsm Matthew Radford and R. W. Hamlet.
WILLIAM D. FAILE to LOUIZA PEARCE 29 Jun 1850. Bdsm William D. Faile and William M. Hooks.
DAVID C. CARINGTON to TEMPERANCE RAIFORD 8 Jul 1850. Bdsm David C. Carington and Henry Gearheardt.
ELIAS LAMB to JANE PARRISH 2 Aug 1850. Bdsm Elias Lamb, Stanly Kirby and James Davis.
CLEM EVANS to MARTHA SANDERS 25 Jul 1850. Bdsm Clem Evans and Gerard T. Johnson.

JOHNSTON COUNTY MARRIAGES

LARKIN STANSEL to MILLY HAYLE 20 Aug 1850. Bdsm Larkin Stansel and Stephen Hicks.
J. R. DRAUGHAN, JR. to NANCY J. WEAVER 26 Aug 1850. Bdsm J. R. Draughan, Jr. and William Peacock.
GEORGE HARRISON to SARAH WOODARD 27 Aug 1850. Bdsm George Harrison and Asa Barny.
JOEL HORN to BETSY SPIVEY 27 Aug 1850. Bdsm Joel Horn and Stanly Kirby.
JOHN WHITMAN to MARY W. JOHNSON 18 Sep 1850. Bdsm John Whitman and Allen W. Johnson.
KIMON STEVENSON to SARAH WHIOVGR? 12 Sep 1850. Bdsm Kimon Stevenson and David Steppenson .
ALSEY JOHNSON to LUCY STEPHENS 17 Sep 1850. Bdsm Alsey Johnson and M. L. Collins.
ISAAC LANGLY to BETSY LAMB 23 Sep 1850. Bdsm Isaac Langly and Ransom Kirby.
JAMES MONDS to PENCY BARBER 24 Sep 1850. Bdsm James Monds and Kinchen Morgan.
WILLIAM H. AVERA to ELIZA ANN CULOM 3 Oct 1850. Bdsm William H. Avera and William A. Culom.
ELBERTON HILL to SUSAN DODD 14 Oct 1850. Bdsm Elberton Hill and William A. Jones.
RANSOM G. ALLEN to SALLEY ALLEN 11 Oct 1850. Bdsm Ransom G. Allen and Josiah Allen.
RANSOM PILKINTON to HANAH SPENCE 4 Oct 1850. Bdsm Ransom Pilkinton and William Scott.
WILLIAM BAREFOOT to ZELPHA SMITH 27 Oct 1850. Bdsm William Barefoot and V. A. Creech.
WESLEY JONES to ALSEY ANN BARBER 20 Oct 1850. Bdsm Wesley Jones and Owen Barber.
JACKSON WALLACE to ELIZA SIMS 17 Oct 1850. Bdsm Jackson Wallace and Calvin P. Wallace.
BRYAN BATTEN to WOFIED CORBET 2 Nov 1850. Bdsm Bryan Batten and John Corbet.
ROBERT MASSINGELL to ELIZABETH LEE 13 Nov 1850. Bdsm Robert Massingill and Barry Green.
GUY W. PHILLIPS to NANCY BROWN 13 Nov 1850. Bdsm Guy W. Phillips and Jesse Parker.
JOEL McLAIN to EVILIN YOUNG 26 Nov 1850. Bdsm Clinton Wood, Jr.
URIAH THOMPSON to CAROLINE COBB 26 Nov 1850. Bdsm John W. Avera and Uriah Thompson.
DANIEL B. INGRAM to INDIANA BRIDGERS 29 Nov 1850. Bdsm Daniel B. Ingram and Henry Pearce.
WILLIAM J. HIGGINS to OLIVE STEVENSON 11 Dec 1850. Bdsm William J. Higgins and Alvin Stephenson.
JOBY STEVENS to BETSY A. SPENCE 14 Dec 1850. Bdsm Joby Stevens and Ransom Bridgers.
DOCTOR D. WOODARD to MARTHA MASSEY 23 Dec 1850. Bdsm Doctor D. Woodard and Henry Woodard.
WILLIAM HASE to ANNIE BAREFOOT 23 Dec 1850. Bdsm William Hase and Dempsy Hase.
JOHN ELDRIDGE to MARY GEORGE 24 Dec 1850. Bdsm John Eldridge and

MARRIAGE BONDS

Moses Lee.
BALDY G. BAILY to PENNY BAILY 28 Dec 1850. Bdsm Baldy G. Baily and Warren Baily.
NATHAN SNIPES to POLLY PEARCE 28 Dec 1850. Bdsm Nathan Snipes and Edwin Hines.
TROY PARRISH to PARRISH 8 Jan 1851. Bdsm Troy Parrish and James Parrish.
ALLISON THORNTON to MARTHA ANN SIMPKINS 9 Jan 1851. Bdsm Allison Thornton.
J. R. COATS to NANCY BYRD 8 Jan 1851. Bdsm J. R. Coats and William H. Coats.
HARRISON FERRELL to LUZUNA DRICE 10 Jan 1851. Bdsm Harrison Ferrell and John A. Ford.
ASHLEY BEASLY to REDLY BYRD 22 Jan 1851. Bdsm Ashley Beasly and Louis Byrd.
EROTUS WELLONS to EVILINE MASSEY 13 Jan 1851. Bdsm Erots Wellons and John Massey.
ALBERT GREEN BINER to ELIZABETH B. PRICE 23 Jan 1851. Bdsm Albert Green Biner and H. G. Price.
WILLIAM H. GREEN to MILLY WOODWARD 25 Jan 1851. Bdsm William H. Green and William W. Morgan.
ELI HONEYCUT to BETTY PARISH 29 Jan 1851. Bdsm Eli Honeycut and George Higgins.
RAFORD LUCAS to ABSELLY DIXON 29 Jan 1851. Bdsm Ruford Lucas and Robert W. Stevens.
WILLIE STRICKLAND to PENELOPE MOORE 31 Jan 1851. Bdsm Willie Strickland and Barzella Blackman.
AUSTON BROWN to GILLY BADEY 31 Jan 1851. Bdsm Auston Brown and Alston Hatcher.
KEDIN BRANNON to EDITH PEAL 31 Jan 1851. Bdsm Kedir Brannon and Bryan Pulley.
GODFREY STANCEL to MARY SANDERS 31 Jan 1851. Bdsm Godfrey Stancel and R. N. Gully.
AVINGTON AVERA to JOANNA EASON 3 Feb 1851. Bdsm Avington Avera and Bryant Harper.
JACOB FLASER, JR. to MARY BARBER 8 Feb 1851. Bdsm Jacob Flaser, Jr and Shadrick B. Lasiter.
WILLIAM PEARSON to JOSEPHINE B. VANTASSEL 10 Feb 1851. Bdsm William Pearson and S. T. Vinson.
STEPHEN PARRISH to VINETTA PLEASANT 11 Feb 1851. Bdsm Stephen Parrish and David Parrish.
LOANNIA LEE to AGILLA WINBORN 18 Feb 1851. Bdsm Loannia Lee and Jesse Winborn.
JOSIAH CONE to WINIFORD GAIN 25 Feb 1851. Bdsm Stanly Kirby.
BUNGAN PARRISH to MERRIA SAVGLY? 25 Feb 1851. Bdsm Ransom Kirby.
JONAS PITMAN to RHODA WATKINS 25 Feb 1851. Bdsm Stanly Kirby.
ELIJAH PARISH to SUSAN KEAN 24 Feb 1851. Bdsm Carrel Langdon.
LOVET PEARCE to CHILLY BASS 25 Feb 1851. Bdsm Ransom Kirby.
JOHN H. WHEELER to CATHERINE FERRELL 4 Mar 1851. Bdsm John H. Wheeler.
WILLIAM MATTHEWS to ELIZABETH CHAMPHIGAN 7 Mar 1851. Bdsm Robert W. Stevens.

JOHNSTON COUNTY MARRIAGES

JOHN SUMMERLIN to DELPHA WILLIAMS 5 Mar 1851. Bdsm Jesse Summerlin.
JOHN WILKINSON to MARINDA PLANIG? 18 Mar 1851. Bdsm John Wilkins and Henry Wilkins.
ENTHAN WIGGS to ELIZABETH STEVENS 1 Mar 1851. Bdsm Eli Sasser.
CUSTIN TALTON to LUCY ANN EDWARDS 2 Apr 1851. Bdsm William Stearling.
ALLEN JOHNSON to PENNY BIRD 25 Mar 1851. Bdsm Amos Johnson.
RIGHT A. JOHNSON to WINIFORD ALLEN 8 Apr 1851. Bdsm Right A. Johnson and Josiah G. Allen.
JONATHAN BAKER to EMILY STANLY 15 Apr 1851. Bdsm Jonathan Baker and N. G. Massengill.
H. F. JOBY to ISABELLE BRIDGERS 15 Apr 1851. Bdsm H. F. Joby and William Summerlin.
BRIGHT HARDY to CAROLINE MORGAN 15 Apr 1851. Bdsm Bright Hardy and Abram Dixon.
WILLIAM G. WAY to RUTHA ANN GREEN 20 Mar 1851. Bdsm William G. Way.
ALFRED E. BEASON to DORCAS BIRD 25 Apr 1851. Bdsm Robert W. Stevens.
DRURY JOHNSON, JR. to MARGARETTE JANE GRIFFIN 25 Jul 1850. Bdsm D. Dupree.
KADER BRANNON to ZELPHA PEARCE 30 Jun 1851. Bdsm Kader Brannon and Bryant Milby.
EZEKIEL RODGERS to MARTHA LOCKART 15 May 1851. Bdsm Ezekiel Rodgers and H. H. Hobbs.
WILLIE BAREFOOT to REBECCA J. SMITH 25 May 1851. Bdsm Joel Lee.
NEEDHAM MORGAN to SALLY GWIN 28 Apr 1851. Bdsm Needham Morgan and Josiah Thomas.
RUFFIN BAILY to CATHERINE WOODWARD 13 May 1851. Bdsm Ruffin Baily and Robert Hatcher.
JOHN JORDAN to ELIZABETH BARBER 25 Jun 1851. Bdsm John Jordan and N. G. Gully.
JOHN C. F. GERHARDT to HARRIET C. CARTER 3 Jul 1851. Bdsm John C. F. Gerhardt and Henry Gerhardt.
WILLIAM R. HAYS to SARAH PEARSON 2 Aug 1851. Bdsm William Hays and Alsey Perry.
EVERETT FLOWERS to ELIZABETH RHODES 9 Aug 1851. Bdsm Everett Flowers and John R. Causey.
AARON W. MASSINGILL to ANNY HARPER 4 Aug 1851. Bdsm Aaron W. Massengill and Henry C. Johnson.
DALAS CARREL to GILLI ANN PARRISH 11 Aug 1851. Bdsm Dalas Carrel and William Carrel.
MALICA HINTON to ELIZA ANN HOOD 22 Aug 18? Bdsm Malica Hinton and R. Hood.
JOHN CAPPS to NORESSA STALLINGS 20 Sep 1851. Bdsm John Capps and Joshua Creech.
STEPHEN JOHNSON to CEALLY LOW 23 Sep 1851. Bdsm Stephen Johnson and Saul Woody.
DEMPSY ROSE to NANCY DAVIS 23 Sep 1851. Bdsm Dempsy Rose and Stanly Kirby.
JAMES HINNANT to ELIZABETH COPELAND 23 Sep 1851. Bdsm James Hinnant and Gene H. Holland.
EVAN GODWIN to NANCY GARNER 23 Sep 1851. Bdsm Evan Godwin and

MARRIAGE BONDS

Oliver Rains.
JAMES H. LEE to SALLY TINER 24 Sep 1851. Bdsm James H. Lee and Jonathan Tool.
WILLIAM HACKNEY to HELEN HOUSE 13 Oct 1851. Bdsm William Hackney and Robert Christman.
NEWIT R. GODWIN to SALLY BARNES 16 Sep 1851. Bdsm Newit R. Godwin and S. Bagley.
W. H. LAMBERT to MILLY ANN WATKINS 22 Oct 1851. Bdsm W. H. Lambert and Thomas Dupree.
HENRY STANTON to ADLADE HOUSE 22 Oct 1851. Bdsm Henry Stanton and John W. Farrel.
WILLIAM B. SURLES to SARAH M. BYRD 25 Oct 1851. Bdsm William B. Surles and Nathan L. Phillips.
R. B. BAREFOOT to MARY A. LEE 25 Oct 1851. Bdsm R. B. Barefoot and James A. Ellis.
MALACHI WALL to MINDY BATTEN 27 Oct 1851. Bdsm Malachi Wall and William H. Wall.
HENRY JOINER to ELIZABETH PARKER 20 Oct 1851. Bdsm Henry Joiner and Hardy Hinnant.
GARRY SILLAVENT to NANCY ANN JONES 9 Nov 1851. Bdsm Garry Sillavent and Ruffin Sillavent.
RUFFIN SILLAVENT to SARAH SILLAVENT 9 Nov 1851. Bdsm Hardy Sillavant and Ruffin Sillavent.
PHAROAH PARKER to JANE YOUNG 25 Nov 1851. Bdsm Pharoah Parker and Rill C. Williamson.
WILLIAM H. ELLIS to MARY E. HOOD 21 Nov 1851. Bdsm William H. Ellis and Edwin Batten.
JOHN HAGENS to POLLY CRAFFORD 27 Nov 1851. Bdsm John Hagens and Robert Masingil.
EPHRAIM R. EVANS to ELIZABETH BLACKMAN 27 Nov 1851. Bdsm Ephraim R. Evans and Robert Masingell.
SIR WILLIAM BLACKMAN to ELIZABETH BRUNT 4 Dec 1851. Bdsm Sir William Blackman and George P. Rose.
WILLIAM H. CULLUM to ESTHER ANN AVERA 4 Dec 1851. Bdsm William H. Cullum and Stephen Sneed.
WILLIAM P. BLACKMAN to ELIZABETH PRICE 12 Dec 1851. Bdsm William P. Blackman and John P. Cook.
AUDIE DAVIS to ELIZABETH EDWARDS 8 Dec 1854. Bdsm Aduie Davis and John Davis.
JESSE B. STRICKLAND to SALLY ANN WIGGINS 20 Dec 1851. Bdsm Jesse B. Strickland and E. O. Beasly.
QUINTON STEPHENSON to MARYAN ELIZABETH CREECH 20 Dec 1851. Bdsm Quinton Stephenson and Kimmon Stephenson.
JOHN W. HUTSON to ELIZABETH JOHNSON 24 Dec 1851. Bdsm John W. Hutson and J. J. Johnson.
ALFRED RYALS to REBECCA MOORE 24 Dec 1851. Bdsm Alfred Ryals and Thomas G. Bezzel.
JOHN H. WHEELER to CATHERN FERRELL 4 Mar 1851. Bdsm John Wheeler and Noah Wheeler.
ALEXANDER MESSER to PEGGY STEPHENSON 30 Dec 1851. Bdsm Alexander Messer and John B. Johnson.
WILLIAM MORGAN to REBECCA BAREFOOT 1 Jan 1852. Bdsm William Morgan

JOHNSTON COUNTY MARRIAGES

and Henry I. Belle.

JEREMIAH CORBETT to MILLY BROWN 2 Jan 1852. Bdsm Jeremiah Corbett and James Corbett.

JOHN ALLEN STATON to SUSAN ELDRIDGE 13 Jan 1852. Bdsm John Allen Staton and Troy Eldridge.

HENRY W. THARP to ARMANDATT WILLEY 11 Jan 1852. Bdsm Henry W. Tharp and John W. Avera.

PERRY GODWIN to MARY HANE 14 Jan 1852. Bdsm Perry Godwin and John E. Earp.

LEWIS MANKER to MARY LYNCH 21 Jan 1852. Bdsm Lewis Manker and Sele Wilkins.

HENRY BAGLY to PATIENCE ATKINSON 15 Jan 1852. Bdsm Henry Bagly and Alvin Bagley.

THOMAS ATKINSON to ELIZABETH GODWIN 26 Jan 1852. Bdsm Thomas Atkinson and Jesse Parker.

JOHN H. CRAWFORD to PATIENCE A. A. STEVENS 29 Jan 1852. Bdsm John H. Crawford and H. H. Hobbs.

NATHANIEL MOORE to SALLY RAPER 28 Jul 1852. Bdsm Nathaniel Moore and B. R. Hinnant.

SAMUEL CROCKER to SALLY ADAMS 3 Feb 1852. Bdsm Samuel Crocker and Josiah Gay.

JAMES H. ROADS to PHEROBY TOMPSON 5 Feb 1852. Bdsm James H. Roads and A. J. K. Roads.

HENRY PEARCE to ANN ELIZA PARRISH 10 Feb 1852. Bdsm Henry Pearce and Thomas Ingram.

WILLIAM HENRY WEAVER to ELIZABETH LEE 10 Feb 1852. Bdsm William H. Weaver and Ransom Langdon.

JOHN A. FORD to CATHERINE MUNDEN 13 Feb 1852. Bdsm John A. Ford and H. T. Bell.

JAMES G. ALLEN to ELIZABETH WOODALL 20 Feb 1852. Bdsm James G. Allen and Robert W. Stevens.

BARDEN NARON to RINDA TALTON 24 Feb 1852. Bdsm Barden Naron and Samuel W. Woody.

JONATHAN T. PIKE to MARY ANN JOHNSON 6 Feb 1852. Bdsm Jonathan Pike and Henry T. Bole.

JOHN HODGES to REBECCA E. SANDERS 8 Mar 1852. Bdsm John Hodges and Edward Sanders.

ELIAS ROSE to MISS EVELINE HEDGEPETH 13 Mar 1852. Bdsm Elias Rose and Calvin Upchurch.

WILLIAM E. THORNTON to PENNY HARRIET CREECH 20 Mar 1852. Bdsm William E. Thornton and Eli Olive.

HARRIS ATKINSON to CAROLINE BAILEY 1 Mar 1852. Bdsm Harris Atkinson and A. W. Richardson.

WILLIAM T. MARTIN to MARTHA ADAMS 26 Mar 1852. Bdsm William T. Martin and Robert W. Stevens.

HENRY O. EDWARDS to NANCY OVEBA 5 Apr 1852. Bdsm Henry O. Edwards and Joshua Creech.

WILLIE P. STANSEL to MARTHA STANSEL 10 Apr 1852. Bdsm Willie P. Stansel and James H. Earp.

JOHN WINBURN to ELIZABETH FULGHAM 17 Apr 1852. Bdsm John Winburn and Perry Rentfrow.

ABSALUM BARBER, JR. to MARY ANN LASSETER 15 Apr 1852. Bdsm Absalum

MARRIAGE BONDS

Barber, Jr. and B. Brannon.
JOSEPH T. WESTBROOK to PHEREBON ELKRIDGE 1 May 1852. Bdsm Joseph T. Westbook and Troy Elkridge.
JAMES ELLIS to JUNE RAIFORD 6 May 1852. Bdsm James Ellis and Henry Cole.
GEORGE MITCHEL to NANCY HOWELL 7 Jul 1852. Bdsm George Mitchel and Henry G. Edwards.
GREEN PARKER MESSER to MARY E. STEPHENSON 14 May 1852. Bdsm Green Parker Messer and Osborn Messer.
WILLIAM H. WEST to TEMPY LEE 22 May 1852. Bdsm William H. West and William R. Stanly.
WESLEY I. HIGGINS to ELIZUR HONEYCUT 26 May 1852. Bdsm Wesley I. Higgins and John Ruffus Coats.
JAMES DAVIS to PATIENCE KIRBY 25 May 1852. Bdsm James Davis and Stanly Kirby.
RUFFIN BALLANCE to ELIZA SASSER 27 Apr 1852. Bdsm Ruffin Ballance and Stephen Bagly.
JESSE PARKER to MARTHA RENTFROW 26 May 1852. Bdsm Jesse Parker and William H. Joyner.
JESSE R. BLACKMAN to ELIZABETH E. MASSINGELL 29 May 1852. Bdsm Barna Gwin and Jesse R. Blackman.
B. R. HINNANT to TRECINDA BAGLEY 14 Jun 1852. Bdsm B. R. Hinnant and J. B. Beckwith.
BARDIN CROCKER to HAWKINS EASON 29 May 1852. Bdsm Bardin Crocker and Calvin R. Wallace.
RUFFIN GRISWELL to MATILIDA BAILEY 18 Jun 1852. Bdsm Ruffin Griswell and Stephen Boykins.
CALVIN HOLLAND to POLLY ROWE 18 Jun 1852. Bdsm Curtis Holland and Calvin Holland.
IZIAH PERDUE to LITHA ROSE 26 Jun 1852. Bdsm Iziah Perdue and Jethro Howell.
VINE ALLEN JOHNSON to MARY JOHNSON 1 Jul 1852. Bdsm Vine Allen Johnson and Alexander Young.
JAMES A. SMITH to MARTHA BRYD 11 Jul 1852. Bdsm James A. Smith and Jeremiah Jones.
CHESLEY SMITH to MARTHA GARDNER 10 Jul 1852. Bdsm Chesley Smith and Perry Rentfrow.
WILLIE MITCHELL to POLLY ANN PEARCE 20 Jul 1852. Bdsm Willie Mitchell and William Radford.
JETHRO HOLLAND to LYDIA JUMP 17 Jul 1852. Bdsm Jethro Holland and Uriah Holland.
STEPHEN STANSELL to RHODAY RENTFROW 21 Jul 1852. Bdsm Stephen Stansell and Everett Stevens.
SAMUEL GAME to APSABETH EDWARDS 26 Jul 1852. Bdsm Samuel Game and John Harrel.
DELIA JOHNSON to SUSAN BAILEY 15 Aug 1852. Bdsm Delia Johnson and Stephen Johnson.
HINNANT MITCHEL to MARY PARNEL 10 Jul 1852. Bdsm Hinnant Mitchel and William Rains.
JAMES N. ELLIS to MARY BLACKMAN 10 Aug 1852. Bdsm James N. Ellis and P. W. Hutson.
A. E. LOCKART to ELIZA BARCUM 22 Sep 1852. Bdsm A. E. Lockart and

JOHNSTON COUNTY MARRIAGES

George N. Tharp.
WILLIAM W. PERKINSON to MARIAH BALLENGER 4 Sep 1852. Bdsm William W. Perkinson and A. A. Dance.
WILLIAM PENDON to ANNA RADFORD 15 Aug 1852. Bdsm William Pendon and William Rains.
BRYANT JORDAN to JULIA ANN LEE 1 Sep 1852. Bdsm Bryant Jordan and Duncan Johnson.
AMOS J. PEDIN to ELIZABETH CREECH 7 Sep 1852. Bdsm William J. Pedin and Amos J. Pedin.
AARON WOODALL to SARAH LEE 22 Sep 1852. Bdsm Aaron Woodall and Alexander Woodall.
WILLIAM H. LANGDON to EMELY JANE CAPPS 30 Sep 1852. Bdsm William H. Langdon and Jacob H. Barnes.
JAMES MURRY to ELIZA RYALS 1 Oct 1852. Bdsm James Murry and R. H. Stewart.
SAMUEL MUNSON to MARY HONEYCUTT 7 Oct 1851. Bdsm Samuel Munson and Robert W. Stevens.
JOHN J. LEE to CATHRIN CAROLINE BRYAN 13 Oct 1852. Bdsm John J. Lee and Barnaby Green.
WILLIAM SKINE to ELIZABETH WALLACE 2 Nov 1852. Bdsm William Skine and Chris J. Bingham.
GEORGE P. ROSE to NANCY BRUNT 19 Oct 1852. Bdsm George P. Rose and S. W. Blackman.
RYAL COATS to SARAH DODD 3 Nov 1852. Bdsm Ryal Coats and A. S. Dodd.
ALSEY PARISH to EMILY HOCOTT 24 May 1852. Bdsm Alsey Parish and A. W. Richardson.
GEORGE PHILLIPS to HELEN KELLY 12 Nov 1852. Bdsm George Phillips and J. L. Collins.
HINNANT RENTFROW to ZELPHIA WATSON 13 Nov 1852. Bdsm Hinnant Rentfrow and Stephen Rentfrow.
WYATT EARP to MARIAH FOUNTAIN 4 Nov 1852. Bdsm A. W. Richardson and Wyatt Earp.
JOHN L. WOOD to PENNARY WALL 1 Dec 1852. Bdsm John L. Wood and William G. Parish.
STEPHEN SNEAD to MATILDA V. ENNIS 24 Nov 1852. Bdsm Stephen Snead and John R. Thomson.
THOMAS D. SNEAD to ELIZABETH SANDERS 1 Dec 1852. Bdsm Thomas D. Snead and Stephen Snead.
GRIFFIN BAILY to REDDY WALLS 27 Dec 1852. Bdsm Griffin Baily and James Manning.
WILLIAM MITCHELL to ELIZABETH T. HOOD 15 Dec 1852. Bdsm William Mitchell and Ransom Brannon.
JAMES J. FERRELL to ADELAH C. ELLINGTON 13 Dec 1852. Bdsm James J. Ferrell and Augustus W. Parrish.
HORATIO B. HODGES to SARRAH GILES 29 Dec 1852. Bdsm Horatio B. Hodges and William M. Ryals.
GABRIEL FARREL to NELLY WATSON 27 Dec 1852. Bdsm Gabriel Farrel and W. B. Bell.
JOSIAH G. ALLEN to ELIZABETH ALLEN 30 Dec 1852. Bdsm Josiah G. Allen and Alexander Allen.
RICHARD RASBERRY to RACHEL EDWARDS 27 Dec 1852. Bdsm Richard

MARRIAGE BONDS

Rasberry and Richard Edwards.
BENJAMIN SMITH to MARY OLIVER 4 Jan 1852. Bdsm Benjamin Smith and Westly Massey.
WILLIAM CORBIN to REBECCA WISE 5 Jan 1853. Bdsm William Corbin and Mordica Lee.
MORDICA J. PARRISH to HARRIET PEACOCK 8 Jan 1853. Bdsm Mordica J. Parrish and James R. Young.
STARLING BAKER to LOUSINDA BAKER 7 Jan 1853. Bdsm Starling Baker and Ransom Temple.
HARDY HINNANT to JEMIMA PARRISH 8 Jan 1853. Bdsm Hardy Hinnant and William Watson.
WILLIAM WATSON to PENELOPE KIRBY 8 Jan 1853. Bdsm William Watson and Hardy Hinnant.
WILLIAM MORGAN to MARTHA ANN HICKS 12 Jan 1853. Bdsm William Morgan and Delia Johnson.
HENRY BATTEN to ZELLA PRICE 10 Jan 1853. Bdsm Henry Batten and Henry Starlin.
JOHN REVEL to ELIZABETH GODWIN 20 Jan 1853. Bdsm John Revel and James Davis.
NEEDHAM FIELDS to ZELPHA BLACKMOND 26 Jan 1853. Bdsm Needham Fields and Lewis J. Williams.
J. HENDERSON EARP to EMILY JOHNSON 27 Jan 1853. Bdsm J. Henderson Earp and Everet T. Roberson.
ALEXANDER ALLEN to EMILY ELIZABETH JOHNSON 27 Jan 1853. Bdsm Alexander Allen and Ransom G. Allen.
JOHN TINER to SALLY CAPPS 29 Jun 1853. Bdsm John Tiner and Calvin Simpkins.
RANSOM KIRBY to CELIA HOLLAND 1 Feb 1853. Bdsm Ransom Kirby and William Watson.
NEEDHAM G. BAKER to POLLY STANLY 5 Feb 1853. Bdsm Needham G. Baker and Lewis Stanly.
ARTHUR A. BLACKMAN to ALDIE JERNIGAN 8 Feb 1853. Bdsm Arthur A. Blackman and Aaron Lee.
ALLEN PORTER to ELIZUR HOLLANDWORTH 7 Feb 1853. Bdsm Allen Porter and John Porter.
RICHARD AVERA to LUCATTA JONES 12 Feb 1853. Bdsm Richard Avera and William H. Turner.
CALVIN RAEPER to ELIZABETH SULLOMAN 15 Feb 1853. Bdsm Calvin Raeper and Garry Sulloman.
WILLIAM NICHOLS to SARRAH ANN TERRY 18 Feb 1853. Bdsm William Nichols and F. S. Smith.
LARKIN PEDEN to MARY SASSER 26 Feb 1853. Bdsm Larkin Peden and Wilie W. Peden.
BRYANT MORGAN to SALLY JOHNSON 19 Feb 1853. Bdsm Bryant Morgan and Alexander Johnson.
JOHN COOPER to BETSY PARRISH 16 Mar 1853. Bdsm George Parrish.
NATHAN PEELE to MARTHA PEELE 28 Feb 1853. Bdsm Nathan Peele and Noel Barnes.
JACOB BARNES, SR. to ANNA GREEN 28 Feb 1853. Bdsm Jacob Barnes, Sr. and Noel Barnes.
RICHARD HILL to SUSAN BARBER 28 Feb 1853. Bdsm Richard Hill and George Barber.

JOHNSTON COUNTY MARRIAGES

DIXON KIRBY to MARTHA PEEBLE 28 Feb 1853. Bdsm Dixon Kirby and Stanly Kirby.

ALDRIDGE H. DIXON to MIMMY BARBER 4 Mar 1853. Bdsm Aldridge H. Dixon and Robert W. Stevens.

JAMES B. DUNN to ELIZABETH FORD 11 Mar 1853. Bdsm James B. Dunn and Needham Morgan.

RUSSEL SILAVANT to MATILDA TALTON 23 May 1854. Bdsm Russel Silavent and Hardy Silavant.

WILLIAM R. JOINER to ELIZABETH COLE 23 May 1854. Bdsm William R. Joiner and Furney Langston.

JAMES H. JOHNSON to FANNY MORGAN 17 Mar 1853. Bdsm James H. Johnson and Henry C. Johnson.

JONATHAN STEPHENSON to SARAH PLEASANT 12 Mar 1853. Bdsm Jonathan Stephenson and Tunnel Heath.

RIGHT H. JOHNSON to JOCIE SURLES 18 Mar 1853. Bdsm Right H. Johnson and Sir William Johnson.

LEVY L. BRADY to HARRIET DAVIS 17 Mar 1853. Bdsm Levy L. Brady and Dixon Davis.

JOHN HONEYCUT to ELIZABETH KEMP 30 Mar 1853. Bdsm John Honeycut and John W. Liles.

GEORGE D. BUNDY to MARY AUSTON 29 Mar 1853. Bdsm George D. Bundy and William W. Shepard.

HENDERSON PRICE to CELIA HOGG 7 Apr 1853. Bdsm Henderson Price and Carson Oneal.

NATHAN ADAMS to ELIZABETH S. HOBB 1 Apr 1853. Bdsm Nathan Adams and James H. Pool.

MATTHEW GILES to ELIZABETH ROBERTS 14 Apr 1853. Bdsm Matthew Giles and John Broadshaw.

JAMES COLE to ELIZABETH WEAVER 9 Apr 1853. Bdsm James Cole and Lewis Williams.

SIR WILLIAM LASETTER to TABITHA BYRD 20 Apr 1853. Bdsm Sir William Lasetter and William Lasetter.

WILLIAM H. TOMLINSON to MARTHA ELLINGTON 23 Apr 1853. Bdsm William H. Tomlinson and P. R. Tomlinson.

JOHN P. WILLIFORD to SALLY ROBERTS 28 Apr 1853. Bdsm John P. Williford and R. D. Atkinson.

WILLIAM H. HONEYCUT to POLLY ANN PENDER 25 Apr 1853. Bdsm William H. Honeycut and John P. Sandford.

WILLIAM SCOTT to MARY ANN PILKINTON 18 Mar 1853. Bdsm William Scott and Ransom Pilkinton.

DEBREAN D. TALTON to AZKETTA HEDGEPETH 19 Mar 1815/1851. Bdsm Debrean D. Talton and Young Thornton.

LUCIAN H. JONES to TRANQUILLA JOHNSON 28 Mar 1853. Bdsm Lucian H. Jones and William Hill.

JOHN P. WELLEFORD to SALLY ROBERTS 28 Apr 1853. Bdsm John P. Welleford and R. D. Atkinson.

JOHN ROSE to CATHERINE GAY 3 May 1853. Bdsm John Rose and Calvin Upchurch.

WILLIE WELLONS to ZELPHA OLIVER 12 May 1853. Bdsm Willie Wellons and R. M. Oliver.

GASTON JOHNSON to MARY JANE CARROL 14 May 1853. Bdsm Gaston Johnson and Drury Johnson.

MARRIAGE BONDS

GEORGE HAMELTON to TRANQUILLA SMITH 24 May 1853. Bdsm George Hamelton and Amos Coats.
WILLIAM BLACKMAN to SALLY WEBB 25 May 18?. Bdsm William Blackman and George Keen.
JAMES H. STEPHENS to SUSAN COATS 4 Jun 1853. Bdsm James H. Stephens and Grue P. Messer.
AUGUSTUS W. PARRISH to HARRIET HOCUTT 6 Jun 1853. Bdsm Agugustus W. Parrish and Matthew Boykins.
BRYANT HOLLAND to POLLY LEE 15 Jun 18?. Bdsm Bryant Holland and W. S. Ballenger.
RICHARD D. MEADEN to JULIA M. NORTHHOUSE 21 Jun 1853. Bdsm Richard D. Meaden and Bryan E. Raiols.
JOHN H. COTTER to K. LOUIZER MORGAN ? 1853. Bdsm John H. Cotter and Henry J. Bell.
CASWELL PARRISH to ELIZABETH JONES 18 Jun 1853. Bdsm Caswell Parrish and David Parrish.
ELI WILKINS to EVALINE HILL 19 Jul 1853. Bdsm Eli Wilkins and Henry Wilkins.
JOHN G. GURLEY to FRANCIS E. NICHOLS 21 Jul 1853. Bdsm John G. Gurley and William W. Nichols.
BENEJAH WILLIAMS to SALLY LEWIS 22 Jul 1853. Bdsm Benejah Williams and Arthur Wiggs.
WILLIAM LYNCH to MARTHA JANE DENNING 30 Jul 1853. Bdsm William Lynch and Lewis Williams.
BRYANT POPE to AQUILLA SELEVANT 5 Aug 1853. Bdsm Bryant Pope and Jesse Parker.
WILLIAM BARBER to PENCY LASHLEY 5 Aug 1853. Bdsm William Barber and Ashley Barber.
GEORGE STEPHENSON to MARY LASETTER 5 Aug 1853. Bdsm George Stephenson and William H. Coats.
GEORGE EDWARDS to AXEY STRICKLAND 9 Aug 1853. Bdsm George Edwards and Larkin Creech.
JONES WALKER to ALSEY POWELL 29 Aug 1853. Bdsm Jones Walker and Bennett Blackmore.
WILLIAM HILE to SARRAH E. JONES 1 Sep 1853. Bdsm William Hile and Lucian H. Jones.
WILLIAM RAEPER to CELIA MOORE 2 Sep 1853. Bdsm William Raeper and Thomas Woodard.
EVERET CROCKER to AVA MARELLEN CORBET 3 Sep 1853. Everet Crocker and James M. Corbet.
RAIFORD PEARCE to EVALINE HINTON 5 Sep 1853. Bdsm Raiford Pearce and Henry Hales.
ALSEY ADAMS to NANCY BAKER 9 Sep 1853. Bdsm Alsey Adams and N. G. Massingell.
ARTHUR WIGGS to MARTHA CASEY 13 Sep 1853. Bdsm Arthur Wiggs and William Beard.
STEPHENSON OGBURN to MARY ANN PRICE 27 Sep 1853. Bdsm Stephenson Ogburn and William Lasetter.
URIAS BAUCUM to SALLY TURNER 28 Sep 1853. Bdsm Urias Baucum and C. W. D. Hutchens.
JOHN A. SMITH to LOUIZIER JOHNSON 11 Oct 1853. Bdsm John A. Smith and S. W. Pate.

JOHNSTON COUNTY MARRIAGES

JEREMIAH JONES to UNITY BRYD 11 Oct 1853. Bdsm Jeremiah Jones and James A. Smith.

THOMAS ALLEN to ELIZABETH MUNDS 11 Oct 1853. Bdsm Thomas Allen and James Munds.

WILLIAM B. HOCUTT to MARY JANE RICHARDSON 21 Oct 1853. Bdsm William B. Hocutt and W. B. Richardson.

DUNCAN UPCHURCH to ELIZABETH EDWARDS 23 Oct 1853. Bdsm Duncan Upchurch and Jonathan Nowell.

NATHANIEL BARBER to LANCY DIXON 26 Oct 26 1853. Bdsm Nathaniel Barber and Kinchen Morgan.

WILLIAM J. BRADDY to MATILDA BARBER 26 Oct 1853. Bdsm William J. Braddy and Gideon Barber.

SETH WOODARD to MARY TOMLINSON 29 Oct 1853. Bdsm Seth Woodard and B. A. Woodard.

LEVY BATTEN to LOUIZA WALL 29 Oct 1853. Bdsm Levy Batten and William H. Wall.

JESSE HINNANT to CAROLINE WHITLEY 9 Nov 1853. Bdsm Jesse Hinnant and Michael Whitley.

BURWELL TEMPLE to ELIZABETH WHITLEY 13 Nov 1853. Bdsm Burwell Temple and A. W. Richardson.

EVERT A. BIZZELE to BETHANY BARNES 14 Nov 1853. Bdsm Benjamin Wellons and Evert A. Bizzele.

NEEDHAM MORGAN to MARTHA JOHNSON 15 Nov 1853. Bdsm Needham Morgan and James B. Dunn.

WILLIAM J. CREECH to POLLY MASSENGILL 17 Nov 1853. Bdsm Warren J. Creech and Herron Creech.

WALTER W. GULLY to LOUISA WALL 20 Nov 1853. Bdsm Walter W. Gully and Quean Earp.

JOHN J. BARNES to EVALINE JOHNSON 29 Nov 1853. Bdsm John J. Barnes and S. W. Pate.

WILLIAM H. MULLINS to CLARY A. BATTON 26 Nov 1853. Bdsm William H. Mullins and Willie A. Boykins.

JOSEPH STAFFORD to CHILLY A. DENNING 20 Nov 1853. Bdsm Joseph Stafford and J. G. Rose.

STARKY KING to PATSEY STANLY 30 Nov 1853. Bdsm Starky King and William Stanly.

JOSEPH BOYTT to LARKEY BRYANT 9 Dec 1853. Bdsm Joseph Boytt and Pitts Kirby.

ROBERT B. DEBNAM to EVALINE WATSON 10 Dec 1853. Bdsm Robert B. Debnam and James Munds.

WILLIAM GREEN to ALLEY ELIZABETH JONES 10 Dec 1853. Bdsm William Green and Samuel Jones.

MERCIN D. BRITT to ELIZABETH H. HORN 12 Dec 1853. Bdsm Mercin D. Britt and William G. Gully.

WILLIAM H. SELLERS to HARRIET E. RAIFORD 21 ? 1853. Bdsm William H. Sellers and Daniel A. Sellers.

RANSOM CREECH to ELIZABETH ATKINSON 29 Dec 1853. Bdsm Ransom Creech and Clark F. Garrell.

JOSEPH J. ADAMS to LUCETTA ANN OGBORN 2 Jan 1854. Bdsm Joseph J. Adams and John A. Adams.

JOHN ALLEN to SALLY JOHNSON 2 Jan 1853. Bdsm John Allen and Robert Masingile.

MARRIAGE BONDS

CLAUDIUS B. SANDERS to ZELLEY E. WHITLEY 4 Jan 1854. Bdsm R. D. Atkinson.
JACKSON BAKER to NANCY R. STANLY 4 Jan 1854. Bdsm Jackson Baker and W. R. Stanly.
YOUNG J. LEE, JR. to ANN ELDRIDGE 4 Jan 1854. Bdsm Young J. Lee, Jr. and Joel Lee.
EDMOND WILSON to POLLY BLALOCK 4 Jan 1854. Bdsm Edmond Wilson and Brittan Stephenson.
MACK HONEYCUT to POLLY SMITH 7 Jan 1854. Bdsm Mack Honeycut and William Lambert.
ANDERSON THOMAS to RACHEL ANN WOOD 7 Jan 1854. Bdsm Anderson Thomas and John Stewart.
HENRY FERRELL to MOLLEY ANN WILDER 10 Jan 1854. Bdsm Henry Ferrell and Harrison Dean.
SAMUEL POLLARD to PENELOPE ALLEN 13 Jan 1854. Bdsm Samuel Pollard and Edmond Johnson.
GEORGE W. DAVIS to PATIENCE KIRBY 16 Jan 1854. Bdsm George W. Davis and Joseph Raeper.
KINCHEN MORGAN to POLLY JOHNSON 16 Jan 1854. Bdsm Kinchen Morgan and Bright Hardee.
JOHN W. STRICKLAND to ALTENY E. WORLEY 17 Jan 1854. Bdsm John W. Strickland and W. R. Stanly.
LINSEY LEE to PATSEY RAP WINBORN 18 Jan 1854. Bdsm Linsey Lee and Linford Lee.
REUBEN WALLIS to AMMY AUSTIN 26 Jan 1854. Bdsm Reuben Wallis and William W. Shephard.
MABRY GARNER to MARGARET STANSELL 28 Jan 1854. Bdsm Mabry Garner and Amos Parker.
GEORGE W. CORBET to MOURNING CROCKER 30 Jan 1854. Bdsm George W. Corbet and James Corbet.
WILLIAM DURHAM to AMMY MASSINGILL 4 Feb 1854. Bdsm William Durham and Joel H. Massingill.
JAMES HARRISON to LORENDA JOHNSON 8 Feb 1854. Bdsm James Harrison and Troy Bridgers.
WALTER D. MARTIN to ELIZABETH H. RAPER 18 Feb 1854. Bdsm Walter D. Martin and Josiah W. Price.
HAYWOOD MEDLIN to WINIFRED BATTEN 16 Jan 1854. Bdsm Haywood Medlin and Richardson Oneal.
BURWELL W. TEMPLE to MARTHA R. BLACKMORE 18 Feb 1854. Bdsm Burwell W. Temple and Needham G. Massingill.
MAC RUFFIN SMITH to MARY JANE HODGES 27 Feb 1854. Bdsm Mac Ruffin Smith and John G. Hodges.
HENRY HANE to SALLY STANSELL 28 Feb 1854. Bdsm Henry Hane and Milton M. Godwin.
IREDEL GODWIN to MARY E. WOODALE 7 Mar 1854. Bdsm Irdele Godwin and Zachariah Lee.
ELI STANLY to SUSAN EMILY STANLY 7 Mar 1854. Bdsm Eli Stanly and N. G. Masingele.
BRIGHT HARDY to MARY JANE JOHNSTON 11 Mar 1854. Bdsm Bright Hardy and Kinchen Morgan.
JOSIAH PRICE to SUSAN MOODY 16 Mar 1854. Bdsm Josiah Price and Levy B. Hogg.

JOHNSTON COUNTY MARRIAGES

JOHN HOLT to HENRIETTA JONES 27 Mar 1854. Bdsm John Holt and Alsey Parnell.

WILLIAM G. HOLLAND to MARY DUPREE 28 Mar 1854. Bdsm Ransom M. Stephenson.

ELIJAH SMITH to RODA JOHNSON 29 Mar 1854. Bdsm Elijah Smith and James Hinnant.

BRYANT JONES to MARTHA CLIFTON 3 Apr 1854. Bdsm Bryant Jones and Westly Jones.

RUEL A. HOLLAND to AMANDA HOLLAND 8 Apr 1854. Bdsm Ruel A. Holland and Exum H. Holland.

ISAAC STALLINGS to MOURNING SELLERS 12 Apr 1854. Bdsm Isaac Stallings and Herrin Creech.

WILLIAM R. WHITLEY to REXEY CHAMBLEE 15 Apr 1854. Bdsm William R. Whitley and William Hinnant.

JOHN MORGAN to POLLY BARBER 15 Apr 1854. Bdsm John Morgan and Kinchen Morgan.

BRITAIN STEPHENSON to MARTHA BLALOCK 14 Apr 1854. Bdsm Britian Stephenson and William Grimes.

SIMPSON EVANS to ELIZABETH HODGE 20 Apr 18?. Bdsm Simpson Evans and James E. Meden.

MOSES HILL to ABSELLA HOWELL 25 Apr 1854. Bdsm Moses Hill and S. W. Whitley.

ALSEY PARNELL to POLLY HOLT 26 Apr 1854. Bdsm Alsey Parnell and Willie Deans.

MATTHEW BOYKINS to SARAH ANN E. PARRISH 3 May 1854. Bdsm Matthew Boykins and S. F. Johnson.

JOHNSON B. WALL to LEVINA GAY 6 May 1854. Bdsm Johnson B. Wall and Robert N. Gully.

CURTIS JOHNSON to SARAH INGRAM 6 May 1854. Bdsm Curtis Johnson and Sir William Ingram.

JOSIAH DEANS to PENELOPE SASSER 9 May 1854. Bdsm Josiah Deans and Perry Rentfrow.

RANSOM LEE to LUCY ROSE 16 May 1854. Bdsm Ransom Lee and John F. Sanders.

JAMES PEEDEN to LUCRETIA SELLERS 16 May 1854. Bdsm James Peeden and Monrow Peeden.

JAMES H. POOL to DELEA ANN DRAUGHAN 16 May 1854. Bdsm James H. Pool and Alfred Holland.

ARTHUR D. YOUNG to JENCY RAINES 22 May 1854. Bdsm Arthur D. Young and James Beasley.

ERASTUS E. POWELL to NANCY JANE BARKAM 30 May 1854. Bdsm Erastus E. Powell and William H. Cullom.

JAMES H. ADAMS to ESTHER LEE 14 Jun 1854. Bdsm James H. Adams and Joseph E. Rhodes.

JAMES P. WEDDEN to JULIA M. TERRY 15 Jun 1854. Bdsm James P. Wedden and H. H. Hobbs.

GABRIEL PARKER to SUSAN FIELDS 17 Jun 1854. Bdsm Gabriel Parker and Benjamin F. Hutson.

HUGHEY BARBER to PATSEY REAVES 17 Jun 1854. Bdsm Hughey Barber and William A. Reaves.

WILLIAM H. ALLEN to NANCY INGRAM 19 Jan 1854. Bdsm William H. Allen and Samuel Pollard.

MARRIAGE BONDS

ALEXANDER JOHNSON to SARAH STANSEL 26 Jun 1854. Bdsm Alexander Johnson and Daniel W. Ryals.
JOHN T. FAISSON to POLLY V. JOHNSON 17 ? 1854. Bdsm John T. Faisson and Harry Johnson.
SILVESTER R. PEARCE to ? 27 Aug 1854. Bdsm Silvester R. Pearce and Charles Creech.
LEVY B. HOGG to JENSEY PRICE 28 Jul 1854. Bdsm Levy B. Hogg and John C. Allen.
JAMES W. BAKER to MARTHA GRIFFIN 4 Aug 1854. Bdsm James W. Baker and George Kean.
REDMAN PARKER to LOUISA LASSETER 5 Aug 1854. Bdsm Redman Parker and John J. Barnes.
GUION EARP to JINSEY HOLLAND 8 Aug 1854. Bdsm Guion Earp and Everett P. Robertson.
HENDERSON ROBERT to ELIZABETH DODD 8 Aug 1854. Bdsm Henderson Robert and Ephraim Page.
DEVEREAUX POOL to MARY ANN PRICE 12 Aug 1854. Bdsm Devereaux Pool and Ashley Price.
ALLEN BAKER to REBECCA STANLY 28 Aug 1854. Bdsm Allen Baker and Starky King.
JOSEPH E. RHODES to ELIZABETH LEE 5 Sep 1854. Bdsm Joseph E. Rhodes and Elam Lee.
JESSE FULGHAM to POLLY PEACOCK 8 Sep 1854. Bdsm Jesse Fulgham and Levi Barden.
THOMAS INGRAM to JANE E. STALLINGS 12 Sep 1854. Bdsm Thomas Ingram and Malachi Wood.
DAVID WILLIAMS to MARY ANN DUPREE 14 Sep 1854. Bdsm David Williams and James H. Dupree.
NATHANIEL DUPREE to ELIZABETH TURLINGTON 20 Sep 1854. Bdsm Nathaniel Dupree and Thomas Dupree.
CASWELL D. MASSEY to MATILDA HUSTON 26 Sep 1854. Bdsm Caswell D. Massey and B. F. Whitley.
JOHN HAWLEY to SALLY KIRBY 27 Sep 1854. Bdsm John Hawley and Pitts Kirby.
KINCHEN BATTEN to NANCY E. HODGE 27 Sep 1854. Bdsm Kinchen Batten and Matthew Batten.
JAMES H. CORBET to ELIZABETH ADAMS 28 Sep 1854. Bdsm James H. Corbet and Harris H. Atkinson.
JOHN WEBB to SUSAN BAKER 4 Oct 1854. Bdsm John Webb and Henry Gwin.
JESSE PARNELE to PENELOPE BARCUM 4 Oct 1854. Bdsm Jesse Parnele and John E. Earp.
ELISHA B. JORDAN to NANCY EZZELE 4 Oct 1854. Bdsm Elisha B. Jordan and D. W. Hood.
JOHN D. TALTON to YANNCY NARON 13 Oct 1854. Bdsm Johon D. Talton and Bardin Naron.
HANDY H. ENNIS to BETSY ANN WHITMAN 13 Oct 1854. Bdsm Handy H. Ennis and John H. Ennis.
HIRAM W. JOYNER to SALLY E. HARMAN 4 Oct 1854. Bdsm Hiram W. Joyner to William D. Joyner.
WILLIAM B. STANLY to SARAH BLACKMAN 17 Oct 1854. Bdsm William B. Stanly and Jackson Baker.
MILLS BRITT to TABITHA TADLOCK 17 Oct 1854. Bdsm Mills Britt and

JOHNSTON COUNTY MARRIAGES

Robert Hood.
AMBERS LEE to KITREY JONIRKIN 21 Oct 1854. Bdsm Ambers Lee and Right H. Lee.
BRIGHT BAREFOOT to LOUISA HOLMES 27 Oct 1854. Bdsm Bright Barefoot and William R. Holmes.
B. A. WOODALL to ELIZA WELLONS 31 Oct 1854. Bdsm B. A. Woodall and William H. Wellons.
WILLIAM C. BROWN to EMILY JONES 1 Nov 1854. Bdsm William C. Brown and S. F. Johnson.
COUNCIEL KEEN to CALY RENTFROW 6 Nov 1854. Bdsm Counciel Keen and Roberson Raper, Jr.
AHASURUS VINSON to MARY TURNER 6 Nov 1854. Bdsm Ahasurus Vinson and James T. Vinson.
YOUNG STRICKLAND to LOTTY STANLY ?? 1854. Bdsm Young Strickland and John W. Stanly.
BRYANT ONEAL to JULIA WHITLEY 18 Nov 1854. Bdsm Bryant Oneal and Hardy H. Hinnant.
MATTHEW BAKER to NANCY BAKER 21 Nov 1854. Bdsm Matthew Baker and James Baker.
AMOS COATS to TABITHA TURLINGTON 23 Nov 1854. Bdsm Amos Coats and James B. Johnson.
RUFUS JOHNSON to EDITH STEPHENS 23 Nov 1854. Bdsm Rufus Johnson and James B. Johnson.
HENDERSON JONES to PATSY PARRISH 26 Nov 1854. Bdsm Henderson Jones and A. P. Clifton.
ROBERT B. HOOD to MARY M. THORNTON 25 Nov 1854. Bdsm Robert B. Hood and Elias J. Jones.
MAJOR DIXON to MARTHA WOODALE 27 Nov 1854. Bdsm Major Dixon and Kinchen Morgan.
THOMAS WADDLE to MARCELINE WHITLEY 2 Dec 1854. Bdsm Thomas Waddle and James A. Vinson.
JETHRO HOWELL to LORENDA BATTEN 14 Dec 1854. Bdsm Jethro Howell and Jennett Holland.
ASHLEY CREECH to PENELOPE BAGLEY 5 Dec 1854. Bdsm Ashley Creech and Daniel A. Sellers.
NAPOLEAN B. HORN to REBECCA ANN JONES 6 Dec 1854. Bdsm Napolean B. Horn and and B. F. Barber.
PARROT CREECH TO SARAH JANE CANADAY 7 Dec 1854. Bdsm Parrot Creech and Bartley Harper.
MOSES A. LEE to KETSY ELDRIDGE 11 Dec 1854. Bdsm Moses A. Lee and Elam Lee.
JULIUS NICHOLS to MARY N. FERRELL 11 Dec 1854. Bdsm Julius Nichols and Berbin Liles.
WILLIAM H. EASON to ELIZABETH TALTON 11 Dec 1854. Bdsm William H. Eason and H. H. Talton.
WILLIAM P. EDWARDS to NANCY RICHARDSON 15 Dec 1854. Bdsm William P. Edwards and Henry Gerhardt.
FURNEY MILLINDER to SUSAN BROWN 18 Dec 1854. Bdsm Furney Milllinder and John Dunn.
HARRISON FERRELL to NANCY LEVY 19 Dec 1854. Bdsm Harrison Ferrell and Henderson Grayham.
ELI TURLINGTON to SARAH WOODALE 20 Dec 1854. Bdsm Eli Turlington

MARRIAGE BONDS

and Alfred Holland.
BRYANT ALLFORD to MARY ROSE 21 Dec 1854. Bdsm Eli Elengen? and Perry Rentfrow.
JOHN FULGHAM to ZELPHA MASSEY 16 Nov 1854. Bdsm John Fulgham and William Rains.
WILIE ALFORD to SARAH THOMPSON 27 Dec 1854. Bdsm Wilie Alford and B. B. Alford.
SAMUEL CLEMONS to GREZZY ANN DANIEL 29 Dec 1854. Bdsm Samuel Clemons and Edmond Howard.
JESSE H. GODWIN to WILLY WALL 3 Jan 1854. Bdsm Jesse H. Godwin and Irvin L. Godwin.
WILLIAM BUNN to JUNE E. HINTON 8 Dec 1854. Bdsm William Bunn and A. Hinton.
BENJAMIN LEATH to ELIZABETH DANIEL 17 Jan 1855. Bdsm Benjamin Leath and Edmund Howard.
GEORGE W. DUNN to SUSAN LASETTER 24 Jan 1855. Bdsm George W. Dunn and Jesse H. Stanly.
ALEXANDER MUNDS to ELIZUR BARBER 24 Jan 1855. Bdsm Alexander Munds and James M. Carter.
RUFFIN BOYKINS to MARZELLA GREEN 26 Jun 1855. Bdsm Ruffin Boykins and Willie A. Boykins.
JAMES A. GODWIN to LOUIZA ATKINSON 27 Jan 1855. Bdsm James A. Godwin and Jacob H. Godwin.
GIDEON ALLEN to LUCY JUNE MASSINGELE 30 Jan 1855. Bdsm Gideon Allen and William B. Massengill.
HAYWOOD JOHNSON to NANCY H. JOHNSON 8 Feb 1855. Bdsm Haywood Johnson and W. H. Jernigan.
ALEXANDER McLEOD to ELIZUR ANN WHITINGTON 22 Feb 1855. Bdsm Alexander McLeod and H. A. Williams.
ELISHA PITMAN to EDNEY CREECH 26 Feb 1855. Bdsm Elisha Pitman and Alvin Bagley.
ASA CARRELL to MARY H. JOHNSON 27 Feb 1855. Bdsm Asa Carrell and Gaston Johnson.
ROBERSON RAPER to NANCY RENTFRO 27 Feb 1855. Bdsm Roberson Raper and John C. Allen.
ALEXANDER WOODALL to JULIA BARBER 28 Feb 1855. Bdsm Alexander Woodall and Benjamin Godwin.
BRITTAN SMITH to SALLY ANN NORRIS 3 Mar 1855. Bdsm Brittan Smith and John L. Smith.
JAMES RENTFROW TO RAINEY MORRIS 13 Mar 1855. Bdsm James Rentfrow and H. H. Hawley.
AARON W. MASSENGALL to NANCY WILLEY HARPER 15 Mar 1855. Bdsm Aaron W. Masengale and Harrison Ferrell.
WILLIAM S. EARP TO ANN EASON ? Bdsm William S. Earp and John E. Earp.
DIXON PEARCE to EXEY STANSELL 20 Mar 1855. Bdsm Dixon Pearce and John E. Earp.
ISAAC DENNING to MAHALA MANOR 26 Mar 1855. Bdsm Isaac Denning and Jeremiah Blackman.
WRIGHT BLOW to NANCY ONEAL 27 Mar 1855. Bdsm Wright Blow and William H. Oneal.
WILLIAM GRIFFIN to HARRIET STEPHENSON 27 Mar 1855. Bdsm William

JOHNSTON COUNTY MARRIAGES

Griffin and Calvin R. Wallace.
TURNER JONES to MARGARET CREECH 21 Mar 1855. Bdsm Turner Jones and Jacob Brazzel.
ROBERSON RAPER to MARTHA HINNANT 28 Mar 1855. Bdsm Roberson Raper and Joseph Raper.
HENDERSON CROCKER to VINEY CORBET 11 Apr 1855. Bdsm Henderson Crocker and Josiah Gay.
WILLIAM C. POOLE to PHEREBEE ANN HARRISON 16 Apr 1855. Bdsm William C. Poole and John Harrison.
ISAAC PARRISH to EMALINE GODWIN 17 Apr 1855. Bdsm Isaac Parrish and David Parnes.
HELLMAN H. MEDLEN to LUCY M. STRICKLAND 17 Apr 1855. Bdsm Hellman H. Medlen and Loverd Eldridge.
MABRY T. WALL to LOUIZE J. TALTON ? Bdsm Mabry T. Wall and William B. Talton.
THOMAS WHITE to MARY GOODSON 27 Apr 1855. Bdsm Thomas White and Zachariah Hocutt.
LARRY ROSE to ELIZABETH GAY 7 May 1855. Bdsm Larry Rose and Alvin Bagley.
LUCIUS H. BRYAN to ELIZABETH ELLIS 11 May 1855. Bdsm Lucius H. Bryan and P. P. Medlin.
JOHN HOLT to LUQUINNY BARBER 12 May 1855. Bdsm John Holt and Thomas H. Barber.
JOHN R. GOWER to ELIZABETH HOPKINS 15 May 1855. Bdsm John R. Gower and Adam A. Gower.
JOSEPH EDWARDS to SARAH TALTON 15 Mar 1855. Bdsm Joseph Edwards and Howard Edwards.
RICHARD W. SELLERS to ELIZABETH HEDGEPETH 16 Mar 1855. Bdsm Richard W. Sellers and Bryant Taylor.
JOHN BLACKMAN to THENA STRICKLAND 22 May 1855. Bdsm Thomas Lockart.
WILLEY ALFORD to ELIZABETH EDWARDS 28 May 1855. Bdsm Willey Alford and B. B. Alford.
DEMPSEY W. BOON to ALICE H. BOON 29 May 1855. Bdsm Dempsey W. Boon and Wiley S. Boon.
WILIE W. COX to MARY ANN POOLE 29 May 1855. Bdsm Lewis Poole and Sanders E. Cox.
ERASLUS H. GULLY to ELIZABETH HINNANT 29 May 1855. Bdsm Eraslus H. Gully and Joseph J. Wall.
WILLIAM HARTOFIELD to MARY CARTER 5 Jun 1855. Bdsm William Hartofield and J. C. F. Gerhardt.
CHURCHWELL HARRIS to MARY M. BEASLEY 9 Jun 1855. Bdsm Churchwell Harris and Parker R. Tomlinson.
WYATT H. POWELL to MARY WEEKS 11 Jun 1855. Bdsm Wyatt H. Powell and Washington Weeks.
YOUNG R. LEE to MARY E. MORGAN 2 Jul 1855. Bdsm Young R. Lee and John H. Collins.
ZECHARIAH HILL to VIRGINIA WHITLEY 7 Jul 1855. Bdsm Zechariah Hill and Alfred Holland.
THOMAS G. BOWLS to SARAH JANE SMITH 14 Jun 1855. Bdsm Thomas G. Bowls and James M. Carter.
SIDNEY A. SMITH to MARY E. WILLIAMS 16 Jul 1855. Bdsm Sidney A. Smith and John B. Beckwith.

MARRIAGE BONDS

BARDIN WATKINS to CINTHA HORN 23 Jul 1855. Bdsm Bardin Watkins and Elijah Atkinson.
JAMES H. WILDER to KISISH C. BARNES 30 Jul 1855. Bdsm James H. Wilder and John Gully.
JOSEPH H. LEE to MARY ANN BARBER 8 Jul 1855. Bdsm Joseph H. Lee and William E. Thornton.
RUBIN R. CLIFTON to SUSAN JANE GRIFFIN 10 Jul 1855. Bdsm Rubin R. Clifton and Bryant Jones.
JOHN POLLEARD to HARRIET HARPER 10 Aug 1855. Bdsm John Polleard and Cannon Canaday.
LEN C. STALLINGS to THETUS BAUCUM 10 Aug 1855. Bdsm Len C. Stallings and Thomas D. Ingram.
HINTON EVANS to WINIFRED WALL 28 Aug 1855. Bdsm Hinton Evans and B. C. Richardson.
ALVIN J. SHALLINGTON to ABSELLA SNIPES 28 Aug 1855. Bdsm Alvin J. Shallington and David Snipes.
JEREMIAH LEE to ALLEY WATKINS 5 Aug 1855. Bdsm Jeremiah Lee and William H. Massingell.
JOHN B. INGRAM to NANCY WALTSON 19 Sep 1855. Bdsm John B. Ingram and James E. Lee.
THOMAS SHANE to FRANCIS AVERA 12 Sep 1855. Bdsm Thomas Shane and Joseph Barham.
EPHRAIM O. BEASLY to ELIZABETH TOOL 13 Sep 1855. Bdsm Ephraim O. Beasly and Ashley Blackman.
WILIE KEEN to MILLY HORN 21 Sep 1855. Bdsm Wilie Keen and Blackman Ballance.
THOMAS HOLLAND to MARY GARRELL 1 Oct 1855. Bdsm Thomas Holland and Wilie Watson.
ISAAC GARRELL to MARY GARRELL 13 Oct 1855. Bdsm Isaac Garrell and Enos Garrell.
WILLIAM WEBB to LUCINDA YOUNG 24 Oct 1855. Bdsm William Webb and James N. Ellis.
HENRY BARNES to JENSEY WOODARD 7 Nov 1855. Bdsm Henry Barnes and Irvin Woodard.
WILLIAM H. WALL to APPY BATTEN 15 Nov 1855. Bdsm William H. Wall and James Wall.
WILLIAM THAIN to JULIA ANN CULLUM 15 Nov 1855. Bdsm William Thain and W. H. Cullum.
CEPHAS BARBER to TEMPERANCE LOCKART 17 Nov 1855. Bdsm Cephas Barber and A. E. Lockart.
R. D. HOLT to ELIZABETH LOCKART 17 Nov 1855. Bdsm R. D. Holt and A. E. Lockart.
WILLIAM H. JACKSON to PIETY J. JACKSON 27 Nov 1855. Bdsm William H. Jackson and John C. Hood.
LEVY COX to PATIENCE PARKER 3 Dec 1855. Bdsm Levy Cox and William H. Joyner.
ALEXANDER SHANE to LUCY ANN ENNIS 11 Dec 1855. Bdsm Alexander Shane and William H. Avera.
LEVY CARMACK to CHELLY HOWELL 15 Dec 1855. Bdsm Levy Carmack and Elijah Atkinson.
WILLIAM H. COLE to SARAH THOMPSON 28 Dec 1855. Bdsm William H. Cole and John Dunn.

JOHNSTON COUNTY MARRIAGES

JOHN WIGGS to PENELOPE BROUGHTON 31 Dec 1855. Bdsm John Wiggs and Barna Lane.
ALFORD PEARCE to MALINDA SMITH 3 Jan 1856. Bdsm Alford Pearce and Gaston Hinnant.
JOHN OVERBY to SALLY COLLINS 12 Jan 1856. Bdsm John Overby and Henry G. Edwards.
MARION W. LEE to MARGARET JORDAN 19 Dec 1855. Bdsm Marion W. Lee and B. B. Lee.
GEORGE B. BALLENGER to SARAH R. HINNANT 26 Dec 1855. Bdsm George B. Ballenger and William H. Sellers.
MORRACE EDWARDS to MARTHA CONE? 16 Jan 1856. Bdsm Morrace Edwards and John Edwards.
JONATHAN BAKER to LEWANY WALLACE 17 Jan 1856. Bdsm James Baker, Jr.
WILLIAM J. SPENCER to EDITH OLIVER 22 Jan 1856. Bdsm William J. Spencer and John Peedin.
JESSE WELLONS to DRUZELLA SHEPHERD 23 Jan 1856. Bdsm Jesse Wellons and W. D. Wood.
JAMES H. ABELL to LUCY J. ELDRIDGE 25 Jan 1856. Bdsm James H. Abell and Alfred Holland.
JUSTUS PARRISH to MARTHA GODWIN 28 Jan 1856. Bdsm Justus Parrish and John C. Gully.
JAMES WILKINS to CINDA PARNELL 31 Jan 1856. Bdsm James Wilkins and Deveraux Parnell.
JOHN T. WIGGS to PENELOPE STEPHENSON 1 Feb 1856. Bdsm John T. Wiggs and Kimmons Stephenson.
WILLIAM M. LYNN to ANNE ELIZA CHAMBLEE 6 Feb 1856. Bdsm William M. Lynn and William Chamblee.
EDMUND HOWARD to MEDY ANN PARRISH 12 Feb 1856. Bdsm Edmund Howard and Kerney Wilder.
W. R. YOUNG to J. PEACOCK 16 Feb 1856. Bdsm W. R. Young and P. R. Tomlinson.
MILES V. BAREFOOT to MARY JOHNSON 26 Feb 1856. Bdsm Miles V. Barefoot and W. H. Massingele.
JOEL BAREFOOT to ESTHER A. BAREFOOT 26 Feb 1856. Bdsm Joel Barefoot and W. H. Massingill.
AMOS PARRISH to NANCY PEOPLES 26 Feb 1856. Bdsm Stephen Parker.
ALFRED HOLLAND to CAROLINE AVERA 5 Mar 1856. Bdsm Alfred Holland and John H. Daniel.
GEORGE MASSINGILL to NANCY ANN JERNIGAN 6 Mar 1856. Bdsm George Massingill and Isaac Ingram.
SIMON WILKINS to ELIZABETH DAUGHTRY 14 Mar 1856. Bdsm John R. Thompson.
JOHN R. BAREFOOT to NANCY G. JACKSON 17 Mar 1856. Bdsm John R. Barefoot and Loverd Eldrige.
ELI GODWIN to ZELPHA ROSE 19 Mar 1856. Bdsm Eli Godwin and Thomas G. Raiford.
WILLIAM P. BARBER to ZELLA STEPHENSON 25 Mar 1856. Bdsm William P. Barber and Amos Coats.
WILLIAM D. SHEPPERD to ELIZUR ANN HINTON 25 Mar 1856. Bdsm William D. Shepperd and William Chamblee.
AQUILLA BYRD to CATHERINE STEWART 25 Mar 1856. Bdsm Aquilla Byrd and Edward Byrd.

MARRIAGE BONDS

YOUNG MORGAN to ZELPHA GURLEY 27 Mar 1856. Bdsm Young Morgan and D. McPherson.
JOSEPH P. BELL to HARRIET BAILY 29 Mar 1856. Bdsm Carsen Oneal.
ASHLEY B. EVANS to HELEN WILKINS 31 Mar 1856. Bdsm Ashley B. Evans and George Brazell.
JOHN R. THOMPSON to EVELINE M. RICHARDSON 1 Apr 1856. Bdsm John R. Thompson and Stephen Snead.
WILLEY P. WIGGS to EDNEY PEEDIN 5 Apr 1856. Bdsm Willey P. Wiggs and Nathan Wiggs.
WILLIAM M. JERNIGAN to POLLY ANN COATS 8 Apr 1856. Bdsm William M. Jernigan and Loverd Eldridge.
LARRY PACE to CINTHY BATTEN 8 Apr 1856. Bdsm Larry Pace and Bartley Pace.
WILLIAM B. OLIVER to MARY PERLIUS PEEDEN 8 Apr 1856. Bdsm William B. Oliver and Thomas Oliver.
JOSEPH OVERBY to SALLY CREECH 25 Apr 1856. Bdsm Joseph Overby and Henry G. Edwards.
BENJAMIN B. BAKER to MARTHA WHITAKER 21 Apr 1856. Bdsm Benjamin B. Baker and James S. Holt.
SIMON R. MORGAN to MANEZUS SIMPKINS 7 May 1856. Bdsm Simon R. Morgan and Alfred Holland.
ALLEN STEPHENSON to JENNET WILSON 10 May 1856. Bdsm Allen Stephenson and Amos Coats.
WILLIAM JORDAN to ELIZABETH JOHNSON 1 Apr 1856. Bdsm William H. Massingill.
JESSE N. JOHNSON to MARTHA J. E. FARSON 17 May 1856. Bdsm Jesse N. Johnson and B. F. Farson.
ALLEN S. STANSELL to HARRIET RENTFROW 17 May 1856. Bdsm Allen S. Stansell and Jesse Hinnant.
JOHN B. BECKWITH to JULIA M. SANDERS 20 May 1856. Bdsm John B. Beckwith and Stephen Snead.
THOMAS HOGG to POLLY M. LEE 20 May 1856. Bdsm Thomas Hogg and Joseph Bell.
DAVID HOLLY to LYDIA A. COLE 22 May 1856. Bdsm David Holly and Ransom Lawhan.
JOHN M. HAYSE to AGGY NOLES 24 May 1856. Bdsm John M. Hayse and Noah B. Barefoot.
JOHN A. ENNIS to WINIFRED ENNIS 26 May 1856. Bdsm John A. Ennis and John E. Ennis.
RANSOM DUNCAN to LUCINDA BOON 27 May 1856. Bdsm Ransom Duncan and George M. Duncan.
LINCOLN LEE to WILLEY EATMAN 30 May 1856. Bdsm Lincoln Lee and Alvin H. Atkinson.
CASWELL HOCUTT to HAWKINS BRANNON 3 Jun 1856. Bdsm Caswell Hocutt and Henry Price.
RAY PHILLIPS to NANCY JONES 5 Jun 1856. Bdsm Ray Phillips and William H. Joyner.
JOHN G. HODGES to HARRIET E. JERNIGAN 9 Jun 1856. Bdsm John G. Hodges and William H. Jernigan.
CHARLES CARRELL to MARTHA KING 18 Jun 1856. Bdsm Charles Carrell and Benjamin Baker.
MARRION LASSITER to AEBELLA ELLIS 18 Jun 1856. Bdsm Marrion

JOHNSTON COUNTY MARRIAGES

Lassiter and John B. Lassiter.
HENESBURY COLIN to WELTHY HODGE 24 May 1856. Bdsm Henesbury Colin and L. Richardson.
JOSEPH JONES to MARY ROBERTS 10 Jul 1856. Bdsm Joseph Jones and Perry Renfrow.
LOVIT RAYNER to KESEAH JERNIGAN 11 Jul 1856. Bdsm Sir William Johnson.
ELIJAH STANLY to JENSEY STANLY 12 Jul 1856. Bdsm Eli Stanly.
JOHN A. ENNIS to MARY ANN WHEELER 24 Jul 1856. Bdsm John A. Ennis and Benjamin Godwin.
SAMUEL EVANS to SALLY HOBBIT 28 Jul 1856. Bdsm Samuel Evans and Silvester Pearce.
WILLIAM YOUNG to MARY H. ADAMS 8 Aug 1856. Bdsm William Young and Amos Coats.
CRAWFORD FUTRELL to CAROLINE PEEDIN 8 Aug 1856. Bdsm Crawford Futrell and Daniel A. Sellers.
JAMES RAYNER, JR. to JANE E. BEASLEY 11 Aug 1856. Bdsm James Rayner, Jr. and William Hutson.
JAMES W. STRICKLAND to HESTER ANN INGRAM 21 Aug 1856. Bdsm James W. Strickland and Jesse H. Stanly.
RUFUS WOODARD to MARY MASSEY 25 Aug 1856. Bdsm Alexander Brown.
GEORGE W. MASSENGILL to ALCINDA ALLEN 26 Aug 1856. Bdsm George W. Massengill and George Keen.
D. L. JONES to SARAH L. JERNIGAN 26 Aug 1856. Bdsm D. L. Jernigan and L. M. Surles.
JOAB LEE to SUSAN LEE 27 Aug 1856. Bdsm Joab Lee and Allen J. Lee.
JONATHAN COPELAND to BETHANY GODWIN 23 Sep 1856. Bdsm Jonathan Copeland and Gaston Hinnant.
WILLIAM McLANE to MARTHA LEE 29 Sep 1856. Bdsm William McLane and James Lash.
DANIEL SELLERS to SARAH ANN BLACKMAN 13 Oct 1856. Bdsm Daniel Sellers and Ransom Taylor.
SIR WILLIAM JOHNSON to RACHEL H. ALLEN 11 Oct 1856. Bdsm Sir William Johnson and Lovet Rayner.
ASHLEY JOHNSON to LUCINDA MASSENGILL 22 Oct 1856. Bdsm Ashley Johnson and Gideon Kean.
JOHN W. BEASLEY to CHARLOTTA F. HOOD 5 Nov 1856. Bdsm John W. Beasley and B. R. Hood.
JOHN R. BRANNON to POLLY ANN POOL 17 Nov 1856. Bdsm James R. Ellis.
JOHN F. S. RHODES to MARY E. CROCKER 4 Oct 1856. Bdsm John F. S. Rhodes and John H. Daniel.
MARSHALE H. BEZZELE to ELIZABETH COLE 24 Nov 1856. Bdsm Marshale H. Bezzele and Marshaville Bezzele.
WILLIAM ROBINS to NANCY SCHSOINS? 25 Nov 1856. Bdsm William Robins and Vine Edwards.
WILLIAM N. HARPER to PHEREBE SMITH 25 Nov 1856. Bdsm Albert Parrish.
ROBERT D. CHRISMAN to MARY A. HINNANT 25 Nov 1856. Bdsm Robert D. Chrisman and B. C. Richardson.
JOHN R. HARRISON to MARTHA UPCHURCH 26 Nov 1856. Bdsm John R. Harrison and James H. Bryan.
ASA L. SASSER to ELBERT D. HOLT 26 Nov 1856. Bdsm Asa L. Sasser and

MARRIAGE BONDS

Henderson Grayham.
LEONIDIAN H. PENNY to ELIZABETH BYRD 6 Dec 1856. Bdsm Leonidian H. Penny and Richard Byrd.
G. W. LAWRENCE to MARY E. BIZZELL 10 Dec 1856. Bdsm G. W. Lawrence and Samuel Bizzell.
JOHN PARRISH to CIVIL A. STEPHENSON 15 Dec 1856. Bdsm John Parrish and J. Marion Stephenson.
CORNELIUS STEPHENSON to MARY E. COATS 18 Dec 1856. Bdsm Cornelius Stephenson and Joel H. Massingell.
JOEL PITMAN to JULIA ROSE 29 Dec 1856. Bdsm Joel Pitman and S. H. Pitman.
HARDY SILAVENT to ISABELL BASS 30 Dec 1856. Bdsm Hardy Silavent and William Rains.
MERRIT LANGDON to MARGARET J. STEPHENSON 30 Dec 1856. Bdsm Merrit Langdon and J. R. Harper.
WESTLY HUBBARD to NANCY S. ATKINSON 31 Dec 1856. Bdsm Westly Hubbard and James D. Hinnant.
NATHAN WIGGS to ELIZABETH MASSEY 31 Dec 1856. Bdsm Nathan Wiggs and Philip H. Oliver.
WILLIAM A. SMITH to POLLY ANN MUNSON 31 Dec 1856. Bdsm William A. Smith and T. W. Whitley.
STEPHEN WATSON to PIETY HINNANT 6 Jan 1857. Bdsm Stephen Watson and Tobias Godwin.
ROBERT D. LUNCEFORD to CORNELIA A. POWELL 7 Jan 1857. Bdsm Stephen Snead.
JOHN OLIVER to EVALINE WATSON 10 Jan 1857. Bdsm William J. Spencer.
GEORGE BARBER to ROBIN BLANCHET 12 Jan 1857. Bdsm Benjamin Godwin.
S. P. TEMPLE to PENELOPE MASSINGILL 14 Jan 1857. Bdsm S. P. Temple and Blackman Coats.
JOHN A. COLE to ADELINE BEASLEY 15 Jan 1857. Bdsm John A. Cole and James H. Abell.
STARLING BAKER to CAROLINE GRIFFIN 21 Jan 1857. Bdsm Starling Baker and Benjamin Wellons.
NOAH G. BAREFOOT to SUSAN A. JOHNSTON 28 Jan 1857. Bdsm J. R. Barefoot.
ROBERT M. OLIVER to MARY A. W. STARLING 31 Jan 1857. Bdsm Robert M. Oiver and R. P. Raiford.
JACOB STANLY to REBECCA ANDREWS 4 Nov 1856. Bdsm William H. Massingill.
JOHN W. BROWN to SARAH GARNER 3 Feb 1857. Bdsm Ruffin Brown.
FRANCIS BRIDGERS to SARAH LOUISE ? 4 Feb 1857. Bdsm William Pearce.
URIAH DENNING to ELIZABETH STAFFORD 9 Feb 1857. Bdsm Needham Fields.
JOHN B. GREEN to ESTHER S. DODD 11 Feb 1857. Bdsm John B. Green and Henry F. Boon.
BENJAMIN STRICKLAND to POLLY ANN DAUGHTRY 11 Feb 1857. Bdsm John Daughtry.
H. F. PORTER to PENELOPE LEE 23 Feb 1857. Bdsm H. F. Porter and J. A. Porter.
NEEDHAM PARCIE to ELIZA WOODELL 3 Jan 1857. Bdsm B. C. Richardson.
SAMUEL L. YOUNG to PHEBY McLUM 24 Feb 1857. Bdsm A. D. Young.
JOHN DODD to PENELOPE JOHNSTON 24 Feb 1857. Bdsm Aventon Avera.

JOHNSTON COUNTY MARRIAGES

JAMISON H. ELLIS to ESTHER HUTSON 25 Feb 1857. Bdsm J. W. Hutson.
CRAWFORD WATKINS to ANNA PEARCE 25 Feb 1857. Bdsm James W. Sasser.
JOHN HOBBS to BYTHA ANN BARBER 25 Feb 1857. Bdsm Larkin Barber.
JASON YELVINGTON to SARAH PHILLIPS 9 Mar 1857. Bdsm Guy H. Phillips.
JOHN CLARK to RUTHA POWELL 10 Mar 1857. Bdsm John Clark and Willis A. Bell.
WILLIS COLE to CAROLINE COGDALE 10 Mar 1857. Bdsm John Britt.
CULLEN CREECH to ESTHER HIX 18 Mar 1857. Bdsm John B. Creech.
B. F. WHITLEY to MARY PARRISH 1 Mar 1857. Bdsm Raiford Williamson.
LARKIN G. BOYETT to CHLOE ANN BAGLEY 24 Mar 1857. Bdsm Larkin G. Boyett and Seth Pitman.
JOHN J. WALL to ELIZUR JANE HOCUTT 24 Mar 1857. Bdsm John H. Bryan.
HAYWOOD RAINS to MARY PEARCE 26 Mar 1857. Bdsm Moses Hill.
HENRY S. LASETTER to ELENOR DIXON 15 Apr 1857. Bdsm William Lasetter.
BARTLEY DEANS to ELIZABETH ANN PEARCE 20 Apr 1857. Bdsm Hinton Evans.
JOHN R. JONES to CATHARINE A. JOHNSON 20 Apr 1857. Bdsm John J. Barnes.
REUBEN JOHNSON to ELIZABETH STANLY 21 Apr 1857. Bdsm Reuben Johnson and George Keen.
HOBSON BROWN to NANCY BATTEN 22 Apr 1857. Bdsm John Brown.
BRYANT H. CREECH to LUCINDA HOLLEMAN 27 Apr 1857. Bdsm Bryant H. Creech and William H. Joyner.
RANDAL MOORE to ESTHER BARBER 21 May 1857. Bdsm Randal Moore and Haywood Moore.
WILLIAM HUTSON to CAROLINE HARPER 8 May 1857. Bdsm William Hutson and Jeremiah L. George.
J. C. MONK to EUPHEMIA EASON 9 May 1857. Bdsm J. C. Monk and Everett Thornton.
JOEL HUTSON to SARAH ELDRIDGE 19 May 1857. Bdsm Joel Hutson and William Hutson.
ALLEN R. DUNN to ANGERONAH W. HINTON 1 May 1857. Bdsm Allen R. Dunn and Samuel P. Holton.
WILLIAM HIN to SARAH STANSEL 8 Jun 1857. Bdsm Nehemiah Hin.
W. H. JERNIGAN to SUSAN ALLEN 7 Jun 1857. Bdsm W. H. Jernigan and Budd Jernigan.
WILLIAM G. STRICKLAND to NANCY THARP 15 Jun 1857. Bdsm Norfelt T. Bell.
WILLIAM A. HOCUTT to JOANNA WILLIAMSON 16 Jun 1857. William A. Hocutt and Jesse Hinnant.
JESSE WHEELER to CATHARINE JOHNSON 22 Jun 1857. Bdsm Jesse Wheeler and W. D. Wood.
WILLIAM SMITH to RINDA ADAMS 22 Jun 1857. Bdsm Josiah Atkinson.
REGDON H. F. ELLEN to MARY JANE DUPREE 15 Jul 1857. Bdsm Charles Beasley.
WILLIAM A. LANGSTON to NANCY M. BLACKMAN 17 Jul 1857. Bdsm Raiford Harres.
STEPHEN A. CREECH to ELIZABETH CREECH 17 Jul 1857. Bdsm Stephen A. Creech.
JOHN MUNDEN to JULIA Y. HINES 31 Jul 1857. Bdsm Henderson Graham.

MARRIAGE BONDS

HILLIMAN LEWIS to SARAH JOHNSON 2 Sep 1857. Bdsm Hilliman Lewis.
WILLIAM LANE to MARGARET A. WHITLEY 2 ? 1857. Bdsm William Lane and Thaddeus W. Whitley.
WILLIAM GWIN to RHODA BAKER 11 Sep 1857. Bdsm William Gwin and George Keen.
JACOB A. STEVENS to E. L. JOBY 15 Sep 1857. Bdsm James A. Stevens and Young N. Thornton.

JOHNSTON COUNTY MARRIAGES

MARRIAGE RECORDS

RANSOM CREECH to ELIZABETH ATKINS 3 Jan 1854. JP Jesse Parker.
ELISHA PITMAN, JR. to EDNEY CREECH 2 Feb 1855. JP Jesse Parker.
ROBERSON RAPER to MARTHA HINNANT 29 Mar 1855. JP Jesse Parker.
MARBY T. WALL to LOUISA J. TALTON 22 Apr 1855. JP Perry Godwin.
RAY PHILLIPS to NANCY JONES 6 Jun 1856. JP Perry Godwin.
ELIJAH STANLEY to JENCY STANLEY 13 Jul 1856. JP Perry Godwin.
HILLSMAN LEWIS to SARAH JOHNSON ? Sep 1857. JP Perry Godwin.
WILLIAM LANE to MARGARET R. WHITLEY 3 Sep 1857. JP B. Gifford.
BOURBON IVEY to FANNY MARTIN 31 Dec 1857. JP R. Massingell.
THOMAS R. ROSE to LEACEY ALLEN 18 Nov 1857. JP R. Massingell.
JORDAN GODWIN to ELIZABETH FUTRELL 17 Dec 1857. JP Willie Wellons.
G. W. BAREFOOT to ELIZABETH LEE 26 Nov 1857. JP R. Massingell.
ARCHIBALD ARTIS to NANCY HATCHCOCK 26 Nov 1857. JP J. C. Wood.
NEWRY DINKINS to EVALINE C. BOON 30 Nov 1857. JP J. F. Ellington.
WILLIAM JORDAN to EDITH A. ADAMS 8 Oct 1857. JP J. H. Kennedy.
JAMES B. REAVES to NANCY E. HICKS 1 Dec 1857. JP Robert A. Gully.
LARKIN BROWN to NANCY BATTEN 3 Dec 1857. JP Willie Wellons.
JOHN A. SMITH to MARTHA E. BEASLEY 22 Oct 1857. JP John C. Wood.
JAMES D. HINNANT to MARY A. BARNES 8 Oct 1857. JP R. A. Gully.
NEEDHAM FREEMAN to BETTY ROE 26 Sep 1857. William Potter, Minister.
DELIA MITCHELL to MARY HOWELL 29 Sep 1857. JP William Raines.
OWEN WILKINS to REBECCA JOHNSON 26 Nov 1857. JP James H. Sasser.
EDWIN S. TISDALE to LUCINDA ONEAL 22 Dec 1857. JP W. Earp.
N. Y. FREEMAN to RIXEY HORN 24 Sep 1857. JP J. F. Ellington.
AQUILLA NARRON to ELIZA TALTON 23 Sep 1857. JP A. H. Atkinson.
JESSE J. JOHNSON to TOBITHA ELLIS 16 Nov 1857. JP John C. Wood.
RANSOM RYALS to EMILY WOODALL 29 Oct 1857. JP P. Godwin.
WILLIAM CARDELL to POLLY CARDELL 21 Oct 1857.
JOHN B. PARKER to ELIZABETH E. JOHNSON 1 Nov 1857. JP John C. Wood.
D. D. WINDHAM to LYDIA BARBER 12 Nov 1857. JP Amos Coats.
A. F. WHITLEY to MINERVA ANN SMITH 23 Sep 1857. JP J. F. Ellington.
JACOB A. STEVENS to ELIZABETH L. JOBY 16 Sep 1857. JP A. Lane.
M. L. AUSTIN to ANNY HOLT 26 Nov 1857. JP A. J. Leach.
WILLIAM GWIN to PHEBE BAKER 13 Sep 1857. JP George Keen.
E. M. OLIVER to JULIA Y. ADAMS 27 Oct 1857. JP George Keen.
JOHN MUNDEN to JULIE HINES 31 Aug 1857. JP B. A. Wellons.
WILLIAM H. JERNIGAN to SUSAN ALLEN 18 Jun 1857. JP P. Godwin.
JESSE WHEELER to CATHERINE JOHNSON 2 Jul 1857. JP F. Garrard.
WILLIAM RAINS JR. to BETSY JANIO CREECH 23 Nov 1858. JP Jesse Parker.
NEEDHAM L. KNOX to PATSY S. PILKINTON 26 Oct 1858. JP Perry Godwin.
THOMAS WOOD to PENNY MASSINGILL 9 Jan 1858. JP R. Massingell.
JESSE HINNANT to CHERRY BARNES 24 Feb 1857. JP L. G. Boyette.
ABRAM DIXON to SARAH BATTEN 18 Feb 1858. JP P. Godwin.
JESSE HODGE to LUCENNA WALL 10 Feb 1858. JP B. C. Richardson.
GASTAN HINNANT to JOANNE COPELAND 7 Jan 1858. JP Jessie Parker.
ROBERT J. BYRD to HELLOW WELLONS 10 Mar 1858. JP J. H. Kennedy.
THOMAS FURLEY to RIDLEY ELLIS 15 Jan 1858. JP J. F. Ellington.
JAMES MILWALL? to MARY BROUGHTON 2 Jan 1858. JP Robert A. Gulley.

MARRIAGE RECORDS

EXUM H. HOLLAND to SARAH SASSER 11 Feb 1858. JP Jesse Parker.
HARRY BRYAN to SPICEY McLAN 8 Apr 1858. JP John C. Hood.
WILLIAM F. HALL to ELIZA IVEY 16 Feb 1858. JP P. Godwin.
JOHN WOOD to SARA A. CROP 21 Feb 1858. JP W. F. Holderman.
EVERETT PEARCE to KEZIAH WHITEHEAD 24 Nov 1858. JP Willie Holt.
WILLIAM R. STEPHENSON to MARTHA A. MITCHINER 10 Feb 1858. JP William E. Bell.
RICHARD BATTEN to TEMPY ATKINSON 24 Jan 1858. JP P. Godwin.
MR. J. L. BANKS to MISS PHEREBA H. TOMLINSON 30 Sep 1858. JP Thomas D. Snead.
JOSIAH PULLEY to MILLY RICHARDSON 21 Nov 1858.
JAMES D. WALL to NANCY E. BROUGHTON 28 Jul 1857 JP A. Gully.
CALVIN BROUGHTON to MARY E. LASSITER 24 May 1858. JP J. R. Ellington.
JOHN BATTEN to MARTHA BATTEN 27 May 1858.
STERLING JOHNSON to ARAMINTA GOWER 12 Sep 1858. JP D. H. Holton.
QUILLY PRICE to MARY PARKER 11 Mar 1858. JP L. G. Boyett.
RANSOM GODWIN to CEANY GODWIN 30 May 1858. JP James Faulk.
THOMAS BARBER to SARAH TOMLINSON 7 Mar 1858. JP F. Garrard.
JOHN R. CREECH to EVALINE OLIVER 6 Jan 1857. Barnes, Minister.
W. H. DURHAM to AMELIA TURNER 21 Dec 1858. JP J. F. Garrard.
HARRY LEE to NANCY WOOD 4 Nov 1858. JP R. Massingill.
HENRY AUSTIN to SOPHIA MITCHENER 14 Dec 1859. JP J. F. Ellington.
SETH PENNY to MARY C. BRYD 15 Jan 1859. JP Robert W. Stevens.
ALLEN S. STANSEL to ELIZABETH SYLLIVANT 24 Dec 1855. JP T. G. Boyette.
HAYWOOD BARBER to HARRIET MORGAN 26 Dec 1858. JP Robert W. Stevens.
HAYWOOD JOHNSON to ELIZABETH ONEAL 28 Nov 1858. JP S. W. Moody.
JAMES UNDERWOOD to MARY J. SCOTT 11 Nov 1858. JP John C. Hood.
WILLIAM H. CANADY to ELIZABETH BARBER 15 Apr 1858. JP B. Goodwin.
JACOB H. GODWIN to AURELIA BARBER 6 May 1857. JP P. Godwin.
JAMES HICKS to MARY E. MURPHREY 11 Apr 1858. JP Thomas Snead.
JAMES D. T. WELLONS to ALICE BLACKMAN 9 Mar 1858. JP John C. Hood.
NATHAN T. LANGLEY to WINNY POPE 6 May 1858. JP P. Godwin.
HENRY H. HOBBS to MARY A. NORTHANS 1 Jun 1858. JP William C. Bell.
JOSIAH L. BLACKMAN to MARY SMITH 27 Apr 1858. JP A. B. Peacock.
G. W. REAVES to WINNY WHEELER 13 Apr 1857. JP W. F. Han.
YOUNG A. STANCELL to SUSAN C. GODWIN 22 Aug 1858. JP R. Godwin.
M. F. HOOD to M. HINTON 29 Jun 1858. JP B. E. Richardson.
ALFRED PEARCE to PATIENCE HINNANT 28 Mar 1858. JP Jesse Parker.
WILLIAM G. BARBER to PIETY PAGE 10 Aug 1858. JP P. Godwin.
GARRY HORNE to MILLICENT RAIFORD 18 Mar 1858. JP Jesse Parker.
JAMES H. SAULES to FRANCES WHEELER 30 Dec 1858. JP W. F. Holt.
LEWIS B. OLIVER to JULIE H. TINER 21 Oct 1858. JP George Keen.
WILLIS A. BELL to AUGUSTA JANE LANGHORN 22 Dec 1858. JP George Keen.
YOUNG LEE AND FANNY INGRAM 11 Jul 1858. JP George Keen.
JOSIAH MASSINGILL to ANNY BARBER 18 Dec 1858. JP George Keen.
SIR WILLIAM DUNN to RIDLEY STANLY 15 Aug 1858. JP George Keen.
ABSALOM BARBER to POLLY ANN MASSINGELL 4 Dec 1858. JP George Keen.
RICHARD D. BYRD to ELEANOR McGEO 16 Sep 1858. JP P. Godwin.
RANSOM POOL to ELIZABETH SIMMONS 25 Sep 1858. JP J. A. Stevens.

JOHNSTON COUNTY MARRIAGES

JOHN W. POOL to MARGARET PEACOCK 26 Oct 1858. JP John H. Kennedy.
WILLIAM H. STEVENS to SARAH MARTIN 28 Oct 158. JP J. W. Whitley.
W. D. PHILLIPS to MARTHA FITZGERALD 19 Oct 1858. JP Willie Williams.
ABEL GOWER to CLARKEY HOLLIMAN 1 Dec 1858. JP B. A. Williams.
WILLIAM D. HOLT to KEZIEH C. CAPPS 29 Apr 1858. JP Edwin Boykins.
TROY W. WOODALL to EMILY H. BIZZELL 14 Dec 1858. JP J. J. Hobby.
JOHN R. DUNN to MARY A. FAIL 12 Aug 1858. JP John C. Hood.
HENRY SCOTT to CHARLOTTE BAREFOOT 29 Aug 1858. JP John C. Hood.
THOMAS S. HOLLIMAN to NANCY M. HOLT 14 Jun 1858. JP Edwin Boykins.
NEEDHAM L. BARNES to MARY A. W. M. YOUNGBLOOD 15 Oct 1858. JP R. W. Gulley.
LEWIS CREECH to ALLY CRAWFORD 24 Jun 1858. JP Edwin Boykins.
LOVETT LEE to WINIFORD GRANT 5 Sep 1858. JP R. Massingill.
PATRICK CREECH to CALLY JONES 1 Dec 1859. JP William Brown.
JOHN HAMILTON to TRANQUILLA PRICE 3 Nov 1859. JP William Brown.
PETER C. DUPREE to MARTHA W. BRITT 16 Oct 1858. JP John Harper.
BYTHAN BAREFOOT to JANE BRYANT 29 Dec 1859. JP John C. Hood.
JAMES W. ALLEN to PARTHENON H. MASSINGILL 4 Mar 1859. JP George Keen.
WILLIE SEABERRY to NANCY POWELL 4 Dec 1859. JP Ransom Lee.
WILLIAM GWIN to POLLY BLACKMAN 1 May 1859. JP George Keen.
BENJAMIN J. DUNN to LUCY C. LASSITER 6 Feb 1859. JP George Keen.
BLACKMAN COATS to NANCY LEE 24 Apr 1859. JP George Keen.
JOHN W. BASS to PATIENCE ANN DEANS 17 Mar 1859. JP Jesse Parker.
JOSEPH BATTEN to AMANDA PITMAN 3 Nov 1859. JP P. Godwin.
ALSEY PARNOLD to LONENZA HOLT 17 Nov 1859. JP Robert W. Stevens.
JOHN A. ENNIS to ABI WHEELER 13 Oct 1859. William Holt, Elder.
R. K. FERRELL to MARY ANN VINSON 9 Nov 1859. JP J. F. Ellington.
WILLIAM HUGHES to NANCY WOOLEY 13 Jan 1859. JP B. Lane.
GASTON JONES to S. E. JOHNSON 19 Jan 1859. JP J. F. Ellington.
W. G. MURPHY to SARAH C. HINTON 10 Feb 1859. JP R. N. Gulley.
JAMES H. CLIFTON to MARTHA CORDELL 24 Feb 1859. JP Robert W. Stevens.
WILIE JACKSON to CLARKEY BAREFOOT 20 Feb 1859. JP R. Massingill.
JAMES E. LEE to DICY A. GWIN 17 Feb 1859. JP R. Massingill.
JESSE GODWIN to KETSY JACKSON 20 Feb 1859. JP R. Massingill.
JOHN G. RANIER to ELIZABETH BEASLEY 20 Feb 1859. William F. Holt, Elder.
NATHANIEL GILES to ANNA HOLMES 25 Jan 1859. W. F. Holt, Elder.
P.P. COATS to SUSAN JOHNSON 6 Mar 1859. JP William J. Brigham.
CHARLES C. MASSEY to MARY W. TOLER 24 Feb 1859. JP Thomas H. Atkins.
NATHAN GREEN to HOPETTINE TOLTON 26 Jan 1859. JP J. F. Ellington.
PINKNEY WILKINS to PHOEBE McLAN 11 Jul 1858. JP Right Ryals.
BENJAMIN J. HINES to ALTNEY JANE ADAMS 28 Apr 1859.
E. R. OLIVER to SUSAN L. TINER 13 Jan 1859. JP George Keen.
HAYWOOD MOORE to DARKESS GREEN 6 Jan 1859. JP George Keen.
THOMAS H. ATKINSON to MARTHA A. R. RICHARDSON 12 Oct 1859. Lemmon Shell, Minister.
JOSEPH JOHNSON to LUCINDA GAY 11 Dec 1859. JP Wilie Wellon.
JOHN DUNN to SARAH JUMP 28 Apr 1859. JP Jesse Parker.

MARRIAGE RECORDS

WILLIAM GAY to SARAH H. WALL 6 Dec 1859 JP R. N. Gulley.
JETHRO THAIN to AMANDA ALLEN 6 Sep 1859. JP R. D. Lunceford.
JACKSON SOUTHARD to ANN SMITH 12 Jun 1859 JP Jesse Parker.
J. P. PICKETT to MARY EATMAN 4 Aug 1859. JP Charles W. Lee.
CALVIN PITMAN to RANZY GAY 25 Sep 1859. JP Jesse Parker.
WILLIAM H. BRYAN to SARAH A. E. VINCENT 16 Nov 1859. Lemmon Shell, Minister.
WILLIAM G. MORGAN to MARTHA WOOD 3 Nov 1859. JP John C. Hood.
WILLIAM ADAMS to MARTHA GREEN 7 Jul 1859. JP Right Ryals.
BENNET WALL, JR. to RIXEY CARROLL 4 Jul 1859. JP R. N. Gulley.
THOMAS MORGAN to PATSY FREEMAN 24 ? 1859. Lemmon Shell, Minister.
JOHN F. BATTEN to MARY ANNE COLLIN 18 Sep 1859. JP L. G. Boyette.
CURTIS BRYD to PARAGADAN PARISH 11 Sep 1859. JP F. F. Ellis.
A. H. ROSE to ELIZABETH ELDRIDGE 9 Jun 1859. JP John Harpin.
STEPHEN E. BOYETTE to ELIZABETH BROUGHTON 30 Aug 1859. JP William B. Wall.
W. H. MINDLEN to HARRIET JOHNSON 14 Apr 1859. JP B. A. Wellons.
J. J. REID to HARRIET ANN MILLINIER 8 Nov 1859. JP R. D. Lunceford.
ERASMUS LEE to LUCINDA ALLEN 15 Apr 1859. JP B. A. Woodall.
GASTON HARP to SARAH ANN E. WHITLEY 31 Mar 1859. JP W. H. Massingill.
W. M. PEEDEN to LUCINDA STARLING 7 Apr 1859. JP William Brown.
JAMES A. RYALS to PHEBE WOODALL 28 Apr 1859. William T. Hall, Elder.
ALLEN CAPPS to CHARLOTTE DAVIS 19 May 1859. William Brown.
HENRY JOHNSON to HARRIET BEASLEY 16 Aug 1859 JP C.J. Brigham.
ELISHA DAVIS to SARAH GORMAN 24 Mar 1859. JP B. R. Hinnant.
WILLIAM M. MURPHY to LUCRETIA GAY 24 Nov 1859. JP William B. Wall.
DUPREE HOWELL to MILLY GAY 15 Nov 1859. JP James H. Sasser.
W. H. WEBB to ELIZABETH E. FLOWERS 13 Jul 1859. JP N. Ingram.
SIMEON H. GOWER to EVALINA S. BARBER 21 Jul 1859. JP D. H. Holt.
ANDERSON S. POOL to LOUISA JONES 17 Mar 1859. J. F. Ellington.
JESSE LEE to HENRIETTA TART 7 Apr 1859. JP John A. Smith.
WILLIAM J. JONES to HARRIET A. SANDERS 30 Mar 1859. JP T. F. Ellington.
ABRAHAM BATTEN to MILLY H. TALTON 5 Feb 1859. JP Wilie Wellons.
A. C. SPENCER to PATSY N. WATSON 31 Mar 1859. JP Wilis Wellons.
LEVI BATTEN to QUILLY GERALD 8 Mar 1859. JP Wilie Wellons.
GASTON BRITT to ELIZABETH HOUSE 10 Mar 1859. John Dupmar.
BARDEN BROWN to HONOR H. JOHNSON 31 Mar 1859.
JOHN CARROLL to PENNY A. JONES 8 Mar 1859. Moore Stephenson.
JAMES W. HODGES to ELIZABETH RAINEN 28 Apr 1859. JP R. Massingill.
JOHN H. LEE to ELIZABETH GWIN 12 Mar 1859. JP R. Massingsill.
AMOS DUNN to ELIZA LEE 2 Jun 1859. JP R. Massingill.
DANIEL A. SELLERS to PATSY JAINE PEEDEN 30 Jun 1859. JP Wilie Wellons.
RAINS LEE to R. L. BLACKMAN 3 Mar 1859. JP R. Massingill.
JAMES B. JERNIGAN to ALLYCOLLO LEO 3 Apr 1859. JP R. Massingill.
EZEKIEL CREECH to ELEANOR GODWIN 3 Jul 1859. JP B. A. Woodall.
NATHAN JOHNSON to DIANAH RHODES 30 Jun 1859 JP Edwin J. Sanders.
JAMES C. WILLIAMS to THINY ELDRIDGE 3 Mar 1859. JP John C. Hood.

JOHNSTON COUNTY MARRIAGES

HENRY M. JOHNSON to NANCY A. BEASLEY 10 Mar 1859. JP John C. Hood.
WILLIAM HAYLES to ELIZABETH FERRELL 6 Mar 1859. William B. Wall, Esq.
NATHAN PARISH to EDITH PARISH 16 Mar 1859. Moore Stephenson.
JAMES MUNIFORD to NANCY WATSON 17 Mar 1859 JP James Faulk.
DAVID NICHOLS to HARRIET CROCKER 18 Jan 1859. JP Edwin Boykins.
J. S. KIRBY to MARGARET EASON 4 Jan 1859. JP P. Godwin.
EDEN RHODES to JOANNA JOYNER 23 Dec 1859. JP Ransom Lee.
LEROY BYRD to RIDLEY BARBER 28 Dec 1859. JP R. W. Stevens.
DAVID BROWN to SUSAN JONES 20 Oct 1859. JP D. H. Holt.
DAVID P. JOHNSON to CATHERINE M. TINER 1 Jan 1851. JP B.A. Wellons.
AUGUSTUS CORBET to LAURINDA GAY 30 May 1860. Edwin S. Stoers.
HENDERSON BATTEN to JOANNE PITMAN 21 Feb 1860. JP P. Godwin.
MORDECAI HELME to SARAH ENNIS 26 Apr 1860. JP George Keen.
JOSHUA KENNEDY to AMY ANN COATS 4 Mar 1860. JP George Keen.
WILLIAM A. WOODARD to REBECCA A. JOHNSON 25 Feb 1860. J. F. Ellington.
NEEDHAM FAIL to PHEREBEE HOWELL 22 Mar 1860. James. H. Sasser Minister.
STEPHEN H. HOCUT to ELIZABETH BAILEY 11 Jul 1860. JP S. Woody.
WILLIAM G. WILDER to MILLY JANE HINTON 10 Jun 1860. JP S. Woody.
JAMES O. LASSITER to ELEANN JOHNSON 15 Jan 1860. JP Robert W. Stevens.
JACKSON S. BARBER to SMITHY A. GODWIN 1 Jan 1860. JP R.W. Stevens.
JOHN W. ROBERTSON to SERENA J. ONEAL 8 Mar 1860. M. G. Todd.
WILLIAM H. HOLT to LEREY JOHNSON 7 Mar 1860. JP W. Stevens.
KINCHEON H. BATTEN to NANCY WALLACE 3 Apr 1860. JP McNab Earp.
JAMES PARISH to LOUISA STEPHENSON 8 Mar 1860. Moore Stephenson, Elder.
JAMES. H. BARBER to ALCINDA BARBER 17 Jan 1860. JP Robert W. Stevens.
ELIJAH Y. THOMPSON to SARAH A. OLIVER 31 Jan 1860. William Brown.
JOHN W. BALLANCE to PINETTS HOLLAND 26 JuL 1860. JP James Faulk.
WILLIAM STEPHENSON to MARY E. GRIFFIN 25 Feb 1860. JP C. J. Brigham.
RUFUS VAN to EDITH BRYAN 9 Feb 1860. JP John C. Hood.
WILLIAM H. JONES to MARIA BARBER 12 Jan 1860. JP J. W. Hodges.
CASWELL TEMPLE to MARY H. MASSINGILL 25 Mar 1860. JP George Keen.
STEPHEN CLARKE to SUSAN BAREFOOT 16 Feb 1860. JP James H. Adams.
DENNIS GRANT to MARY J. TAYLOR 9 Feb 1860. JP Ransom Lee.
NEEDHAM PRICE to NANCY DRIVEN 24 Jun 1860. JP S. Woody.
HENRY HOLT to DELIA S. JONES 25 Jan 1860. Lemmon Shell, Minister.
W. R. JOHNSON to M. A. E. PENNY 19 Apri 1860. JP Amos Coats.
CHARLES T. BARBER to E. A. BEASLEY 2 May 1860. JP Amos Coats.
CALVIN LASSITER to ELEANOR WOODALL 20 May 1860. JP John H. Kennedy.
DANIEL KING to MARY PEARCE 23 May 1860. JP W. D. Holt.
W. T. MASSINGILL to MARTHA BLACKMAN 23 Feb 1860. JP George Keen.
A. G. MASSINGILL to SARAH A. TEMPLE 12 Feb 1860. JP George Keen.
PHILLIPS WILKINS to JULIA ANN DAVIS 14 Aug 1860. JP J. A. Stevens.
BRIGHT WILLIAMS to MARY ANN STANLY 12 Aug 1860. JP James H. Adams.
J. A. DEAN to LISHA A. WILDER 13 Sept 1860. JP S. W. Woody.
A. J. HOPKINS to ELIZABETH WILDER 16 Sept 1860. JP S.W. Woody.

MARRIAGE RECORDS

CHARLES JONES to MAHALA WATKINS 24 Aug 1860. JP Jesse Parker.
WILLIAM WILKINSON to ELIZABETH OLIVER 13 Sept 1860. JP Jesse Parker.
THOMAS STANCELL to DELANAS C. SASSER 15 Jul 1860. JP Roy Phillips
L. W. HOOD to RACHAEL STEVENS 4 Sep 1860. JP R. D. Lunceford.
JOHN W. BENSON to SARAH BARBER 16 Sep 1860. JP B. A. Woodall.
HARRY BARBER to SMITHY BRYD 14 Aug 1860. JP Robert W. Stevens.
CHRISTOPHER RADFORD to MARY ANN UPCHURCH 7 Nov 1860. JP Robert W. Stevens.
ISHAM WOODALL to REBECCA E. DRAUGHON 31 Oct 1860. JP W. A. Wellons.
GEORGE JONES to NANCY ELLIS 24 Oct 1860. JP J. F. Ellington.
GEORGE P. SNEAD to MARY R. SANDERS 22 Nov 1860. JP J. F. Ellington.
KEDAR BRANHAM to MARTHA PRICE 15 Sep 1860 JP William B. Wall.
JOHN W. M. STANLEY to NANNIE STANLY 13 Dec 1860. JP James H. Adams.
JOHN B. RAND to CHARITY BAUCOM 12 Dec 1860. Stincen Ivy.
WILLIAM HINNANT to SARAH E. WILLIAMSON 1 Jan 1860. JP W. Earp.
RUFUS M. NEEDHAM to DORCAS BENSON 22 Nov 1860. JP B. A. Woodall.
HAYWOOD CAPPS to JULIA MOORE 12 Sep 1860. JP Right Ryals.
THEOPHILIUS GODWIN to ESTHER JONES 24 Oct 1860. JP A. H. Atkinson.
WILLIAM A. LYNCH to MARY HUGHES 11 Dec 1860. JP B. Laws.
JOSEPH A. LASSITER to MARTHA WOODALL 18 Nov 1860. John Kennedy.
ALEXANDER BYRD to MARY F. CAPPS 29 Jul 1860. JP Robert W. Stevens.
WILLIAM F. WESTBROOK to PENNINA SMITH 29 Nov 1860. JP R. Massingill.
MATTHEW I. DEANS to RILDA PACE 22 Dec 1860. JP P. Godwin.
JAMES B. WILLIAMS to MARY P. MILLIFORD 3 Jul 1860. JP Perry Godwin.
JOHN PILKINTON to NANNIE DAUGHTRY 1 Jan 1861. JP William Brown.
JOHN S. WOOD to NANCY J. PARKER 23 Oct 1860. JP John C. Hood.
BENJAMIN HOLMES to LUCINDA PARKER 23 Feb 1860. JP John C. Hood.
LINSEY TINER to SARAH A.E. THOMPSON 23 Dec 1860. JP W. A. Smith.
WILLIAM B. T. EDWARD to MARY OVERBY 16 Dec 1860. JP William Brown.
RUEBEN WEAVER to KIZIAH INGRAM 2 Dec 1860. JP John Harper.
NEEDHAM MORGAN to ELIZABETH WORLEY 1 Oct 1860. JP B. A. Wellons.
S. R. MORGAN to MARTHA A. THORNTON 31 Jan 1860. JP R. D. Lunceford.
W. J. TALTON to MARY YELVINGTON 17 Oct 1860. JP Jonathan Hodgens.
JETHRO YELVINGTON to ELIZABETH J. JOHNSON 16 Oct 1860. JP J. W. Hodges.
JACKSON STRICKLAND to SARAH H. HOCUT 2 Dec 1860. JP S. W. Woody.
SIR WILLIAM HONEYCUTT to NANCY E. ENNIS 4 Oct 1860. JP C. J. Brigham.
WILLIAM W. CAPPS to EASTER PRICE 9 Feb 1861. JP B. Lane.
BRAZELL HUGHES to ELIZA HAMILTON 7 Jan 1861. JP B. Lane.
JOHN F. PARISH to DELLANY HOCUT 13 Jan 1861 JP W. Earp.
CALVIN RICHARDSON to MARY HALL 23 Jan 1861. JP W. Earp.
GIDEON LEE to MARY ANN HOOD 9 Apr 1861. JP James H. Adams.
L. D. STEPHENSON to A. M. MITCHENSON 5 Mar 1861. Thomas G. Witaker, Minister.
THOMAS W. ROSE to NANCY RYALS 25 Apr 1861. William F. Hale, Elder.
RUFFIN CAPPS to NANCY NORRIS 28 Apr 1861. William F. Hale, Elder.
ALFRED STEPHENSON to WINIFRED M. DODD 15 Sep 1861. JP Thomas D. Snead.
GEORGE G. GULLEY to JOANNAH DENISE 8 Dec 1861. JP Thomas D. Snead.

JOHNSTON COUNTY MARRIAGES

LEROY JONES to ELIZABETH BARBER 19 Dec 1861. JP Thomas D. Snead.
JOSIAH CREECH to MARY FUTURELL 12 Dec 1861 JP Wilie Wellons.
JAMES AYCOCK to MARTHA ATKINS 23 Feb 1861. JP Jesse Parker.
E. S. TISDALE to EMILINE PULLEY 21 Nov 1861. JP J. R. Brown.
D. W. BOYKINS to AGNES SNEAD 18 Jun 1861. JP John R. Brooks.
JACOB J. HARPER to MILLY JANE ATKINSON 17 Jan 1861. JP N. G. Gully.
JOSIAH G. ALLEN to NANCY JANE MASSINGILL 31 Mar 1861. JP James H. Adams.
GAVINS B. POWELL to SARAH A. KENNEDY 26 Mar 1861. JP R. D. Lunceford.
NAPOLEON B. HEARNE to HENRIETTA JONES 14 Oct 1861. JP J. W. Hodges.
JACKSON BARBER to ZILPHA J. OLIVER 13 May 1860. JP George Keen.
ELWOOD COLLIER to EDITH LITTLETON 5 Nov 1861. JP Jettman Lewis.
GEORGE D. JOHNSON to GRIZZY STEWART 24 Oct 1861. Elder Moore Stephenson.
JONATHAN APPLEWHITE to LUCRETIA A. WHITLEY 15 Oct 181. James Mahoney.
RICHARD PARISH to CEELIA ANN JOHNSON 21 Aug 1861. JP W. H. Lambert.
ELISHA JOHNSON to CATHERINE V. T. HARPER 18 Aug 1861. W. H Lambert.
M. H. GRANTHAN to CAROLINE BRIDGERS 28 Mar 1861. J. R. Brook.
HAYWOOD JONES to MARTHA PARISH 12 Mar 1861. JP W. H. Lambert.
HILNEY BOYKINS to MILLY NARRON 6 Jul 1861. JP A. H. Atkinson.
WILLIAM B. BARBER to CATHERINE BARBER 22 May 1861. JP W. H. Lambert.
LEMUEL B. LANGDON to MARGARET LASSITER 1 May 1861. JP George Keen.
L. D. BYRD to MARTHA J. DRAUGHON 11 Apr 1861. Isaac Furnago, Elder.
JOHN LEACY ELLIS to L. ELDRIDGE to 30 Apr 1861. JP L. West.
JAMES BARKER, JR. to MARTHA J. BARKER 19 May 1861. JP Right Ryals.
HARDY FORD to CAROLINE KELLY 9 Jan 1861. JP J. F. Ellington.
NEHEMIAH HICKS to WILLY JANE NEANNING 24 Jan 1861. JP A. H. Atkinson.
JAMES R. SPENCER to HARRIET RENFROW 8 Jan 1861. JP B. Phillips.
JOHN W. PARKER to ALLIE WOOD 17 Jan 1861. JP A. H. Atkinson.
W. A. CROCKER to CHRISTIAN BOYKINS 7 Jan 1861. JP A. H. Atkinson.
NOAH B. PARKER to JANE E. TART 27 Jan 1861. JP John C. Hood.
AVERA E. GODWIN to MARTHA J. EASON 24 Dec 1861. JP N. G. Gully.
WILLIAM H. WOODARD to REBECCA CAPPS 30 Jan 1861. JP W. A. Smith.
WHITNEY MESSER to WINIFORD STEPHENSON 12 Dec 1861. JP Robert W. Stevens.
ISAAC DODD to LOUGENIA TURLEY 6 May 1816. JP J. F. Ellington.
WILLIAM B. MASSINGELL to MARY LASSITER 16 Feb 1861. JP George Keen.
DANIEL AMMONS to LOUISA LEE 11 Jun 1861. JP George Keen.
WILLIAM PEARCE to ELIZABETH LANE 8 Aug 1861. JP W. D. Holt.
GEORGE BRASWELL to KEZIAH MASSEY 12 May 1861. JP William Brossion
GEORGE L. PRICE to LOUCINDA ATKINSON 17 Jan 1861. N. G. Gulley.
THOMAS TURNER to PHEREBE DODD 7 Feb 1861. JP J. F. Ellington.
W. S. LONG to L. W. SANDERS 22 May 1861. JP P. H. Batton.
WILLIAM BRYAN to ELIZABETH DUNN 18 Mar 1861. JP R. Massingill.
HENRY M. JOHNSON to CHARLOTTA A. PEACOCK 3 Dec 18161. JP J. C. Eason.
JOHN W. THOMPSON to SARAH P. PEEDEN 30 Jan 1862. JP Willam Brown.
SAMUEL JONES to MARTHA LASSITER 5 Jan 1862. JP Calvin Lassiter.

MARRIAGE RECORDS

AMOS T. JOHNSON to WILSEY A. BARBER 23 Sep 1862. JP Robert W. Stevens.
ISHAM McLAIN to HARRIET WEBB 17 Sep 1862. JP Robert W. Stevens.
W. P. ELLINGTON to MARTHA EASTMAN 6 Jul 1862. JP James H. Bryan.
MALEDICK THORNTON to CUSTICO FRUZIN 28 May 1862. JP John A. Smith
JAMES BRUCE to CLARRISA BLACKMAN 14 May 1862. JP J. E. Eason.
FRANCIS M. MUSGRAVES to MINERVA A. WALL 10 Apri 1862. Wright Blow.
WILLIAM WOOD to AVEY ANN PARKER 6 Feb 1862. JP R. Massingell.
JAMES W. CREECH to PENELOPE STEPHENSON 25 Apri 1862. JP Robert W. Stevens.
THEOPHILUS H. BARBER to ROSA T. BARBER 6 Apr 1862. JP W. H. Lambert.
SANDFORD CREECH to MARY BROUGHTON 2 Apr 1862. JP James H. Bryan.
JOHN ATKINSON to ZILPHIA AYCOCK 25 Sep 1862. James H. Sasser Minister.
ISAAC W. JONES to MARTHA BRANHAM 13 Apr 1862. JP A. G. Gulley.
JOHN T. CAPPS to HAWKINS TALTON 26 Aug 1862. JP W. P. Raiford.
ATLES HOCUT to ELLEN CARROLL 9 Oct 1862. JP Jethro Lewis.
HAYWOOD NORRIS to SALLIE ANN HOLMES 2 Sep 1862. JP William F. Holt Elder.
CALVIN SIMPKINS to JOANNA RHODES 10 Aug 1862. JP Needham Ingram.
L. J. RAINES to ZELPHA CLAMMUND 22 Dec 1862 JP Jesse Parker.
JESSE ADAMS to MARY MITCHELL 16 Dec 1862. JP B. A. Willams.
EDWIN YOUNG to ELIZABETH FAIRLEY 30 Aug 1862. JP W. D. Holt.
JESSE BARBER to CASSEY BARBER 16 Mar 1862. JP N. B. Barber.
ADEN DAUGHTERY to EMILY STRICKLAND 1 May 1862. JP John R. Brooks.
JOSHUA EDWARDS to HAWKINS TALTON 9 Jan 1862. JP Jethro Lewis.
BERRY HOLLIMAN to MARGARET JONES 16 Jan 1862. JP Roy Phillips.
DAVID H. PRICE to ELIZABETH SKENE 20 Feb 1862. JP N. G. Gulley.
J. A. BROWN to ISLIE J. WINBORN 11 Apr 1862. JP J. R. Brown.
MALCOMB JOHNSON to POLLIE ANN ATKINSON 4 Feb 1862. JP N. G. Gulley.
L. CHRISMAN to MARTHA MILLENDEN 21 Jan 1862. JP McNab Earp.
JOHN COOPER to MORNING STANCELL 31 Jan 1862. JP S. W. Woody.
SAMUEL B. THAIN to PASHA ELIZA WOODARD 4 Jun 1863 William Brown Elder.
NAZRA STEPHANSON to CHELLY JOHNSON 27 Feb 1862. JP Robert W. Stevens.
M. W. GREGORY to MARY ANN BRAZIN 11 Mar 1862. JP Robert W. Stevens.
WILLIAM SAULS to JOANNA P. KATE 24 Jun 1862. JP John R. Coats.
JOSEPH WOODARD to ANNA WIGS 24 Dec 1863. JP Willis Holt.
SIR T. WILLIAM ALLEN to NARCISSA ADAMS 7 Jun 1863. JP R. Massingill.
JOHN B. GRIFFIN to HAWKINS HONEYCUT 29 Dec 1863. John R. Coats.
A. T. STEVENS to MARY ANN OGBORN 24 Sep 1863. Aldridge Partin.
NEEDHAM T. BYRD to NARCISSA WEST ? Nov 1863. JP Robert W. Stevens.
JAMES M. HOLT to SARAH ANN LEE 27 Dec 1863. JP Robert W. Stevens.
SETH T. LEE to MARTHA WOODALL 24 Nov 1863. JP Robert W. Stevens.
P. F. MASSEY to LAURA SNEAD 1 Sep 1863. L. S. Burkehead Minister.
EDWARD S. PARKER to ELLEN C. NORTHAN 23 Dec 1863. JP L. S. Burkehead.
JOHN A. JOHNSON to NANCY C. PEACOCK 17 Nov 1863. JP James H. Adams.
RANSOM WALLIS to ELIZABETH STANLY 26 Feb 1863. JP R. Massingill.

JOHNSTON COUNTY MARRIAGES

A. J. H. LEE to ELIZABETH ALLEN 8 Oct 1863. JP James H. Adams.
THOMAS J. FERRELL to MARTHA ONEAL 16 Sep 1863. JP J. F. Ellington.
BURKHEAD BROWN to MARSALINE EASON 26 Feb 1863. JP McNnab Earp.
PATRICK DIXON to LUCY WOODALL 2 Mar 1863. JP P. Godwin.
LARKIN NARRON to MARTHA STALLINGTON 30 Jul 1863. JP J. Lewis.
JAMES ROBERTSON to JULIA ELLINGTON 15 May 1863. M. G. Todd, Minister.
JAMES H. WHITLEY to RHODA E. RICHARDSON, 16 Jul 1863. M. G. Todd, Minister.
EVERETT WADDELL to DELITHA LANGLEY 21 Jul 1863. JP J. T. Pike.
SILAS HOLLOWELL to NARRICUS HINES 30 Jul 1863. JP W. D. Holt.
MATTHEW PEELS to MARY JONES 19 May 1863. JP Jesse Parker.
WILLIAM W. NICHOLS to SARAH A. ROBERT 6 Apr 1863. JP William H. Morris.
JOHN HINNANT to ELIZABETH WALL 25 Jan 1863. JP N. G. Gulley.
WILIE PEEDEN to POLLIE ANN DAVIS 4 Jan 1863. JP T. T. Ellis.
JOHN R. BROOKS to JULIA A. HASTING 23 Jun 1863. JP L. S. Burkehead.
ALLEN HATCHEN to REBECCA STRICKLAND 28 Jan 1863. JP Ramson Lee.
THOMAS AYRES to SARAH POWELL 16 Jan 1863. JP Ranson Lee.
JAMES H. LEE to MARY H. PRICE 31 May 1863. JP B. A. Wellons.
THOMAS B. JEFFERYS to CORA ELVINA WORLEY 11 Aug 1863. JP J. A. Stevens.
RICHARD COLLENS to SARAH STARLING 26 May 1863. JP W. D Holt.
HENRY M. JOHNSON to EDITH A. ALLEN 4 Jan 1863. JP P. Godwin.
JAMES FOWLER to ELIZABETH CROWDEN 13 May 1863. JP J. A. Stevens.
JOSEPH EDWARDS to LINEY RENFROW 30 Apr 1863. JP T. Lewis.
THOMAS McLAN to JUDA C. BEASLEY 10 Jan 1864. JP R. A. Adams.
L. W. PERDUE to ANNIE E. UTLEY 20 Jan 1864. JP L. S. Burkehead.
JAMES A. BARNETT to MARY E. WHITLEY 20 Jan 1864. JP L. S. Burkehead.
SAMSON DUNN to MIZVAINE LANGLEY 28 Feb 1864. JP R. Massingill.
FREDERICK E. WAYNE to MARTHA E. GRAHAM 10 Mar 1864.
ARTHUR LANGLEY to ELIZABETH THOMPSON 17 Apr 1864. JP W. A. Smith.
WALTER R. MOORE to AMANDA BARBER 28 Jun 1864. JP Robert W. Stevens.
SAMUEL PARISH to DELANY GARDNER 27 Jan 1864. JP Jesse Parker.
JOHN PLEASANT to MARGARET E. CUTTS 3 Apr 1864. JP John R. Coats.
ALVIN BARBER to TEMPY JONES 31 Mar 1864. JP W. H. Lambert.
GEORGE W. BAREFOOT to MARY L. HUTSON 24 Mar 1864. JP John A. Smith.
JEREMIAH BLACKMAN to UNITY JANE BARNHOLT 5 Jun 1864. JP John Harper.
JOHN M. COX to PATTIE POOL 4 May 1864. J. F. Ellington.
WILLIAM J. Y. THURSTON to TILPHA GULLEY 3 May 1864. J. F. Ellington.
RUFUS R. CLIFTON to MARZILLA BYRD 17 Feb 1864. JP W. H. Lambert.
WILLIAM HINNANT to MARY ANN RAINS 12 Feb 1864. JP Jesse Parker.
B. V. SMITH to JANE E. ATKINSON 6 Mar 1864. JP W. A. Smith.
THOMAS J. D. PATE to SUSAN ANN HOLLAND 17 Aug 1864. JP William Rains.
P. P. BARBER to LUCY C. JOHNSON 13 Aug 1864. JP Right Ryals.
WILLIAM H. R. LEE to MARTHA ANN EASON 9 Aug 1864. JP R. Massingill.
RICHARD PEARCE to NANCY BASS 10 Aug 1864. JP William Rains.
WILLIAM PEARCE to SALLY WALKER 8 Sep 1864. JP William Rains.

MARRIAGE RECORDS

NEEDHAM M. BEASLEY to EDITH HOLMES 27 Sep 1864. JP Robert W. Stevens.
JOSEPH C. ELLINGTON to BETTIE B. TOMLINSON 15 Nov 1864. L. S. Burkehead, Minister.
DAVID T. MOORE to ELIZABETH B. SMITH 9 Nov 1864. L. S. Burkehead, Minister.
JOHN W. YOUNGBLOOD to JOSEPHINE HOLT 10 Nov 1864. L. S. Burkehead, Minister.
ROBERT W. STEVENS to DORCAS WINDHAM 25 Oct 1864. JP C. Langdon.
H. L. JOHNSON to MARY F. PENNY 22 Nov 1864. JP D. H. Holt.
STEPHEN JOHNSON to MARTHA BASS 20 Nov 1864. JP William Rains.
ELISHA STARLING to PATSEY SPENCER 1 Dec 1864. JP W. H. Wellons.
SAMUEL P. HORTON to REBECCA S. TEFLAIR 15 Dec 1864. L. S. Burkehead, Minister.
BARNA LANE to S. J. WHITLEY 29 Dec 1864. L. S. Burkehead, Minister.
WILLIAM W. MARKLAND to HARRIET A. REID 5 Jan 1865. JP P. Godwin.
A. N. OWEN to NANIE PILKINGTON 22 Jan 1865. JP Josiah Strickland.
JAMES JEFFREY to JULIA ANN ONEAL 1 Dec 1864. JP J. R. Brown.
PLEASANT BATTEN to LUCINDA DAVIS 12 Mar 1864. JP R. Massingill.
C. C. PEACOCK to CYNTHIA A. JESSUP 14 Dec 1864. JP W. H. Wellons.
MATTHEW JENNET to PHEREBE FAIL 14 Dec 1864. JP W. H. Wellons.
CHARLES KENYON to ZILPHIA STANCELL 22 Dec 1864. JP Jethro Lewis
JAMES M. PARISH to ELIZA A. JOHNSON 31 Dec 1864. JP John R. Coats.
HENRY JOHNSON to MARY COATS 11 Jan 1865. JP John R. Coats.
H. A. HODGES to SARAH R. BAREFOOT 25 Dec 1864. JP John A. Smith.
ROBERT NORRIS to FRANCES SUGGS 13 Dec 1864 JP Robert W. Stevens.
WILLIAM D. JONES to WILLY HORNE 12 Mar 1865 JP Jesse Parker.
JOSHUA DIXON to ELIZABETH HOLLAND 17 Jan 1865. JP Jesse Parker.
B. R. MASSINGILL to JULIA LITTLE 15 Dec 1864. R. Massingill.
BENJAMIN HOWELL to ANNIE HOOD 9 May 1865. JP W. D. Holt.
JOEL P. DAVIS to ELIZA STARLING 14 Nov 1865. JP Wilie H. Wellons.
ISAAC SAMPSON to KEZIAH PEEDEN 2 Sep 1865. JP W. D. Holt.
JOHN WILKINS to POLLIE ANN EDWARDS 14 Apr 1864. JP W. D. Holt.
MOSES NICHOLS to EMILY HILL 13 Jan 1865. JP W. D. Holt.
ALFRED WILKINS to WILLY PILKINGTON 14 Dec 1863. JP W. D. Holt.
MATTHEW RADFORD to ELIZABETH EDWARDS 23 Sep 1865. JP W. D. Holt.
WILLIAM T. EDWARDS to CATHERINE E. JONES 9 Jan 1864. JP W. D. Holt.
JESSE GREEN BAREFOOT to NICY BAREFOOT 26 Nov 1865. JP John A. Smith.
WESLEY WHITLEY to EASTERN GODWIN 7 Dec 1865. JP William Thain.
THOMAS KIRBY to TEMPIA HOLLAND 8 Oct 1865. JP B. R. Hinnant.
J. G. WOODALL to EMILY ELDRIDGE 21 Nov 1865. John J. Harper Minister.
LOVETT INGRAM to AUGUSTINO RHODES 8 Oct 1865. JP S. B. Thain.
HENRY E. THAIN to SUSAN D. BEASLEY 4 Jan 1866. JP W. B. Jones.
THOMAS L. ROBERTSON to SUSAN MAINARD 28 Sep 1865. JP John R. Brooks.
R. M. BARLOW to MARY E. ROBERTSON 28 Sep 1865. JP John R. Brooks.
JACKSON RAINS to F. D. PERRY 18 May 1865. Wilie Wellons.
ROMULUS H. CREECH to LOUISA GODWIN 19 Oct 1865. JP P. Godwin.
RAMSON M. STEPHENSON to MARY JARRELL FAIRCLOTH 12 Oct 1865. JP John

JOHNSTON COUNTY MARRIAGES

R. Coats.
RUFUS W. SMITH to NANNIE W. GULLEY 12 Sep 1865. Joseph Wheeler Minister.
HAYWOOD W. GODWIN to PEITY E. GODWIN 1 Oct 1865. JP B. Hinnant.
WILLIAM L. JOHNSON to SARAH PENNY 13 Sep 1866. JP John R. Coats.
STARLING WILSON to MARTHA CAPPS 23 Jul 1865. John J. Harper Minister.
HENRY ADKINS to LOUCINIDA WATSON 22 Aug 1865. JP Barna Creech.
AARON HENRY to CAROLINE FUTRELL 24 Aug 1865. JP Barna Creech.
ISAAC J. SMITH to LUCY C. ALLEN 3 Oct 1865. JP P. Godwin.
E. J. PEARCE to CLARKEY GODWIN 23 Jul 1865. JP B. R. Hinnant.
THEOPHILUS HINNANT to MARTHA WATSON 18 Jul 1865. JP B. R. Hinnant
SIDNEY S. TINER to JULIA H. OLIVER 30 Jul 1865. JP P. Godwin.
JOSEPH D. BALLNGER to LAURA L. BRIDGERS 6 Jul 1865. Joseph Wheeler, Minister.
THOMAS J. BARHAM to FRANCIE HINES 31 Aug 1865. JP D. S. Avera.
JOHN RYALS to PHEBIE WILKINS 8 Oct 1865. JP P. Godwin.
JAMES T. TART to AILEY JOHNSON 1 Oct 1865. JP Thomas D. Snead.
JOHN JONES to SUSAN J. COATS 20 Aug 1865. Rev Parrot Creech.
ALEXANDER WARD to LUCINDA TISDALE 24 Sep 1865. JP B. R. Hinnant.
JACOB FULGHAM to POLLEY ROSE 14 Sep 1865. JP B. R. Hinnant.
LEWIS M. JERNIGAN to ELIZABETH McLANE 19 Feb 1865. Rev Parrot Creech.
JOSEPH MOORE to MARY JANE PALMER 21 May 1865. Joseph Wheeler, Minister.
RANSOM GODWIN to NANCY HAYLES 11 Oct 1865. JP James Faulk.
JOSIAH LEE to LEANNA SMITH 28th Nov 1865. JP R. Massingill.
AMOS DUNN to MARY JANE LEE 5 Nov 1865. JP R. Massingill.
WILLIAM KENNEDY to JOANNA DUNN 5 Nov 1865. JP R. Massingill.
R. J. BAKER to ATINCY F. WEST 14 Sep 1865. JP Needham Ingram.
HARRY DEARHAM TO MISOURI ANN E. STICKLAND 26 Oct 1865. JP Jethro Thain.
HARRY JOHNSON to ELIZABETH T. HARPER 4 Jan 1866. J. F. Ellington, Minister.
JESSE W. HINTON to RIDLEY R. JOHNSON 15 Dec 1865. J. F. Ellington Minister.
DAVID HONEYCUT to REBECCA HOOD 12 Dec 1865. J. F. Ellington Minister.
J. M. WHITE to Mrs. M. E. TOMLINSON 16 Jan 1866. W. B. Jones, Minister.
EDWARD BROWN to ELIZABETH MORGAN 25 Jan 1866. W. B. Jones.
JOHN W. TALTON to ERMA L. PARISH 25 Jan 1866. JP I. D. Davis.
J. G. ALLEN to LUCINDA JOHNSON 7 Jan 1866. JP B. A. Woodall.
WILLIS H. SMITH to MARTHA GURLEY 4 Jan 1866. JP Simon Godwin.
JAMES POOLE to JULIA H. OLIVER 2 Jan 1866. Rev Parrot Creech.
ABSALOM BARBER to TOBITHA LASSITER 4 Jan 1866. Rev Parrot Creech.
JAMES N. BARBER to CATHARINE BARBER 31 Dec 1865. Rev Parrot Creech.
WILLIAM BASHAM to JENCY STRICKLAND 10 Jan 1866. Joseph Wheeler Minister.
J. F. ELLINGTON to LOUISA J. BOYKINS 4 Jan 1866. Joseph Wheeler Minister.
RANSOM HINNANT to MARGARET A. PITMAN 11 Feb 1866. JP Willie Wellons.

MARRIAGE RECORDS

J. N. CROCKER to JULIA WORLEY 21 Dec 1865. JP Wilie Wellons.
RANSOM BATTEN to ELIZABETH PARISH 4 Feb 1866. JP Wilie Wellons.
LARRY B. LANIM to CATHARINE BATTEN 18 Feb 1866. JP Wilie Wellons.
JAMES WALLACE to LOUISA BENSON 15 Feb 1866. JP N. Ingram.
RAIFORD DRIVAN to MARSALINE GREEN 25 Jan 1866. Rev. E. Mecons.
JAKE TISDALE to PATSY HOCUT 19 Dec 1865. Rev E. Mecons.
GEORGE SMITH to SARAH MITCHINER 13 Jan 1866. JP William Thain.
JOHN R. BARBER to ELIZA ANN CANADY 22 Feb 1866. Rev Parrot Creech.
JAMES R. BENSON to SUSAN GODWIN 15 Feb 1865. Rev Parrot Creech.
WILLIAM T. WALTON to KOZIAH E. DUPREE 4 Jan 1866. JP John Coats.
DAVID FERRELL to ANNIE E. ENNIS 21 Dec 1865. JP John R. Coats.
J. H. J. NEIGHBORS to LOUISA RYALS 1 Feb 1866. James Turnage.
WILLIAM LANGLEY to JULIA A. PARNOLD 17 Dec 1865. JP B. R. Hinnant.
WORLEY CREECH to MARTHA HARE 22 Feb 1866. JP B. R. Hinnant.
D. F. MASSEY to MELVINA FINLAYSON 6 Feb 1866. JP W. D. Holt.
W. H. HOOD to FANNY DANIEL 30 Nov 1865. JP W. D. Holt.
R. F. GURLEY to MARY L. KING 25 Jan 1866. JP W. D. Holt.
WILLIAM TALTON to ELIZABETH HOBBS 14 Jan 1866. JP W. D. Holt.
MERRIT WHITLEY to ADALAID EVANS 26 Dec 1865. JP W. D. Holt.
WILLIAM B. JONES to HAWKINS JONES 6 Feb 1866. F. T. Ellington, Minister.
JOHN H. DANIEL to MARY POOL 7 Dec 1865 JP Thomas D. Snead.
S. H. BRADDY to SALLIE ANN BRASWELL 22 Jan 1866. JP J. Phillips.
JOHN TROY JONES to MARTHA MASSEY 26 Dec 1865. JP F. Phillips.
W. H. CULLOM to POLLY BARHAM 31 Jan 1866. W. B. Jones, Minister.
DR. J. G. ROSE TO EMMA E. NORTHAM 31 Jan 1866. Joseph Wheeler, Minister.
W. W. RICHARDSON TO ELIZABETH PEARCE 7 Jan 1866. Rev William Nowell.
HAYWOOD DIXON to LUCINDA BARBER 21 Dec 1865. JP P. Godwin.
J. W. FLOWERS to NANCY F. DODD 4 Jan 1866. JP Jethro Thain.
JOHN PEACOCK to POLLIE ANN SPIVEY 4 Jan 1866. JP James H. Sasser.
SIR WILLIAM BEASLEY to SPICY BAREFOOT 24 Dec 1865. JP John A. Smith.
CULLEN REGISTER to NANCY BAREFOOT 14 Jan 1866. JP John A. Smith.
JULIUS A. LEE to PARTHENA J. ALLEN 14 Jan 1866. JP James H. Adams.
NEEDHAM PARKER to POLLY PRICE 25 Jan 1866. JP S. W. Woody.
SOLOMON WATSON to MINERVA RUFFIN 12 Apr 1866. JP John W. Lee.
JOEL HUTSON to ELIZABETH E. WESTBROOK 27 Feb 1866. JP J. C. Eason
WILLIAM H. RAINER to POLLIE ANN JERNIGAN 7 SEP 1865. JP R. Massingill.
HUGHEL HINTON to PERMINA HAYLES 15 Mar 1866. Rev Ellin Mecons.
DANIEL SANDERS to CHERRY ELDRIDDGE 25 Mar 1866. Rev Parrot Creech.
JOHN W. BARBER to FRANCES BARBER 28 Mar 1866. Rev Parrot Creech.
WILLIAM R. STRICKLAND to SARAH A. GEORGE 19 Apr 1866. Rev Parrot Creech.
HANDY F. PEEDEN to TRECINDA RAIN 3 Apr 1866. JP Wilie Wellons.
WINIFREE NORRIS to AMY ELIZA RANSEN 25 Mar 1866. JP Josiah Coats.
JAMES A. WOODALL to ELIZABETH WHITLEY 1 Mar 1866. Joseph Wheeler Minister.
JONES FAULK to ANNIE KIRBY 15 Mar 1866. JP B. R. Hinnant.
HENRY LEE to DELIA HOLT 22 Mar 1866. JP John W. Lee.

JOHNSTON COUNTY MARRIAGES

DIXON DAVIS to MARY POOLE 26 Mar 1866. JP W. B. Jones.
THOMAS WATSON to SEARCY PEELE 25 Mar 1866. JP Roy Philips.
HENAN HATCHER to NANCY BROWN 27 Feb 1866. JP J. F. Pike.
WILLIAM BAILEY to MARTHA HILLIARD 1 Mar 1866. JP Jesse Hinnant.
JOSEPH HOLT to CHARLOTTE LEE 9 Mar 1866. JP J. W. Stephenson.
JOB WHITLEY to WINIFRED BARNETT 22 Feb 1866. JP Seth Woodall.
ALISON HOCUT to CLARA ENNIS 24 Feb 1866. J.F. Ellington, Minister.
JOHN H. SASSER to PASHO A. RAINES 17 Apr 1866. JP B. R. Hinnant.
WILLIAM WORLEY to CATHARIN CROOKER 15 Apr 1866. JP James C. Ballard.
HILLARY HINNANT to MARY J. COBET 6 Apr 1866. JP William C. Nowell.
THOMAS WHITFIELD to BETTIE BROWN 18 Apr 1866. JP W. B. Jones.
WILLIAM W. MESSER to LOUINIZA PARNOLD 12 Apr 1866. JP John M. Stephenson.
ROBERTSON STANCELL to MARY STANCELL 25 Feb 1866. JP Ransom Hare.
RAMSON BEASLEY to CATHERIN McLAIN 4 Feb 1866. JP P. Godwin.
THOMAS SASSER to ELIZA JANE CREECH 30 Dec 1865. William Brown Elder.
BENJAMIN EDWARDS, JR. to EVALINE OVERBY 6 Feb 1866. William Brown, Elder.
LEVI P. CREECH to EVALINE BRASWELL 16 Nov 1865. William Brown, Elder.
THOMAS CARDLE to LUCRIETTA ADAMS 8 Feb 1866. William R. Johnson.
BENNET KING to RETTA JANE BLALOCK 21 Feb 1866. JP William R. Johnson.
JOHN M. COLLINS to ELIZA HAMILTON 20 Feb 1866. JP W. R. Johnson.
JAMES B. GRIFFIN to ELIZA JANE HOLT 22 Feb 1866. JP W. R. Johnson.
WILLIAM R. CREECH to NANCY E. THOMPSON 14 Dec 1865. William Brown, Elder.
KEDAR J. BALLARD to REBECCA WARREN 3 Oct 1865. William Brown, Elder.
BENJAMIN BRADY to CHERRY OLIVER 30 Dec 1865. William Brown, Elder.
NEEDHAM WARREN to FARINIA HOLT 7 Feb 2866. William Brown, Elder.
STEPHEN STANCELL to SALLIE BARKER 31 Jan 1866. James Wilson, Elder.
WILLIAM H. WALL to RUTHA E. BATTEN 22 Feb 1866. JP Josiah Hinnant.
MERRIT BLOW, (col) to RACHAEL O'NEAL (col) 1 May 1866. JP McNab Earp.
EZEKIEL BAREFOOT to MARY ELDRIDGE 3 May 1866. John J. Harper, Minister.
C. C. PEACOCK to BETHANN JONES 18 Apr 1866. James H. Sasser.
B. TOMLINSON to S. G. RENFROW 1 May 1866. W. B. Jones, Minister.
JAMES T. PRICE to MARTHA A. ELLIS 1 Apr 1866. J. F. Ellington, Minister.
JOHN H. PARKER to ELIZABETH MASSEY 1 May 1866. JP J. C. Ballard.
COUNSEL AYRES to MARY CARROLL 3 May 1866. JP B. R. Hinnant.
S. BOYKINS to MILBRY BOYKINS 28 Apr 1866. JP S. W. Woody.
DAVID TURNER to ALICE C. MITCHINIER 9 May 1866. JP W. B. Jones.
WILLIAM JOYCE to NARCISSA WILLIAMS 30 Apr 1865. John J. Harper Minister.
PUTNEY PARISH to EMILY PEACOCK 6 Feb 1866. JP John C. Hood.
HENDERSON SANDERS to LYDIA SANDERS 21 Apr 1866. JP Jethro Thain.
DR. THOMAS A. WOODLY to GEORGIA ANNE HIGGINS 28 Mar 1866. Rev.

MARRIAGE RECORDS

Hook.
FERDINAND KINSTER to RIXCY FREEMAN 10 May 1866. Sincrom? Ivy.
BRYANT A. SMITH to SARA F. COATS 20 May 1866. JP I. M. Ogborn.
GREEN ANDREWS (col) to SYLVIA WARD (col) 13 May 1866. JP James Hay.
CALVIN A. HOLT to ELIZABETH HOWELL 27 May 1866. JP James Hay.
JOHN H. HINNANT to SARA JONES 24 Apr 1866. JP J. F. Pike.
HENRY C. ROSE to SARAH FULGHAM 5 Apr 1866. JP J. F. Pike.
W. B COLE to SERENA W. LANGSTON 30 May 1866. John J. Harper, Minister.
PETER R. TEMPLE to EVALINE PRICE 7 Jun 1866. JP B. R. Hinnant.
J. R. JACKSON to ANN E. INGRAM 21 Dec 1865. JP Green Flowers.
W. H. LASSITER to LOUISA JOHNSON 2 Jun 1866. JP Calvin Lassiter.
JULIUS A. LEE to CHARLOTTE L. PEACOCK 22 Feb 1866. JP R. Massingill.
JESSE EDWARDS to JUDIE BEASLEY 21 Dec 1866. JP R. Massingill.
WRIGHT UNDERWOOD to ELIZABETH BARBER 11 May 1866. JP J. E. Ballard.
YOUNG L. LAROHORO to MARY A. LEE 10 May 1866. JP R. Massingill.
HARRIS JOHNSON to ELIZABETH J. STRICKLAND 22 Apr 1866. JP R. Massingill.
BIRKEE JONES to MARY JONES 20 May 1866. J. F. Ellington Minister.
W. C. BENSON to SARAH A. DIXON 17 Jun 1866. JP P. Godwin.
ISAAC MECAL to OLIVIA RUFFIN 14 Jun 1866. JP John W. Lee.
WESLEY OVERBY to SUSAN ALLEN 30 May 1866. JP John R. Coats.
GILES WATSON (col) to MARIA ATKINSON (col) 27 Jun 1866. JP W. A. Smith.
DICK ATKINSON (col) to JANE LANGSTON (col) 4 July 1866. JP W. A. Smith.
JAMES W. HOLMES to DARTHA YOUNG 7 June 1866. Isaac Wheeler Minister.
JOSEPH A. BARBER to CAROLINA HUTSON 10 Jul 1866. John I. Harper, Minister.
WILLIAM RICHARDSON to MARY E. ATKINSON 27 Jun 1866. Joseph Wheeler, Minister.
RANSOM HARE to SARAH A. C. BAGLEY 22 May 1866. JP Roy Phillips.
WILLIAM S. HOBBY to MARIA SNEAD 30 Aug 1866. JP Seth Woodall.
GASTON W. BRITE to ELIZABETH MORGAN 26 Aug 1866. JP James Hay.
RICHARD RADFORD to CELIA ANN SMITH 31 May 1866. JP J. F. Pike.
JESSE M. BARBER to BRAZILLA BARBER 7 Aug 1866. JP B. A. Woodall.
TIMOTHY ALLEN to EASER TOMPKINS 16 Aug 1866.
HANDY BEST (col) to JENIMNA JERNIGAN 10 Aug 1866.
RUFFIN HINNANT (col) to ALLEY TISDALE (col) 15 Aug 1866. JP Jesse Hinnant.
AQUILLA NARRON to POLLY LEE 26 Aug 1866. JP S. W. Woody.
BENJAMIN LYNCH to SALLY BASS 26 Aug 1866. Elisha Holland, Minister.
GEORGE A. WITT to ANNIE BECKWITH 17 Sep 1866. W. B. Jones, Minister.
J. W. LEE to CHILLY HOLMES 18 Sept 1866. W. F. Hall, Minister.
MADISON ATKINSON (col) to PHERBE TOLER (col) 1 Sep 1866. JP Bryant Williams.
DOCTOR ALTMAN (col) to CHARLOTTE BENTON (col) 22 Sept 1866. JP Bryant Williams.
KELLY TISDALE to SALLIE ANN THOMPSON 3 Apr 1866. JP W. C. Sellers.

JOHNSTON COUNTY MARRIAGES

WILLIE HODGE (col) to FANNY LASSITER (col) 8 Sep 1866. JP E. D. Snead.
MOSES EARP (col) to JANE WALL (col) 9 Jun 1866. JP McNab Earp.
JOSEPH CARROL (col) to CAZILLA TOMLINSON (col) 27 Sep 1866. JP William Hastings.
ZECHARIAH HOCUT to SARA L. RICHARDSON 26 Apr 1866. JP William Hinnant.
JAMES CARROLL to BETSY WALL 17 Sept 1866. W. C. Nowell.
NATHAN SMITH (col) to ANN HEATH (col) 13 Oct 1866. JP A. J. Heath.
PETER BOYLAN (col) to ISABELLE SMITH (col) 13 Oct 1866. JP Adam J. Heath.
BUCK ONEAL (col) to LEASY RICHARDSON (col) 7 Sep 1866. Josiah Hinnant.
HAYWOOD VINSON (col) to ISABELL WATSON (col)18 Oct 1866. JP McNab Earp.
GREEN HELME (col) to OLIVE SMITTS (col) 27 Sep 1866. Joseph Wheeler, Minister.
JAMES WHITLEY (col) to ADALADE WATSON (col) 29 Sep 1866. Elisha Holland, Minister.
A. R. DUNCAN to BETTIE TURNER 16 Oct 1866.
NEANDY B. JERNIGAN to POLLIE GRANT 21 Aug 1866. JP R. Massingill.
NATHAN INGRAM to CATHARINE A. ADAMS 23 Aug 1866. JP R. Massingill.
N. E. ALLEN to LONENZA ADAMS 19 Jul 1806. JP R. Massingill.
ALEXANDER EASON to JOANNA BATTEN 15 Nov 1866. JP William Hastings
RUFUS A. JOHNSON to MARGARET JOHNSON 30 Sep 1866. JP Abram Dixon.
JOHN C. STANCELL to ELIZA ANN CREECH 30 Sep 1866. JP W. D. Phillips.
RICHARD CRABTREE to MARY E. GRISWOOD 1 Nov 1866. J. F. Ellington, Minister.
S. D. LEE to URSULA SMITH 13 Oct 1866. JP J. C. Eason.
JAMES T. RENFROW to MARY BOYKINS 11 Nov 1866. JP S. W. Woody.
JOHN WARREN (col) to CATHARINE FURNER (col) 22 Nov 1866. JP James Hay.
MARK JONES (col) to ANN BARBER (col) 28 Oct 1866. JP S. H. Hood.
GREEN McCULLENS (col) to REBECCA McCULLENS 10 Nov 1866. JP S. H. Hood.
STEPHENS SIMMONS to SYLLA LANGSTON 9 Oct 1855. JP Bryant William.
PARISH B. PARISH to NANCY E. LANGDON 14 Oct 1866. JP James A. Smith.
WILLIAM COX (col) to CAROLINE MITCHENER (col) 12 Nov 1866. J. F. Ellington, Minister.
JAMES A. ALLEN to MARTHA MASSINGILL 9 Sep 1866. JP James H. Adam.
EDWARD LEE to MARTHA A. LEE 25 Sep 1866. JP Joel Lee.
JOHN T. HINNANT to ADALINE SUGGS 9 Oct 1866. JP W. H. Wellons.
JONATHAN COLYER to MARTHA ANN SELLERS 20 Nov 1866. JP W. H. Wellons.
JACOB R. WALL to GRIZZY ANN BOYETTE 15 Nov 1866. JP Jesse Hinnant.
DENNIS WHITLEY (col) to 'LOU' EATMAN (col) 8 Dec 1866. JP Jesse Hinnant.
RANSOM RICHARDSON (col) to SALLY ANN WATSON (col) 2 Dec 1866. JP McNab Earp.
URIAH THOMPSON to LOUISA WALLACE 6 Dec 1866. JP B. A. Wellons.

MARRIAGE RECORDS

ANTHONY BELL (col) to WILLY HOLLAND 20 Dec 1866. JP Jethro Thain.
HENRY L. WATSON to ANNIE MOORE 20 Dec 1866. W. B. Jones, Minister.
MOSES STANCELL to EMILY MASSINGILL 11 Dec 1866. Rev. Parrot Creech.
LEVI COLE to SARAH N. GUESS 20 Dec 1866. JP W. P. Raiford.
DOCTOR R. BARBER to MARY JOHNSON 15 Oct 1866. W. F. Hall, Minister.
WILIE F. GERALD to SARAH PHILLIPS 26 Feb 1867 JP James Hay.
EZEKIEL BARBER to MARY F. JOHNSON 14 Feb 1867. Rev Parrot Creech.
JOSEPH G. EDGERTON to CELIA O. SNIPES 21 Feb 1867 JP W. D. Holt.
WILLIAMS T. HOLLAND to MARY J. STEPHENSON 20 Dec 1866. JP N. A. Clifton.
ELDRIDGE STEPHENSON to SARAH LEE 20 Dec 1866. JP N. A. Clifton.
JOHN P. STEPHENS to BARTILLIE HOLLAND 24 Dec 1866. JP N. A. Clifton.
GEORGE GODWIN to LEATHY ANN SMITH 20 Dec 1866. JP John A. Smith.
JAMES GREEN to SEANY LEE 20 Feb 1867. JP M. K. Grantham.
JOHN A. WOODALL to LUCY JOHNSON 24 Jan 867 N. B. Barber, Minister.
N. G. PRICE to A. ROBERTSON 17 Jan 1866. Rev H. Hocut.
IRVIN BARBER to MARY JONES 19 Dec 1866. JP A. R. Duncan.
T. B. HARRISON to BETTIE JOHNSON 13 Dec 1866. JP A. R. Duncan.
STEPHEN MORRIS to CAROLINE GRANTHAM 6 Feb 1867. JP Bryant Williams.
STEPHEN S. FAIRCLOTH to PENNY GAINAS 21 Feb 1867. JP Bryant Williams.
DAVID BOOTH to SARAH STEVENS 30 Apr 1865. JP H. H. Hinnant.
WILLIAM BRITT to MARY PRICE 13 Dec 1866. JP B. Williams.
JOHN B. HOOD to MISOURI B. LEE 22 Jan 1867. JP S. W. Blackman.
JOHN C. WEST to SARAH E. ROSE 14 Feb 1867. JP Bryant Williams.
HEZEKIAH WARWICK to MARTHA STEPHENS 6 Dec 1867. JP Bryant Williams.
GARRY MEEKS to SUSAN ELDRIDGE 19 Feb 1867. JP Bryant Williams.
JOSEPH LEE to MARTHA G. BRYANT 18 Nov 1866. JP P. Godwin.
THOMAS D. BARBER to ELIZABETH BARBER 27 Jan 1867. Rev Parrot Creech.
JAMES A. T. JONES to SARAH E. BARNES 20 Feb 1867 Rev B. B. Walden.
W. N. APPLEWHITE to VIRGINIA WHITLEY 27 Nov 1866. A. J. Finlayson Minister.
JOHN B. PEACOCK to ELIZABETH JOHNSON 22 Jan 1867. JP P. Godwin.
IRVIN HOCUT to BETTIE BARHMAN 8 Mar 1866. Rev W. Hocut.
WALTER JOHNSON to PARAZADINE JOHNSON 3 Jan 1867. JP J Thain.
LEONARD PARKER to ESTHER ANN INGRAM 6 Jan 1867. JP James H. Adams.
HARDY FAIRCLOTH to MARTHA MESSER 10 Jan 1867. JP John R. Coats.
ANDREW WATTON to MARY C. HONEYCUT 23 Dec 1866. JP John R. Coats.
RAYMOND ENNIS to EMILY STEPHENS 19 Dec 1867. JP John R. Coats.
JAMES H. SMITH to MARTHA ANN SMITH 5 Dec 1866. JP John R. Coats.
JOHN W. BATTEN to CHERRY SNIPES 11 Oct 1866. JP W. D. Holt.
JAMES N. NOWELL to ELIZABETH JOHNSON 7 Aug 1855. JP W. D. Holt.
RICHARD MILLS NOWELL to ELIZA SOLACE 24 Jul 1866. JP W. D. Holt.
KIMBRELL EATSMAN to NANCY M. BATTEN 4 Dec 1866. JP John Broadwall.
JOHN S. EASON to ELIZABETH BROWN 17 Jan 1867. JP John Broadwall.
BENJAMIN HILLARD to LOUISA HINNANT 6 Dec 1866. William C. Nowell, Minister.
RANSOM BRANNON to HARRIET PARRISH 2 Sep 1866. W. C. Nowell.
GEORGE R. HARPER to F. E. SMITH 12 Dec 1867. JP P. T. Massey.
JAMES WOOD to ELIZABETH JONES 30 Nov 1866. J. F. Ellington,

JOHNSTON COUNTY MARRIAGES

Minister.
DEVEREAUX PARNOLD to MARTHA PARNOLD 20 Jan 1867. JP W. F. Gerald
JAMES K. WHITLEY to NANCY WOODARD 3 Jan 1867. JP William Hinnant.
WOODRUFF MURPHY to AMANDA EASON 29 Jan 1867. JP Jesse Hinnton.

INDEX

-A-
AARON, Henry, 11
ABELL, James H., 112, 115
ADAM, James H., 132
ADAMS, Adin, 20
 Alford, 50
 Alsey, 93, 103
 Altney Jane, 120
 Betsey, 19
 Betsy, 48, 50
 Bryan, 40
 Bryant, 4, 18, 49
 Catharine A., 132
 Colin, 58
 Cudncy, 48
 David, 55, 65, 77
 David B., 87, 88
 Edith A., 118
 Edwin, 79
 Eleanor, 88
 Elizabeth, 107
 Frances, 12
 Green, 44, 50
 Hardy, 33, 39, 93
 Howell, 4, 9, 12
 J. I., 85
 James, 21, 41, 58, 133
 James H., 106, 122, 123, 124, 125, 129
 Jesse, 35, 40, 43, 88, 125
 John, 47, 89
 John A., 70, 104
 John H., 63
 Joseph Ann, 91
 Joseph J., 65, 69, 104
 Joshua, 69
 Josiah, 41
 Julia Y., 118
 Kinchen Q., 45
 Lewis, 14
 Lonenza, 132
 Louisa, 63
 Lucrietta, 130
 Lucy, 50
 Martha, 98
 Mary, 89
 Mary H., 114
 Mary Jane, 65
 Narcissa, 125
 Nathan, 102
 Nicey, 61
 Pruella, 10
 R. A., 126
 Rebecca, 61
 Reddick, 64
 Redley, 58
 Right A., 64, 88
 Right H., 64
 Rinda, 116
 Sally, 98
 Sally A., 86
 Sarah, 9
 Sidney, 58, 63
 Susan, 67
 Vine H., 61
 William, 63, 90, 121
 William G., 71
 William H., 67
 William M., 65
 Winifred, 46
ADKERSON,
 Elizabeth, 15
 Mary, 4
 Micajah, 4
ADKINS, Henry, 128
ADKINSON,
 Charlotte, 18
ALEXANDER, Adam, 13, 28
ALFORD, B. B., 109, 110
 Bythan, 84
 Nancy, 54
 Peyton, 20
 Wilie, 109
 Willey, 110
ALFRED, John, 91
ALLEN, Ahab, 61
 Alcinda, 114
 Alexander, 100, 101
 Aley, 90
 Alfred, 70
 Amanda, 121
 Aon, 48
 Betsy, 59
 Bryan, 49, 50
 Caroline, 76
 Edith A., 126
 Elizabeth, 25, 26, 37, 100, 126
 Esther, 4
 Giddeon, 20, 29
 Gideon, 50, 60, 61, 62, 109
 Gidion, 2
 Harriet, 84
 J. G., 128
 James, 50, 58, 61
 James A., 132
 James G., 98
 James R., 46
 James W., 120
 John, 50, 59, 104
 John A., 78
 John B., 54, 56, 59, 86
 John C., 107, 109
 John E., 74
 Joseph E., 71
 Josiah, 58, 94, 124
 Josiah G., 96, 100
 Leacey, 118
 Lucinda, 121
 Lucy, 1
 Lucy C., 128
 Mary, 11, 78
 Mary Ann, 60
 Meady, 34
 N. R., 132
 Nancy, 69
 Nathan, 14, 54
 Nathan L., 72
 Nathan T., 50, 65
 Parthena J., 129
 Penelope, 105
 Penny, 64
 Phereby, 52
 Polly, 22, 49, 60, 66
 Rachel H., 114
 Ransom G., 78, 94, 101
 Ridley, 83
 Salley, 94
 Sally, 36
 Sarah, 18, 53
 Siddy, 33

JOHNSTON COUNTY MARRIAGES

Sir T. William, 125
Sir William, 83
Susan, 69, 85, 116, 118, 131
Thomas, 4, 39, 53, 85, 104
Timothy, 131
William, 16, 21, 28
William B., 66
William H., 106
Winiford, 96
Winifred, 65, 67
Young, 1
ALLFORD, Bryant, 109
ALMOND, Sarah, 12
ALSTEN, W. F. S., 88
ALSTON, W. F. S., 73
ALTMAN, Doctor, 131
Edith, 13
Joel, 4
Mourning, 11
Nathan, 11
Phereby, 38
Willie, 89
Zilpah, 11
AMMONS, Daniel, 124
ANDERSON, Frederick, 33
ANDREWS, Green, 131
Nancy, 85
Rebecca, 115
APPLEWHITE, Jonathan, 124
W. N., 133
ARMSTRONG, Clement, 10
Elpsaha, 12
ARNOLD, William, 62
ARRSTON, Asa, 8
ARRUNDEL, Ann, 1
ARTEST, Luke, 38
ARTIS, Archibald, 118
ARTUS, Luety, 83
ASHE, Thomas S., 24
ASHLEY, William, 58
ATKERSON, Amos, 6, 7, 10
ATKINS, Elizabeth, 118
Isaac, 9
John, 21
Josiah, 16
Martha, 124
Thomas, 31
Thomas H., 120
ATKINSON, A. H., 118, 123, 124
Alvin H., 113
Amos, 13, 45
Ashley, 80
Avie, 13
Blake, 58, 63
Cary, 38
Dick, 131
Edith, 13
Elias, 3
Elijah, 77, 80, 111
Elizabeth, 104
Elizabeth J., 78
Harris, 98
Harris H., 107
Jane E., 126
Joanny, 87
John, 12, 16, 38, 49, 50, 55, 60, 63, 125
Josiah, 116
Loucinda, 124
Louiza, 109
Lucinda Hawkins, 77
Madison, 131
Maria, 131
Martha, 81
Mary E., 131
Milly, 73, 83
Milly Jane, 124
Nancy Ann, 82
Nancy S., 115
Nathan, 18, 38, 54
Patherly, 66
Patience, 98
Pollie Ann, 125
R. D., 102, 105
Sarah, 56
Seney, 79
Tempy, 119
Thomas, 12, 98
Thomas H., 120
Wancey, 17
William, 10, 77
Willie, 40
Willis, 18
AUSTIN, Alsey, 51
Alvin, 64
Ammy, 105
Arrison, 51
Betsy, 43
Elbert, 76
Henry, 119
James, 72
M. L., 118
AUSTON, Alsey, 47, 51
Arison, 46
John, 20, 36
Mary, 102
Polly, 36
AUTON, John, 47
AVEALS, Isham, 7
Mary, 7
AVERA, Alexander, 3, 17
Anne, 8
Anny, 11
Aventon, 11, 24, 115
Avington, 95
Betsy, 64
Boling G., 58
Cader, 37, 41
Caroline, 112
Catharine, 71, 87
Celah, 21
Christian, 59
Cynthia, 25, 26
David, 23, 25
Dempsey, 21
Edith, 1, 6, 18, 30
Elizabeth, 12, 74, 93
Esther, 21
Esther Ann, 97
Francis, 111
Gilly, 37
Hardy, 29, 37, 40, 58

INDEX

Harry, 64, 67
Henry, 4, 23, 25
Jacob, 2
Jane, 90
John, 26, 31, 33, 39, 40, 85
John C., 63
John W., 94, 98
Jonathan, 3
Kedar, 22, 28, 40
Lelah, 5
Levana, 10
Lewis, 9
Lizy, 53
Louensa, 65
Louiser, 80
Lucrecy, 9
Maria, 66
Martha, 60
Mary, 8
Matthew, 62, 67, 68, 70, 85
Nancy, 61, 68
Olive, 4
Patience, 12
Peggy, 21
Polly, 18, 64
Polly Ann, 91
Rachel, 92
Richard, 48, 101
Sally, 11, 58
Samuel, 2, 4, 13, 21
Sander, 13
Sarah, 85
Sarah Ann, 80
Susan, 81
Thomas, 12, 21, 30
Viny, 25
William, 4
William H., 94, 111
Wimey, 21
Winifred, 13, 85
AVERET, Edith, 7
AVERGET, Sally, 4
AVERY, John, 41
  Polly, 63, 91
AVERYETT, Edith, 59
AVERYT, Alexander, 25

Daniel, 14, 26
Edith, 89
Elizabeth, 17
James, 61
Keziah, 16
Lizzy, 51
Patience, 50
AVERYTT, Jonathan, 33
  Winifred, 33
AYCOCK, Albert, 90
  Daniel, 81
  James, 19, 124
  Simon, 75
  William H., 75
  Zilphia, 125
AYRES, Counsel, 130
  Thomas, 126

-B-

BABOCK, Phebe T., 74
BACKHAM, James, 7
BADEY, Gilly, 95
BAGGET, Alsey, 12
  Edith, 5
  Josiah, 9
  Roda, 14
BAGGETT, Josiah, 27
BAGLEY, Alvin, 98, 109, 110
  Ann, 2
  Chloe Ann, 116
  Edmund, 34
  Edney, 74
  Harriet, 77
  Henry, 72, 73
  Joanny, 90
  Patsy, 70
  Penelope, 108
  S., 97
  Sarah A. C., 131
  Stephen, 87
  Theophilius, 33, 81
  Theophilus, 34, 38
  Thiny, 25
  Thomas, 68, 70, 91
  Trecinda, 99
BAGLY, Henry, 98

Stephen, 99
BAGSDALE, Thomas L., 45
BAGWELL, Mary, 63
BAILEY, ?, 9
  Anna, 55
  Arnold, 21
  Arthur, 9, 38
  Baldy G., 79
  Beedy, 31
  Caroline, 98
  Celah, 17
  David B., 2
  Deanmiah, 8
  Elizabeth, 49, 79, 122
  Everett, 30
  Gilly, 88
  Griffin, 82
  Hardy, 25
  Hinton, 64
  Hudson, 67
  Hutson, 64
  Isom, 9
  Jamaey, 11
  Jesse, 3, 23, 26, 30, 53, 55
  John, 15
  Leasy, 48
  Levi, 23
  Lunceford, 72
  Matilda, 99
  Micajah, 23
  Milly, 55
  Nancy, 55, 69
  Olief, 89
  Pherebe, 65
  Phereby, 9
  Piety, 69
  Polly, 75
  Rene, 28
  Richard, 5
  Sally, 31
  Sarah, 14
  Susan, 99
  Thomas, 56
  Warren, 31, 38, 64, 69
  Warren W., 75
  William, 8, 130
BAILY, Baldy G., 95
  Catharine, 82

JOHNSTON COUNTY MARRIAGES

Charity, 48
Dilny, 59
Gastin, 71
Griffin, 100
Hardy, 52
Harriet, 113
Hilliard, 52
Mary, 71
Nicy, 52
Osborn, 82
Penny, 95
Ruffin, 96
Warren, 95
BAINES, Sarah, 36
BAKER, Allen, 107
Anne, 30
Benjamin, 113
Clem, 45, 66
Clement, 48, 52
Dileah, 58
Elijah, 11, 19, 30, 38, 61
Elizabeth, 3, 91, 93
Haywood, 75
Jackson, 105, 107
James, 45, 59, 108, 112
James W., 107
John, 48, 88
Jonathan, 96, 112
Louisinda, 101
Lucy, 87
Matthew, 108
Nancy, 103, 108
Needham G., 101
Phebe, 118
R. J., 128
Rhoda, 117
S., 77
Starling, 101, 115
Sukey, 22
Susan, 107
Wammer, 3
William, 3, 66
BALANCE, Blackman, 66
Martin, 82
Teel, 46
Tegal, 60
BALDWIN, Samuel, 7,

8
BALKAM, Ichabod, 22
Seth, 19
BALKCOM, Ichabod, 43
BALKHAM, Ichabod, 19
BALLANCE, Amy, 89
Blackman, 111
Fanny, 51
Harriet, 84
John W., 122
Ruffin, 99
BALLARD, J. C., 130
J. E., 131
James C., 130
Kedar J., 130
Peter, 16
Rebecca, 39
BALLENGER, A. L., 81
Allen, 19, 28, 59, 64
Allen L., 35, 44, 46, 69
Allen S., 19, 48, 65, 66
Allen T., 38, 57
Apsabeth, 14
Beverly O., 73
Elizabeth, 19
George B., 112
John, 8
Joseph D., 128
Mariah, 100
Mary A., 93
W. S., 88, 103
William, 7, 8, 14
William S., 84, 89
BAMCUMB, Martha, 60
BAMDAM, Sally, 76
BANKS, Adam, 50
J. L., 119
BARBER, Absalom, 35, 76, 119, 128
Absalum, 98
Adeline, 76
Alcinda, 122
Alsey Ann, 94
Alvin, 126
Amanda, 126

Amy, 22
Angeline, 81
Ann, 132
Anna, 46
Anny, 119
Ashley, 84, 88, 91, 103
Aurelia, 119
B. F., 108
Bailie, 75
Brazilla, 131
Britton, 77
Burwell, 12, 14, 22, 59, 75
Bytha Ann, 116
Casandra, 70
Cassey, 125
Catharine, 128
Catherine, 124
Celia, 62
Cephas, 111
Charles T., 122
Coream, 91
Doctor R., 133
Drury, 24
Dudley, 92
Edith, 38
Elizabeth, 43, 45, 64, 96, 119, 124, 131
Elizabeth H., 88
Elizur, 109
Emeline C., 82
Esther, 116
Evalina S., 121
Ezekiel, 133
Frances, 129
George, 7, 16, 21, 24, 47, 55, 71, 91, 101, 115
Gideon, 62, 104
Hardy, 15, 75, 86
Harry, 38, 64, 123
Hawkins, 76
Haywood, 119
Hughey, 106
Irvin, 133
Isaac, 62
Isabel, 88
Jackson, 124
Jackson S., 122

138

INDEX

James, 59
James H., 122
James K., 47, 49, 58
James N., 128
Jesse, 125
Jesse H., 67
Jesse M., 131
John, 40, 45, 58, 65, 67, 75
John R., 129
John W., 129
Joseph A., 131
Julia, 91, 109
Larkin, 77, 81, 84, 116
Lucinda, 129
Luquinny, 110
Lusey, 38
Lydia, 118
Maria, 122
Mary, 84, 95
Mary Ann, 111
Matilda, 104
Matthew, 58
Mimmy, 102
N. B., 125, 133
Nancy, 75
Nathaniel, 62, 104
Nathaniel B., 82
Owen, 16, 21, 58, 94
P. P., 126
Patsy, 43
Pency, 94
Penelope, 46
Penny, 65
Peola, 75
Pheby, 18
Phina, 9
Plyer, 15, 38, 49, 53, 62, 66, 90
Polley, 9
Polly, 106
Pyler, 35, 59, 91
Reuben, 7, 33, 43, 58, 62
Ridley, 122
Rosa T., 125
Sally, 33, 53
Sarah, 123
Simon, 70, 91
Susan, 101
Susannah, 65
Tempy C., 76
Terry, 40, 54, 56, 64, 65
Theophilus, 33, 88
Theophilus H., 125
Thitorson, 48
Thomas, 12, 14, 20, 26, 29, 32, 34, 37, 43, 59, 64, 77, 119
Thomas D., 133
Thomas H., 110
Welthy Ann, 80
William, 103
William B., 124
William G., 119
William J., 86
William P., 112
Wilsey A., 125
Young, 70, 74
Young A., 84
BARBEY, Phereby, 9
Ruth, 9
BARCUM, Eliza, 99
Penelope, 107
BARDEN, Levi, 107
BAREFOOT, Amy, 76
Annie, 94
Bright, 108
Bythan, 120
Charlotte, 46
Clarkey, 120
Esther A., 112
Ezekiel, 130
Fanny, 80
G. W., 118
George W., 126
Hardy, 69
J. R., 115
Jane, 69
Jesse Green, 127
Joel, 112
John, 9, 34, 90
John R., 112
Miles, 34
Miles V., 112
Nancy, 129
Nicy, 127
Noah B., 113
Noah G., 115
Pherebe, 63
Polly, 30
R. B., 97
Rebecca, 97
Sally, 65
Sarah R., 127
Spicy, 129
Susan, 60, 122
Thomas, 60
William, 94
Willie, 90, 96
BARFIELD, Bryan, 88
Bryant, 88
Cullen, 61
BARHAM, Benjamin A., 47
Joseph, 111
Polly, 129
Thomas J., 128
BARHMAN, Bettie, 133
BARHORN, Eldridge, 66
BARKAM, James E., 91
Nancy Jane, 106
BARKER, James, 124
Martha, 124
Sallie, 130
BARLOW, R. M., 127
Wilson, 42
BARNES, Archeleus, 5
Bennet, 91
Bethany, 104
Catharine, 77
Cherry, 118
Edith, 40
Elias, 20, 65, 70
Elizabeth, 28
Harry, 89
Henry, 111
J., 119
Jacob, 47, 71
Jacob H., 100
Jesse, 5
Joanna, 84
John, 31, 101

JOHNSTON COUNTY MARRIAGES

John J., 104, 107, 116
Joseph, 91
Kisish C., 111
Levy, 30
Mary A., 118
Mynck, 30
Needham, 71, 87
Needham L., 120
Noel, 82, 101
Patience, 72, 90
Patsy, 20
Rebecca, 49
Redick, 39
Rildy, 76
S., 56
Sally, 97
Sarah, 88
Sarah E., 133
Solomon, 91
Stephen, 37, 49, 55, 56
William, 69
Zelpha, 93
Zilpah, 18
Zilpha, 80
BARNETT, James A., 126
Moses, 35
Sandy, 86
Winifred, 130
BARNHOLT, Unity Jane, 126
BARNY, Asa, 94
Cynthia, 64
BARRISON, James, 7
BARTLETT, Henry, 39
BARTLEY, Wealthy, 44
BASHAM, William, 128
BASS, Andrew, 47
Betsy, 21
Caty, 37
Chilly, 95
Isabell, 115
John W., 120
Katy, 26
Martha, 127
Matthew, 67
Nancy, 126
Sally, 66, 131

William A., 61, 67
BATEMAN, Nancy, 23
BATTAN, John, 15
Nathan, 15
BATTEN, Abraham, 30, 40, 44, 54, 121
Amos, 26, 40
Anny, 58
Appy, 111
Aziel, 93
Betsy, 48
Bridgers, 29
Bryan, 94
Carolin, 93
Catharine, 129
Charles, 36
Cinthy, 113
Edny, 53
Edwin, 87, 97
Elizabeth, 61
Ephraim, 83
Hardy, 40
Henderson, 122
Henry, 101
James, 58
Joanna, 132
John, 28, 30, 40, 61, 62, 119, 133
John F., 121
Joseph, 120
Josiah, 82
Kinchen, 107
Kincheon H., 122
Levi, 121
Levy, 104
Lorenda, 108
Louiza, 78
Lucinda, 87
Martha, 119
Matthew, 61, 80, 107
Mindy, 97
Nancy, 116, 118
Nancy M., 133
Patience, 51
Patsey, 87
Pleasant, 57, 78, 127
Ransom, 129
Richard, 119

Robert, 76
Rutha E., 130
Saley, 50
Samuel, 28, 29, 40, 60, 62
Sarah, 118
Simon, 34
Starling, 57
Strawdry, 61
William, 36, 50
William W., 78
Winifred, 105
Zilpha, 76
BATTIN, Dolly, 90
James H., 90
John T., 90
BATTON, Clary A., 104
P. H., 124
BAUCOM, Bennett, 34
Charity, 123
Isham, 14
Mary, 67
Urias, 34
BAUCUM, Thetus, 111
Urias, 103
BAULKAM, Ichabod, 29
BAVADRIL, Elizabeth, 9
BAVRY, Polly, 30
BAYLEY, Elizabeth, 78
BEAD, James, 21
BEAL, Elizabeth, 57
John, 33, 48, 57
Siddy, 83
BEAMAN, David, 25
Isaac, 26, 30
Jacob, 22, 25
Nathan, 27
Samuel, 43
Welthy, 30
BEARD, Comsill, 47
Council J., 45
Sally, 50, 55
William, 22, 103
BEARFOOT, John, 35
Miles, 35
Nancy, 32
BEASLEY, Adeline, 115

INDEX

Anna, 62
Ceelia Ann, 75
Charles, 116
E. A., 122
Elizabeth, 120
Ephraim O., 89
Harriet, 121
Isaac, 41
James, 106
Jane E., 114
Jesse, 62, 85
John W., 114
Juda C., 126
Judie, 131
Judith, 78
Martha E., 118
Mary M., 110
Nancy A., 122
Needham M., 126
Ransom, 130
Sir William, 129
Susan D., 127
BEASLY, Ashley, 95
E. O., 97
Ephraim O., 111
Isaac, 82
James, 86
Kindrick, 60
Mary Ann, 89
BEASON, Alfred E., 96
BECKWITH, Annie, 131
J. B., 99
John B., 86, 91, 110, 113
BEDDIN, Elisha, 41
BEDDON, ?, 26
BEDERYFIELD, Desa, 4
BEDINGFIELD, Betsy, 58
John, 4, 6, 58, 60
Kern, 52
Lucy, 6
Mary, 63
BEEL, Edna, 70
Nancy, 53
BELL, Ann Mariah, 85
Anthony, 133

Benjamin, 36, 48
D., 36
David, 2, 5, 6, 39, 53, 90
Elizabeth, 56, 75
Etheldred, 33, 35, 36, 37, 43
Ethelred, 39
H. T., 98
Hardy, 34
Henry, 32, 65, 86, 103
Henry I., 74
Joseph, 113
Joseph P., 113
Martilla, 38
Mary, 53
Mary E., 86
Norfelt T., 116
Patsy, 84
Thomas, 46
W. B., 100
William C., 119
William E., 119
Willis A., 116, 119
BELLE, Henry I., 98
Mony, 91
BELLINGTON, Ezekiel, 7
BENNET, Nancy, 42
William, 49
William K., 83
BENSON, Caty, 22
Charles, 35
Dorcas, 123
James R., 129
John W., 123
Louisa, 129
Mary, 62
Nancy, 51
W. C., 131
William, 61, 63
BENTON, Charlotte, 131
BER, Sherod, 44
BEST, Handy, 131
BEZZEL, Thomas G., 97
BEZZELE, Marshale H., 114
Marshaville, 114

BIMDIE, Mark, 39
BIMS, Tobias, 40
BINER, Albert Green, 95
BINGHAM, Charles J., 80
Chris J., 100
BINN, James, 47
BINV, Cinith, 50
BIRD, Benton, 26
Dorcas, 96
Emily, 78
Lemmuel, 86
Penny, 96
Rachel, 62
BISHOP, Asa, 33
Moses, 45
Polly, 33
BIZZELE, Evert A., 104
BIZZELL, Emily H., 120
Mary E., 115
Montraville, 82
Samuel, 115
BLACKBURN, George, 16
BLACKMAN, Aley, 37
Alice, 119
Anna, 36
Arthur A., 101
Ashley, 78, 111
B. C., 83, 84
Barzella, 50, 54, 60, 79, 89, 95
Barzilla, 46
Bennett, 17
Clarrisa, 125
Cullen, 61
Edith, 51
Edmond, 19, 32
Elena V., 60
Elizabeth, 5, 97
Esther, 11
Harry, 78, 91
Icabod, 13
Ichabod, 4, 16, 18
Jeremiah, 36, 44, 51, 54, 109, 126
Jerusha, 32
Jesse R., 99

JOHNSTON COUNTY MARRIAGES

John, 3, 11, 18, 54, 61, 110
Joseph, 29
Josiah, 17, 85, 119
Kedar, 57
Lelah, 19
Lewis, 61
Martha, 122
Mary, 10, 63, 99
Nammy, 4
Nancy M., 116
Patsey, 81
Polly, 34, 120
Powell, 84, 85, 86
R. H., 72
R. L., 121
Rachel, 44
Richard, 66
S. W., 100, 133
Sally, 60, 90
Sarah, 14, 107
Sarah Ann, 114
Sir William, 73, 89, 97
Susan, 74
Tabitha, 54
William, 16, 19, 103
William P., 97
Wimmy, 80
Zilphia, 27
BLACKMOND, Zelpha, 101
BLACKMORE, Bennet, 103
  Martha R., 105
BLACKWELL, Betsy, 57
  Josiah, 42
  Thomas, 77
BLACKWOOD, N. H., 68
BLALOCK, Martha, 106
  Polly, 105
  Retta Jane, 130
BLANCHET, Robin, 115
BLANEFORD,
  Winifred, 88

BLANKETSHIP,
  Lythia, 23
BLENKET, Tempy Ann, 71
BLENSON, Thomas, 19
BLINSON, William, 66
BLOW, Merrit, 130
  Wright, 109, 125
BLUNT, Benjamin, 24
  William, 9, 17
BLURTON, Henry, 7, 17
BODDERY, Elizabeth, 43
BODDIE, John, 34
  Nathan V., 35
  William Willis, 34
BODDIR, Bennet, 59
BODERY, Isaac, 60
BODIARY, Nancy, 44
BOLE, Henry T., 98
BOLTEN, John, 37
  Polly, 37
BON, Daniel, 85
BOND, Emily, 64
BOON, Alice H., 110
  Bennet, 48
  Dempsey, 34
  Dempsey W., 110
  Eliza, 41
  Eliza C., 60
  Elizabeth, 12
  Erdena V., 61
  Evaline C., 118
  Henry F., 115
  John, 33
  John W., 77, 83
  Joseph, 2, 7, 12, 14, 27, 44
  Julia A., 68
  Louisa, 69
  Lucinda, 113
  Patsy, 39
  Pereby M., 77
  Sally, 39, 58
  Wiley S., 110
  Willie S., 73
BOOTH, David, 133
  Levi, 84
BOOTHE, Isaac, 49, 52
BORDEN, Abram G., 64
BOSWETH, Catheran A., 73
BOVEY, George W., 80
BOWLER, Peggy, 50
BOWLS, Thomas G., 110
BOYET, Fereby, 41
  John, 22
BOYETT, Chosa, 71
  George, 58
  Harriet, 77
  Isaac, 58, 69, 75
  L. G., 119
  Larkin G., 116
  Moses, 28, 29
  Patsy, 59
  Penelope, 55
  Temperance, 32
  Zilphia, 56
BOYETTE, Grizzy Ann, 132
  L. G., 118, 121
  Stephen E., 121
  T. G., 119
BOYKINS, Christian, 124
  D. W., 124
  Edwin, 61, 69, 74, 80, 120, 122
  Harris, 90
  Hilney, 124
  Jesse, 90
  John S., 77, 90
  Louisa J., 128
  Mary, 132
  Matthew, 103, 106
  Milbry, 130
  Ruffin, 109
  S., 130
  Stephen, 90, 99
  Willie A., 104, 109
BOYLAN, Peter, 132
BOYLE, Cally, 54
BOYT, Nanny, 54
BOYTT, Joseph, 104
BRADDY, Abner, 59
  James, 5, 70

INDEX

Nathan, 46
Robert, 46
S. H., 129
Sally, 46
William, 11
William A., 71
William J., 104
William M., 83
Winifred, 59
Winnifred, 10
BRADY, Benjamin, 130
Betsy, 51
Blake, 20, 25
Grace, 1
John, 2, 6, 27
Levy L., 102
Lewis, 2
Nathan, 55
Patience, 34
Polly, 37
William, 55
BRAMMON, Allen, 70
BRANHAM, Kedar, 123
Martha, 125
BRANNAN, Anne, 6
James, 7
William, 3
BRANNON, Allen, 47, 82
B., 99
Betsy, 27
Caron, 59
Hawkins, 113
John, 21
John R., 114
Josiah, 63, 87
Kader, 96
Kedan, 38
Kedar, 28
Kedin, 95
Leroy, 18
Mary, 38
Olive, 64
Ransom, 82, 100, 133
Sally, 46
Thomas, 33, 38
Welly, 13
William, 13, 18, 47, 48
Willie, 48

BRANTLY, Edwin, 34
Sarah, 35
BRASHAM, Wilson, 32
BRASSEL, George, 74, 90
Jacob, 90
BRASSELL, Polly, 68
BRASWELL, Betsy, 4, 27
David, 19, 27
Evaline, 130
George, 124
Jacob, 75
Laney, 23
Lercy, 35
Levy, 22, 25
Lewis, 40
Martha, 22, 25
Nancy, 35
Polly, 3
Sallie Ann, 129
Sally, 39
William, 11, 15
BRATCHER, Tabithy, 4
BRAXTEN, Willie, 77
BRAZELL, George, 113
BRAZIN, Mary Ann, 125
BRAZZEL, Jacob, 110
BRENT, Betsy, 41
Catty, 39
Nancy, 31
BRETT, Polly, 39
Rachel, 24
BREWER, Alice, 52
Fathy, 8
Jenny, 5
BRICE, N. L., 45
Neil, 42
BRIDGERS,
Abesebeth, 32
Benjamin, 3
Betsy, 57
Braswell, 39, 43, 48, 57
Caroline, 124
Charity, 10
David, 33
David H., 72
Francis, 61, 115

Indiana, 94
Isabelle, 96
Jane, 21, 66
Jane E., 81
Laura L., 128
Margaret, 8
Martha, 79
Mary, 59
Mary Ann, 12
Ransom, 72, 76, 94
Sally, 14, 40
Thomas, 57, 64
Thomas D., 48, 50, 52
Troy, 105
William, 7, 9
Young, 10, 23, 26, 62, 63, 64, 79
BRIGGS, John, 25
BRIGHAM, C. J., 121, 122, 123
William J., 120
BRINT, Richard, 48
BRITE, Gaston W., 131
BRITT, Amy, 31
Cynthia, 26
Elizabeth, 3
Gaston, 121
Harry, 49
Jessy, 19
John, 116
Jonathan, 20, 29, 38, 43, 58
Martha W., 120
Mercin D., 104
Mills, 107
Nancy, 24
Patience Ann, 79
Patsy J., 66
Rebecca Maria, 71
Reddam, 34
Sally, 50
William, 133
Winifred, 29
BROADSHAW, John, 102
BROADSTREET,
Allama, 64
Caroline, 54

JOHNSTON COUNTY MARRIAGES

Edith, 63
Edney, 56
Liany, 48
Milley, 14
Robert, 32
William, 14
BROADWALL, John, 133
BROADWELL, John, 38, 83
William, 81
BROGDEN, Cruzzy, 37
John, 40
BRONSON, Benjamin B., 80
BROOK, J. R., 124
BROOKS, Benjamin S., 53
Charity W., 58
Jacob, 19
John R., 124, 125, 126, 127
John W., 53
Nancy, 31
Nicy, 55
BROSSION, William, 124
BROUGHTON,
Benjamin, 63
Betsy, 36
Calvin, 119
Elizabeth, 74, 121
Jesse, 66
John, 59
Joseph, 14, 18
Mary, 118, 125
Nancy E., 119
Penelope, 112
Sally, 59
Stephen, 66
Steven, 64
BROWN, Abedience, 80
Aden, 91
Alexander, 114
Ann, 16
Auston, 95
Barden, 121
Betsy, 23
Bettie, 130
Burkhead, 126

Celia, 57
David, 51, 122
Edward, 128
Elisha, 7
Elizabeth, 45, 133
Hobson, 116
J. A., 125
J. R., 124, 125, 127
James, 32
Jesse, 92
John, 29, 49, 50, 51, 67, 116
John A., 41
John W., 87, 115
Joseph, 11, 12, 13, 14, 25, 26, 37, 43
Josiah, 61
Larkin, 118
Lee, 51
Little Berry, 43
Mildred, 9
Milly, 98
Nancy, 23, 70, 94, 130
Needham, 88
Ruffin, 115
S., 23
Sally, 13
Samuel, 21, 29
Stephen, 20, 39, 60, 83, 91
Susan, 108
Thomas, 53, 56, 92
Thomas A., 32
Vicy, 20
Willey, 83
William, 48, 50, 54, 61, 62, 74, 76, 120, 121, 122, 123, 124, 125, 130
William C., 108
BRUCE, James, 125
BRUI, Frederick, 11
BRUNT, Charlotte, 44
Elizabeth, 97
Nancy, 70, 100

BRYAN, Aley, 62
Arthur, 1, 9
Asa, 1, 30
Asptie, 2
Benjamin, 4, 23
Betsy, 33
Bythan, 46, 53, 59, 64
Cathrin, 18
Cathrin Caroline, 100
Celah, 17
Charlotte, 10
Cynthia, 66
David, 48
David H., 38, 57, 60
Drenny, 5
Drury, 10, 18
Edith, 58, 122
Edward, 46
Edwin, 70
Elbert A., 78, 87
Elisbra, 46
Elizabeth, 1, 2, 20
Elvin, 68
Emy, 60
Frederick, 28, 39
Hardy, 3, 4, 10, 11, 12, 18, 29
Harry, 119
Henry, 11, 27
Jacob, 37
James, 30, 39
James B., 91
James H., 114, 125
Joel, 35
Johannah, 40
John, 10, 67
John Arthur, 25, 28
John H., 72, 77, 116
John L., 90
John M., 93
Larry, 23, 25, 37
Lewey, 84
Lewis, 2, 16, 33
Lisba, 9
Lotty, 38

144

INDEX

Lucius H., 110
Lunnon, 46
Mary, 8
Nancy, 35, 51, 65
Nathan, 33
Needham, 1, 27, 30, 49, 63, 64, 66, 68, 70
Needham G., 64
Patsey, 38, 42
Pherebe, 34
Redley, 4
Robert, 52, 66
Samuel A., 52, 65
Sarah, 70
Simon, 38, 58
Susannah, 1
Ulrica, 38
William, 1, 2, 8, 9, 15, 16, 25, 33, 39, 51, 67, 124
William H., 121
William W., 30, 45, 46
Willy, 71
BRYANT, Elbert, 88
Jane, 120
John, 17
Larkey, 104
Lewis, 3
Martha G., 133
BRYD, Martha, 99
Mary C., 119
Redder, 33
Right, 60
Smithy, 123
BUBSY, Barnaby, 30
BUCK, Lewis, 28
Polly, 25
BUCKMAN, William H., 76
BUCKS, Betsy, 28
BULL, Barnaby, 30
David, 7
BULLOCK, Ann, 7
Elizabeth, 24, 36
BULLS, Barna, 52
Barnaby, 5, 11, 20, 34
Betsy, 20
Cloe, 44

Elizabeth, 83
Esther, 30, 35
Jethro, 6, 16, 17
Nancy, 45
Nancy J., 67
Rachel, 18
Rebecca A., 68
Sally, 30
Tilphria, 6
William, 6, 17, 35
William H., 31, 41
BUNCH, James H., 75
BUNDY, George D., 102
William, 82
BUNN, William, 109
BUNTING, William, 62
BURCKET, Lemuel, 62
BURK, Goldy, 66
BURKEHEAD, L. S., 125, 126, 127
BURNETT, Barna, 38
BURRIETT, Eliza, 47
BUSBEE, Alfred, 49
Alsey, 40
Charles M., 88
Johnson, 29
Kinchen, 45
Nancy, 55
Ransom, 45
Thomas, 60
Wilson, 37
BUSBY, Daniel, 30
Jonathan, 25
Winnowfield, 1
BUSH, John, 1
BUTCHER, John, 34
BUTLER, James, 2
Samuel, 66
BUTTS, Wilson, 53
BYRD, Alexander, 123
Aquilla, 112
Betsy, 21
Bright, 36, 46
Curtis, 121
Edward, 112
Elizabeth, 115
George, 34, 37, 56
James, 74
John, 19, 22, 24, 47, 49
L. D., 124
Leroy, 122
Lewis, 77
Louis, 95
Mary, 67
Marzilla, 126
Nancy, 68, 95
Needham T., 125
Olive, 47
Pherebe, 65
Redder, 21
Redding, 36
Redly, 95
Richard, 19, 24, 115
Richard D., 119
Robert J., 118
Sarah M., 97
Susan, 37
Sutton, 89
Tabitha, 102
Thomas, 70
Unity, 104
William, 48

-C-
CABLE, Amanda, 74
CADELL, Banks, 46
CALVET, Mary, 3
CANADA, Susan, 60
CANADAY, Cannon, 111
Sarah Ann, 108
CANADY, Eliza Ann, 129
William, 4
William H., 119
CANBERT, Martha, 74
CANNON, Samuel, 59
CANWELL, Charity, 2
CAPPE, Nancy, 37
CAPPS, Allen, 58, 88, 121
Barbara, 11
Betsy, 52
Edith, 42
Elijah, 76, 86, 90

JOHNSTON COUNTY MARRIAGES

Elizabeth, 35
Emely Jane, 100
Esther, 84
Haywood, 123
Henry, 34, 36
Jeremiah, 35, 36, 58
John, 96
John T., 125
Kezieh C., 120
Laley, 42
Lewis, 84
Littleton, 48
Martha, 128
Mary F., 123
Matthew, 51
Needham, 29
Patsey, 75
Rebecca, 124
Ruffin, 123
Sally, 101
William, 6, 27, 29, 35, 56, 84, 88
William H., 86
William W., 123
Winifred H., 76
CAPS, Ann, 28
Phereby, 20
CAPSE, Rebeckah, 6
CAR, Nancy, 24
Samuel H., 24
CARDELL, Polly, 118
William, 118
CARDLE, Thomas, 130
CAREL, Mary Ann, 28
CARINGTON, David C., 93
CARLILE, Edward, 35
CARLILES, Nancy, 10
CARMACK, Levy, 111
CARMADY, Cannon, 62
CARR, Blanery, 61
James, 26
CARREL, Benjamin, 39
William, 96
CARRELL, Aley, 51
Asa, 109
Beedy, 49
Benjamin, 22, 27, 31, 43, 62, 87

Britain, 43
Ceborn, 59
Charles, 113
Dalas, 96
Dallas, 72
David, 54, 57
Dennis, 3
Dolly, 55
Elizabeth, 37
Gincy, 66
James, 4, 9, 13, 17, 25, 26, 49, 52, 62
Jane, 14
John, 3, 4, 11, 14, 24, 27, 43, 68
John R., 83
July, 75
Mitchell, 22
Peggy, 32
Ransom, 72
Reuben, 57
Rhoda, 66
Ruffin, 81
Sally, 22
Sarah, 66
Simeon, 63
Simon, 66
Sintha, 76
Susanna, 43
Thomas, 12
Upton, 60
William, 15, 17, 27, 47, 64
Winifred, 3
CARROL, Joseph, 132
Mary Jane, 102
CARROLL, Benjamin, 19
Delilah, 19
Ellen, 125
James, 132
John, 121
Mary, 130
Rixey, 121
CARTER, Ader, 14
Charles, 32
Charlotte, 8
Emily, 59
Emily Jane, 88
Harriet C., 96

Irvin, 14
Isiah, 12
James M., 109, 110
John, 32, 36, 39, 77
Joseph, 61
Kindred, 11, 14
Lucy, 25
Lydia, 14
Mary, 74, 78, 110
Polly, 36
Reuben, 15
William, 30, 34, 42
William M., 53
Young, 56
CARTWRIGHT, Lydia, 32
CASEY, Martha, 103
CASSE, Annie, 10
Lucretia, 7
William, 7
CAUDELL, Cammell, 39
Carmel, 34
Harmon, 34, 54
Isabel, 64
Lewis, 44
Susan, 79
CAUDLE, Amy, 55
Benjamin, 30
Hammon, 30
John, 22, 30, 92
Jonathan, 30
Nancy, 30
Polly, 62
CAUSEY, John R., 96
CAVENDER, Polly, 32
CELLARS, Cally, 41
CHAMBERLEE,
Freeman, 70
Hiram, 70
CHAMBERS, James, 16
Polly, 5
Susannah, 17
Thomas, 6
CHAMBLEE, Anne
Eliza, 112
Patience, 92
Rexey, 106
William, 73, 112

INDEX

CHAMBLER, Hiram, 64
CHAMLEY, John, 26
CHAMPANE, Elijah L., 47
CHAMPHIGAN, Elizabeth, 95
CHAMPION, Henry, 22
  Isaac, 24
CHANCE, Evans, 75
CHIANS, Thomas, 1
CHILES, Edith, 13
CHILIS, Matthew, 4
CHRISMAN, L., 125
  Robert D., 114
CHRISTAINBURY, Thomas, 77
CHRISTIFER, Christer, 58
CHRISTMAN, Robert, 97
CHRISTOPHERS, Christopher, 60
CHURCHILL, William, 85
CLAMMUND, Zelpha, 125
CLANEY, Phereby, 5
CLARK, Abisha, 68
  Ann, 7
  Arabella, 86
  Eli, 30
  Emily, 88
  Francis, 19
  Gracy, 25
  Harris, 8, 34
  Helen Mariah, 65
  James, 36
  John, 116
  Lewey, 29
  Stephen, 62, 122
CLARKE, Martha, 10
CLEMMONS, Peggy, 16
CLEMMY, Pherebe, 55
  William, 20
CLEMONS, Samuel, 109
CLERK, Susanna, 10
CLIFTON, A. P., 108
  Acril P., 91
  Aeriel P., 74
  Ann, 56
  Azel, 13

Candis, 74
Elizabeth, 61
Emily N., 73
Henry A., 68, 76
J., 91
James, 9
James H., 120
Joel, 26, 29, 44, 48, 68, 76, 84
Joel B., 67
John, 58
John B., 48
Joseph, 59, 63, 67
Martha, 106
N. A., 133
Rubin R., 111
Rufus R., 126
Thomas C., 47
William, 9
CLIMMY, Mary, 4
COALTS, Ann, 5
COATS, Amos, 60, 103, 108, 112, 113, 114, 118, 122
  Amy Ann, 122
  Blackman, 60, 115, 120
  Burwell, 30
  Cynthia, 64
  Emily, 87
  J. R., 95
  John, 15, 31, 52, 129
  John R., 125, 126, 127, 133
  John Ruffus, 99
  Josiah, 69, 129
  Mary, 31, 127
  Mary E., 115
  Nancy, 3
  P. P., 120
  Penny, 86
  Polly Ann, 113
  Ryal, 100
  Sally, 26
  Sara F., 131
  Susan, 103
  Susan J., 128
  Thomas, 81
  William, 4, 24,

36, 48
William H., 60, 75, 86, 87, 95, 103
Zilla, 64
COBB, Barsheby, 2
  Caroline, 94
  James, 68
  John Petty, 17
  Sally, 4
  Willis, 55
COBBS, John, 47
  Thomas, 47
COCHRAN, Thomas, 5
COCKRELL, Celah, 27
  Ervin, 92
  John, 35
  Jonathan, 66
  Mary, 29
  Nancy, 49
  Piety, 93
  Ruffin, 92
  Sally, 51
  Samuel, 15, 35
  Sarah, 13
  Simon, 24, 27, 48, 52, 58
  Stephen, 20
  Thomas, 15, 58, 59
  William, 25
COGDALE, Caroline, 116
COGDELL, John S., 67
COLE, Betsy, 51
  Elizabeth, 64, 102, 114
  Henry, 99
  James, 102
  John, 61
  John A., 115
  Josiah, 51
  Levi, 133
  Lydia A., 113
  Nancy, 49
  Patsey, 37
  Rebekah, 18
  Sarah, 51
  Thomas, 66, 78
  W. B., 131
  William H., 111

JOHNSTON COUNTY MARRIAGES

Willis, 15, 20, 41, 63
Willis A., 116
COLIN, Henesbury, 114
COLLENS, Richard, 126
COLLERS, Patty, 5
COLLIER, Elwood, 124
  John, 58
  Mezaney, 85
COLLIN, Mary Anne, 121
COLLINER, George, 92
COLLINS, Alexander, 50
  Andrew, 17
  Betsy, 35
  Cardis, 52
  D. G., 68
  Deal, 6, 29, 54
  Deal D., 20
  Elizabeth, 39
  Frances, 12
  George, 18
  J. L., 100
  John H., 110
  John M., 130
  Lewis, 17
  M. L., 94
  Mark, 88
  Matthew, 27
  Milly, 62
  Nancy, 22, 33
  Patience, 18
  Polly, 75, 88
  Sally, 112
  Samuel, 1
  Thomas, 17
  Uriah D., 68
  Urias, 17
  Warren, 49
  Zachariah, 30
COLTON, Ally, 47
  Leanna, 50
COLYER, Jonathan, 132
CONE, Josiah, 95
  Martha, 112
CONEGY, Owen, 80

COOK, John, 19, 21
  John P., 97
COOL, Anderson, 58
COOLEEN, Anny, 87
COOPER, Ann, 34
  Betsy, 30
  Betty, 43
  Henry, 53
  John, 32, 53, 101, 125
  Mary, 35
  Sally, 55
  Tabitha, 30
COPELAND, Charles, 6, 14, 15
  Elizabeth, 96
  Hezekiah, 39
  Joanne, 118
  Jonathan, 114
  William, 6
COPPER, John, 51
  Solly, 56
CORBET, Augustus, 122
  Ava Marellen, 103
  George W., 105
  James, 31, 85, 105
  James H., 60, 87, 107
  James K., 89
  James M., 89, 103
  John, 77, 94
  Joshua, 34
  Lodrick, 89
  Lordrick A., 85
  Mary, 40
  Mary J., 130
  Nancy, 45, 89
  Richard, 35
  Sealy, 44
  Viney, 110
  Wofied, 94
CORBETT, James, 98
  Jeremiah, 98
  Mary Ann, 78
  Susannah, 34
CORBIN, William, 101
CORDDE, Abby, 53
CORDELE, John, 77
CORDELL, Henry L.,

80
  John, 69, 70
  Martha, 120
  Nancy, 53
  Sally, 69
CORDLE, Harmon, 49
CORE, Penelope, 47
COREY, Thomas, 15
CORKE, Patsy, 47
COTTER, John H., 103
COTTON, John, 1
  Polly, 54
  Thena H., 48
COURDELL, Candiss, 45
COWELL, Jordan, 63
COX, John M., 126
  Levy, 111
  Mary, 69
  Mecajah, 79
  Sanders E., 110
  Wilie W., 110
  William, 132
CRABTREE, Richard, 132
CRAFFORD, Amy, 67
  Polly, 34, 97
  Winifred, 2
CRAVY, Hugh, 4, 11, 18
CRAWFORD, Ally, 120
  Catherine, 23
  Ceela, 54
  Charles, 48, 53
  Daniel, 52
  Edith, 33
  Elizabeth, 15
  John H., 98
  Julia, 86
  Sarah, 29
  William K., 77
CRAWLEY, John, 26
CREACH, Ezekiel, 27
  Joshua, 27
  Rebecca, 35
CREECH, Alvin, 74, 89
  Apsabeth, 49
  Ashley, 108
  Barna, 80, 128
  Benjamin, 20

INDEX

Bennet, 58
Betsy Janio, 118
Bryant H., 116
Catharine, 69
Catherine, 88
Charles, 107
Cullen, 116
Doctor L., 93
Edney, 109, 118
Eli, 70
Eliza Ann, 132
Eliza Jane, 130
Elizabeth, 100, 116
Ezekiel, 46, 57, 75, 76, 92, 121
Haywood, 72
Herrin, 106
Herron, 74, 104
James, 92
James W., 125
Jesse, 13, 38, 71, 76
Joannah, 61
John, 57
John B., 116
John R., 119
Joseph, 49
Joshua, 16, 17, 20, 28, 37, 58, 69, 75, 90, 96, 98
Josiah, 124
Kedar, 69, 75, 83
Lany, 37
Larkin, 72, 89, 103
Levi P., 130
Lewis, 120
Louisa, 70
Lousee, 49
Margaret, 70, 110
Maryan Elizabeth, 97
Nancy, 45, 50
Parrot, 108, 128, 129, 133
Patrick, 120
Penny Harriet, 98
Ransom, 104, 118
Romulus H., 127
Sally, 20, 113
Sandford, 125
Standford, 71
Stanford, 85, 87
Stephen, 116
Susan, 59, 66
Tempy, 90
V. A., 94
William, 84, 92
William H., 82, 83
William J., 104
William R., 130
Willy, 66
Wimmy, 68
Worley, 129
CRISTMAN, Mary J., 73
CROCKER, Bardin, 99
Catty, 50
Elizabeth H., 81
Everet, 103
Harriet, 122
Harry, 88
Henderson, 85, 110
J. N., 129
James, 50, 53
Joel, 42
John, 62
Linsey, 86
Mary E., 114
Mattie, 89
Milly, 91
Morning, 69
Mourning, 105
Nancy, 80
Samuel, 40, 42, 98
Thena, 63
W. A., 124
CROFORD, Sally, 40
CROOKER, Catharin, 130
CROP, Sara A., 119
CROSS, Lugenia, 72
Peggy, 48
Sarah, 71
CROWDEN, Elizabeth, 126
CRUISE, Lewis, 54
CRUMPLER, Asa, 19
Benjamin, 6
Charity, 40
Edmond, 20
Garry, 71, 81
John, 36
Kinchen, 61
William, 20, 36
CULLEN, Matthew, 85
CULLOM, W. H., 129
William H., 106
CULLON, Mortimer, 84
William Henry, 84
CULLUM, Julia Ann, 111
W. H., 111
William H., 97
CULOM, Eliza Ann, 94
William A., 94
CUTTS, Margaret E., 126

-D-

DANCE, A. A., 100
DANIEL, Delilah, 11
Elizabeth, 109
Fanny, 129
Grezzy Ann, 109
John, 78
John H., 72, 73, 112, 114, 129
Joshua, 45
Josuah, 41
Nancy, 33
DARCIL, Mary, 61
DARDEN, Leweney, 67
DAUGHTEREY, Apsabeth, 80
DAUGHTERY, Aden, 125
Arthur, 34
Hardy, 45
Henry, 34
Jacob, 50
Patience, 35, 36
Richards, 35
Robert, 46
Thomas, 52
DAUGHTRY, Benjamin, 65
Elizabeth, 112
George, 86

John, 86, 115
Nannie, 123
Polly Ann, 115
Sally, 70
Solomon, 75, 84
DAVIDSON, Peggy, 33
DAVIS, Arthur, 9
Audie, 97
Betsy, 24
Charlotte, 17, 121
Cintha, 89
Dixon, 40, 51, 58, 102, 130
Elisha, 34, 121
Elizabeth, 71, 80
George W., 105
Harriet, 102
Henry, 9, 11
Henry H., 60
I. D., 128
Jacob, 10, 75
James, 4, 34, 59, 84, 93, 99, 101
Jesse, 67
Jessie, 56
Joel P., 127
John, 40, 97
Jones, 37
Joshua, 70
Julia Ann, 122
Lucinda, 127
Mariah, 59
Martha, 29
Mary Ann, 17
Molly, 79
Mourning, 61
Nammy, 4
Nancy, 42, 96
Patty, 10
Polley, 12
Pollie Ann, 126
Polly, 69
Rebecca, 68
Rebena, 88
Sally, 36
Susan, 56
Thaney, 60
Thomas, 34, 55, 61
William, 23, 36
DAVISON, Joseph, 46

DAWSON, Sarah, 2
Stephen, 86
William, 2
DEAN, Calvin, 67
Cassandra, 64
Harrison, 105
Henry, 66
J. A., 122
John, 15
DEANS, Bartley, 116
Clary, 51
Josiah, 106
Matthew I., 123
Nancy, 36
Patience Ann, 120
Polly, 56
Willie, 64, 106
DEARHAM, Harry, 128
DEBERY, Benjamin, 62
DEBNAM, Edward, 62, 67, 78
James A., 62
Robert B., 104
William, 67
DEES, Daniel, 6, 10, 31, 42
Drury, 3
Edmond, 27
Edmund, 16
Eliza, 45
Hilliard, 20
Ridgon, 47
DELK, Jacob, 4
DELOACH, Britain, 30
Jerusha, 19
John, 3
Joseph, 3, 5, 12
Polly, 27, 55, 59
Samuel, 27
DEMENT, Ann, 18
DEMING, Nathan, 85
DEMONT, Margaret, 5
DENBY, Henry, 28
James, 28
DENISE, Joannah, 123
DENKINS, Winifred, 41
DENNING, Chilly A., 104

George, 78
Isaac, 109
Martha Jane, 103
Robert, 86, 93
Thomas, 93
Uriah, 115
DENNIS, James, 60
DEVOLT, Polly, 19
DEW, Anne, 23
DICKENS, Susan, 62
DICKERSON,
Alexander, 31
DIMKINS, Henry, 85
DINKINS, Newry, 118
DINMORE, John, 10
DIVIN, John, 14
DIXON, Abram, 63, 68, 75, 78, 96, 118, 132
Abselly, 95
Aldridge H., 102
Elenor, 116
Elizabeth, 79
Emily, 82
Haywood, 129
John, 11, 50, 68
Joshua, 127
Lancy, 104
Lemmuel, 74
Major, 108
Mary, 88
Nancy, 92
Patrick, 126
Penny, 77
Sarah A., 131
Tabith, 90
DODD, A. S., 100
Bennett, 34
Dempsey, 3
Edny, 62
Elizabeth, 88, 107
Esther S., 115
Hisy, 29
Isaac, 124
Jane, 5
John, 5, 8, 88, 115
Lithy, 33
Matthew, 62
Nancy, 36, 82
Nancy F., 129

INDEX

Pherebe, 124
Phereby, 3
Polly, 31
Reuben, 35, 37, 44
Robert, 2
Sarah, 25, 100
Susan, 94
Theophilius, 69
Theophilus, 64
William, 1, 20
Willie, 88
Winifred, 39
Winifred M., 123
DODDE, Bennett, 29
DOUGHDY, Matthew, 66
DOUGLAS, Rhodham, 23
Thomas, 20
DOUGLASS, Frances, 24
DOWDEN, John, 23
DOWDY, Benjamin, 47
Betsy, 41
Fanny, 71
DOWNING, Mary, 5
DOXEY, Polly, 32
DOXY, Nancy, 41
DOZIER, Edmond, 58
DRAKE, David, 18
DRAMHAM, Richard, 35
DRAPER, Mary, 3
DRAUGHAM, Hailey, 30
DRAUGHAN, Delea Ann, 106
J. R., 94
DRAUGHON, Martha J., 124
Rebecca E., 123
DRAUGHORN, John, 49
DRICE, Luzuna, 95
DRIVEN, Nancy, 122
DRIVER, Gilbert, 54
John, 10, 17, 40, 51, 54
Jonathan, 40, 60
William, 75
DUIK, Beady, 23
Elizabeth, 32

James, 32
Polly, 13
DUN, Benjamin, 120
Elizabeth, 72
DUNCAN, A. R., 132, 133
Alexander, 70
Betsy, 64
Everett, 50
G. W., 81
George, 50, 87
George M., 113
George W., 70
Henry, 16, 61, 87
John, 34
Luzanna, 90
Winifred, 87
DUNN, Allen R., 116
Amos, 121, 128
Barnaba, 65
Barnaby, 38
Benjamin, 39
Elizabeth, 124
George, 60, 61, 71
George W., 109
Harriet, 88
James B., 102, 104
Joanna, 128
Joel, 50
John, 108, 111, 120
John R., 120
Nancy, 46, 51
Nathaniel, 40
Priscilla, 39
Reney, 83
Richard S., 86
Robert, 64
Sally Ann, 68
Samson, 126
Sir William, 119
Thomas, 57
DUPMAR, John, 121
DUPREE, D., 96
James H., 107
John, 54
Koziah E., 129
Mary, 106
Mary Ann, 107
Mary Jane, 116

Nathaniel, 107
Peter, 21
Peter C., 120
Sally, 53
Thomas, 97, 107
DURDEN, James, 61
DURHAM, Anne, 21
Betsy, 23, 67
Christian, 11
Creasey, 32
Edney, 61
Hardy, 50
Harry, 71
James, 4, 21, 30, 70
James H., 79, 85, 86, 88
Letty, 3
Louisa, 87
Lusanna, 22
Matthew, 32
Polly, 43
Samuel, 59
Sorind, 70
Thomas, 59, 69, 70, 84, 86
W. H., 119
William, 3, 7, 16, 18, 62, 105

-E-

EADOM, Harriet, 34
EARP, Ailsy, 60
Alsey, 66, 67
Berry, 55
Betsy, 57
Burwell, 15, 62, 75
Elizabeth, 58
Emeline, 81
Guion, 107
Harriet, 68
Hutson, 35, 66
Izeriah, 31
J. Henderson, 101
James H., 98
John, 7, 66, 74
John E., 98, 107, 109
Jonathan, 15
Maria, 76
Martha, 41, 73

JOHNSTON COUNTY MARRIAGES

Mary, 82
McNab, 122, 124, 125, 130, 132
Moses, 132
Nancy, 43, 68
Penny, 27
Quean, 104
Sally, 35
Sherad, 13
W., 118, 123
William, 11, 63, 66
William S., 109
Wyatt, 75, 79, 100
EASON, Adin, 46
Alexander, 132
Aley, 47
Alsey, 28, 31
Ann, 109
Avera, 77
Benjamin, 23, 30, 36
Edith, 27
Elisha, 30
Emily W., 71
Euphemia, 116
Faranrich, 28
Frances, 66
George, 77
Hardy, 64
Hawkins, 99
Henry W., 47
J. C., 124, 129, 132
J. E., 125
James, 55, 76
Jesse, 59
Joanna, 95
John, 4, 8, 9, 16, 28, 44, 51, 55, 61, 64
John S., 133
Kearney, 70
Margaret, 122
Marsaline, 126
Martha Ann, 126
Martha J., 124
Mary, 2, 38
Moses, 35
Nancy, 38
Olive, 38

Othorial, 2
Penny, 82
Polly, 63
Sally, 35
Sanders, 89
Sarah, 15
Sarah A. E., 87
Shadrock, 12
Smithy, 86
Temperance, 41
Theaney, 30
Thomas, 62, 63
Viney, 55
William, 36, 59
William H., 108
EASTMAN, Martha, 125
EATMAN, Alsey, 58
Crisy, 82
Cynthia, 83
Deliah, 35
Eatty, 47
John, 35
Labon, 68
Lou, 132
Mary, 121
Thomas, 17, 23
Willey, 113
EATMON, Kimbrel, 69
Nancy, 63
EATON, Pordi, 51
EATSMAN, Kimbrell, 133
EAVEN, Seth T., 84
EAVENS, Polly, 84
EAVINS, Daniel, 27
EDGERTON, Joseph G., 133
Thomas, 91
EDMOND, Samson, 21
EDWARD, Celia, 50
Elizabeth, 9, 11
Henry, 74
William B. T., 123
EDWARDS, Amy, 77
Apsabeth, 99
Benjamin, 12, 39, 66, 130
Caroline, 89
Delaney, 71
Edith, 51, 62

Elizabeth, 97, 104, 110, 127
Elvy, 91
Emily, 80
George, 103
Henry, 84
Henry G., 70, 99, 112, 113
Henry O., 98
Howard, 110
Jacob, 12, 17, 49
Jesse, 18, 40, 131
John, 7, 70, 89, 112
Joseph, 4, 5, 6, 23, 35, 40, 53, 110, 126
Joshua, 125
Lucy, 60
Lucy Ann, 96
Martha, 82
Mary, 63
Mecajah, 47
Mechajal, 29
Morrace, 112
Nancy, 23, 49, 69
Nancy Ann E., 83
Needham, 68
Newsom, 61
Patsy, 19, 44
Patty, 3, 22
Piety, 87
Pollie Ann, 127
Polly, 35, 37
Rachel, 100
Raiford, 81
Rebecca, 67
Richard, 101
Robbin, 84
Robert, 74, 80, 84, 90
Sally, 44
Sampson, 39, 63, 68, 69
Sarah, 5, 17
Sarrah, 77
Stephen, 29, 68
Thomas, 13, 37, 57, 69, 76
Vine, 70, 114
Vinson, 70

152

INDEX

William, 36, 69
William E., 68
William P., 108
William T., 127
Zachariah, 82
EGERTON, Thomas, 88
ELDRIDGE, Ann, 105
  Betsy, 85
  Cherry, 129
  Elizabeth, 44, 121
  Emily, 127
  John, 94
  Ketsy, 108
  L., 124
  Lizzy, 82
  Loverd, 32, 53, 56, 57, 110, 112, 113
  Lucy J., 112
  Mary, 48, 130
  Ryals, 39
  Sarah, 116
  Susan, 98, 133
  Thiny, 121
  Troy, 98
  Young, 61
ELENGEN, Eli, 109
ELIOT, John, 5
ELKRIDGE, Pherebon, 99
  Troy, 99
ELLEN, Regdon H. F., 116
ELLINGTON, Adelah C., 100
  Betsy, 49
  Edith, 59
  F. T., 129
  J. F., 118, 121, 122, 124, 128, 130, 131, 132
  J. R., 119
  Jesse, 27
  Joel, 44
  John F., 14, 59
  Joseph C., 127
  Julia, 126
  Kindred C., 57
  Martha, 102
  Nancy, 57
  Polly, 65

Sally, 27
W. P., 125
Worsham, 27
ELLIOT, Sally, 19
ELLIS, Abel, 83
  Aebella, 113
  Edney, 21, 48
  Elijah, 18
  Elizabeth, 110
  F. F., 121
  Ferdinand, 79
  German, 21
  James, 54, 99
  James A., 97
  James N., 99, 111
  James R., 62, 68, 114
  Jamison H., 116
  John, 4, 18, 22, 24, 48, 62, 80
  John Leacy, 124
  Lecy, 67
  Lofton, 81
  Luly, 62
  Martha, 36
  Martha A., 130
  Nancy, 77, 123
  Ridley, 118
  T. T., 126
  Tobitha, 118
  William, 68, 70
  William H., 97
ENNIS, Annie E., 129
  Clara, 129
  Handy H., 107
  Henry C., 61
  John A., 113, 114, 120
  John E., 113
  John H., 107
  Lucy Ann, 111
  Matilda V., 100
  Nancy, 86, 92
  Nancy E., 123
  Needham, 63
  Ransom, 62, 63
  Raymond, 133
  Sarah, 122
  Winifred, 113
ERRANT, Betsy, 53
ETHELDRED, ?, 16

Edward, 14
ETHERIDGE, William J., 91
ETHRIDGE, Edward, 15
  Jency, 64
  Levey, 11
  Loverd, 37
  Thomas, 64
  William, 66
EVANS, Adalaid, 129
  Ashley B., 113
  Athy, 58
  Betsy Ann, 70
  Betsy E., 81
  Caroline, 79
  Charlotte, 78
  Clem, 93
  David, 14, 24, 35
  Dicy, 75
  Edith, 80
  Elinor, 62, 67
  Ephraim, 31
  Ephraim R., 97
  Etheldred, 22
  Francis, 5
  Hinton, 111, 116
  Jeremiah, 54
  Jesse, 5
  Joanna, 60
  John, 24, 31, 61
  John B., 66
  Jonathan, 67
  Josiah, 80, 87
  Peggy, 62
  Sally, 45
  Samuel, 114
  Simpson, 106
  Zilpha, 38
EVERYTT, William, 40
EZZEL, Fanny M., 82
EZZELE, Nancy, 107

-F-

FAIL, Ailsey, 74
  Dixon, 11
  Edith Ann, 59
  Elizabeth, 66
  Jonathan, 59, 61
  Julia, 81
  Lewis, 41

Maria, 70
Mary A., 120
Nancy, 24, 76
Needham, 83, 122
Patsy, 83
Pherebe, 127
Phereby, 50
Polly, 52
Rachel, 68
Sally, 25
Sarah, 67
William, 20, 38
William D., 93
FAILE, Anne, 2
  Phereby, 14, 17
  Thomas, 14, 17
  William D., 93
FAIRCLOTH, Hardy, 133
  Mary Jarrell, 127
  Stephen S., 133
FAIRLEY, Elizabeth, 125
FAISSON, John T., 107
FARMER, Benjamin, 24
  Betsy, 53
  Edith, 29
  Henry, 81
  James J., 85
  Jenkins, 13, 14, 22
  John, 19, 20, 25, 53
  Jonathan, 26
  Joseph, 41, 55, 57, 74
  Kinchin, 25
  Polly, 16
  Sally, 63
  Sarah, 22
  Susannah, 19, 31
  Thomas, 66
  William, 14, 16
FARRAR, Eliza, 56
  William, 21
FARREL, John W., 97
FARRELL, Gabriel, 100
FARROR, William, 44
FARROW, Catharine, 70
FARSON, B. F., 113
  Martha J. E., 113
FARVER, Sally, 32
FAULK, Creacy, 36
  Elizabeth, 7, 50
  Henry, 3
  James, 12, 77, 90, 119, 122, 128
  John, 3
  Jones, 129
  Nicholas, 23
  Sarah, 44
FEARRELL, James, 85
FEDDER, Penny, 19
FELICK, James, 48, 50
  Jane, 61
FELLOW, S. E., 62
FELLOWS, John, 19, 31, 53
FERREL, James, 89
FERRELL, Aley, 24
  Betsy, 22
  Catherine, 95
  Cathern, 97
  David, 129
  Elizabeth, 66, 122
  Ephramin, 24
  Harrison, 95, 108, 109
  Henry, 105
  Isaac, 2
  Jacob, 15
  James J., 100
  John, 37
  John W., 79, 81
  Leacy, 62
  Levi, 55
  Mary, 4
  Mary N., 108
  Merrit, 63
  Miriam, 7
  Nancy, 27
  Polly, 60
  R. K., 120
  Susannah, 19
  Temperance, 33
  Tempy, 50
  Thetus, 64
  Thomas J., 126
  Ulrica, 86
  Willie, 36
  Willis, 64
  Winifred, 68
FETCH, Jane W., 93
FEWTRELL, Bud, 71
FIBIASH, Morning, 46
FIELD, Lucy, 59
FIELDS, Needham, 101, 115
  Susan, 106
FILLION, William, 5
FINCH, Berty, 33
FINET, Patty, 4
FINLAYSON, A. J., 133
  Melvina, 129
FINLEY, Thomas, 34
  Zilphia, 37
FISH, Abigail, 17
  John, 8, 17
  Sally, 17
  William, 10, 62
FISHER, Polly, 24
FITZGERALD, Martha, 120
FIVASH, Patsy, 43
FLASER, Jacob, 25, 95
FLOID, Aven, 89
  Betsy, 89
FLOWERS, Bedy, 62
  Benjamin, 24
  Elizabeth E., 121
  Ellender, 12
  Emily, 62
  Everett, 96
  Green, 131
  Harriet, 65
  Henry, 13, 15, 46
  J. W., 129
  Jacob, 13, 24, 26, 86
  Joel, 60
  John, 68
  Martha, 77
  Mary, 63
  Michael, 22
  Nathan, 70
  Needham, 9

INDEX

Sally, 46
Tempe, 68
Winifred, 41
FLUELLER, Amy, 15
 Archibald, 16
 Nancy, 86
 Piety, 15
 Sarah, 44
FLUELLERS, James, 43
FOLK, Polly, 35
 Thomas, 21
 William, 21
FOLSOM, Thomas, 3, 25
FORD, Elizabeth, 102
 Hardy, 124
 Jane, 75
 John, 75
 John A., 95, 98
 Patience, 44
FOREHAND, Lewis, 35
 Patsy, 35
FOUNTAIN, Mariah, 100
FOWLER, Charles, 58
 James, 126
 Patrick, 58
 Wesley, 75
FRANKLIN, William, 25
FREEMAN, David, 38
 Mark, 69
 N. Y., 118
 Needham, 118
 Patsy, 121
 Rixcy, 131
FROST, Cathran, 20
 Jonas, 24, 25
 Rachel, 30, 34
 Ryal W., 58, 59
 Sarah, 57
FRUZIN, Custico, 125
FULGHAM, Charles, 22
 Edith, 29
 Elizabeth, 98
 Jacob, 128
 Jesse, 107
 John, 109

Joseph, 22
 Sarah, 131
FULGHRAM, Jacob B., 92
FULLER, John, 10
FURLEY, Apey, 65
 Betsy, 14
 Polly, 30
 Richard, 8
 Thomas, 118
FURNAGO, Isaac, 124
FURNELL, James A., 61
FURNER, Catharine, 132
FURR, Isaac, 11
FUTERAL, Etheldred, 21
 Nathaniel, 36
 Solomon, 21
FUTRELL, Caroline, 128
 Crawford, 59, 63, 65, 114
 Drusilla, 57
 Elizabeth, 118
 Etheldred, 23, 34, 48, 49, 56
 Exum, 53, 54
 Jesse, 67
 Mary, 60, 75
 Nathaniel, 43, 54
 Needham, 20
 Solomon, 40, 50, 67
 Wilkerson, 35, 48
FUTURELL, Mary, 124

-G-
GAIN, Winiford, 95
GAINAS, Penny, 133
GALE, Clarey, 15
GALES, Solomon, 7
GAMALIAN, Polly, 31
GAME, Elizer, 92
 Josiah, 51
 Peggy Ann, 76
 Samuel, 51, 57, 99
GANNER, Christean, 15
 Elisha, 21

Sarah, 21
GARDNER, Delany, 126
 Eli, 68
 Larry, 81
 Levery, 13
 Martha, 99
 Penelopia, 10
GARLAND, Louize, 58
 Mary, 30
GARNER, Asa, 61, 66
 Bedy, 67
 Betsey, 21
 Betsy, 17, 58, 62
 Cintha, 90
 Cinthia, 74
 Cynthia, 48
 Daniel, 73
 Dicy, 24
 Eli, 83
 Elisha, 13
 Elizabeth, 5, 61, 64
 Ely, 85
 Gideon, 54
 Henderson, 87
 James, 64, 67, 87
 Joel, 83
 Josiah, 50
 Levi, 55
 Lydia, 13
 Mabry, 105
 Mary, 52
 Moses, 29, 55
 Nancy, 22, 96
 Patey, 58
 Polly, 68
 Sally, 58
 Sarah, 115
 William, 6, 13, 64, 68, 87
 Willie, 13
 Willis, 20, 24, 25
 Winifred, 6
 Zilpha, 46
GARRALD, Ann, 7
 Enos, 34, 42, 43
 John, 2
 Nancy, 33
 Willie, 59
GARRARD, F., 118,

155

JOHNSTON COUNTY MARRIAGES

119
GARRELL, Clark F., 104
  Enos, 111
  Isaac, 111
  Mary, 111
  Thared, 32
  Willey, 33
  Willis, 32
GATLIN, James, 34
  Zilpha, 50
GAY, Betsy, 57
  Catherine, 102
  Elizabeth, 110
  Josiah, 82, 85, 98, 110
  Laurinda, 122
  Levina, 106
  Lucinda, 120
  Lucretia, 121
  Milly, 121
  Ranzy, 121
  Rutha, 53
  William, 56, 121
  Willis, 36
GEARALD, Delany, 89
GEARHEARDT, Henry, 93
GEORGE, Betsy, 41
  Charity, 50
  David, 34
  Elias, 2
  Isaac, 67
  Isaac L., 77
  Jeremiah L., 82, 89, 116
  Mary, 94
  Nancy, 53
  Sarah A., 129
  Winifred, 54
GERALD, Quilly, 121
  W. F., 134
  Willie, 58
GERHARDT, Henry, 96, 108
  J. C. F., 110
  John C. F., 96
GERHEARDT, Henry, 75, 88
GERMILLON, Polly, 19
GERRALD, Anne, 67
  Clark, 70
  Disey, 69
  Edney, 56
  Enos, 67
  John, 1
  Marion, 49
  Patsey, 45
  Willie, 45
  Willie F., 133
  Willy, 65
GERRALL, John, 26
GESBORN, Catherine, 38
GIBBS, Holly, 47
GIFFORD, B., 118
GILES, Bersheba, 3
  Elisabeth, 2
  Jacob, 5
  John, 29, 49
  Judith, 27
  Matthew, 47, 102
  Nammy, 10
  Nathaniel, 5, 12, 120
  Sally, 49
  Sarrah, 100
  William, 5, 10, 18, 29, 49
GILMAN, Harbard, 6, 25
  Harland, 21
  Herbert, 32
  Winifred, 52
GIMETT, Betsy, 57
GIMMET, Mary, 72
GLASGLOW, James, 3
GLOVER, Benjamin J., 78, 83
GODWIN, Aaron, 9, 52
  Alexander, 29
  Amanda, 76
  Avera E., 124
  B., 130
  Beady, 27
  Benjamin, 82, 88, 109, 114, 115
  Bennet, 64
  Bethany, 114
  Cady, 19
  Ceany, 119
  Clarkey, 128
  Cozzy, 70
  Creacey, 22
  Cresy, 25
  Eastern, 127
  Edith, 56
  Edmond, 27
  Edney, 74
  Edny, 86
  Eleanor, 121
  Eli, 56, 112
  Elias, 30
  Elijah, 65
  Elizabeth, 98, 101
  Emaline, 110
  Ephraim, 5
  Evan, 96
  G. W., 72
  George, 133
  Gracy, 36
  Griffin M., 80
  Griffin W., 81
  Haywood W., 128
  Henderson, 73
  Hinton M., 79
  Iredel, 105
  Irvin L., 109
  Jacob H., 109, 119
  James, 22, 48
  James A., 109
  Jemby, 85
  Jesse, 120
  Jesse H., 109
  John, 74
  Jordan, 118
  Louisa, 127
  Margaret, 93
  Martha, 77, 112
  Milby, 32
  Milton M., 105
  Minton M., 87
  Muntean M., 81
  Nancy, 35, 61
  Newit R., 97
  P., 119, 120, 122, 123, 127, 129, 131, 133
  Perry, 98, 118
  Piety, 61
  Piety E., 128
  Polly, 39, 43, 51

INDEX

Raney, 69
Ransom, 119, 128
Rhoda, 3
Samuel, 11, 13
Silas, 26
Silvy, 25
Simon, 82, 128
Smithy A., 122
Stephen, 68
Stephenson, 60
Susan, 129
Susan C., 119
Theophilius, 123
Tobias, 40, 115
Uriah, 6
Wiley, 85
Willie, 61, 65
GOODRICH, Betsy, 41
 Catern, 5
 George, 19
 James, 40
GOODSON, Mary, 110
GORMAN, M., 36
 Sarah, 121
GOTMAN, Kinbard, 68
GOWER, Abel, 120
 Adam A., 110
 Araminta, 119
 Caron, 82
 Daniel, 28
 Esther, 9
 Gideon, 52
 John R., 110
 Lewis, 13
 Lydia, 8
 Pherebe, 8
 Polly, 27
 Reuben, 47, 72
 Simeon H., 121
 William, 13, 28, 74
 Zachariah, 28, 29, 44
GRAHAM, Henderson, 79, 116
 Martha E., 126
GRANT, Dempsey, 89
 Dennis, 122
 Pollie, 132
 Winiford, 120
GRANTHAM, Alley, 63
 Barna, 69

Caroline, 133
Dicy, 70
Frederick, 72
M. H., 124
M. K., 133
Whitley, 62
GRAVES, Polly, 15
GRAY, Alexander, 7
 Henry, 13, 18
 Thomas, 5
 William, 19
GRAYHAM, Henderson, 108, 115
GREEN, Anna, 101
 Barnaba, 62
 Barnaby, 100
 Barry, 94
 Betsy, 51
 Bryan, 28
 Bryant, 12
 Caroline, 92
 Clary, 38
 Darkess, 120
 Dempsey, 25, 56
 Edith, 17
 Ervin, 53
 Fernifold, 63, 65, 67
 Henry, 67, 69
 Henry S., 72
 James, 54, 70, 133
 James H., 93
 Jane, 81
 Jesse, 57
 John, 7, 17, 83
 John B., 115
 Labon, 44
 Marsaline, 1291
 Martha, 121
 Mary, 3, 14
 Mary C., 32
 Marzella, 109
 Milly, 59
 Nancy, 30, 34, 53, 58
 Nathan, 120
 Penny Jane E., 93
 Polly, 59
 R., 77
 Reding, 56
 Reley, 44

Reter, 31
Richard, 86, 93
Rutha Ann, 96
Sally, 37, 45, 51
Sion, 12
Sir, 30
Susan, 31
Thomas, 6
William, 7, 49, 51, 54, 58, 63, 104
William H., 95
Willie, 44, 57
GREGGEL, Mary, 21
GREGORY, James, 13, 34
 John, 71
 M. W., 125
 Patty, 17
 Uz, 15
GRICE, Calvin, 60
 Cynthia, 30
 David, 76
 Deliah, 10
 Garry, 49, 50, 55
 James, 36
 Jesse, 42
 Piety, 68
 Stephen, 15, 21, 22, 24, 28, 29
 Tempy Ann, 53
 Thomas F., 67
 Thomas T., 85
 Zilpha, 8, 61
GRIFFIN, Atlis, 58
 Caroline, 115
 Edmond, 10
 Elizabeth, 45
 George W., 65
 James B., 130
 John A., 90
 John B., 125
 Labon, 38, 43, 46
 Major, 46, 58
 Margarette Jane, 96
 Martha, 107
 Mary E., 122
 Susan Jane, 111
 Tranquilla, 69
 William, 109
GRIFFITH, Sally, 82

GRIGERY, James, 39
GRIMES, Elizabeth, 63
  Lucy, 55
  Matilda, 62
  Sally, 62
  William, 12, 106
GRISUE, Sally, 90
GRISWELL, Ruffin, 99
GRISWOLD, Nancy, 84, 86
GRISWOOD, Mary E., 132
GRIZZEL, Brammister, 43
GRIZZLER, Brammister, 26
GUESS, Sarah N., 133
GUION, Elizabeth, 8
GULLEY, A. G., 125
  Bethena, 42
  Elizabeth, 12
  George, 18
  George G., 123
  George S., 64
  John, 16, 32
  John G., 35
  Matthew T., 68
  Mead, 13
  N. G., 126
  Nannie W., 128
  Nathan, 3, 12
  Nathaniel, 7
  Needham, 83
  Patsy, 36
  Patty, 12
  Polley, 14
  R. N., 120, 121
  R. W., 120
  Robert, 2, 11, 13, 14, 16, 17, 18, 25, 29, 41
  Robert N., 69
  Robin, 7
  Tilpha, 126
  William B., 84
GULLY, A., 119
  Aney, 38
  Elizabeth, 46
  Eraslus, 110

  George, 51, 64
  Harriet, 62
  John, 111
  John C., 57, 112
  John G., 60, 62, 88
  Martha, 88
  Mary Ann, 81
  Meed, 44
  N. G., 96, 124
  Polly, 42
  R. A., 118
  R. N., 95
  Robert A., 118
  Robert N., 47, 48, 61, 66, 82, 93, 106
  Sally, 39, 46
  Samuel S., 61
  Tranquilla, 39
  Walter W., 104
  William G., 104
  Zilpha, 59
GURLEY, Arthur, 28
  Betsy, 21
  Daniel, 69, 70
  Elizabeth, 5, 33, 75
  Frederick, 27
  Henry, 65
  Jeremiah, 18, 26, 29, 40
  John G., 103
  Jonathan, 28
  Joseph, 65, 66
  Keziah, 26
  Lydia, 61
  Maniss, 26
  Martha, 128
  Mary H., 72
  Maurice, 33
  Monroe, 68
  Morris, 28
  Nancy, 32
  Polly, 34
  R. F., 129
  Raiford, 76, 77
  Susannah, 6
  Willie, 61
  Zelpha, 113
GURLY, Daniel, 59
  Mary Jane, 72

  Robert, 34
GUY, Henry, 34, 38, 39
  John C., 31, 33, 36, 38
  John L., 36, 37
  Josiah, 62
  Nancy, 40
  Narcissy, 50
  Sukey, 36
  William, 29, 35, 74
  William H., 41, 45, 66
  Winifred, 34
GWIN, Abraham, 23
  Barna, 86, 99
  Dicy A., 120
  Elizabeth, 121
  Henry, 83, 107
  Sally, 96
  William, 117, 118, 120

-H-

HACKNEY, Celah, 20
  James A., 73
  Martha, 16
  Piety, 27
  William, 4, 15, 16, 19, 97
HADLEY, Benjamin, 32
  Susannah, 14
  Thomas, 46
HAGAN, Smithey, 73
HAGENS, John, 97
HAILS, Chatman, 20
  Henry, 20
  William, 30
HAINES, Anne, 28
HAISTIP, Betsy, 24
  Jeremiah, 26
HALE, William F., 123
HALES, Gillis, 83
  Henry, 103
HALL, Bedy, 83
  Delany, 43
  Edith, 54
  Fernifold, 61
  Martin, 39

INDEX

Mary, 123
Matthew, 76
Phereby, 40
Sally, 84
Sarah, 63
Susan, 35
W. F., 131, 133
William, 74, 119
William G., 90
William T., 121
Willoughby, 63
Zilpha, 49
HALLIMAN, James, 2
HALLINGS, Sally, 11
HALLY, John C., 92
HAMBLETON, Henry, 46, 57, 87
HAMELTON, Edith, 60
George, 103
HAMILTON, Barnaba, 59, 65
Eliza, 123, 130
Henry, 69, 91
John, 120
Sally, 35
HAMLET, R. W., 93
HAMMONTREE, Peter, 68
Stephen, 68
HAMPER, Bartlett, 77
HAN, W. F., 119
HANDY, Major, 75
Matthew, 20, 21, 22
Matthias, 21
HANE, Henry, 105
Mary, 98
HARDCASTLE, James, 10
HARDEE, Bright, 105
HARDY, Bright, 96, 105
Holmes, 47
Martha, 73, 76
Nelly, 48
Sally, 30
Sarah, 90
HARE, John, 81, 90
Joseph, 90
Martha, 129
Ransom, 130, 131

Rebecca, 71
Sally, 77
HARMAN, Rhoda, 23
Sally E., 107
HARMON, James, 31
HARP, Gaston, 121
HARPER, Absalom, 55
Anny, 96
Banister, 58
Bannister, 43
Bartlet, 88
Bartley, 69, 108
Bryan, 62, 68, 92
Bryant, 95
Caroline, 116
Catherine V. T., 124
Daniel, 55
Devereaux, 91
Elizabth T., 128
Frederick, 33
George R., 133
Harriet, 111
J. R., 115
Jacob J., 124
John, 24, 41, 120, 123, 126
John B., 88
John I., 131
John J., 127, 130, 131
John R., 91
Joseph, 33
Leverley, 9
Martin, 55
Mary, 55
Milly, 92
Nancy, 15
Nancy Willey, 109
Phereby, 35
Polly, 39
Westly, 91
William N., 114
Wilsey, 81
HARPIN, John, 121
HARPS, John, 9
HARREL, John, 99
HARRELL, Ann, 51
Asa, 41, 48
Betsy, 50
Charlotte, 4
Cinith, 67

Elizabeth, 16
Elizabeth, 55
Frances, 37, 39
Francis, 18, 22, 23, 25, 26, 50, 51, 59
Henry, 3
Jacob, 23
John, 51, 69
Levy, 20
Patty, 23
Samuel, 16
Susanna, 57
William, 26, 37, 57
HARREN, Anna, 29
HARRES, Raiford, 116
HARRIS, Churchwell, 110
Matthew, 9
William, 23
HARRISON, Betsy, 50
Della, 85
Elias, 66
Elisha, 46, 61, 63, 64, 66, 68
Elizabeth, 10
George, 94
James, 33, 105
John, 110
John R., 114
Pherebee Ann, 110
T. B., 133
Zachariah, 64
HART, Catharine, 52
John, 21
Polly, 37
HARTOFIELD,
William, 110
HARVILLE, Isham, 33
Moses, 33, 41
HASE, Dempsy, 94
Pritsey, 76
William, 94
HASTING, Julia A., 126
HASTINGS, Howell, 51
William, 84, 132
William H., 63, 84

JOHNSTON COUNTY MARRIAGES

HATCHCOCK, David, 68
　Eveline, 77
　Sally, 66
HATCHEN, Allen, 126
HATCHER, Alston, 95
　Austen, 69
　Austin, 70
　Auston, 68, 87
　Beedy, 6
　Benjamin, 9, 15, 21, 39, 42, 44, 56, 59
　Betsy, 16
　Charles, 83
　Henan, 130
　James, 68
　John, 6, 41, 68
　John T., 60, 69, 83
　Lee, 81
　Mary, 6
　Patty, 15
　Robert, 60, 69, 96
　Sally, 39
　Sarah, 56
　William, 15, 21
HATCHOCK, Nancy, 118
HAWKINS, Elizabeth, 65
HAWLEY, H. H., 109
　Harris, 90
　John, 107
　Polly, 90
HAY, James, 131, 132, 133
HAYES, Amos, 69
　Elizabeth, 91
　John, 5
　Rhobra, 72
　Willis, 50
HAYLE, Anny, 35
　Milly, 94
HAYLES, Culia, 28
　Cynthia, 32
　Enoch, 33
　Gilbert, 80
　Guilford, 76
　Henry, 9, 81
　Henry H., 78

　Ira, 31
　Isiah, 31
　John, 3, 10
　John T., 46
　Lucas, 57
　Matthew, 31
　Nancy, 128
　Penny, 43
　Permina, 129
　Polly, 66
　Susannah, 32
　William, 46, 65, 122
　William H., 86
　Zilpha, 44
HAYS, Betsy, 14
　Dempsey, 80
　William R., 96
HAYSE, John M., 113
　Levina, 13
HAYWOOD, John Lee, 58, 61
HEARN, Jonathan, 59, 62
　Joseph, 31
HEARNE, Betsey, 12
　Joseph, 22
　Mason, 12
　Napoleon B., 124
HEATH, A. J., 132
　Ann, 132
　Martha, 73
　Milbany, 23
　Tunnel, 102
HEDGEPETH, Azketta, 102
　Elizabeth, 110
　Eveline, 98
HEITH, Carl, 3
HELME, Caroline, 60
　Green, 132
　Mordecai, 122
　Phereby, 59
　Ravena, 91
　Robert H., 28, 39, 40, 47, 59
　Robt H., 52
　Roy, 36, 38, 48
HENDERSON, Robert, 107
HENDRICK, Jeremiah, 1

HENRY, Aaron, 128
HENS, Reddick, 37
HERITAGE, James, 79
HERRING, Joel, 29
　John, 16, 28
　Matchet, 4
　Rachel, 21
HETH, James, 21
HICKS, Aley, 50
　Bishop, 71
　Emily, 79
　James, 55, 119
　Martha Ann, 101
　Matthew, 55
　Mecajah, 6
　Nancy E., 118
　Nehemiah, 124
　Sally, 69
　Sarah, 39
　Stephen, 55, 64, 66, 67, 71, 94
　Thomas, 51
HIGDON, Daniel, 3
　John, 3
HIGGINS, George, 95
　Georgia Anne, 130
　Wesley I., 99
　William J., 94
HIGH, Alsey, 51
　John, 20
　John B., 78
　Martha, 62
　William, 52
　Winifred, 19
HILE, William, 103
HILL, Abner, 18
　Benjamin, 3, 7, 18
　Betsy, 31
　Elberton, 94
　Emily, 127
　Evaline, 103
　Green, 14, 26, 32, 71
　John, 44
　Joseph, 58
　Leon, 26
　Moses, 106, 116
　Moses Lloyd, 39
　Rebeckah, 45
　Richard, 101
　Sam, 33

INDEX

Sarah, 45
Savel, 19
Scely, 31
Sim, 44
Thomas, 5
Willilam, 102
Zechariah, 110
HILLARD, Benjamin, 133
HILLIARD, Ezekiel, 41
  George, 22
  Henry, 19
  James, 37, 47, 50, 54
  Martha, 130
  William, 62, 76
HILLINGSMITH, Ion, 8
HILLINGSWORTH, John, 9
  Truman, 31
HIN, Nehemiah, 116
  William, 116
HINES, Benjamin, 120
  Edwin, 95
  Francie, 128
  Julia Y., 116
  Julie, 118
  Narricus, 126
HINNANT, Amelia, 12
  B. R., 98, 99, 121, 127, 128, 129, 130, 131
  Barney B., 86
  Berry, 58
  Bryan B., 73
  Bryan R., 76, 85
  Bryant R., 87
  Cally, 48, 62
  Elizabeth, 30, 110
  Gastan, 118
  Gaston, 112, 114
  George W., 81
  H. H., 133
  Hardy, 49, 97, 101
  Hardy H., 108
  Henry, 82, 87
  Hepsebah Jane, 64

Hillary, 130
James, 62, 64, 72, 78, 79, 80, 86, 96, 106
James D., 115, 118
James H., 77, 87
Jesse, 51, 61, 62, 64, 65, 69, 70, 104, 113, 116, 130, 131, 132
John, 11, 28, 126
John H., 131
John T., 132
Jonathan, 47
Jones, 87
Josiah, 36, 42, 47, 48, 50, 74, 82, 90, 130, 132
Larry, 68
Louisa, 133
Lucy, 54
Mabry, 71, 77, 82
Martha, 110, 118
Mary A., 114
Morning, 47
Nancy, 85
Needham, 20
Patience, 43, 119
Piety, 115
Ransom, 128
Rany, 73
Robert D., 68
Ruffin, 131
Sally, 52, 66
Sarah R., 112
Stephen, 33, 77
Theophilus, 128
Thomas G., 88
William, 20, 23, 24, 27, 30, 31, 34, 42, 106, 123, 126, 132, 134
Williamson, 62, 78, 81
HINNAT, Jesse, 118
HINNIARD, Mary, 7
HINNNAT, Jesse, 68
HINTER, Emily G., 48

HINTON, A., 109
  Angeronah, 116
  Betsey, 44
  Betsy, 31
  Delany, 45
  Edith, 9, 52
  Eliza Jane, 67
  Elizabeth, 12, 22, 48, 58, 93
  Elizur Ann, 112
  Esther, 26
  Evaline, 103
  George, 9, 15
  George G., 16
  Hardy, 6
  Harriet, 53
  Henry, 21
  Hughel, 129
  Isaac, 4, 47
  Jacob, 19
  James, 44
  Jesse W., 128
  John, 6, 8, 12, 55
  Joseph, 26, 55
  Joseph H., 53
  June E., 109
  Kiddy, 23
  Levey, 20
  Lucy M., 60
  Lydia, 23
  M., 119
  Maleke, 27
  Malica, 96
  Mary Ann, 37, 48
  Matilda, 47
  Matthew, 37
  Milly, 38
  Milly Jane, 122
  Phereby, 16
  Polly, 14, 43, 58
  Ransom, 63, 77, 89
  Rini, 24
  Salina, 75
  Sally, 23
  Sarah, 2
  Sarah C., 120
  Thomas O., 47
  William, 8, 17, 20, 23, 26, 33, 45, 56, 59

Willie, 63
Willis, 11, 37, 55
Wimberly, 52
HIX, Esther, 116
HOALT, Samuel, 20
  William, 41
HOBB, Elizabeth S., 102
HOBBIT, Sally, 114
HOBBS, Battling G., 26
  Bolling G., 40
  Elizabeth, 129
  H. H., 73, 96, 98, 106
  Henry H., 82, 93, 119
  John, 116
  Sally, 91
  William, 6, 10, 31
  Willie, 92
HOBBY, Anna, 24
  Edna, 69
  Edny, 21
  Henry, 21, 26
  J. J., 120
  John, 40
  Jonathan, 32
  Mary, 19
  Patsy, 49
  Pherebe, 34
  Piety, 64
  Sally, 25
  William, 14, 17
  William S., 131
HOCUT, Alison, 130
  Atles, 125
  Benjamin, 42, 66
  Betsy, 44
  Bryan, 64, 92
  Crecy, 62
  Dellany, 123
  Emily, 100
  H., 133
  Irvin, 133
  Juanna, 72
  Lemuel, 60
  Mary, 49
  Nancy, 52, 62
  Patsy, 129

Rilda, 69
Sarah H., 123
Stephen, 122
W., 133
William B., 28, 37
William Brown, 18
Zechariah, 132
HOCUTT, ?, 47
  Benjamin, 30
  Betsy, 20
  Caswell, 113
  Elizabeth, 8
  Elizur Jane, 116
  Emily, 100
  Harriet, 103
  Mary, 11
  Sarah, 14
  William, 14
  William A., 116
  William B., 30, 104
  William Brown, 15
  Zachariah, 110
HODGE, Allen, 33
  Curtis, 91
  Elizabeth, 106
  Jesse, 118
  Nancy E., 107
  Welthy, 114
  Westly, 64
  Willie, 132
HODGENS, Jonathan, 123
HODGES, Deliah, 20
  H. A., 127
  Horatio B., 100
  J. W., 122, 123, 124
  James, 65
  James W., 121
  John, 98
  John G., 105, 113
  Joseph, 18
  Mary Jane, 105
HODGSON, Isabel, 3
HOGG, Celia, 102
  Levy B., 105, 107
  Richard, 47
  Smitha, 80
  Temperance, 68
  Thomas, 113

HOLDER, Catherine, 59
  Celah, 54
  James, 16, 18
  John, 17
  Jonathan, 4, 27, 31
  Josiah, 10, 16
  Prudence, 18, 19
HOLDERMAN, W. F., 119
HOLLAND, Alfred, 106, 109, 110, 112, 113
  Amanda, 106
  Bartillie, 133
  Benajah, 70
  Betsy, 47, 53
  Bryant, 78, 103
  Calvin, 99
  Celia, 101
  Charles, 77
  Curtis, 51, 69, 99
  Daniel H., 85
  David H., 73
  Eason, 77
  Elisha, 47, 131, 132
  Elizabeth, 127
  Enos, 47
  Exum, 73
  Exum H., 106, 119
  Eziekel, 80
  G. H., 84
  Gene H., 96
  Green, 61
  Green H., 83
  James, 74, 78
  Jennet, 66
  Jennett, 108
  Jesse, 79, 85
  Jethro, 99
  Jimmett, 73
  Jinsey, 107
  Louisa, 75
  Marie, 79
  Mary, 22, 70
  Matilda, 89
  Nancy, 42, 51
  Pinetts, 122
  Ruel A., 106

INDEX

Saper, 92
Susan Ann, 126
Tempia, 127
Tempy, 77
Thomas, 46, 73, 76, 111
Uriah, 99
Warren, 80
William, 48, 87
William G., 106
William T., 133
Willy, 133
Zilpha, 90
HOLLANDWORTH,
  Elizur, 101
HOLLEMAN, Celia, 3
  David, 2
  Edney, 42
  Frederick, 6
  Jesse, 53
  Lucinda, 116
  Mary, 29
  Richard, 2
  Seth, 6
  William, 9
HOLLEMON,
  Frederick, 4
  Mary, 3
HOLLIMAN, Berry, 53, 125
  Cally, 31
  Clarkey, 120
  Clary, 87
  David, 19
  Elizabeth, 32
  Frederick, 18
  James, 1, 17
  Jesse, 15, 52
  Jonathan, 51
  Josiah, 49, 54, 69
  Larry, 58
  Mickey, 25
  Mildred, 16
  Ransom, 72
  Seth, 19
  Thomas S., 120
  Tobias, 18, 27, 32, 44
  William, 9, 90
  Willie, 51
HOLLIMON,
  Frederick, 5
  Josiah, 62, 84
  William, 69, 72
HOLLINGSWORTH,
  Lucy, 66
  Nathaniel K., 31
  Rebecca, 75
HOLLIOWELL, Thomas T., 60
HOLLOMAN, Asa, 46
  Berry, 52
  Celia, 44
  Garry, 57
  Griffin, 41
  James, 52, 58
  John, 57
  Josiah, 57
  Patsey, 58
  Patsy, 57, 58
  Ransom, 81
  Rhoda, 57
  Winiford, 46
HOLLOMON, Bardam, 46
  Elizabeth, 42
  Garry, 46
  Larkin, 52
  Patsy, 46
HOLLOWELL, Polly, 46
  Silas, 126
HOLLY, David, 113
HOLMES, Anna, 120
  Benjamin, 19, 123
  Berseba, 70
  Chilly, 131
  Edith, 127
  Frederick, 11, 14, 21, 85
  Hardy, 20
  Heron, 60
  James, 89
  James W., 131
  Jane, 66
  John, 49, 84
  Louisa, 108
  Polly, 32, 34
  Sallie Ann, 125
  Sally, 21
  William R., 108
HOLMS, Heron, 89
  Hiram, 82
  James, 89
HOLOMAN, Nancy, 30
HOLT, Anny, 118
  Beddy, 58
  Calvin A., 131
  D. H., 121, 122
  Delia, 129
  Elbert D., 114
  Eliza Jane, 130
  Ethedred, 61
  Etheldred, 24, 28, 33, 34, 39, 40, 55
  Ethelred, 38
  Farinia, 130
  H., 127
  Harriet, 74
  Henry, 122
  James, 86
  James M., 125
  James S., 113
  Jesse, 60, 71
  John, 4, 49, 58, 81, 90, 106, 110
  Joseph, 130
  Josephine, 127
  Lonenza, 120
  Nancy, 39
  Nancy M., 120
  Osborn, 49
  Polly, 52, 106
  R. D., 111
  Richard, 12, 58
  Sally, 92
  Sophia, 60
  W. D., 124, 125, 126, 129, 133
  W. F., 119
  William, 22, 42, 120
  William D., 120
  William F., 125
  William H., 122
  Willie, 73, 74, 77, 78, 80, 93, 119
  Willis, 88, 125
HOLTON, D. H., 119
  Salathiel, 5
  Samuel P., 116
HONEYCUT,
  Alexander, 70

Britain, 45
Candis, 55
David, 128
Dilley, 83
Edmond, 56
Eli, 95
Elizur, 99
Hawkins, 125
James, 75
John, 102
Lucy, 63
Mack, 105
Mary C., 133
William, 39, 45, 53
William H., 102
Winifred, 73
HONEYCUTT, Betsy, 15
Cherry, 22
Mary, 100
Sir William, 123
William, 15
HOOD, Annie, 127
B. R., 114
Bold R., 49
Bold Robin, 41, 47, 51
Bryan, 29, 62
Caswell, 74
Charles, 10, 27, 31
Charlotta F., 114
D. W., 107
Eliza Ann, 96
Elizabeth T., 100
John B., 133
John C., 65, 84, 86, 88, 111, 119, 120, 121, 122, 123, 124, 130
Joshua, 51
L. W., 123
M. F., 119
Mary Ann, 123
Mary E., 97
Nathaniel, 6
Pearce, 23
R., 96
Rebecca, 128
Robert, 70, 107

Robert B., 108
S. H., 132
W. H., 129
William, 32
HOOK, Rev., 131
William, 35
HOOKS, Hardy, 60
Harriet, 86
Jacob, 27
Robert, 6
William M., 93
HOPKINS, A. J., 122
Elizabeth, 110
Nancy, 79
Sarah, 47
William M., 40
William W., 39, 41
Wilthy, 87
HORN, Benajah, 63
Benejah, 64
Beryeak, 49
Celah, 38
Charity, 1
Cintha, 111
Elizabeth H., 104
Emily, 64
Henry, 31
Hilliard, 73
Jesse, 64
Joel, 49, 94
Martha Ellen, 87
Milly, 111
Napolean B., 108
Polly, 61
Priscalla, 21
Richard, 1
Rixey, 118
Sally, 42, 54
Sarah, 28, 67
Silas, 63
Slimey, 24
Zilpha, 44
HORNE, Benajah, 69
Garry, 119
Henry, 23
Jesse, 54
Willy, 127
HORTON, Bedith, 20
S. P., 74
Samuel P., 75, 127

HOSEA, Henry, 28
HOUDLER, Ruffin, 67
Unity, 56
HOUGHTON, Joshua, 3
Thomas, 3
HOULDEN, James, 16
HOULDER, Edith, 45
Isarel, 66
Josiah, 47, 59, 64
Morning, 46
Rhoda, 41
Willy, 40
Zachariah, 89
HOUSE, Adalade, 97
Elizabeth, 121
Helen, 97
Warren, 19
HOWARD, Drusilla, 51
Edmond, 109
Edmund, 109, 112
Jane, 60
Joseph P., 60
Polly, 50
HOWELL, Absella, 106
Ann Retor, 4
Barnaba, 79
Benjamin, 127
Burwell, 51
Catharine, 76, 78
Charles, 85
Chelly, 111
Cherry, 77
Chilly, 46
David, 48
Dupree, 121
Edmond, 24, 33, 37
Edmund, 16
Elizabeth, 131
Jasper, 41
Jethro, 99, 108
John D., 82
Mary, 118
Nancy, 99
Osburn, 24, 37
Pherebee, 122
Sarah, 13
Tibithy, 73
Willie, 79

INDEX

HOWLEY, Tempe, 69
HOYLES, Polly, 25, 26
HUBBARD, Westly, 115
HUDSON, Benjamin F., 84
  Joel, 116
  Joel Green, 90
  William, 116
HUGHES, Benjamin, 29
  Brazell, 123
  Drusilla, 60
  Ganzada, 82
  Mary, 123
  William, 120
HUGHS, Aquilla, 69
  Benjamin, 62
HUMPHRIES, Nammy, 11
HUSTED, Hiram W., 81
  K. N., 69
HUSTON, Matilda, 107
HUTCHENS, C. W. D., 103
HUTCHER, Austen, 88
HUTCHINS, Isaac, 54
HUTSON, B. F., 85
  Benjamin F., 106
  Carolina, 131
  Esther, 116
  J. J., 85
  J. W., 116
  Joel, 129
  Joel G., 88
  John W., 97
  Mary, 89
  Mary L., 126
  P. W., 99
  William, 114

-I-
INGRAM, Alice, 46
  Alsy, 28
  Ambrose, 29
  Ann, 7
  Ann E., 131
  B., 33
  Barnaby, 28, 29, 31
  Barney, 13
  Bethania, 75
  Betsy, 27, 49
  Betsy E., 83
  Chilly, 67
  Cornelia, 28
  Daniel B., 94
  Edith, 88
  Elizabeth, 21
  Ellinder, 55
  Esther Ann, 133
  Fanny, 119
  Harry, 67
  Henry, 81
  Hester Ann, 114
  Isaac, 12, 54, 87, 112
  Issac, 8
  John B., 111
  Joseph, 5, 32, 41, 64
  Joseph A., 73
  Julia, 81
  Kiziah, 123
  Lecy, 91
  Loverd, 32
  Lovett, 127
  Michael, 52
  N., 121, 129
  Nancy, 16, 25, 48, 82, 106
  Nathan, 132
  Needham, 71, 125, 128
  Polly, 1, 28, 65
  Sally, 19, 31
  Sarah, 56, 106
  Shaderick, 27
  Sir William, 71, 106
  Susan, 83
  Theny, 64
  Thomas, 98, 107
  Thomas D., 111
  William, 12, 32, 48, 52, 59
  Wimmy, 18
  Winifred, 58
  Zilphia, 2
INMAN, Mary, 1
IRVIN, Joseph, 9, 14
IRWIN, Joseph, 16, 17
IVEANS, Sally, 76
IVEN, Joseph, 8
IVES, Thomas, 81
IVEY, Bourbon, 118
  Eliza, 119
  Elizabeth, 50
  James, 57
  Lovell, 11
  Vine A., 72
IVY, David, 27
  David, Jr., 26
  Hartwell, 28, 38
  James, 49
  Julia, 64
  Peter, 33
  Peyton, 45
  Silvey, 25
  Sincrom, 131
  Stincen, 123

-J-
JACKSON, Calvin, 93
  Edin, 60
  J. R., 131
  James, 32
  James T., 63
  John, 42, 61, 64, 69
  Jordan, 33
  Ketsy, 120
  Lewis, 33
  Nancy G., 112
  Piety J., 111
  Sally, 69
  Wilie, 120
  William, 6, 42, 51
  William H., 111
  Willie, 46
JAMES, Charlotte, 21
  Tempia, 1
  William, 84
JARRELL, Delanie, 29
  Isaac, 24, 29
  John, 4, 12
  Patience, 14
JEFFERS, Sally, 56

JEFFERYS, Thomas
  B., 126
JEFFREY, James, 127
JEFFREYS, James, 73
  Ruffin, 73
JEFFRYS, Willie, 58
JELKS, John, 32
JENKINS, Jane, 48
  Lewis, 49
  Lewis W., 63, 64
  Reding, 84
  Sally, 46
JENNET, Matthew, 127
JENNING, Hezekiah, 16
JENNINGS, Mary, 9
  Ryal, 8, 9
JERALD, Matilda, 45
JERNIGAH, Bud, 86
JERNIGAN, Aldie, 101
  Alexander, 20
  Allen, 25, 37
  Arthur, 2
  Asa, 31
  Betsey, 85
  Betsy, 74
  Bright, 41, 48, 49, 65
  Budd, 116
  Calvin, 50, 76
  Charlotte, 26
  Elizabeth Ann, 70
  Esther, 70
  George, 66
  Harriet E., 113
  James B., 121
  Jenimna, 131
  Joseph, 58
  Kedar, 84
  Keseah, 114
  Lewis, 24
  Lewis M., 128
  Lovy, 58
  Mary, 8, 84
  Nancy, 16
  Nancy Ann, 112
  Neandy B., 132
  Pollie Ann, 129
  Polly, 86
  Sarah L., 114
  W. H., 109, 116
  William H., 113, 118
  William M., 113
  Zilpah, 16
JERNIGON, Saran, 93
JESSUP, Cynthia A., 127
JETER, Henry M., 60
JIMMET, John, 32
JINSEE, Rhoda, 26
JOBY, E. L., 117
  Elizabeth L., 118
  H. F., 96
JOHNS, William, 32
JOHNSON, Aaron, 3, 15
  Ailey, 128
  Alexander, 47, 101, 107
  Aley, 51
  Alford, 82
  Alfred, 28, 70, 83, 85
  Allen, 18, 20, 40, 47, 64, 96
  Allen W., 94
  Alsey, 3, 61, 70, 80, 94
  Altara, 59
  Alvan, 64
  Amanda, 70
  Amantha, 80
  Amos, 3, 4, 41, 92, 96
  Amos T., 125
  Amy, 18, 33
  Ann, 48
  Anny, 78
  Aquilla, 68
  Arthur, 46
  Arthur Baile, 2
  Arthur Bailey, 12
  Ashley, 114
  Badeath, 12
  Balaam, 1
  Barnaby, 39
  Barty, 52
  Bedly, 40
  Berry, 49
  Berty, 82
  Betsy, 20, 29, 44
  Bettie, 133
  Bridgon, 29
  Brigdon, 21
  Bulany, 59
  Burwell, 24, 48, 53, 55
  Caleb, 6
  Carrell, 31, 59
  Cary, 60, 61
  Catharine, 116
  Catharine A., 116
  Catherine, 118
  Ceela, 76
  Ceelia Ann, 124
  Charlotte, 27
  Chelly, 125
  Cordelia, 31
  Crecy, 39
  Culey, 37
  Curtis, 106
  David, 20, 65
  David P., 122
  Delia, 99, 101
  Delitha, 72
  Dorcas, 8, 29
  Drury, 27, 52, 54, 96, 102
  Duncan, 32, 72, 100
  Edith, 39, 57, 59, 62
  Edmond, 39, 64, 105
  Edmund, 70
  Edny, 31, 93
  Eleann, 122
  Elijah, 80
  Elijah B., 78
  Elijah P., 83
  Elisha, 124
  Eliza A., 127
  Elizabeth, 20, 24, 58, 70, 82, 97, 113, 133
  Elizabeth J., 123
  Elizabth E., 118
  Emily, 64, 101
  Emily Elizabeth, 101
  Esther, 29
  Etheldred, 8
  Evaline, 104

INDEX

Fanny, 47, 52
Frederick, 57
Garry, 79
Gaston, 102, 109
George D., 124
Gerard T., 93
Green, 82
H. L., 127
Hardy, 51
Harriet, 89, 121
Harris, 131
Harrot, 33
Harry, 20, 61,
 67, 69, 71, 91,
 107, 128
Haywood, 109, 119
Henry, 21, 28,
 30, 42, 75, 83,
 121, 127
Henry C., 96
Henry M., 122,
 124, 126
Henry S., 72
Henry W., 66, 67
Heron, 67
Honor H., 121
Irene, 21
Isaac, 3, 18, 27,
 62, 63, 64
Isham, 14
Isom, 9
J. J., 97
Jacob, 3, 31, 32,
 62, 65, 85
James, 11, 31,
 47, 64, 68, 83
James B., 87, 108
James H., 102
Jarold, 50
Jarret T., 89
Jeremiah, 36
Jesse, 1
Jesse J., 118
Jesse N., 113
Joel, 14
John, 33, 38
John A., 125
John B., 82, 97
John W., 33, 62,
 63, 65, 67, 68,
 77
Jonathan, 21

Joseph, 59, 120
Joshua, 24, 88
Josiah, 65
Judy B., 51
Keziah, 58
Kirby, 79
Leacy, 5, 70
Lerey, 122
Lilipah, 15
Littleton, 33,
 40, 56
Lizzie, 38
Lorenda, 105
Louisa, 131
Louizier, 103
Luanna, 61
Lucinda, 128
Lucy, 53, 90, 133
Lucy C., 126
Lucy H., 74
Luvensy, 47
Lydia, 75
Malcomb, 125
Margaret, 47, 89,
 132
Mark, 45
Martha, 6, 8, 104
Martin, 9
Mary, 9, 57, 78,
 99, 112, 133
Mary Ann, 98
Mary F., 133
Mary H., 109
Mary W., 94
Matthew, 32
McCoy, 89
Merritt, 70
Milly, 50
Moses, 2, 10, 15
Moses A., 89
Myrach, 60
Nancy, 7, 43, 46,
 48, 56, 64
Nancy H., 109
Nathan, 37, 121
Nathaniel, 49, 50
Noah, 14
Noel, 3
Obed, 28, 31
Olive, 37
Osborn, 64
Parazadine, 133

Patsey, 62, 81
Patsy, 51, 77
Peggy, 44
Pency, 57
Penny, 48, 67
Peter, 19
Pheba, 40
Pherebe, 71
Phereby, 6, 13,
 86
Philip, 10, 15,
 25, 29, 30, 37,
 42
Phillip, 53
Polly, 28, 34,
 56, 105
Polly V., 107
Rachel, 13
Ransom, 70
Rebecca, 118
Rebecca A., 122
Rebeckah, 36
Redden, 28, 29
Redder, 12
Redly, 61
Reuben, 51, 61,
 116
Richard, 6, 40,
 47
Richardson, 28
Ridley R., 128
Rigdon, 21, 64
Right A., 96
Right H., 102
Robert, 7
Roda, 106
Rufus, 108
Rufus A., 132
Ryan, 14
S. E., 120
S. F., 106, 108
Sally, 20, 21,
 22, 38, 41, 43,
 65, 101, 104
Samuel, 22, 27,
 32, 75
Sandy, 75
Sarah, 3, 14, 16,
 26, 75, 117, 118
Seth, 33
Siddy, 15
Sir William, 102,

JOHNSTON COUNTY MARRIAGES

114
Solomon, 35, 42, 51
Staton, 90
Stephen, 86, 96, 99, 127
Sterling, 119
Surary, 3
Susan, 89, 120
Thiana, 47
Thomas, 48
Tranquilla, 68, 102
Uriah, 10
Urias, 18
Vine Allen, 99
W. R., 122
Walter, 133
Warren, 31, 50, 63
West, 32
Whitmill, 32
Whitwell, 42
Wiley, 3
William, 7, 15, 22, 25, 27, 32, 33, 36, 39, 42, 45, 50, 51, 56, 62, 72, 76, 80, 86
William L., 128
William P., 60
William R., 130
William W., 67
Willie, 28, 40, 60, 70
Willis, 88
Wilsy, 39
Wily, 33
Winifred, 34, 63
JOHNSTON, Alfred, 82
Angelina, 88
Beading, 25
Celey, 93
Deliah, 61
Edmund, 85
German G., 82
Henry C., 92
Isaac, 89
Jesse, 23
Kesiah, 73

Mary, 84
Mary Jane, 105
McKoy, 92
Moses, 4, 14
Penelope, 115
Reading, 37
Rebecca, 14
Staton, 73
Stephen, 73, 93
Susan, 35, 85
Susan A., 115
William, 82
Winifred, 26
JOINER, Benjamin, 33
Betsy, 61
Edith, 9
Henry, 97
Jesse, 7, 32
Joel, 75
John, 20, 31, 33
Milly, 42
Patience, 67
Reddin, 71
Southey, 39
Stephen, 59
Thomas, 7, 14
Turner, 73
William R., 102
JOLLY, Charles, 78
JONES, Allen, 32, 58
Alley Elizabeth, 104
Amanda M., 68
Augustus, 85
Augustus G., 79
Barnaby, 6
Benjamin, 4, 37, 64, 85
Bennet, 52
Bethana, 65
Bethaney, 61
Bethann, 130
Betsy, 37
Birkee, 131
Bryan, 54
Bryant, 106, 111
Bud, 47
Burwell, 14, 33, 61
Cally, 120

Catherine E., 127
Charles, 2, 123
Charlotta, 48
Creacy Ann, 91
D. L., 114
Delia S., 122
Dianna, 79
Doctor C., 81
Dorcas, 54
Edward, 32
Edwin, 60
Elias J., 108
Elihugh, 74
Elizabeth, 37, 49, 52, 71, 103, 133
Elly, 83
Emily, 108
Esther, 123
Etheldred, 2
Gaston, 120
George, 123
Hardy, 40
Harrison, 64
Hawkins, 129
Haywood, 124
Henderson, 108
Henrietta, 106, 124
Henry, 27
Isaac, 14, 16, 26
Isaac W., 74, 125
James, 49, 50, 64, 77
James A. T., 133
James Alvin, 82
James H., 74
James R., 72, 74
Jane E., 70
Jeremiah, 99, 104
Jesse, 2
John, 11, 15, 85, 128
John R., 116
John Troy, 129
Joseph, 114
Josiah, 81
Judith, 21
Lemmuel, 70
Lemuel, 69
Leroy, 124
Levy, 68

INDEX

Lotty, 47
Louisa, 121
Lucatta, 101
Lucian H., 102, 103
Lydia, 12
Margaret, 125
Martha, 47
Mary, 6, 16, 126, 131, 132, 133
Mary Ann, 90, 93
Matthew, 14, 22, 27, 30, 41
Milly, 23
Mimmie, 19
Nancy, 49, 68, 82, 113, 118
Nancy Ann, 97
Nathaniel, 30
Nicy, 67
Patsey, 75
Pency Villia, 44
Penny A., 121
Penny H., 28
Phillip, 62
Polly, 15, 65
Rachel, 16, 27
Rebecca Ann, 108
Redley, 91
Retty, 62
Revell, 70
Rhoda, 91
Roy, 70
Sally, 49
Samuel, 104, 124
Samuel M., 79
Sara, 131
Sarrah E., 103
Simon, 81
Susan, 77, 122
Susetta, 77
Sysvester, 76
Tempy, 126
Thomas, 3, 31, 32, 49, 77
Turner, 110
W. B., 127, 129, 130, 131, 133
W. T., 75
Wesley, 94
Westly, 106
Willey, 87
William, 13, 22, 27, 37, 43, 61, 67
William A., 84, 94
William B., 129
William D., 127
William H., 122
William J., 121
William W., 43, 49, 52
Willie, 50, 57, 74, 85
Willie T., 82
Willis, 28, 40
Wimmy, 59
Zachariah, 79, 82
Zilpha, 79
JONIRKIN, Kitrey, 108
JORDAN, Abner, 4
Bedie, 19
Berlin, 72
Bersheba, 22
Betsy, 32
Bryant, 100
Dixon, 22
Elisha B., 107
Elizabeth, 16
Green, 58, 83
Henry, 15, 33, 39, 45, 52, 53
James C., 78
John, 33, 96
Margaret, 112
Mary, 4
Moses, 45, 55
Nancy, 62, 64, 86
Nichols, 62
Rebecca, 70
Reuben, 13
Susan C., 74
Thomas L., 86
Vicy, 39
William, 113, 118
Winifred, 62
JORDEN, Nicholas, 92
JORNIGAN, Cathina, 11
JOY, David, 24, 25
Peyton, 25
JOYCE, William, 130
JOYNER, Hiram W., 107
Joanna, 122
Joel, 79, 82
Martha J., 87
Temple, 83
Turner, 87
William D., 107
William H., 99, 111, 113, 116
JUMP, Lydia, 99
Sarah, 120

-K-

KATE, Jonanna P., 125
KEAL, Polly, 23
KEAN, Crecy, 68
George, 72, 80, 90, 91, 107
Giddeon, 90
Gideon, 78, 114
Ridley, 78
Susan, 95
KEARNI, John, 7
KEARSI, John, 6
KEEN, Alsey, 41
Caty, 35
Counciel, 108
George, 5, 32, 38, 75, 77, 79, 91, 103, 114, 116, 117, 118, 119, 120, 122, 124
Isaac, 11, 32
John, 32, 38, 39
Mary, 22
Olea, 49
Sally, 37
Tilpha, 49
Wilie, 111
KELLY, Alice, 83
Caroline, 124
Celah, 28
Helen, 100
James, 56
John, 21, 28, 37, 40
Pherebee, 84
Polly, 15

JOHNSTON COUNTY MARRIAGES

Preston, 70
Quinton, 67, 77
William, 28, 31
KEMP, Elizabeth, 102
  Green, 79
KENEDY, Elizabeth, 60
KENNEDY, Henry H., 61
  J. H., 118
  Jesse, 56
  John, 123
  John H., 120, 122
  Joshua, 122
  Sarah A., 124
  William, 21, 128
KENT, Glatha H., 77
  Mary, 90
  Milby, 90
  Nelson, 65, 68, 90
  Roberson, 50
  William, 31
KENYON, Charles, 127
KERN, Elizabeth, 68
KILGO, Keziah, 19
KILLINGSWORTH,
  Betsy, 33
  Dicy, 26
  Freeman, 9
  John, 9, 14, 22
  Polly, 19
  Rachel, 18
KINDALL, Isaac, 11
KINDRALL, Isaac, 19
KING, Bennet, 130
  Daniel, 122
  Harriet, 65
  Henry, 17
  James, 57
  Martha, 113
  Mary L., 129
  Starky, 104, 107
KINGRY, William, 41
KINSTER, Ferdinand, 131
KIRBY, Annie, 129
  Dixon, 102
  Erasmus, 74
  J. S., 122

  Jacob, 71
  James, 3, 18
  Jesse, 11, 46, 57
  Judith, 11
  Martha, 85, 87
  Molly, 57
  Nancy, 43
  Patience, 99, 105
  Penelope, 101
  Pitts, 79, 89, 104, 107
  Ransom, 94, 95, 101
  Sally, 107
  Stanley, 74, 77
  Stanly, 90, 93, 94, 95, 96, 99, 102
  Thomas, 32, 127
KITTINGSWORTH,
  Betsy, 32
  Freeman, 5, 32
  John, 12
  Kathrin, 13
KNOWL, Patsy, 33
KNOX, Needham L., 118

-L-

LABORN, Westly, 73
LAMB, Betsy, 94
  Calvin, 75
  Elias, 93
  Isaac, 87
  Silas, 75
  Zilpha, 47
LAMBERT, W. H., 97, 124, 125, 126
  William, 105
LAMLERS, Alexander, 71
LANCASTER, Elijah, 88
LANCEFORD, David, 39, 79
LANDERS, Alexander, 37
  Nancy, 59
  Reuben, 40
LANE, B., 120, 123
  Barbaby, 17
  Barna, 112, 127

  Barny, 93
  Elizabeth, 124
  Harry, 50
  Henry, 56
  Nancy, 61
  William, 117, 118
  Winifred, 26
LANESTER, Wm. K., 92
LANFORD, Eaney, 30
LANGDON, Betsy, 14
  Britain, 42
  Briton, 54
  Brittain, 32
  Britton, 62
  C., 127
  Carrel, 92, 95
  Carrell, 68, 78
  Casandra, 80
  Caswell, 82, 92
  Edith, 53
  James, 2, 3, 5, 9, 10
  Lemuel, 124
  Merrit, 115
  Nancy, 52
  Nancy E., 132
  Polly, 33
  Ransom, 98
  Rhoda, 88
  Sally, 43
  William H., 100
  Winifred, 25
  Zachariah, 82
LANGFORD, James, 13
LANGHAM, Betsy H., 92
  Francis, 92
LANGHON, Francis, 86
LANGHORN, Augusta Jane, 119
LANGIER, John, 23
LANGLERY, Miles, 7
LANGLEY, Arthur, 88, 126
  David, 50
  Delitha, 126
  Isaac, 43
  Loverd, 69
  Martin, 60
  Miles, 21, 31, 70

INDEX

Mizvaine, 126
Nathan T., 119
Ozwell, 40
Polly, 43
Sally, 70, 80
William, 70, 129
LANGLY, Isaac, 94
LANGSDON, James, 18
LANGSTER, Furney, 75
LANGSTON, Betsy, 20
  Elias, 60
  Furney, 102
  Jane, 131
  John, 3
  Joseph, 3, 11, 15, 18, 22, 26, 68
  Serena W., 131
  Sylla, 132
  Westbrook, 79
  William A., 116
LANIM, Larry B., 129
LARNER, Polly, 58
LAROHORO, Young L., 131
LARVER, Sally, 56
LARVIR, Betsy, 49
LASETTER, Henry S., 116
  Mary, 103
  Sir William, 102
  Susan, 109
  William, 102, 103, 116
LASH, James, 114
LASHLEY, Cassandra, 85
  Daniel, 39
  John, 86
  Pency, 103
  William, 20
LASITER, Shadrick, 95
LASSER, Henry, 37
LASSETER, Louisa, 107
  Lucy, 31
  Mary Ann, 98
LASSITER, Alfred, 70, 79

Ann E., 71
Calvin, 122, 124, 131
Campbell, 60
Elijah, 59
Elisha, 49
Elizabeth, 70
Fanny, 132
George, 24
James, 48, 49, 50, 53, 55, 82
James O., 122
Jason, 48
John B., 114
Joseph A., 123
Lucy C., 120
Margaret, 124
Marrion, 113
Martha, 124
Mary, 55, 124
Mary E., 119
Penny, 50
Renfrow, 36
Shadrack B., 76
Shadreck, 53
Tobitha, 128
W. H., 131
William, 41, 50, 76, 79
LASTER, Sarah, 72
LAUHORN, Anna, 57
LAWHAN, Ransom, 113
LAWHORN, Sarah, 1
LAWRENCE, G. W., 115
LAWS, B., 123
LEACH, A. J., 92, 118
  Jack A., 62
  Jackson A., 59
  James F., 62
  James T., 81
  John, 30, 41
  Louisa, 68
  Mary, 18
  Nancy, 14
  Polly, 30
  Sally, 14
  Susan, 50
  Thomas, 12
LEARCEY, Asa, 20
  John, 20

LEARCY, Fereby, 28
  John, 20, 23, 29
LEAREY, J. W., 13
  John, 5, 8
LEATH, Benjamin, 109
LEATS, Benjamin, 15
LEE, A. J. H., 126
  Aaron, 67, 101
  Abesebeth, 32
  Alexander J., 87
  Alford, 84
  Alfred, 52
  Allen J., 114
  Ambers, 108
  Ambrose, 64, 66
  Amy, 13
  Anna, 55
  Anne, 1
  Anny, 40
  Atha, 51
  B. B., 112
  Barsheba, 42
  Barthma, 32
  Bayley R., 76
  Betsy, 31, 34, 87
  Blackman, 63
  Boykin, 55
  Brian, 54
  Bryant, 7
  Burchett, 22
  Calvin, 59
  Caty, 54
  Charles M., 73
  Charles W., 121
  Charlotte, 80, 130
  David, 32, 55
  Eady, 76
  Edith, 32, 61
  Edward, 15, 23, 24, 31, 49, 50, 132
  Elam, 107, 108
  Elijah, 59
  Elisha, 52
  Eliza, 121
  Elizabeth, 52, 69, 90, 94, 98, 107, 118
  Erasmus, 121
  Esther, 53, 106

JOHNSTON COUNTY MARRIAGES

Fereby, 52
Gideon, 123
Harry, 119
Henry, 30, 31, 42, 62, 91, 129
Henry H., 70
Hopkins, 12
Hugh, 52, 57
Ingram, 22, 25, 79
Isaac, 49, 52
Ivey, 63
J. W., 131
James, 1, 6, 7, 8, 32, 43, 55
James E., 111, 120
James H., 80, 84, 97, 126
Jane, 15
Jaob, 30, 114
Jeremiah, 12, 20, 24, 111
Jesse, 121
Joanna, 47
Joel, 63, 67, 74, 82, 96, 105, 132
John, 4, 11, 22, 24, 25, 31, 39, 41, 47, 50, 54, 65, 70, 71, 73, 74, 105
John H., 70, 121
John J., 100
John W., 129, 131
Jonathan, 32
Joseph, 81, 133
Joseph A., 73
Joseph H., 111
Josiah, 128
Julia Ann, 100
Julius A., 129, 131
Kedar, 43, 49, 52, 55
Keziah, 8
Lansford, 80
Larkin, 79
Lemmuel, 54
Lewis, 40
Lincoln, 113
Linford, 105

Linsey, 105
Littleton, 81
Loannia, 95
Louisa, 124
Lovet, 31
Lovett, 120
Lowanna, 92
Marion W., 112
Martha, 32, 55, 114
Martha A., 132
Martha E., 73
Mary, 79
Mary A., 97, 131
Mary Jane, 128
Misouri, 133
Misouri B., 133
Moidica, 1011
Moses, 95
Moses A., 108
Nancy, 46, 56, 70, 79, 120
Nathan, 4
Nicholas, 46, 48, 71, 91
Nichols, 49
Patsy, 55
Penelope, 115
Penny, 15
Peter, 31, 55, 58, 59, 65
Pherebe, 54
Pherebee, 73
Phereby, 20
Polly, 27, 46, 49, 80, 103, 131
Polly M., 113
Rains, 121
Rams, 49
Ransom, 76, 106, 120, 122, 126
Rebecca, 66
Right H., 108
Robert, 12
S. D., 132
Sally, 14, 34, 50, 83, 86
Samuel, 7, 8, 15, 19, 20, 25, 26, 27, 32, 34, 35, 46, 51, 53, 55, 61, 66, 71

Sarah, 71, 100, 133
Sarah Ann, 125
Seany, 133
Seth T., 125
Simon, 58
Simon P., 78
Stephen, 6, 8, 51
Strange, 26
Susan, 44, 60, 89, 114
Susannah, 30, 87
Tabitha, 2, 12
Tempy, 99
Thomas, 46, 59
Westbrook, 63, 83
William, 7, 13, 50, 52, 68
William H. R., 126
William R., 74, 77, 83
Winifred, 8, 34, 92
Young, 119
Young J., 92
Young R., 110
Zachariah, 19, 22, 105
Zilphia, 35
LEGAN, Lucy, 60
Norcisa, 92
LEGON, Fanny, 87
Nancy, 50
Samuel, 93
Thomas H., 90
Thomas M., 69
LEO, Allycollo, 121
LESSERD, Willey, 56
LESSORD, Jane, 90
LEVERY, Dudiniah, 10
LEVY, Nancy, 108
LEWIS, Berry, 42
Bryan, 59
David, 9
Elizabeth, 1
Griffin, 32
Henry, 9, 41
Hilliman, 117
Hillsman, 118
James, 29

INDEX

Jane, 60
Jethro, 79, 125, 127
Jettman, 124
Lydia, 36
Robert, 35
Sally, 103
Susanna, 9
T., 126
William, 12
LIGHTFOOT, Ann, 7
LIGON, Thomas, 76
  Thomas H., 87
LILES, Basham, 26
  Berbin, 108
  Chloe, 14
  John W., 102
  Mechajah, 5
  Michajah, 14
LILLINGTON, Polly, 60
LIMSDEN, George W., 70
LIMSDON, George W., 55
LINDSEY, Jerusha, 65
  Louis, 88
LITTLE, Julia, 127
  Lowellen, 68
LITTLETON, Charlie, 12
  Edith, 124
  Joel, 47
  Savage, 47
LLOYD, A. J., 74
LOCKANY, Christian, 89
LOCKART, A. E., 99, 111
  Martha, 96
LOCKHART, A. E., 111
  Britain, 13
  Edith, 24, 28
  Elam, 31, 32, 45, 48
  Eleanor, 81
  Eliza, 45
  Elizabeth, 111
  Gaston, 59, 62
  Harriet G., 85

James, 7, 16
Julia, 52
Lucy, 50
Osborn, 13, 16, 24
Patsy, 23
Rachel, 84
Sarah, 41
Solomon, 60, 61, 69, 85, 88
Stephen, 24
Temperance, 111
Thomas, 24, 30, 38, 39, 41, 43, 47, 55, 57, 65, 68, 80, 110
LOCKOBOY, Elinor, 72
LONG, George, 24
  Patsy, 57
  W. S., 124
LOTHROP, Francis, 23
LOVE, Cissaley, 72
  Elizabeth, 66
  Ephraim, 49
  Hinson, 66
  James, 10
  John A., 75
  Jonathan, 61
  Nancy, 61
LOVET, Barnaba, 41
  Cornelius, 25
LOVETT, Barnaby, 56
LOW, Ceally, 96
LOWELL, Clayton, 9
LUCAS, Civil, 68
  Lizzy, 82
  Radford, 95
LUCUS, William, 74
LUIS, Sarah, 92
LUNCEFORD, Caroline, 87
  David, 69
  Miriam, 76
  R. D., 121, 123, 124
  Robert D., 115
  Susan, 67
LUNSFORD, Polly Ann, 79
LUSBY, John, 62

LUSS, Polly, 27
  Sally, 30
LUSTENE, Jane, 41
LYLES, Bryan, 89
  Drury, 19
LYNCH, Ailsey, 71
  Benjamin, 131
  Betsy, 63
  Bryan, 32, 33
  Cornelius, 35
  Edith, 26
  Harriet, 68
  Mary, 98
  Nicholas, 42
  William, 27, 103
  William A., 123
LYNET, Susan, 29
LYNETT, Cornelius, 15
LYNN, William M., 112

-M-

MCCALESS, James, 22
MCCLAM, Thomas, 69
MACCLAMS, Jane, 61
MCCLEMEY, Charity, 21
MCCLEMMY, Samuel, 22
MCCLEOD, John, 47
MCCLIM, William, 68
MCCLINTON, Jesse, 18
MCCLOUD, Roderick, 19
MCCONIC, Ferebe, 18
MCCULLARS, Patsy, 30
MCCULLEN, George, 53
  Lewis, 51
MCCULLENS, Green, 132
  Rebecca, 132
MCCULLERS, Edwin, 61
  Edwin S., 62
  Elizabeth, 45
  Feraba, 1
  John, 1
  Lucy Ann, 84

JOHNSTON COUNTY MARRIAGES

Mary, 1
Matthew, 62, 63, 82
Phereba, 39
Polly, 25
Promulus, 93
Sally, 36
Susan, 66
William, 57, 61, 84
William H., 71, 75
William K., 86
William W., 93
Winifred, 38
MCDUGALD, A. A., 71
MACE, Equila, 11
 Equilla, 27
 Harriet, 75
 Jonas, 27
MCGEE, Thomas, 84
MCGEO, Eleanor, 119
MCGLAWHON, Jerusah, 11
 William, 5, 35
MCHONDIKES, John, 15
MCKAY, Deliah, 13
MCKIMMEL, Sarah, 74
MCKINNCE, Robert, 32
MCLAIN, Catherin, 130
 Isham, 125
 Joel, 94
MCLAN, Phoebe, 120
 Spicey, 119
 Thomas, 126
MCLANE, Elizabeth, 128
 Isham, 71
 John, 88
 Robert, 74
 Sally, 72
 William, 71, 74, 114
MCLEAN, John, 68
MCLEOD, Alexander, 109
 John, 31, 43, 70
 John W., 57
MACLEOD, William, 79
MCLUM, Pheby, 115
MCPHERESON, Duncan, 71
MCPHERSON, D., 113
 Duncan, 63, 72, 75
MAELEMORE, Nancy, 63
MAHONEY, James, 124
MAINARD, John, 50
 Susan, 127
MAINORD, Olive, 44
MALABY, Samuel, 63
MAMMERY, James, 65
 John, 65
MANDLEY, William, 11
MANERY, Heritt, 48
MANKER, Lewis, 98
MANN, Jonas, 15
MANNING, James, 100
 Richard, 83
MANOR, James, 28
 John, 48
 Judith, 22
 Mahala, 109
MARCH, Tabitha, 7
MARKLAND, William W., 127
MARSHALL, Edith, 4
 Elizabeth, 15
 William, 17
MARTIN, Aaron, 82
 Aley, 25, 37
 Alley, 26
 Benjamin, 34, 43, 62, 67
 Charlotte, 78
 Fanny, 118
 Gibson, 52
 Hayward, 83
 Haywood, 63, 65, 66, 67, 68, 82, 83
 John H., 46
 Lewis, 9
 Martha, 46
 Rose, 7
 Sarah, 63, 120
 Susana, 42
 Sylvear, 52
 Walter D., 105
 William, 43
 William T., 98
MASINGELE, N. G., 105
MASINGELL, Robert, 97
MASINGIL, Robert, 97
MASINGILE, Robert, 104
MASON, Jemima, 58
 John, 79
 William, 66
MASSE, Thomas, 26
MASSENGALE, Henry, 68
MASSENGALL, Aaron W., 109
MASSENGILL, Aaron, 81
 Betsy, 37
 Elizabeth, 91
 George, 40, 54
 George W., 114
 Jane, 39
 Lucinda, 114
 Mournen, 19
 N. G., 96
 Needham G., 79
 Polly, 20, 59, 104
 Rebekah, 39
 Robert, 66, 77, 83, 89, 91
 Robert H., 77
 Robert T., 71
 Sally, 30
 Starling, 87, 88
 Thena, 54
 William B., 109
 Wilsey, 84
MASSEY, Caswell D., 107
 Charles, 67
 Charles C., 120
 D. F., 129
 Drury, 4
 Elizabeth, 115, 130
 Eviline, 95
 Isaiah, 35

INDEX

Isiah, 36, 37
John, 26, 49, 69, 84, 95
Keziah, 124
Lucy, 1
Martha, 94, 129
Mary, 114
P. F., 125
P. T., 133
Peggy, 37
Peleg, 90, 92
Polly, 35, 59
Sally, 62
Wesley, 67
West, 79
Westly, 101
William, 49, 80
Zelpha, 109
Zilpha, 36
MASSINGALE, Laney, 67
Lucy, 49
Nancy Jane, 124
Needham, 60
Starling, 60, 69
Warren, 49
MASSINGELE, Lucy June, 109
W. H., 112
MASSINGELL,
Elizabeth E., 99
Joel H., 115
Lucy, 35
N. G., 103
Nancy, 88
Polly Ann, 119
R., 118, 125
Robert, 94
Thiny, 29
William B., 124
William H., 111
MASSINGIL,
Etheldred, 5
George, 5
MASSINGILL, A. G., 122
Aaron, 31, 55
Aaron W., 96
Ammy, 105
Avey, 31
B. R., 127
Emeline, 90

Emily, 133
Etheldred, 11, 29
George, 19, 31, 112
Jane, 44
Joel H., 105
Josiah, 119
Lucinda, 62
Margaret, 38
Martha, 132
Mary H., 122
N. G., 93
Naomi, 19
Needham G., 105
Parthenon H., 120
Penelope, 115
Penny, 118
R., 120, 123, 124, 126, 127, 128, 129, 131, 132
Robert, 11, 50
Robert M., 93
Starling, 88
W. H., 112, 121
W. T., 122
William H., 113, 115
MASSY, Charles, 46
Cogdell, 46
Lelia, 48
MATTHEW, Tempe, 68
MATTHEWS, Delaney, 89
Elizabeth E., 92
Isaac, 63
Israel, 77
Jacob, 22
John, 6, 27
Joseph, 67
Joseph J., 66
Lazarus, 50, 52
Margaret, 57
Martha, 64
Middy, 58
Polly, 54
Sarah, 11
Thomas, 6
William, 95
MAY, Bryan A., 66
Little Berry, 15, 17

Sally, 15
MEADEN, Richard D., 103
MECAL, Isaac, 131
MECONS, E., 129
Ellin, 129
MEDDYATT, Celah, 42
Micajah, 42
MEDDYETT, Asa, 33
Mecajah, 55
MEDEN, James E., 106
MEDIN, Alfred, 27
MEDLEN, Drury, 14
Hellman H., 110
MEDLIN, Drury, 26
Haywood, 105
Johnson, 50
P. P., 110
MEDYETT, Anna, 39
Asa B., 48
MEEKS, Ann, 6
Garry, 133
MEGEL, Samuel, 31
MEHAMS, Raiford R., 78
MELSER, Thomas, 29
MERBLINS, Drenny, 14
MERCER, Jacob, 40
William G., 41
MEREDITH, Sally, 21
MESSER, Aldridge, 60
Alexander, 97
Amy, 42
Bryant, 52
Edith, 37
Elizabeth, 32
Green Parker, 99
Grue P., 103
John, 47, 52, 56, 60, 85, 86
Martha, 133
Osborn, 99
Sally, 52
Tedy, 84
Thomas, 53
Whitley, 47, 85
Whitney, 124
William, 9, 32, 56

175

JOHNSTON COUNTY MARRIAGES

William W., 130
MICHINER, Lewis, 38
MICKLEROY,
  Avington, 2
  William, 2
MIDYETT, Asa, 36
MILBY, Bryant, 96
MILLENDEN, Martha, 125
MILLIFORD, Mary P., 123
MILLINDER, Furney, 108
MILLINER, Cintha, 91
  Fernifold, 71
  Henry, 75
  Margaret, 68
  Nicy, 70
MILLINIER, Harriet Ann, 121
MILWALL, James, 118
MIMDEN, Elizabeth, 65
MINDEN, John, 86
MINDLEN, W. H., 121
MINNCHEL, James, 46
MINOR, George, 18
MISBURN, Laty, 34
MITCHEL, George, 99
  Hinnant, 99
MITCHELL, Anzy, 42
  Crawford, 62
  Delia, 118
  Frederick, 55
  George, 47
  Henry, 18
  John, 52
  Mary, 125
  Rachel, 26
  Sally, 61
  William, 80, 100
  Willie, 99
MITCHENER,
  Caroline, 132
  Samuel, 17
  Sophia, 119
MITCHENSON, A. M., 123
MITCHINER, Agrissa, 82
  Edith, 65

Elizabeth, 67
Festus, 81
John, 81
Martha A., 119
Mary, 55
Samuel, 23, 59
Sarah, 129
MITCHINIER, Alice C., 130
MITCHNER, Samuel, 47
MOBLEY, Edward, 1
  William, 1
MOIDON, Learcey, 12
MONDS, James, 94
MONK, J. C., 116
  Willis, 9
MONTAGUE, John, 65
  John C., 45, 61, 63, 65
MOODY, David, 19, 22
  James, 29
  S. W., 119
  Susan, 105
  Susannah, 29
  William, 60, 72
MOON, John, 1
  Lewis, 1
MOONAHAM, John, 53
  Priscilla, 36
  William, 53
MOORE, Annie, 133
  Bedy, 62
  Benjamin, 39, 50, 90
  Celia, 103
  Clara, 60
  Crecey, 38
  David T., 127
  Eliza, 78
  Fanny, 85
  Haywood, 116, 120
  Henry, 75, 86
  James, 72
  John, 13
  Josefus, 71
  Joseph, 128
  Julia, 123
  Lany, 81
  Lewis M., 24
  Lotty, 55

  Mariney, 4
  Mary, 82
  Molly, 5
  Nancy, 17, 18, 81
  Nathaniel, 98
  Olive, 12
  Penelope, 95
  Randal, 116
  Randolph, 10
  Rebecca, 97
  Right, 59
  Sarah, 38
  Stansill, 20
  Walter R., 126
  Welthy, 17
MORGAN, Allen, 45, 81
  Anne, 65
  Bryant, 101
  Caroline, 96
  Eli, 89
  Elizabeth, 128, 131
  Fanny, 11, 102
  Harriet E., 119
  Henry C., 102
  James W., 80
  Jesse, 4
  John, 14, 49, 81, 106
  Julia C., 73
  K. Louizer, 103
  Kinchen, 94, 104, 105, 106, 108
  Lucy, 26
  Martha, 76
  Mary E., 110
  Nathan A., 46
  Needham, 96, 102, 104, 123
  S. R., 123
  Sampson, 68
  Simon R., 113
  Susanna, 85
  Susannah, 14
  Thomas, 121
  William, 39, 97, 101
  William G., 121
  William H., 86
  William M., 91
  William W., 71,

INDEX

72, 88, 95
Young, 46, 47, 54, 56, 113
MORLEY, Exaline, 66
Needham, 66, 69
MORLY, Rossen, 35
MORNING, William, 68
  William H., 69, 72, 74, 80, 83, 85, 86, 91, 93
MORREY, Duncan, 9
MORRIS, John, 57
  Rainey, 109
  Reddick, 63
  Stephen, 81, 133
  Vincy, 51
  William H., 126
MOSES, Levin, 24
MOTT, Benjamin, 9
MULLINS, William H., 104
MUNDEN, Catherine, 98
  Elizabeth, 63
  Isaac, 71, 80
  John, 116, 118
MUNDS, Alexander, 109
  Elizabeth, 104
  James, 104
MUNIFORD, James, 122
MUNSON, Polly Ann, 115
  Samuel, 100
MURFHREY, John, 67
MURPHEY, James, 56
MURPHREE, Jonathan, 59
MURPHREY, John, 72
  Mary, 63
  Mary E., 119
  Matthew M., 65
  Phereby, 50
  Sally, 50
MURPHY, Polly, 22
  W. G., 120
  William M., 121
  Woodruff, 134
MURRY, James, 100
MUSGRAVE, Joshua,

32, 34
MUSGRAVES, Francis M., 125
MUSSELWHITE, Peggy, 23
MUSSLEWHITE, Drury, 10, 12
  William, 10, 14, 56
MYDELL, Mecajah, 31

-N-

NAHORN, Celia, 62
NAIRR, Augnelia, 9
NARIN, Nancy, 17
NARION, Harriet, 80
NARON, Barden, 98
  Bardin, 107
  Braswell, 14
  Drumy, 53
  John, 84
  Milley, 7
  Richmond, 59
  Susan, 55
  Wriley, 88
  Yanncy, 107
NARRON, Aily, 69
  Aquilla, 49, 118, 131
  Cloe, 32
  Delilah, 22
  Dunny, 58
  John, 45, 48
  Larkin, 126
  Milly, 52, 124
  Polly, 69
NEANNING, Willy Jane, 124
NEEDHAM, Rufus M., 123
NEIGHBORS, J. H. J., 129
NELMS, Polly, 41
  William, 58, 59
  Willis, 20, 23
NELSON, Wilson, 10
NEWBY, Phereby, 38
NEWSOM, Elizabeth, 16, 27
  Reddin, 85
NEWSOME, Moses, 18
NICHOLAS, Allen, 89

Julius, 108
Moses, 24
Noah, 20, 32
NICHOLS, Allen, 82
  Ann, 7
  Benjamin, 41
  David, 122
  Ethedred, 67
  Francis E., 103
  Josiah, 52
  Moses, 127
  Noah, 37, 38, 42
  Sally, 66
  William, 101
  William W., 52, 103, 126
NINV, Beady, 13
NOBY, Celah, 27
NOLES, Aggy, 113
NOLIS, Elizabeth, 27
NOMS, John, 11
NONSWORTHY, Kissey, 11
  Polly, 22
  Samuel, 22
  Winiford, 26
  Winifred, 29
NORRIS, Bryant H., 74
  Haywood, 125
  James, 66
  Nahor, 13
  Nancy, 19, 123
  Robert, 127
  William, 73
  Winifree, 129
NORRISS, Ann, 2
  Betsy, 28
  Charity, 3
  Clarry, 10
  Easter, 3
  Edith, 33
  Frances, 17
  James, 3
  John, 2, 10
  Nahor, 4, 10, 19
  Nancy, 17
  Reuben, 3
  Sally, 29
NORTHAM, Emma E., 129

JOHNSTON COUNTY MARRIAGES

NORTHAN, Ellen C., 125
NORTHANS, Mary A., 119
NORTHHOUSE, Julia M., 103
NOWEL, Martha, 1
NOWELL, Esther, 67
  James N., 133
  John, 38, 41
  Jonathan, 104
  Mark, 39, 45
  Patience, 18
  Polly, 39
  Richard Mills, 133
  W. C., 132
  William, 41, 58, 129
  William C., 130, 133
NOWLS, Martha, 82
NUTT, Bennett, 39

-O-

ODOM, Jacob, 47
  James, 12
  John, 61
  Levy, 47
  Mary, 13
  Patience, 12, 70
  William, 45
OGBORN, I. M., 131
  Lucetta Ann, 104
  Mary Ann, 125
OGBURN, Charlotte, 77
  James, 14, 16
  Lucy, 59
  Sarah, 76
  Stephenson, 103
OGNIM, Elizabeth, 20
OLIVE, Eli, 98
OLIVER, Anny, 80
  Appy, 34
  Asa, 38, 45
  Ashly R., 73
  Betsy, 22
  Cherry, 130
  Crecy, 45
  E. M., 118

  E. R., 120
  Edith, 44, 112
  Eliza, 45
  Elizabeth, 16, 84, 123
  Evaline, 119
  Heddy, 56
  Henry, 18, 71
  James, 59
  Joanna, 92
  John, 3, 5, 115
  Julia H., 128
  Lecrecy, 46
  Levi, 45, 57
  Levy, 53
  Lewis, 49
  Lewis B., 119
  Louisa, 63
  Mary, 68, 101
  McKinne, 57, 69, 93
  Nancy, 62
  Needham, 64, 69
  Patience, 1
  Philip H., 115
  Polly, 13
  R. M., 102
  Robert, 69
  Robert M., 115
  Sarah A., 122
  Stephen, 3, 49, 61
  Thomas, 17, 50, 113
  William, 38, 45, 61, 84
  William B., 113
  Winifred, 72
  Zelpha, 102
  Zilpha, 124
ONEAL, Anne, 67
  Beedy, 34, 47
  Benjamin, 7, 8
  Bryant, 108
  Buck, 132
  Carsen, 113
  Carson, 102
  Condary, 48
  Cornelia, 79
  Elizabeth, 17, 38, 119
  Gilly, 67

  Hopkins, 67
  Hopson, 66
  Isham, 1, 6, 19, 40
  Isome, 1
  James, 25, 29
  Julia Ann, 127
  Lany, 66
  Lindrick, 19
  Lucinda, 63, 118
  Manly, 71
  Martha, 66, 126
  Mary, 6
  Mecajah, 48
  Mechajah, 1
  Micajah, 43
  Milla, 29
  Nancy, 19, 48, 83, 109
  Nathan, 77
  Olive, 36
  Patsy, 69
  Penny, 57
  Piety, 64
  Polly, 40
  Rachael, 130
  Rebecca, 64
  Reldy, 64
  Richard, 52
  Richardson, 63, 78, 79, 89, 105
  Samuel, 4, 25
  Sarah, 7
  Serena, 122
  Stephen, 42
  Susan, 52
  Thomas, 4
  William, 5, 32, 38, 47, 52, 66, 77, 84
  William H., 78, 109
  William K., 82
  Willie, 34
  Willy, 81
  Winifred, 30
ONEIL, Alsobeth, 11
  Alvey, 18
  Benjamin, 21
  Betsy, 21
  Bridgers, 14
  Bryan, 50

INDEX

Creacy, 28
Elizabeth, 23
Frederick, 20
Isom, 13, 29
Kinard, 27
Moses, 27, 29
Nancy, 43
Patsy, 15
Richardson, 77
Samuel, 9, 20, 23
Sarah, 11
Silas, 21, 23
Sodwick, 30
Thomas, 30
Warren, 13
William, 8, 9, 24
OSTON, Clary, 43
OVEBA, Nancy, 98
OVERBY, Anna, 52
  Edwin, 65
  Ephraim, 43
  Evaline, 130
  Jane, 13
  Jesse, 53, 69
  John, 112
  Joseph, 113
  Martin, 43, 44
  Mary, 123
  Parker, 84
  Patsy, 56
  Susannah, 6
  Wesley, 131
OWEN, A. N., 127
  Elijah, 63
  John, 42
OWENS, John, 34

-P-
PACE, Alsey, 49
  Alsy, 64
  Bartley, 76, 113
  John, 53
  Larry, 113
  Rilda, 123
  Stephen, 11
PADEN, Zerilly, 82
PAGE, Allen, 49
  Britain, 22
  Ephraim, 107
  John, 9
  Piety, 119
  Sion, 47

Syndarleigh, 53
Thomas, 9, 21, 22, 55
Tobias, 14
Zelpha, 40
PAIR, Cernontha, 72
PAJON, William, 40
PALMER, Mary Jane, 128
PAMENTER, Nancy, 72
PARCH, Bridgers, 39
  Winifred, 26
PARCIE, Needham, 115
PARE, Nelson D., 78
PARISH, Airy, 68
  Alsey, 100
  Altna, 68
  Augustus, 59
  Bethany, 75
  Betsy, 19
  Betty, 95
  Charles, 6
  David, 44, 53, 56, 64, 67
  David D., 90
  Dilla, 70
  Edith, 122
  Elijah, 95
  Elizabeth, 79, 129
  Erma L., 128
  George, 19
  Isham, 60, 82
  James, 49, 122
  James M., 127
  John F., 123
  Johnson, 42, 70
  Justes, 75
  Martha, 124
  Nathan, 122
  Paragadan, 121
  Parish B., 132
  Peter, 41
  Putney, 130
  Richard, 124
  Samuel, 126
  Simon, 52
  William, 53, 60
  William G., 100
PARKER, Amos, 105
  Ann, 51

Avey Ann, 125
Benjamin, 66
Cherry, 39
Cynthia, 57
Edith, 43
Edward S., 125
Elijah, 65
Elizabeth, 97
Emily, 47
Fanny, 9
Gabriel, 106
Gabrine, 12
Gilly, 42
Hardy, 9, 13, 18
James, 14, 54
Jesse, 66, 71, 79, 80, 86, 93, 94, 98, 99, 103, 118, 119, 121, 124, 125, 126, 127
John B., 118
John H., 130
John W., 124
Leonard, 133
Lucinda, 123
Mary, 119
Matthew, 13, 14, 47, 73
Moaning, 23
Nancy J., 123
Needham, 129
Noah B., 124
Patience, 48, 52, 111
Penny, 36
Pharoah, 97
Powell, 48, 57
Prissy, 44
Redman, 107
Stephen, 13, 71, 112
Tempy, 14
Zilla, 31
PARNEL, Mary, 99
PARNELE, Jesse, 107
PARNELL, Alsey, 106
  Archibald, 28
  Cinda, 112
  Curtis, 65
  Deveraux, 112
  Henry, 34

JOHNSTON COUNTY MARRIAGES

Jeremiah, 58
John, 16
Reldy, 64
PARNES, David, 110
PARNOLD, Alsey, 120
  Archibald, 19
  Clarky, 85
  Devereaux, 134
  Elizabeth, 9, 58
  Gidion, 45
  Henry, 12, 19, 42, 55, 56
  Irvin, 67
  Jeremiah, 35, 36
  Julia A., 129
  Louiniza, 130
  Martha, 134
  Milly, 89
  Moses, 47
  Sally, 51
  Solomon, 24, 55, 89
  Sweeten, 15
  Welthy, 47
  William, 85
PARRISH, Albert, 92, 114
  Amos, 112
  Ann Eliza, 98
  Augustus W., 100, 103
  Betsy, 21, 24, 101
  Bungan, 95
  Caswell, 103
  Caty, 8
  David, 57, 92, 95, 103
  Dicy, 29
  Edith, 34
  Gaston, 63, 64
  George, 18, 21, 101
  Gilli Ann, 96
  Harriet, 78, 133
  Isaac, 110
  James, 95
  Jane, 93
  Jemima, 101
  John, 22, 34, 35, 115
  Johnson, 78

Justis, 15
Justus, 112
Mary, 116
Mason, 63
May, 95
Medy Ann, 112
Mordica J., 101
Nancy, 16
Parrizady, 57
Patsy, 108
Poartock, 28
Ransom, 78, 89
Rody, 78
Sally, 72, 84
Sarah, 10
Sarah Ann E., 106
Simon P., 56
Stephen, 95
Troy, 95
William G., 66
PARROT, Bridgers, 69
PARSON, Nathan, 63
PARSONS, William, 37
PARTIN, Aldridge, 125
  Alfred, 60
  Washington, 76
  William H., 76
PATE, Cynthia, 56
  Edmond, 44
  Hannah, 31
  John D., 86
  Julia, 91
  Nancy, 40, 51
  S. W., 103, 104
  Sally, 36
  Thomas J. D., 126
  Travis, 11
PATTERSON,
  Elizabeth, 9
  Thiny, 32
  Warren, 30
PEACOCK, A. B., 119
  Betsy, 69
  Bryan, 63, 67
  C. C., 127, 130
  Carter, 61
  Celah, 19
  Charlotta A., 124
  Charlotte, 88

  Charlotte L., 131
  David, 10
  Emily, 130
  Harriet, 101
  Iredell, 09, 84
  J., 112
  Jacob, 21
  John, 27, 62, 67, 129
  John B., 133
  Margaret, 120
  Nancy C., 125
  Polly, 107
  Uriah, 44
  William, 67, 92, 94
  William R., 67
  Zadock, 80, 85
PEAK, Mary, 8
PEAL, Edith, 95
PEARCE, Alford, 112
  Alfred, 119
  Ann, 29
  Anna, 116
  Apsilla, 5
  Asa, 24
  Averet, 1
  Bardin, 73
  Cally, 85
  Charlotte, 65
  Clarky, 48
  Dixon, 51, 65, 93, 109
  E. J., 128
  Edwin E., 46
  Eli, 31
  Elizabeth, 21, 28, 42, 129
  Elizabeth Ann, 116
  Everett, 119
  Henry, 94, 98
  Iredell, 69
  James R., 79
  Jesse, 23
  John, 3, 29, 36, 49, 56
  John P., 61
  Kedar, 28, 42
  Larkin, 65, 78
  Laura, 60
  Leavy, 4

INDEX

Lemmuel, 42, 45
Levi, 16
Linda, 80
Louiza, 93
Lovard, 20
Loverd, 35, 47, 56
Lovet, 95
Mary, 116, 122
Patience, 18, 60, 77
Patsy, 35, 78
Philip, 28
Phillip, 1
Polly, 46, 58, 95
Polly Ann, 99
Raiford, 103
Rhoda, 21
Richard, 48, 67, 126
Richmond, 73
Rilda, 77
Sally, 65, 70
Samuel, 20, 21
Sarah, 19, 20, 47
Silvester, 114
Silvester R., 107
Simon, 19, 21, 27, 28, 29, 42
Simon A., 48
Unity, 17, 27
William, 16, 73, 115, 124, 126
Zelpha, 96
Zilphia, 70
PEARSON, John, 29
Lazarus, 91
Peter, 27
Samuel, 3
Sarah, 96
Solomon, 67, 71, 81
William, 95
Zilpha, 91
PEDEN, James, 22
Larkin, 101
Wilie W., 101
PEDIN, Amos J., 100
William J., 100
PEEBLE, Martha, 102
PEEBLES, Lemmel, 39
Lemmuel, 49

Lemuel, 48
Matthew, 80
Patsy, 71
William, 4, 14
PEEDEN, Handy F., 129
James, 106
Keziah, 127
Mary Perlius, 113
Monrow, 106
Patsy Jaine, 121
Sarah P., 124
W. M., 121
Wilie, 126
PEEDIN, Alvin, 83
Amos, 4, 24, 37, 40
Caroline, 114
Edney, 113
Edwards, 57
Elisha, 42
Elizabeth, 37, 87
Handy, 51, 57, 58
Henry, 42
James, 37, 43, 44, 48, 49, 51, 56, 62, 68, 86
John, 34, 42, 75, 112
Martha J., 85, 91
Nancy, 29
Nancy Ann, 86
Newit, 24, 43, 50, 75, 83
Patience, 34
Patsey, 70
Polly, 28
Sally Ann, 71
William, 47, 63
William I., 68
William J., 62, 69
William James, 50
Willie, 86
PEEL, John, 80
Zilphia, 74
PEELE, Martha, 101
Nathan, 101
Piety, 87
Searcy, 130
Stephen, 87
PEELS, Matthew, 126

PEETEVITT, Sarah, 21
PELT, Mary, 28
PENDER, John Core, 5
Nanney, 11
Patty, 18
Polly Ann, 102
PENDON, William, 100
PENNY, Alexander, 6, 21, 24
Aley, 14
Ann, 9
Betsy, 50
Caleb, 47, 51, 70
Caron, 68
Cloe, 50
Edward, 5, 7, 12
Elizabeth, 7
Esther, 24
Frances, 16
Harry, 47, 51
Henry, 16, 66
Isaac, 59
James, 6, 11, 70
Jesse, 14, 30
John, 30
Leonidian, 115
Lotty, 49
M. A. E., 122
Martha, 75, 79
Mary, 13, 70
Mary F., 127
Penud, 25, 43
Ruthy, 37
Sally, 25
Sarah, 27, 42, 63, 128
Seth, 119
Utley, 11
William, 25, 37, 39, 56, 93
PEOPLES, Avey, 92
Drury, 5
Nancy, 112
Penny, 92
PEPKIN, Elizabeth, 2
PEPLES, Archibald, 11
Elizabeth, 29

JOHNSTON COUNTY MARRIAGES

Jarot, 29
PERDUE, L. W., 126
PERKINS, Sally, 31
PERKINSON, William
  W., 100
PERRY, Abraham, 15
  Alsey, 65, 68, 96
  F. D., 127
  Harrod, 79
  Sally, 92
  Stephen, 23
  William, 43
PETTIS, Dorcas, 56
  Eliza, 49
  John, 58
  Polly, 55
  Sally, 54
  Stephen, 37
PHILIPS, Benjamin, 24
  Harry, 1
  Roy, 130
  William, 30
PHILLIPS, Augusta
  C., 79
  B., 124
  Barnaby, 46
  Dickson, 44, 46
  Dixon, 44
  Edith, 45, 69
  Elijah H., 76, 86
  Emma, 70
  Fort T., 84
  Franklin, 59
  George, 100
  Guy H., 116
  Guy W., 94
  Hamilton, 44
  J., 129
  J. W., 85
  John, 47, 51
  Kinedton G., 73
  Lewis Henry, 64
  Mariah, 74
  Nathan L., 97
  Ray, 113, 118
  Roy, 122, 125, 131
  Sarah, 116, 133
  Susan, 65
  W. D., 120, 132
  William, 23, 44

Zilphie E., 67
PICKETT, J. P., 121
PIERCE, Thomas, 13
PIKE, J. F., 130, 131
  J. T., 126
  Jonathan T., 98
PILKERTON, John, 20
PILKINGTON, Mary
  Ann, 102
  Morning, 40
  Nanie, 127
  Ransom, 102
  Willie, 45
  Willy, 127
PILKINTON, Betsy, 51
  Climck, 51
  Elizabeth, 17
  H., 87
  Hardy, 51, 58, 64
  John, 123
  Patsy S., 118
  Ransom, 94
  Richard, 17
  William, 17
PINDER, James, 3
PITMAN, Amanda, 120
  Betsy, 59
  Calvin, 121
  Caroline, 85
  Charity, 76
  Elijah, 41
  Elisha, 45, 109, 118
  Evlina, 73
  Henderson, 93
  Joanne, 122
  Joel, 46, 115
  Jonas, 95
  Joseph, 80
  Leney, 91
  Margaret A., 128
  Piety, 47
  S. H., 115
  Seth, 116
  Thomas, 72, 76, 93
  William H., 72
PITTMAN, Elisha, 37, 43, 86
  Garry, 43

  Harrison, 86
  Harry, 43
  Jeremiah, 80
  Jesse, 19, 23
PLANIG, Marinda, 96
PLEASANT, Jeremiah, 73
  John, 126
  M., 78
  Sarah, 44, 102
  Solomon, 78
  Vinetta, 95
POE, Sally, 45
POLLARD, Samuel, 105, 106
POLLEARD, John, 111
POMON, James, 17
POOL, Albert J., 76
  Anderson S., 121
  Celia, 9
  Devereaux, 107
  Elizabeth, 9, 17
  Fereby, 26
  Frederick, 93
  George, 86
  Gilman K. L., 45
  Hardy, 43, 45, 65, 67
  Henry, 30, 77
  James, 43
  James H., 102, 106
  Jany, 13
  John, 3, 11, 24
  John W., 120
  Jonathan, 65, 67
  Lewis, 71
  Martha, 68
  Mary, 129
  Nammy, 4
  Patsy, 34
  Pattie, 126
  Penny, 81
  Pherebe, 50
  Polly, 40, 45
  Polly Ann, 114
  Ransom, 119
  Rhody, 54
  Sally, 43
  Theo, 19
  William, 21, 43, 52, 70

INDEX

POOLE, James, 128
  Lewis, 110
  Mary, 130
  Mary Ann, 110
  William C., 110
POPE, Bryant, 103
  Delilah, 53
  Edith, 67
  Elizabeth, 65, 71
  Henry, 46
  John, 2, 89
  Mourning, 40
  Nancy, 19
  Nicy, 35
  Patsy, 20
  Pheobee, 74
  Sally A. I., 86
  Simon, 37, 40
  Temperance, 17
  William, 23, 24, 89
  Winny, 119
  Zachariah, 60
  Zelpha, 10
PORCH, Eaton, 64
  Winifred, 69
PORTER, Allen, 101
  H. F., 115
  J. A., 115
  John, 101
  Lotty, 44
  Mary, 83
  Nancy, 50
  Nathan, 50
  Sarah, 27
PORVEL, Lydey, 2
POTTER, William, 118
POWELL, A., 36
  Adin, 48, 49, 53, 54
  Alsey, 103
  Cornelia, 115
  Cynthia, 51
  Edith, 30
  Enos, 19
  Erastus E., 106
  Gavins B., 124
  Jacob, 19, 38
  Jerem, 8
  Jeremiah, 12, 16
  John S., 47

  Kedar, 7
  Kinean, 48
  Margaret, 5
  Nancy, 32
  Nathan, 16, 17, 18
  Patsy, 54
  Ruth, 19
  Rutha, 116
  Sally, 38, 41, 46
  Sarah, 126
  Sophia G., 65
  Stephen, 4
  William, 19, 46, 56
  William A., 79
  Willie, 120
  Wyatt H., 110
POWERS, Jesse, 36
  Lewis, 36
  Rodham, 24
  William, 18, 22
POYNER, Thomas, 8
PRESCOTT, Aaron, 46
PRICE, Allen, 44, 45
  Arthur, 17
  Ashley, 79, 80, 107
  Berry, 65, 80
  Bertha, 79
  Betsy, 25
  Bin, 19
  Bird, 38
  Ceely, 39
  Culy, 48
  Cynthia, 38
  Daniel H., 91
  David, 60
  David H., 125
  Dedemiah, 20
  Dickson, 51
  Dixon, 4, 39, 42
  Easter, 123
  Edny, 80
  Edward, 6, 8, 10, 17, 20, 34, 43, 60, 61, 63
  Elias, 22
  Elizabeth, 97
  Elizabeth B., 95
  Esther, 25

  Evaline, 131
  George, 63, 90
  George L., 124
  Gideon, 46
  Gincy, 60
  Guideon, 48
  H. G., 95
  Henderson, 102
  Henry, 113
  Hilliard, 88
  Icabod, 37
  Ichabod, 52
  James, 8, 37, 43
  James T., 130
  Jane, 77
  Jensey, 107
  John, 4, 16, 23
  Joseph, 61
  Josiah, 86, 105
  Josiah W., 105
  Julia, 45
  Leonard, 10
  Lucius, 6, 7
  Martha, 43, 92, 123
  Martin, 39
  Mary, 133
  Mary Ann, 4, 103, 107
  Mary H., 126
  Mecajah, 10
  Milly, 45
  N. G., 133
  Nancy, 13, 66
  Nathan, 37
  Needham, 59, 122
  Nelly, 64
  Patience, 65
  Patsy, 46
  Penelopia, 15, 16
  Penny, 55
  Perren, 92
  Peysilia, 8
  Polly, 57, 129
  Priscilla, 6
  Quilly, 119
  Retcy, 57
  Rhody, 65
  Rice, 38
  Richard, 7
  Riley, 46
  Royal, 23

JOHNSTON COUNTY MARRIAGES

Rui, 4
Sim, 43
Simon, 9, 14
Stephen, 51
Susan, 79
Susanna, 45
Temperance, 41
Thomas, 4, 6, 8,
  10, 17, 20, 25,
  31, 34, 41, 56,
  60, 65, 71
Tranquilla, 120
William, 26, 79
William Hinton, 78
Willie, 52
Willy, 89
Winifred, 40
Zachariah, 5, 26
Zella, 101
Zilpha, 31, 38
Zilphia, 48
PRICHET, Sarah, 4
PRIDGEN, Hardy, 69
PRIDGIN, William, 50
PRINCE, Richard, 19
PRITCHET, Alsey, 6, 7
  Mary, 11
PRIVET, William Riley, 55
PRIVETT, Penny, 35
  William R., 48
PROCTOR, Clara, 14
  Clarky, 15
  Henry, 13, 25
PUGH, Elizabeth, 59
  Isabel, 55
  Orpah, 41
  Sally, 26
  Tegnal, 28
  William, 53
  Zilphia, 53
PULLEN, Jonathan, 24
PULLEY, Bryan, 83, 95
  Emiline, 124
  John, 22
  Josiah, 119
PURDUE, Iziah, 99

PURVIS, James, 6

-R-
RADFORD, Anna, 100
  Christopher, 123
  Matthew, 93, 127
  Richard, 131
  William, 99
RAEPER, Calvin, 101
  Joseph, 105
  William, 103
RAGAN, Patsy, 52
RAIFORD, Barsheba, 53
  Benjamin W., 67
  Civil, 43
  Drivan, 129
  Harriet E., 104
  Isaac, 43
  James, 50
  James K., 63
  John, 2, 22
  June, 99
  Levi, 77
  Lotty, 57
  Mary Ann, 84
  Millicent, 119
  Nancy, 48, 88
  P., 36
  Philip, 5, 9, 11,
    22, 31, 40, 43, 48
  Philip B., 81
  Phillip, 54
  Polly, 5, 52
  R. P., 115
  Rachel, 37
  Reddin, 45
  Robert, 29, 34, 57
  Sarah, 6, 79
  Temperance, 93
  Thomas G., 112
  W. P., 125, 133
  William, 33
RAIN, Trecinda, 129
RAINEN, Elizabeth, 121
RAINER, James, 70
  James G., 70
  William H., 129
RAINES, Henry, 48,
  83
  Jency, 106
  John H., 80
  L. J., 125
  Nancy, 43
  Pasho A., 130
  William, 83, 118
RAINS, Dilley, 24
  Edney, 51
  Edwin, 49
  Elizabeth, 6, 84
  Emily Jane, 86
  Haywood, 116
  Henry, 2, 19, 28, 65, 73
  J. Oliver, 88
  Jackson, 127
  John, 21, 28, 29, 34
  John H., 63, 76, 78
  Mary Ann, 126
  Molly, 19
  Nancy, 61
  Nelly, 75
  Oliver, 28, 73, 97
  Polly, 21, 22
  Sarah, 2
  William, 61, 65,
    99, 100, 109,
    115, 118, 126, 127
  Zelphia, 57
RAINWATER, William, 7
RAIOLS, Bryan E., 103
RAMS, Ambrose, 5
  Elizabeth, 54
  John, 46, 47
  Polly, 63
  William G., 67
RAND, John B., 123
  William, 1
RANDAL, Mary, 3
RANIER, John G., 120
RANSEN, Amy Eliza, 129
RANSER, Sarah, 46
RANSOM, Duncan, 113

INDEX

RAPER, Elizabeth, 80
  Elizabeth H., 105
  Henry, 78
  John, 43, 81
  Joseph, 78, 80, 90, 110
  Martha, 93
  Mary, 83
  Matthew, 10
  Rebecca, 78
  Roberson, 108, 109, 110, 118
  Robert, 71, 85, 87
  Robertson, 60, 69
  Sally, 98
  William, 75
RASBERRY, Richard, 100
RATCLIFF, Pherebe, 2
  Porter, 2
RAYNER, James, 114
  Lovet, 114
  Lovit, 114
RAYNOR, James G., 81
REAVERS, Levi, 28
REAVES, Betsy, 18
  Civil L., 70
  Elizabeth A., 82
  G. W., 119
  Hudson, 42, 65
  James B., 118
  Lydia M., 82
  Mary Jane, 77
  Patsey, 106
  Sally, 60
  William, 66
  William A., 106
REDDER, Elisha, 21
REDDING, Viney, 59
REDING, Elisha, 54
REED, Elijah, 74
REGISTER, Cullen, 129
REID, Harriet A., 127
  J. J., 121
RENFROW, Harriet, 124

Jacob, 15
James T., 132
Liney, 126
Noel, 19
Perry, 114
S. G., 130
RENFROWE, Everett, 28
  William, 28
RENN, Sarah, 11
RENTFRO, Nancy, 109
RENTFROE, Braswell, 65
RENTFROW, Betsy, 66
  Caly, 108
  Cherry, 81
  Clerety, 91
  Edith, 36
  Harriet, 113
  Hinnant, 100
  James, 43, 109
  Josiah, 43
  Lucy, 72
  Mabry, 79, 91
  Martha, 99
  Merrit, 80
  Patsey, 70
  Perry, 76, 77, 79, 80, 83, 98, 99, 106, 109
  Rhoday, 99
  Stephen, 76, 100
  Willie, 58
  Zilpha, 79
RER, Nancy, 12
RETTER, Henry, 55
  Penny, 34
REVEL, Hardy, 30
  John, 101
  Sally, 49
REVIS, Elizabeth, 7
REYNOLDS, Michael, 5, 17
RHODES, Atlas J. R., 77
  Augustino, 127
  Caroline, 66
  Dianah, 121
  Eden, 31, 122
  Edin, 41
  Elizabeth, 45, 50, 96

Joanna, 125
John, 7, 8, 33, 38, 44
John F. S., 114
Joseph E., 25, 106, 107
Moses, 54
Nathan, 75
Sophia, 69
RICE, Thomas, 41, 42, 44, 59, 65
RICHARDSON, A. W., 83, 98, 100, 104
  Allen, 22, 25, 29, 34, 44, 49
  Applewhite, 13, 40, 65
  B. C., 111, 114, 115
  B. E., 119
  Barsheba, 73
  Barsheby, 4
  Bertie, 68
  Bryant, 24
  Calvin, 52, 58, 89, 123
  Catherine, 73
  Celah, 27
  Clara, 1
  Clarkey, 87
  Creacy, 40
  Elias, 47
  Elizabeth, 25, 29, 58
  Emily, 78
  Eveline M., 113
  Hardy, 27, 40
  Harriet, 52
  Ivy, 44, 47
  James, 30, 42, 77
  Jincy, 89
  John, 25, 26, 31, 55, 57
  Joseph, 12, 16, 30
  Josiah, 81
  L., 76, 114
  Leasy, 132
  Luneford, 63
  Mark B., 62
  Martha, 76
  Martha A. R., 120

JOHNSTON COUNTY MARRIAGES

Mary, 82
Mary Jane, 104
Millicent, 46
Milly, 119
Nancy, 42, 77, 108
Needham, 66
Olive, 13
Patience, 20
Patsey, 62
Patsy, 52
Pharaoh, 69
Polly, 36
Ransom, 63, 132
Rhoda E., 126
Sally, 13
Samuel, 20
Sukey, 26
Thomas, 23
W. B., 104
W. W., 129
William, 8, 81, 131
Zilpha, 49
RIDGLEY, Loyed G., 91
RIVEL, Mary, 75
RIVENBARK, Nancy, 63
RIVERS, Betsy, 28, 64
Ivy, 28
Polly, 40
Richard, 4, 9, 17
Richards, 16
Sally, 25
Susannah, 17
Tabitha, 4
Thomas, 66
William, 9, 37, 45
Willis, 37
Winifred, 45
RIVES, Medley, 7
ROAD, A. J. K., 98
ROADS, James H., 98
John, 3
William, 3
ROBBARDS, William, 82
ROBERD, John, 43
ROBERSON, Everet

T., 101
Nancy, 67
ROBERT, Sarah A., 126
ROBERTS, Adim, 46
Amanda, 93
Betsy, 46
Britain, 44
Ceasy, 33
Cynthia, 55
Daniel, 60
Edith, 88
Elbert, 60, 61, 66, 70
Elizabeth, 54, 102
Ferby, 26
James, 44, 55, 70, 71, 76
John, 44
Joseph, 60
Linsey, 13
Linzery, 5
Martha, 5
Mary, 114
Patsy, 49
Phereby, 41
Rodia, 6
Sally, 20, 102
Thomas, 1, 18
William, 6, 18, 20, 29, 44, 46
ROBERTSON, A., 133
Everett P., 107
Harbard, 9
Herberd, 55
James, 126
John W., 122
Mary E., 82, 127
Molley, 1
Needham, 20
Thomas, 1
Thos. L., 127
William, 46
William F., 82
William T., 65, 78, 82
ROBINS, William, 114
RODGERS, Chereby, 50
ROE, Asa, 44

Betty, 118
Jane, 34
Reddy, 19
ROGERS, Daniel, 12, 13, 15, 17
Ezekiel, 88, 92
Ezikiel, 96
Green, 7
John, 15, 28
Patience, 10
Reubin, 1
Robert, 13, 15
Sampson, 12, 30, 44
Sarah, 7
Susanna, 8
ROLIN, Lewis, 14
ROLLINS, Richard, 37
ROPER, Isaac, 24
John, 5, 21
Sarah, 8
ROSE, A. H., 121
Bardin, 79
Ben B., 82
Benjamin, 25
Dempsy, 96
Elias, 98
George P., 85, 97, 100
Harris, 87, 90
Henry, 49
Henry C., 131
J. G., 104, 129
James, 11, 22, 36, 68
John, 50, 102
John H., 51
Jordan, 41
Julia, 115
Larry, 110
Litha, 99
Lucy, 45, 106
Mark, 37
Martha, 73
Mary, 109
Mary Ann, 22
Milley, 66
Nicholas, 46, 51, 55, 57, 58, 64
Polley, 128
Polly, 62

INDEX

Rebekah, 31
Sarah E., 133
Thomas R., 78, 118
Thomas W., 123
Tobias, 72
William N., 73
Zelpha, 112
ROSN, James, 18
ROWE, Polly, 99
ROWLINE, Patty, 13
RUFFIN, Minerva, 129
  Olivia, 131
RUSSEL, Nancy, 45
RUSSELL, Charles, 18
  Elizabeth, 20
  Polly, 10
  William, 53, 55
RYAL, Price, 16
RYALS, Alfred, 97
  Ann, 6
  Betsy, 74
  Bright, 59
  Britain, 71
  Charles, 6, 14
  Charlie, 12
  Daniel W., 107
  Eliza, 100
  Isom, 13
  James, 44
  James A., 121
  John, 128
  Louisa, 129
  Merrel, 71
  Merrill, 48
  Nancy, 43, 123
  Penelope, 86
  Ransom, 79, 118
  Right, 82, 120, 121, 123, 124, 126
  Sally, 20, 74
  William, 5, 13, 21, 44, 50
  William M., 100
  Young, 60

-S-

SALMON, Daniel, 72
  William, 83
SAMPSON, Isaac, 127
  William, 84
SANDERS, Alexander, 54
  Allen, 90
  Ann, 1
  Ashley, 85
  Baldy, 34, 51, 65, 74
  Betsy, 50
  Bryan, 74, 89
  Bryan S., 82
  Claudius B., 105
  Cynthia, 54
  Daniel, 129
  Deliah, 51
  Edward, 98
  Edwin J., 121
  Elizabeth, 1, 66, 100
  Elizabeth W., 62
  Ellak, 16
  Ellich, 20
  Ellick, 24, 25, 27, 28, 40
  Elliot, 14
  Hardy, 40
  Harriet A., 121
  Henderson, 130
  Jemmia I., 57
  John, 4, 19, 21, 22, 24, 28, 30, 31, 34, 42, 44, 50, 54
  John C., 54
  John F., 80, 106
  Jordan, 90
  Julia M., 113
  Keron Ann, 87
  L. W., 124
  Lucy J., 91
  Lydia, 130
  Lynn B., 85
  Martha, 93
  Mary, 95
  Mary R., 123
  Polly, 21
  Polly Ann, 85
  Ransom, 57, 63, 64, 81, 82
  Rebecca, 70
  Rebecca E., 98
Reuben, 11, 21, 27, 41, 50, 51
Reuben T., 60
Robert, 91
Robert T., 83
Simon T., 41, 52
Sir B., 87
Tranquilla, 34
William, 8, 65
William B., 69, 79, 91
William W., 53
Willis H., 79
Willis J., 93
Willis T., 88
SANDFORD, John P., 102
SANDS, Abner, 5
SASSER, Allen C., 52
  Asa L., 114
  Betsy, 43
  Delanas C., 123
  Delpha, 68
  Eli, 76, 96
  Eliza, 99
  Ely, 92
  Emely, 81
  H., 31, 34, 41
  Henry, 32, 36, 40, 41, 43, 46, 70, 77
  James H., 118, 121, 122, 125, 129, 130
  James W., 116
  John, 43, 49, 50, 68, 81, 90
  John H., 130
  Joseph, 66
  Josiah, 1, 50, 55
  Lewis, 32, 45
  Maria, 89
  Mary, 16, 67, 101
  Monted, 73
  Nancy, 22, 55
  Olim, 48
  Penelope, 106
  Sarah, 119
  Thomas, 35, 130
  William, 27, 32, 49, 84

JOHNSTON COUNTY MARRIAGES

Willis, 52
Xexey, 85
SASSETON, Delitha, 20
  Sally, 28
SAUDERS, Reuben, 31
SAULES, James H., 119
SAULS, Abner, 6, 13
  Daniel, 21, 44
  David, 32
  Eaton, 43
  Phereby, 60
  Polly, 40
  William, 47, 125
SAVGLY, Merria, 95
SAVING, William, 27
SCARSBOROUGH, Enos, 18
SCHOMBLY, Fruman, 64
SCHSOINS, Nancy, 114
SCOTT, Ann, 18
  Benjamin, 1
  Britain, 43
  Emily, 67
  Green H., 43
  Henry, 120
  Irwin, 91
  John, 25
  Mary J., 119
  Nancy, 48
  William, 94, 102
  William J., 75
SEABERRY, Willie, 120
SEARL, Mary, 3
SELEVANT, Aquillia, 103
SELLARS, Alsey, 91
  Benjamin, 6
  Betsey, 13
  Betsy, 90
  Luvensia, 74
  Sally, 11
  Samuel, 49
  Tany, 39
SELLAVENT, Garry, 60
SELLERS, Benjamin, 54
  Daniel, 114
  Daniel A., 104, 108, 114, 121
  James, 39
  Lucretia, 106
  Martha Ann, 132
  Mourning, 106
  Polly, 49
  Richard W., 110
  William H., 104, 112
  Winifred, 4
SELLIVANT, Jesse, 51, 52, 58
  Jonathan, 57, 58
  Nancy, 51
  Russell, 53, 55, 58
SELLS, Polly, 53
SERVING, William, 38
SEVEANEY, Miles, 5
SHALLINGTON, Alvin J., 111
SHANE, Alexander, 111
  Thomas, 111
SHARP, Cathy, 20
  Henry, 26
  Lydia, 26
  Priscilla, 29
SHAW, Clem N., 55
  Clement, 57
  Hugh, 8
  James, 11, 19
  Jane, 52
  Joseph, 38
  Katherine, 19
  Martha, 71
  Mary, 64
  William, 15, 19, 39
SHELL, Lemmon, 121
SHEPARD, William W., 102, 105
SHEPHERD, Druzella, 112
  John, 46
  Jonathan, 31
SHEPPERD, Susan, 62
  William D., 112
SHORE, Ann, 17
SHORT, Starling, 25
SILAVANT, Hardy, 102
  Russel, 102
SILAVENT, Hardy, 115
SILIVENT, Henry, 74
  Willy, 88
SILKS, Melbry, 33
  Phenelah, 10
SILLAVANT, Garry, 90
SILLAVENT, Garry, 97
  Hardy, 97
  Ruffin, 97
  Sarah, 97
SILLIVANT, Jesse, 35
SILLIVENT, Russel, 47
SILLS, James, 27
SILMAN, Jesse, 40
SIMMON, Henry, 37
SIMMONS, Elizabeth, 119
  Stephens, 132
SIMMS, J., 38
  Martha, 15
SIMPKINS, Benjamin, 44
  Betsy, 43
  Calvin, 61, 82, 101, 125
  Edith, 61
  Manezus, 113
  Martha Ann, 95
  Matilda, 60
  Sally, 61
  Tabitha, 40
  Thomas, 34
SIMPSON, Elizabeth, 90
  Ruthy, 71
SIMS, Benjamin, 9, 10
  Edward, 26
  Eliza, 94
  Hester, 10
  Jacob, 26
  Jeremiah, 38
  John, 26

INDEX

Joseph, 2
Marke, 1
Mary, 15
Polly, 41
Priscilla, 19
Zachariah, 53
SKENE, Elizabeth, 125
SKINE, William, 100
SKINNER, Nathan, 42
SLAUGHTER, Scarby, 25
SLOCOMB, Julius G., 69
SMITH, A., 51
 Aaron, 11, 14, 26
 Abner, 25, 28, 31, 37, 56
 Abraham, 8
 Ady, 27
 Alexander, 21, 44, 45
 Ann, 121
 B. V., 126
 Bedith, 4
 Benjamin, 30, 39, 101
 Benjamin A., 82
 Benjamin H., 68
 Betsy, 24, 35
 Britain, 7, 30, 43
 Brittan, 109
 Bryan, 19, 31, 45, 62, 73, 85, 87, 91
 Bryant A., 131
 Bud, 48
 Buny, 60
 Calvin, 55
 Caswell A., 76
 Celia Ann, 131
 Chesley, 99
 Christian, 25
 Clayton, 11
 Cynthia, 68
 Daniel, 31, 72
 David, 2, 19, 73, 87
 Dorothy, 50
 Edith, 20, 42
 Edwin, 27, 28, 45

Elam, 30, 38
Elijah, 106
Eliza, 25, 67
Elizabeth, 2, 7, 48, 74
Elizabeth B., 127
Ephraim A., 75
Esther, 63
Etheldred, 12, 25, 26
Etter, 21
F. E., 133
F. S., 101
Felps, 2
George, 129
Hannah Hawkins, 28
Henry, 4, 29, 39, 82
Isaac, 11
Isaac J., 128
Isabelle, 132
James, 15, 32
James A., 99, 104, 132
James H., 51, 133
Jane, 9
Jaob, 57
Joel, 64
John, 1, 2, 3, 24, 25, 26, 27, 28, 36, 43, 52, 58, 92
John A., 23, 25, 26, 37, 44, 103, 118, 121, 125, 126, 127, 129, 133
John L., 109
Joseph M., 81
Judith, 14
Julia C., 53
Keren, 11
Larkin, 45
Leanna, 128
Leathy, 27
Leathy Ann, 133
Letha, 33
Leucy, 39
Levey, 20
Lewey, 25
Lucinda, 79

Lucy, 12
Ludom, 16
Mac Ruffin, 105
Malinda, 112
Martha, 66
Martha Ann, 133
Mary, 119
Matthew, 26
Mazallian, 92
McCallan, 92
Minerva Ann, 118
Nancy, 93
Nathan, 132
Nehemiah, 10
Peggy, 4
Penelope, 58
Pennina, 123
Perry, 20
Pherebe, 114
Phereby, 12, 47
Polly, 19, 25, 37, 82, 105
Purny Jane, 67
Rebecca J., 96
Reuben, 22
Richard, 23
Rufus W., 128
Ruth, 15
Sally, 20, 27, 31
Samuel, 2, 6, 14, 23, 25, 92
Samuel G., 65
Samuel W., 87
Sarah Jane, 110
Saul, 1
Sidney A., 110
Simon, 50
Tranquilla, 103
Ursula, 132
W. A., 123, 124, 126, 131
William, 17, 37, 40, 116
William A., 115
William I., 83
Willis H., 128
Winifred, 69
Zelpha, 94
Zilpah B., 32
SMITTS, Olive, 132
SNEAD, Agnes, 124
 E. D., 132

JOHNSTON COUNTY MARRIAGES

George, 123
Laura, 125
Maria, 131
Stephen, 100, 113, 115
Thomas, 119, 123, 124
Thomas D., 100, 119, 123, 128, 129
SNEED, Elizabeth, 81
Robert, 48
Robert W., 62, 66
Stephen, 97
SNIPES, Absella, 111
Aley, 22
Bethany, 36
Betsey, 46
Britain, 25, 26, 37
Celia O., 133
Cherry, 133
David, 111
Drury, 47, 56
Jackson, 91
Jesse, 20, 33
John, 8, 19
Mandy, 46
Nathan, 95
Nathaniel, 8
Needham, 15, 86
Polly, 13, 44
Sally, 76
Sindy, 54
Susy, 24
SOLACE, Eliza, 133
SOLOMON, Aaron, 43
Elijah, 3
Elizabeth, 3
Rosey, 11
SOUTHARD, Jackson, 121
SOWELL, Clayton, 4
Elizabeth, 4
Meribeth, 29
Mildred, 26
SPEED, Agatha H., 40
Robert, 43
SPELL, Dempsey, 44

Reddick, 45
SPENCE, Betsy A., 94
Elisha, 51, 52
Hannah, 94
James, 51
Nancy E., 91
SPENCER, A. C., 121
Axcy, 75
Betsy, 56
Cally, 69
Harriet, 76
James, 124
Jesse, 3
John, 45, 53, 54
Nancy, 84
Patsey, 127
Polly, 29
Sally, 75
William, 37, 46, 53
William J., 112, 115
SPERRY, William, 4
SPICER, Elizabeth, 3
James, 8
Joseph, 8
Polly, 24
SPIED, Mildred, 36
SPIER, William, 5
SPIGHT, Thomas, 1
Winifred, 2
SPIGHTS, Edy, 7
SPITT, John, 25
SPIVEY, Betsy, 94
Charlotte, 21
Dickson, 25
Dixon, 80
Edwin, 52, 55, 58
Larkin, 73
Loverd, 53, 63, 64
Lovett, 59
Pollie Ann, 129
Rindy, 80
William S., 43
SPIVY, Edwin, 46, 48, 49
Lovett, 71
Nancy, 22
STACTROCK, David, 50
STAFFORD, Elizabeth, 115
Jesse, 35
Joseph, 104
Polly, 36
STALLING, Richmond, 87
STALLINGS, Betsy, 32, 59
Callen, 59
Callin, 46
Candice E., 91
Candis, 54
Caroline, 72
E., 16
Edith, 65
Elizabeth, 43
Ezekiel, 38
Henry, 60
Henry O., 63, 69
Isaac, 6, 16, 17, 22, 38, 46, 47, 53, 64, 69, 106
Isaac W., 83
Jacob, 6, 8
James, 33, 38, 45, 66, 71, 87
James B., 81, 93
Jane E., 107
John, 43
Judith, 2
Kezia, 68
Len C., 111
Lydia, 68
Mary Ann, 88
Noressa, 96
Polly, 28, 53
Richard, 37
Sally, 19
Ulrica, 64
Willy, 66
Zadoc, 2, 7
Zadock, 1, 18, 19
Zadok, 8, 13
Zalok, 2
Zilpha, 46
STALLINGTON, Martha, 126
STALLION, Elizabeth, 2
STANCEL, Godfrey,

INDEX

95
STANCELL,
  Elizabeth, 71
  Hawkins, 73
  John C., 132
  Martha, 76
  Mary, 130
  Morning, 125
  Moses, 133
  Robertson, 130
  Stephen, 71, 130
  Thomas, 123
  Young A., 119
  Zilphia, 127
STANCIL, Jesse, 65
STANCILL, Edith, 42
STAND, Patsy, 83
STANDEN, Phereby, 74
STANDLEY, Polly, 29
  Sarah, 70
STANLEY, Bartsheba, 83
  Elijah, 118
  Elisha, 39
  Gideon, 74
  James, 19, 35, 44
  Jency, 118
  Jesse, 19, 30, 44
  John, 44, 93
  John W., 78
  Lewis, 42
  Mary, 6
  Nancy, 65
  Sir William, 76, 78
  Sirenty, 26
  W. R., 105
  William, 30, 57, 74
STANLY, Abby, 92
  Eli, 105, 114
  Elijah, 46, 114
  Elisha, 92
  Elizabeth, 116, 125
  Emily, 96
  Jacob, 115
  James, 61
  Jensey, 114
  Jesse, 83
  Jesse H., 109,

114
  John, 88, 91
  John W., 90, 92, 93, 108
  John W. M., 123
  Lewis, 68, 78, 101
  Littleton, 93
  Lotty, 108
  Mariah, 72, 91
  Mary Ann, 122
  Nancy R., 105
  Nannie, 123
  Patsey, 104
  Penny, 88
  Polly, 101
  Rebecca, 107
  Ridley, 119
  Sally Ann, 90
  Sir William, 90
  Susan, 61
  Susan Emily, 105
  W. R., 105
  William, 70, 72, 104
  William B., 107
  William R., 99
STANSEL, Allen S., 119
  Elizabeth, 10, 81
  Larkin, 94
  Lucinda, 90
  Luizer, 80
  Martha, 98
  Sarah, 107, 116
  Stephen, 80, 82
  Willie P., 81, 98
STANSELL,
  Alexander, 62, 82
  Allen S., 113
  Exey, 109
  Godfrey, 85
  John, 19
  John G., 91
  Jonathan, 25
  Margaret, 105
  Nancy, 69
  Sally, 105
  Samuel, 70
  Stephen, 99
STANSIL, Godfred,

69
  Godfrey, 69
  John G., 69
  Polly, 69
STANSILL, John, 8, 15, 37
  Jonathan, 37
  Martha, 82
  Mary, 18
  Nancy, 49
  Nathan, 11, 15
STANTON, Henry, 97
STARLIN, Bidie, 34
  Elisha, 44
  Henry, 101
STARLING, Barbara, 40, 60
  Bedie, 42
  David, 56
  E., 38
  Edith, 56
  Elisha, 56, 68, 127
  Eliza, 127
  Geapler, 29
  George, 28
  Henry, 72, 76
  Hilbert, 45
  Hilbird, 38
  Isaac, 61
  Jesse, 34, 45
  Jimnia, 28
  Lucinda, 121
  Mary A. W., 115
  Milly, 47
  Nancy, 12
  Pecy, 40
  Ruth, 30
  Sally, 62
  Sarah, 126
  William, 74
  Willy, 83
  Zilpha, 74, 84
STATON, John Allen, 98
  Solomon, 9
STEARLING,
  Elizabeth, 92
  William, 96
STEAVNER, John, 17
STENLEY, Nicholas, 71

JOHNSTON COUNTY MARRIAGES

STEPHEN, Jesse, 15
STEPHENS, Edith, 108
  Emily, 133
  James H., 103
  John P., 133
  Lucy, 94
  Martha, 133
  Polly, 9
  Susanna, 8
STEPHENSON, Alfred, 123
  Allen, 83, 113
  Britain, 106
  Brittan, 105
  Britton, 92
  Civil A., 115
  Cornelius, 115
  David, 56
  Edith, 33
  Eldridge, 133
  George, 62, 68, 71, 103
  Harriet, 109
  J. Marion, 115
  J. W., 130
  Jesse, 83
  John, 44
  John M., 130
  Jonathan, 102
  Joshua, 64
  Kimmon, 97
  Kimmons, 112
  L. D., 123
  Lottie, 40
  Lotty, 83
  Louisa, 122
  Margaret J., 115
  Mary E., 99
  Mary J., 133
  Moore, 62, 64, 121, 122, 124
  Nazra, 125
  Peggy, 97
  Penelope, 112, 125
  Quinton, 97
  Ransom M., 127
  Ransom W., 106
  Solomon, 39
  William, 122
  William R., 119
  Winiford, 124
  Zella, 112
STEPPENSON, David, 94
STERLING, Isaac, 63
STETWELL, Thomas, 34
STEVEN, John, 14
STEVENS, A. T., 125
  A. W., 75
  Augustus W., 68, 70
  Bartley, 27
  Bedy, 81
  Benjamin, 28, 29, 35, 36, 37, 48, 50, 70
  Betsy, 33
  Burt, 44
  Caty, 36
  Charles, 3, 21, 23, 29, 41, 42, 53, 55
  David, 21, 37, 47
  Delaney, 28
  Deliah, 24
  E. P., 71
  Edward, 4, 14, 37, 51, 57
  Elizabeth, 5, 26, 27, 55, 96
  Elly, 38
  Emily, 63
  Everett, 99
  Everett P., 83, 84
  Everight P., 41
  Ezekiel, 62, 68
  Harriet, 64
  Henry, 4, 12, 14, 15, 17, 21, 42, 63
  Henry M., 45, 60, 70
  Isom, 24
  J. A., 119, 126
  Jacob, 1, 12, 18, 22, 41, 60
  Jacob A., 75, 89, 117, 118
  James, 51
  Jarrot, 37
  Jenkins A., 68
  Joby, 94
  John, 16, 18, 19, 21, 23, 25, 26, 28, 30, 37, 43, 45
  Julius, 66
  Julius A., 66, 67
  Levy, 66
  Lotty, 34
  Lucy, 66
  Mary, 15
  Mournig, 1
  N. B., 89
  Nancy, 17, 47, 58
  Needham, 63, 67, 73, 87
  Nicy, 84
  P. W., 95
  Patience A. A., 98
  Patsey, 42
  Pattey, 2
  Phereby, 17
  Polly, 23, 28, 29, 35
  Rachael, 123
  Rachel, 59
  Rebecca, 52
  Rhoda, 4
  Rhody, 82
  Richard, 38, 47
  Robert, 48
  Robert W., 65, 72, 73, 74, 78, 79, 81, 84, 86, 89, 90, 91, 92, 93, 95, 96, 98, 100, 102, 119, 122, 123, 124, 125, 127
  Sallie, 3
  Sally, 22, 44, 49
  Sally C., 67
  Sarah, 17, 82, 133
  Sidney, 69
  Simon, 19, 67
  Solomon, 52
  Sophia, 46, 60
  Temperance, 60
  Theney, 5

INDEX

Thomas, 70
W. B., 75
Whitley, 33
William, 8, 9, 10, 16, 17
William H., 67, 120
Williamson, 69
Zachariah, 17
STEVENSON, Alvin, 94
  Amos, 84, 89
  Edith, 41
  Edward, 75
  Garrot, 41
  Henry, 11
  Jackson, 64
  James, 80
  Jenny, 64
  Jesse, 75
  John, 18, 56
  Kimon, 94
  Lewey, 41
  Lilay, 24
  Lucinda, 72
  Olive, 94
  Osbern, 78
  Penny, 73
  Piety, 87
  Ransom M., 84, 89
  Sarah, 61
STEWART, Benjamin, 76
  Catherine, 112
  Charles, 56
  Daniel, 92
  Eldridge, 89
  Grizzy, 124
  James, 60
  Jesse, 72
  John, 105
  R. H., 100
  William, 84
  William A., 73
STINSON, Erasmus, 44
STOAVON, Sarah, 3
STOERS, Edwin S., 122
STOKES, Teresa, 63
STOLT, Alsey, 69
STORKTON, Margaret, 10
STRAPKERS, David, 18
STRICKAND, Jackson, 123
STRICKLAND, Adin, 52
  Axey, 103
  Benjamin, 4, 5, 115
  Bennet B., 76
  Betsy, 52
  Cally, 48
  Calvin, 67
  Charlotte, 78
  Cullen, 83
  David, 60
  Dizy, 46
  Dorcas, 16
  Eli, 52
  Elizabeth J., 131
  Ely, 79
  Emily, 125
  Hartney, 82
  Henderson, 69
  Henry Wright, 91
  Hester, 14
  Hilliard, 69, 77
  Hilliman, 65
  Isabella, 75
  James, 38, 54, 61
  James W., 114
  Jane, 15
  Jeremiah, 5, 57
  Jesse B., 97
  John, 16, 70, 92
  John W., 105
  Jonathan, 61
  Josiah, 92, 127
  Kern, 42
  Lancy, 39
  Levi, 46, 59
  Lewis, 67
  Lotty, 37
  Lucy M., 110
  Mammeduke, 22
  Misouri Ann E., 128
  Nancy, 24, 58
  Nathan, 16, 20, 32, 66
  Patience, 70
  Patsy, 86
  Penny, 11
  Phereby, 16
  Polly, 49
  Rainey, 67
  Rebecca, 90, 126
  Sally, 88
  Samuel, 13, 20, 28, 35, 49, 53, 57, 61
  Thena, 110
  Uriah, 16
  William, 37, 46, 128
  William G., 116
  William R., 129
  Willie, 92, 95
  Wright, 66
  Young, 108
  Zilphia, 59
STUCKEY, Elizabeth, 47
STUEKY, Nancy, 52
STURDIVANT, ?, 81
  Holm, 24
  Matthew, 12
STURIDVANT, Calvin, 60
SUGG, Joshua, 46
SUGGS, Adaline, 132
  Aquilla, 84
  Britain, 13
  Frances, 127
  Rigdon, 42, 52
SULILVAN, Jesse, 43
SULLIVANT, William, 2
SULLOMAN,
  Elizabeth, 101
  Garry, 101
SUMMER, Joseph I., 45
SUMMERLIN, John, 95, 96
  William, 96
SURLES, Jocie, 102
  L. M., 114
  William B., 97
SURLS, Thomas, 67
SWAN, Lucy, 18
SWANSON, Philip, 10
SWEARINGGAME,

Olive, 40
SWING, Elizabeth, 93
SYLLAVENT, Garry, 70
SYLLIVANT, Elizabeth, 119
SYMPKINS, Calvin, 58

-T-
TADLOCK, Tabitha, 107
TAILOR, Nammy, 4
  Susan, 66
TALTON, Arthur, 17
  Cullen, 25, 29, 51
  Custin, 96
  Debrean D., 102
  Elias, 36
  Eliza, 118
  Elizabeth, 59, 65, 71, 108
  H. H., 108
  Hawkins, 125
  James, 12, 22, 63
  Jesse A., 36, 56
  John D., 46, 107
  John W., 128
  Jonathan, 29, 30
  Julia Ann, 71, 81
  Louisa J., 118
  Louize J., 110
  Macle, 73
  Matilda, 102
  Milly H., 121
  Needham, 30
  Nelly, 77
  Reldy, 73
  Rinda, 98
  Sally, 42, 63
  Sarah, 45, 54, 110
  Uley, 68
  W. J., 123
  William, 2, 12, 17, 129
  William B., 110
TANNER, Elizabeth, 2
TANT, Francis, 53

TAPLEY, Adam, 6
TARLET, William, 69
TART, Henrietta, 121
  James T., 128
  Jane E., 124
  John, 83, 92
  Nancy, 68
  Nathan, 76
  Patsy, 65
  Pherebe, 71
  Polly, 86
  Thomas, 67
  William, 76, 81
TAUNT, Reddin, 47
TAYLOR, A. J., 77
  Beneter, 23
  Benjamin, 6, 7
  Bryant, 110
  Clary, 15
  John, 8
  Mary J., 122
  Nancy, 24
  Penny, 29
  Phereby, 42
  Polly, 30
  Ransom, 67, 70, 114
  Richard, 48
  Sally, 54
  Spency, 42
  Susanna, 47
  Thomas, 21, 25
  Willis, 69
TEAL, Lewis, 30
  William, 18, 26, 35, 46
TEDDER, Thomas, 44
TEDER, Stephen, 89
TEFLAIR, Rebecca S., 127
TELFAIR, Abner, 68
TELL, Winifred, 38
TEMPLE, Burwell, 104
  Burwell W., 105
  Caswell, 122
  Elizabeth, 89
  Lucy, 5
  Penny, 93
  Peter R., 72, 81, 131

R. H., 77
Ransom, 101
S. P., 115
Sally, 79
Sarah A., 122
Starling W., 46, 50, 69
Susan, 66
TEMPLER, Polly, 40
TEMPLES, Polly, 60
  Ransom H., 69
  Starling, 19, 63
TERRY, Julia M., 106
  Richard C., 48
  Sarrah Ann, 101
THAIN, Henry E., 127
  J., 133
  Jethro, 121, 128, 129
  S. B., 127
  Samuel B., 125
  William, 111, 127, 133
THARP, George N., 100
  Henry W., 98
  Nancy, 116
THAUGHN, Penelepy, 5
THOMAS, Alexander, 22
  Anderson, 105
  Betsy, 55
  Cloe, 2
  Cynthia, 10
  Edney, 38
  Elisha, 1, 5, 22, 24
  Elizabeth, 65
  Gray W., 82, 89
  James H., 72, 91
  Jesse, 36
  John, 11, 17
  Joseph, 19, 36
  Josiah, 96
  Louiza, 64
  Lucy, 16
  Mecajah, 57
  Nancy, 45
  Nathan, 55

INDEX

Rhoda, 53
Sally, 86
Solomon, 4
Temporam, 7
Wimmey, 24
THOMPSON, Chilly, 34
　David, 34, 36, 53
　Edith, 20
　Elijah, 14, 35
　Elijah Y., 122
　Elizabeth, 126
　Jarrett, 17
　Jarrot, 4
　John, 11
　John R., 112, 113
　John W., 124
　Lewis, 42
　Nancy E., 130
　Nicholas, 7, 14
　Nickey, 89
　Sallie Ann, 131
　Sally, 28
　Sarah, 109, 111
　Sarah A. E., 123
　Stephen, 87
　Stevens G., 80
　Uriah, 94, 132
　William, 26, 42
　William B., 87
THOMSON, Ann G., 86
　Arthur, 69
　Asa, 65
　Betsy, 68
　Daverick D., 76
　David, 58, 59, 60, 66, 79, 81
　Devereaux, 91
　Deverux D., 60
　Elijah, 60
　Harry, 62
　Jesse R., 76
　John R., 85, 91, 100
　Kern, 70
　Lewis, 51, 61, 62, 69
　Mary, 47
　Nicholas, 52, 88
　Rebecca, 86
　Rebeccah, 64
　Roy, 92

Winifred, 52, 61
THORN, Polly, 43
　Sarah, 3
THORNTON, A. G., 85, 92
　Alexander, 68
　Alexander H., 63
　Allison, 95
　Alvin, 88
　Bethina, 31
　Britton, 83
　David, 25
　Eliza, 91
　Elizabeth, 67
　Everett, 116
　Harrod, 27
　Harrold, 40
　Herod, 55
　Maledick, 125
　Martha A., 123
　Mary M., 108
　Michael, 82
　Nathan, 31
　Owen, 40
　Rebecca, 40
　Sally, 47
　Sarah, 10
　Sarah Ann, 72
　Susan Caroline, 82
　Thomas, 64
　Thomas H., 72, 80
　William, 80, 90, 91
　William E., 98, 111
　Young, 102
　Young N., 93, 117
THORP, Celia, 23
　Edith, 68
　Mary, 33
　Nancy, 45
　Patsey, 43
　Phebe, 39
　Rebekah, 25
THURSTON, William J. Y., 126
TIGH, John W., 4
TIMMELL, James, 59
TIMPKINS, Polly, 37
TINER, Catherine M., 122

Jacob, 22
James, 21, 61
Jesse, 11, 34
John, 18, 22, 46, 65, 101
Julie H., 119
Lewis, 42
Linsey, 123
Mariah, 83
Nancy, 34
Patience, 27
Rachel, 29
Ransom, 60
Sally, 43, 97
Sarah, 21
Sarby, 12
Sidney S., 128
Susan L., 120
Willie, 11
Willis, 25
Zachariah, 76, 90
TINNER, Cady, 23
　David, 21
　James, 29
　John, 4
　Mary, 27
　William, 21
TISDALE, Alley, 131
　E. S., 124
　Edwin S., 118
　Elisha, 40, 83
　Jake, 129
　Joel, 78
　Kelly, 131
　Lucinda, 128
TISDELL, Alsey, 53
TOBSON, Thomas, 24
TODD, Elijah, 86
　George, 39
　M. G., 122, 126
　Monroe, 75
　Tempe, 75
　William, 37
TOLAR, Robert, 22
TOLE, Frederick, 26
TOLER, Charlotte, 69
　Clary, 26, 37
　Colie, 89
　Elizabeth, 22
　Mary W., 120
　Pherebe, 131

195

JOHNSTON COUNTY MARRIAGES

Robert, 22
Sarah C., 89
Stephen, 39
Thomas, 62, 63, 68, 69, 70
William H., 77
TOLLER, Stephen, 42
TOLSON, Thomas, 3, 32
TOLTON, Hopettine, 120
TOMLIN, Sarah, 24
TOMLINSON, Allen, 36
Anirilla, 51
Ann, 11
B., 130
Bettie B., 127
Birnice H., 47
Cassandra, 47
Cazilla, 132
Drusilla, 51
Druzilla, 4
Edmond, 3, 8, 13, 26
Harris, 26, 27, 28, 56
Harrison, 34
Harriss, 21, 42
James, 59, 75
M. E., 128
Martha, 47
Mary, 104
P. R., 102, 112
Parker R., 110
Phereba H., 119
Pherebe, 8
Phereby, 33
Polly, 14, 59
Ruffin W., 90, 91
Sally, 5, 41
Sarah, 119
Thomas, 1, 10, 33, 42
William, 67
William H., 102
TOMPKINS, Easer, 131
TOMPSON, Nichols, 5
Pheroby, 98
TOMSON, David, 48
TOOL, Elizabeth,
111
Jonathan, 97
Lodwick, 86
TRAWICH, Emily, 69
TRAYWAY, Nancy, 75
TRAYWICK, George, 15
Olathaniel, 15
TRISDELL, Zardy, 35
TRUMBULL, David, 93
TUCKER, Cary, 57
Elizabeth A., 27
Margaret, 6
Pennington, 27
Rebecca, 63
William, 21, 33
TULE, William, 56
TURLEY, Catharine, 44
Clary, 66
Curdiss, 73
Lougenia, 124
Penny, 55
Richard, 56
Samuel, 62, 68
Samuel M., 68, 77, 81
Thomas, 44, 56, 67
TURLINGTON, Eli, 108
Elizabeth, 107
Tabitha, 108
TURNAGE, James, 129
TURNELL, James A., 61
TURNER, Amelia, 119
Atlas, 61
Betsy, 41
Bettie, 132
David, 42, 72, 130
James, 42
John, 7
John B., 65
Mary, 108
Patsy, 42
Pherebee, 15
Polly, 47
Sally, 103
Samuel, 67
Samuel S., 65, 85

Simon, 88
Sophia, 86
Thomas, 124
William, 42
William H., 93, 101
Willis, 60, 63
Winifred, 63
TYLES, Kincaid, 11
TYNER, Anne, 9
Louisa, 61
Uriah, 69

-U-
UNDERWOOD, James, 119
Thomas, 10
Wright, 131
UPCHURCH, Calvin, 98, 102
Duncan, 104
Martha, 114
Mary Ann, 123
UTLEY, Annie E., 126
Britain S., 65
S. M., 66
Samuel M., 64
Temperance, 69

-V-
VAN, Rufus, 122
VANN, Stephen, 9
VANTASSEL, Josephine B., 95
VASS, Nancy, 23
VIANN, King, 38
VICK, Delany, 33
Jesse, 1
VINCENT, John C., 71
Sarah A. E., 121
Thomas L., 87
William, 33
VINNING, Shadrack, 2
VINSON, Aaron, 6, 7, 8
Abner, 57
Addison, 36
Ahasurus, 108
Amelia, 16

INDEX

Archibald, 15
Drury, 1, 15, 21, 23
Elizabeth, 24, 25
Haywood, 132
Hinton, 42, 52, 53, 58
James, 28, 57
James A., 108
James T., 108
John, 15, 36, 53
Laurinda, 63
Levina, 18
Marseline, 85
Mary, 9, 13, 69
Mary Ann, 120
Needham, 79
Paton, 15
Peyton, 36
S. T., 95
Sally, 54
Sarah, 13
William, 75
Winifred, 14, 26

-W-

W---, Elizabeth, 13
WADDEL, Rachel, 84
WADDELL, Everett, 126
  John, 78
  Rhoda, 28
WADDLE, Thomas, 108
WADE, Hepsabeth, 93
  Mark, 84
WADEL, Everett, 80
WADELL, Edwards, 39
WALDEN, B. B., 133
WALKER, David, 10
  Jacob, 13, 50
  John, 53
  Jones, 103
  Lucy, 11
  Major, 11
  Sally, 126
  William, 79
WALL, Aaron, 50, 51, 57, 59
  Bennet, 50, 67, 121
  Betsy, 132
  Celiah, 25, 37

Elizabeth, 47, 126
Elizabeth Ann, 68
Elizabeth B., 61
Jacob R., 132
James, 111
James D., 119
Jane, 132
Jarrot B., 66
Jesse, 6, 10, 13, 19, 43
John, 14
John J., 116
Johnson B., 106
Jonathan, 50
Jonathan T., 66
Joseph J., 110
Louisa, 104
Louiza, 104
Lucenna, 118
Lucy E., 77
Lydia, 58
Mabry T., 110
Malachi, 72, 97
Marby T., 118
Martha, 91
Martin, 51
Matthew, 80
Milly, 92
Minerva A., 125
Pennary, 100
Perry, 51
Phereby, 67
Polly, 71
Samuel, 68
Sarah, 10
Sarah H., 121
Tempy A., 86
William, 15
William B., 48, 93, 121, 122, 123
William H., 97, 104, 111, 130
Willy, 109
Winifred, 111
WALLACE, Aaron, 65
  Athey, 83
  Calvin, 92
  Calvin P., 94
  Calvin R., 91, 99, 110

Elisha, 61, 91
Elizabeth, 100
Jackson, 94
James, 129
John, 26, 40
Lewany, 112
Lewis, 82
Louisa, 132
Moses, 60, 79
Nancy, 122
Smithy, 65
Susan, 60
WALLIS, Elizabeth, 33
  James, 63
  Jarret, 80
  Moses, 45
  Ransom, 125
  Reuben, 105
WALLS, Reddy, 100
WALSTON, Benjamin, 52, 65
  Elizabeth, 19, 84
  Polly, 45
WALTHAL, William, 10
WALTON, Avera, 56
  F. T., 36
  James S., 81
  Samuel, 25, 26, 91
  Timothy, 14, 52
  William, 2, 11
  William A., 52, 62
  William T., 129
WALTSON, Nancy, 111
WARD, Absalom, 60, 66
  Alexander, 128
  Asa, 62
  Daniel, 34
  Levey, 18
  Martha, 66
  Ryan, 5
  Sally, 67
  Sylvia, 70, 131
  William, 8
WARM, Acculy, 66
WARNER, Gideon, 44
WARREN, Elijah, 1
  Fanny, 54

JOHNSTON COUNTY MARRIAGES

George, 7, 10
John, 132
Needham, 26, 30, 35, 45, 48, 50, 55, 130
Polly, 38, 54
Rebecca, 130
Reddick, 46, 48, 52, 54, 58, 64, 69, 70
Redick, 79
Richard, 1, 10, 30
Ruth, 10
Sarah S., 82
Sophrina, 61
William, 36
WARRICK, John, 79
WARWICK, Hezekiah, 133
WASHINGTON, Richard, 48
WATFORD, David, 46
Hardy, 45, 46, 57
Willie, 56
WATKINS, Allan, 3
Alley, 111
Amos, 18
Bardin, 111
Charity, 56
Crawford, 116
David, 39
Iredell, 51
Ivy, 42
James, 57
Mahala, 123
Milly Ann, 97
Nammy, 48
Nancy, 30
Patience, 84
Pearce, 35
Peggy, 31
Peter, 10
Polly, 12, 44
Rhoda, 60, 95
Robert, 17
Sally, 72
Simon, 62
Susannah, 41
Wiley, 3
Willie, 15, 30
Windsom, 35

WATLEY, Stephen H., 87
WATSON, Adalade, 132
Allen, 29
Alsey, 81
Ancy, 50
Anne, 20
Baal, 5
Betsy, 35, 69
Bridgers, 47
Celah, 36
Cherry, 85
Cuzzy, 58
David, 14, 18, 19
Dempsey, 67
Eavline, 104
Edith, 26
Elizabeth, 1, 41
Evaline, 115
Giles, 131
Harriss, 35
Henry L., 133
Isabell, 132
Isam, 36
Isham, 29
James, 2
Jesse, 52
John, 3, 16, 17, 60
John B., 35, 41
Joseph, 85
Labon, 14
Levan, 10
Littleton, 49
Loucinida, 128
Martha, 50, 84, 128
Milly, 18
Nancy, 80, 87, 122
Nelly, 100
Patsy N., 121
Penny, 71
Priscilla, 40
Quincy, 69
Rachel, 21, 64
Redduck, 18
Robert, 71
Sally, 14
Sally Ann, 132
Simon, 9

Solomon, 64, 86, 129
Stephen, 35, 115
Sylva, 92
Thomas, 130
W., 22
Wilie, 111
William, 2, 35, 36, 101
William H., 61, 63, 65
Willie, 77
Willis, 20, 21, 22, 23, 27, 28, 30, 35
Zadock, 12
Zelphia, 100
WATTON, Andrew, 133
WATTS, Sarah, 25
WAY, William G., 96
WAYNE, Frederick E., 126
WEAVER, Asa, 41
Betsey, 41
Elizabeth, 102
Jesse, 68
Moses, 91
Nancy J., 94
Reuben, 123
William Henry, 98
Zilpha, 86
WEB, Abraham, 3
WEBB, Abraham, 23, 45
Bennet, 67
Harriet, 125
James, 38
John, 107
Mary Ann, 88
Meredith, 38
Nancy, 57
Polly, 30, 39
Reddin, 57, 88
Sally, 103
Seamwell R., 62
Silas, 62, 68, 70, 83
W. H., 121
William, 111
WEDDEN, James P., 106
WEEKS, Mary, 110

INDEX

Washington, 110
WELCH, Milly, 28
  William, 54
WELLEFORD, John P., 102
WELLON, Wilie, 120
WELLONS, B. A., 121, 122, 123, 126
  Benjamin, 88, 104, 115
  Charles, 22, 35, 41, 57, 61
  Clinton, 82
  Curtis H., 65
  Dianna, 41
  Eliza, 108
  Elizabeth, 24
  Erotus, 95
  Exum, 56
  Hellow, 118
  James, 39, 54, 56
  James D. T., 119
  Jesse, 37, 56, 112
  John, 39
  Maleard, 69
  Nancy, 42
  Rebecah, 30
  Sally, 90
  Vetrina, 73
  W. A., 123
  W. H., 127, 132
  Westley, 42
  Wilie, 121, 124, 129
  William, 54
  William H., 108
  Willie, 102
  Zachariah, 30, 45
WELSH, Emily, 64
  Fanny, 83
WEST, Allen, 87
  Atincy F., 128
  Charles, 78
  Handy W., 68
  John C., 133
  L., 124
  Loyed, 76
  Noel, 26, 45, 47, 48, 49, 51, 52, 59, 68
Polly, 61
  Sally, 52
  Spicy, 77
  Vinson, 13
  William H., 99
WESTBROOK, Elizabeth E., 129
  Joseph T., 99
  Mary, 61
  William F., 123
WHEALLER, Martha, 78
WHEELER, Abi, 120
  Frances, 119
  Isaac, 131
  Jesse, 59, 116, 118
  John H., 95, 97
  Joseph, 52, 59, 128, 129, 131, 132
  Mark, 72
  Mary Ann, 114
  Noah, 97
  Winny, 119
  Zerobabel, 72
WHITAKER, Hugh, 16
  Martha, 113
  Samuel, 68
  Thomas G., 123
WHITE, Gilley, 3
  J. M., 128
  John, 69
  Jonathan, 53
  Richard H., 63
  Sally, 4
  Thomas, 83, 110
  W. W., 56
  William, 55
  William N., 54
  Willie N., 34
  Willis N., 33, 38
WHITEHEAD, Keziah, 119
WHITELY, Jesse, 47
WHITENTON, James, 36
  Jonathan, 36
WHITFIELD, Bryan, 1
  George W., 52
  Lewis, 38
Sir. William, 27
  Thomas, 130
WHITINGTON,
  Elizabeth, 6
  Elizur Ann, 109
  John, 42
  Jonathan, 38
  Lucretia, 8
  Mary, 5, 16
  Peggy, 18
  Pensy, 61
  Phaddy, 16
  Richard, 2, 8, 18
  Sally, 18
  Solomon, 28, 33, 41, 58
  William, 35, 38
  William S., 61
WHITLEY, A. F., 118
  Alfred, 35
  Appy, 40, 61
  B. F., 107, 116
  Benjamin, 69
  Bryan, 59
  Bryant, 45
  Caroline, 104
  Celia, 83
  Cynthia, 15
  Daniel, 57
  Dennis, 132
  Easter A., 79
  Elizabeth, 104, 129
  Enoch, 12, 45
  Esther, 50
  Everett D., 73
  Harris H., 85
  Haywood, 70
  J. W., 120
  James, 132
  James H., 126
  James K., 134
  James M., 88
  Jesse, 32, 48, 54, 59
  Jessy, 43
  Job, 130
  John, 7, 10, 30, 35, 45, 48, 71
  John S., 56
  Josiah H., 73
  Julia, 108

JOHNSTON COUNTY MARRIAGES

K. B., 73
Kedar, 19, 87
Kinch, 35
Lucretia, 124
Marceline, 108
Margaret A., 117
Margaret R., 118
Martha, 62
Mary, 85
Mary E., 126
Merrit, 129
Michael, 104
N. R., 76
Nancy, 78
Needham, 6, 15, 49
Obedience, 92
Peter W., 85
S. J., 127
S. W., 106
Sarah Ann E., 121
T., 89
T. W., 115
Temperance A., 67
Thaddeus, 62, 86
Thaddeus W., 117
Virginia, 110, 133
Wesley, 127
William, 19, 54
William R., 106
Willie, 45, 57
Zelley E., 105
Zilly, 85
WHITMAN, Betsy Ann, 107
John, 94
Robert, 66
WHITMOR, Henry, 55
WHITMORE, William, 42
WHITOVGR, Sarah, 94
WHITTEN, Polly, 23
WHITTENTON, Bidy, 71
WHITTINGER, John, 32
WHITTINGTON,
Agatha, 50
Ceny, 85
Cynthia, 65
Elizabeth, 7

James, 44
Jane, 49
Robert, 4, 12
Solomon, 41
William, 45, 50
William S., 53
WIGGINS, Archibald, 33
Sally Ann, 97
William, 44
Willis, 1
WIGGS, Anne, 24
Arthur, 103
Chelly, 85
Enthan, 96
Henry, 80
Isaiah, 87
John, 111
John T., 112
Martin, 36
Nathan, 113, 115
Susan, 82
Willey P., 113
WIGS, Anna, 125
Susannah, 32
WILBURN, Lewis, 30
WILDAIR, Crecy, 36
WILDER, Betsy, 30, 63
Cally, 63
Catherine, 31
Caty, 22, 36
Cullen, 13, 28
David, 21
Dorothy, 15
Elizabeth, 15, 28, 38, 71, 123
Fanny, 26, 57
Harriet, 63
Hillary, 36, 65
Hillery, 55
Irvin, 21, 57
Isham, 63, 64, 87
James H., 111
James William, 68
Jane, 41, 81
John, 13, 21
Kerney, 112
Lisha A., 122
Mary, 38
Matthew, 29, 60, 78, 90

Milly, 33
Molley Ann, 105
Nancy, 48, 64, 78
Olive, 33
Polly A., 81
Reuben, 33, 57, 59, 78
Sally, 33
Samuel, 11, 13, 14, 28
Tell, 21
Temperance, 57
William, 5, 28, 31, 36, 44, 55, 58
William G., 122
William J., 67
Willy, 51
Winifred, 46
Zilpha, 31
WILKERSON, Anne, 9
Benjamin, 2, 9, 15
Calvin, 49
Charity, 19
Charles, 2, 10, 19, 23, 52
Elkeny, 10
Nathan, 15
Reuben, 6, 48
WILKINS, Alfred, 127
Helen, 113
Henry, 96, 103
James, 112
John, 127
Owen, 118
Phebie, 128
Phillips, 122
Pinkney, 120
Sele, 98
Simon, 112
WILKINSON, Berry, 34
Charles, 2
Edith, 52
John, 96
Larry, 42
Micajah, 36, 41, 45
Reuben, 4, 12, 22, 64

INDEX

Roland, 12
William, 123
WILKS, Ann, 8, 10
WILLEY, Armandatt, 98
WILLIAM, Bryant, 132
  Hepsey, 92
  John, 19
WILLIAMS, Adeline, 62
  B. A., 120, 125
  Benajah, 92
  Benejah, 103
  Betsy, 55
  Bright, 122
  Bryant, 83, 131, 133
  Caroline, 75
  David, 107
  Delpha, 95
  Edith, 26
  Elizabeth, 64
  Frederick, 27
  H.A., 109
  Herod I., 8
  Iredell, 31, 42
  Isaac, 25, 44, 45
  Jackson, 77
  James B., 123
  James C., 121
  John, 11, 22, 26, 40, 44
  John P., 60, 69, 83
  Lewis, 72, 102, 103
  Lewis J., 101
  Marmaduke, 38
  Mary, 49, 56
  Mary E., 110
  Nancy, 28
  Narcissa, 130
  Peter, 11, 14, 15
  Polly, 6, 30
  Roland, 12
  Samuel, 1
  Sarah, 16, 17
  Susan, 47
  W. F., 35
  William, 12, 27, 50, 68

Willie, 118, 120
WILLIAMSON,
  Bethany, 69
  Betsy, 57
  Joanna, 116
  K. M. C., 74, 88
  Patience, 36
  Polly, 65
  Raiford, 65, 116
  Rill C., 97
  Sarah E., 123
  Zilpha, 49
WILLIFORD, John P., 102
WILLIS, John, 46, 60
WILLKINS, Eli, 103
WILLOBY, Caden, 29
WILLOUGHBY,
  Solomon, 10
WILLOUGHLEY,
  Elizabeth, 29
  Samuel, 26, 27, 29
WILLOWS, B. A., 118
WILSON, Arthur, 79
  Edmond, 105
  James, 130
  Jennet, 113
  John, 10, 15, 25, 26
  Margaret, 51
  Nancy, 26
  Rhoda, 15
  Sally, 21, 29
  Starling, 128
  William, 13, 39
WIMBERLY, Betsy, 27
  Charity, 31
  George, 16
  Malachi, 1
WIMDEON, William, 54, 69
WIN, Kiddy E., 51
WINBORN, Agilla, 95
  Islie J., 125
  Jesse, 95
  Patsey Rap, 105
WINBURN, John, 98
  Thomas, 20
WINDBORN, Clary, 51
  John, 52

WINDHAM, D. D., 118
  Dorcas, 127
  John, 36, 61
WISE, Casanda, 64
  Isaac, 54
  James, 10
  Nancy, 45
  Rebecca, 101
  Rigdon, 89
  Thomas, 10
WITT, George A., 131
WOOD, Absabeth, 57
  Allie, 124
  Brimmiter, 32
  Clinton, 94
  Elizabeth, 33
  J. C., 118
  James, 133
  Jesse, 31
  John, 2, 5, 8, 26, 67, 119
  John L., 100
  John S., 123
  Lydia, 2, 5
  Malachi, 107
  Martha, 121
  Mary Jane, 70
  Nancy, 49, 52, 119
  Pudisy, 49
  Rachel Ann, 105
  Sally, 59
  Susanna, 49
  Thomas, 118
  W. D., 112, 116
  Whitfield, 65
  William, 35, 38, 63, 125
  William D., 70, 78
WOODALE, Martha, 108
  Mary E., 105
  Sarah, 108
WOODALL, Aaron, 100
  Absalom, 8, 11, 34, 40, 53
  Absalom P., 51
  Alexander, 100, 109
  B. A., 108, 121,

123, 128, 131
Betsy, 40
Carion, 53
Charity, 58
Clement, 52
Easther, 84
Edith, 24
Eleanor, 122
Elizabeth, 98
Emily, 118
Emmeon, 75
Gideon, 50, 55, 90
Harriet, 60
Isham, 123
J. G., 127
Jacob, 8, 15, 16, 20, 27, 50, 54
James, 4, 9, 11, 18, 29, 34, 36, 53, 54, 57
James A., 52, 88, 129
James D., 45
James G., 53, 60, 62, 65
John, 36
John A., 133
Julia A., 80
Lucy, 126
Martha, 123, 125
Martin, 27
Mary, 72
Master, 21
Merrit, 84
Nancy, 56
Nicy, 72
Penny, 58, 62
Phebe, 121
Polly, 54
Sally, 56
Seth, 130, 131
Simeon, 75, 82
Troy W., 120
William, 38, 57, 75
WOODARD, Arthur, 75
B. A., 104
Benjamin, 12, 70
Bertie, 75
Betsy, 83
Doctor D., 94
Elisha, 7
Elizabeth, 28
Emily, 90
Erasmus, 64
Henry, 62, 70, 94
Huldy, 71
Irvin, 111
Jacob, 90
Jensey, 111
Jesse, 58
Jethro, 83
John, 14, 71, 83
Jonathan, 51, 64
Joseph, 39, 83, 91, 125
Mary, 78
Matthew, 27, 34
Micajah, 14
Nancy, 5, 134
Pasha Eliza, 125
Phereby, 9
Rufus, 114
Samuel, 63
Sarah, 94
Seth, 104
Thomas, 103
Tobias, 83
Warren, 45
West, 24, 28
William, 78
William A., 122
William H., 124
Willis, 45
WOODELE, Charles, 12
WOODELL, Eliza, 115
Rany, 93
Zelpha, 20
WOODLY, Thomas A., 130
WOODWARD, Aley, 30
Berry, 57
Catherine, 96
Celia, 66
Edith, 57
Elisha, 43
James, 30
Jesse, 42
John, 32, 36
Jonathan, 46
Milly, 95
Nancy, 46
Sarall, 52
Thomas, 10
Warren, 35
WOODY, S. W., 122, 123, 125, 129, 131, 132
Samuel, 66, 88
Samuel W., 98
Saul, 96
WOOLEY, Nancy, 120
WOOTEN, Berry, 19
James, 1
Jesse, 8
Mary, 7
Sarah, 57, 88
William, 30
WORDALL, Brazzilla, 48
WORLEY, Alteny E., 105
Benjamin, 50
Cora Elvina, 126
Elizabeth, 45, 123
John, 67
Julia, 129
Margaret, 13
Matilda, 83
Nelly Rains, 34
Polly, 37
William, 13, 16, 23, 130
WORTHAM, A. D., 84
WREN, Calvin, 87
Mary, 90
WRIGHT, Aggy, 21
Betsy, 27
Charity, 1
Dionysius, 1
Joseph, 36, 56
Patty, 12
Sihon, 10
Simon, 8
William, 17
WYATT, Sally, 34

-Y-

YALLMAY, Richard, 27
YELVERTON, Seneth, 12
YELVINGTON, Asa, 28

INDEX

Bennet, 75
Dicy, 68
Gidion, 6
Howel, 72
Howell, 83
Jacob, 59
Jason, 49, 116
Jethro, 65, 68, 123
Levi, 46, 49, 77, 80
Levy, 43, 49, 53, 66, 75
Martha, 83
Mary, 123
Penelope, 77
YELVINTON, Amity, 6
Jacob, 2
YOUNG, A. D., 115
Alexander, 99
Allen, 50
Arthur D., 106
Dartha, 131
Edwin, 125
Elizabeth, 47
Elizabeth Ann, 88
Evilin, 94
Ezekiel, 47
Francis, 5, 59
James R., 101
Jane, 97
John, 66
Lucinda, 111
Peggy, 59
Samuel L., 115
Samuel Lee, 49
Thomas, 21, 66
Turner, 57
W. R., 112
William, 114
YOUNGBLOOD, Bird, 50
Edith, 16
Elizabeth, 68
H. H., 76
Ichabod, 25
J. H., 66, 87
James, 59, 76
John W., 127
Mary, 12
Mary A. W. M., 120

Sally, 20
Tabitha, 35
Thomas, 16
Thomas R., 87
William, 8, 12

Other Heritage Books by Charlotte Meldrum:

Abstracts of Bucks County, Pennsylvania Land Records, 1684–1723

*Early Church Records of Burlington County, New Jersey
Volumes 1–3*

Early Church Records of Chester County, Pennsylvania, Volume 2
Charlotte Meldrum and Martha Reamy

Early Church Records of Gloucester County, New Jersey

Early Church Records of Salem County, New Jersey

Early Records of Cumberland County, New Jersey

Johnston County, North Carolina Marriages, 1764–1867

Marriages and Deaths of Montgomery County, Pennsylvania, 1685–1800

www.ingramcontent.com/pod-product-compliance
Lightning Source LLC
Chambersburg PA
CBHW050148170426
43197CB00011B/2005